AF416606

OXFORD MOVEMENT PRIMARY TEXTS
The best writings produced by the Oxford Fathers.
Underwriting their theological project into our own day.

NASHOTAH HOUSE PRESS

Nashotah House Theological Seminary
2777 Mission Road
Nashotah, WI 53058

www.nashotah.edu
www.nashotahhousepress.com

THE

GOSPEL NARRATIVE

OF

OUR LORD'S PASSION

HARMONIZED:

WITH REFLECTIONS.

BY THE

REV. ISAAC WILLIAMS, B.D.

LATE FELLOW OF TRINITY COLLEGE, OXFORD.

"I have heard of Thee by the hearing of the ear; but now mine eye seeth Thee. Wherefore I abhor myself, and repent in dust and ashes."

JOB xlii. 5, 6.

FIFTH EDITION.

LONDON:

RIVINGTONS, WATERLOO PLACE.

1861.

"Grant, O Lord, that in reading Thy Holy Word, I may never prefer my private sentiments before those of the Church, in the purely ancient times of Christianity."—BISHOP WILSON'S PRAYERS.

ADVERTISEMENT.

The present Volume is intended as an experiment, to ascertain how far a Commentary on the Gospels of this kind may be found to answer its purpose. The object has been to introduce something of the depth and devotional thought of ancient interpretation; but these references to early opinions have accumulated on the writer in a manner that renders the narrative more involved, and of less interest, from the continual interruption to the general thread of the subject. With regard to the quotations, it is necessary to state, that in some instances, they are intended rather to convey the meaning of the Author on the point referred to, than to be an exact translation of all his words; and in some passages they are not taken at all from the original authors, but from different Catenas, especially the Catena Aurea. The number and variety of quotations has rendered it impossible to verify all these passages; and indeed, the nature of the work has, it is thought, rendered it unnecessary, as being intended rather for devotional than critical use.

TRINITY COLLEGE,
Feast of the Annunciation,
A.D. 1841.

A 2

CONTENTS.

PART I.

The Hour of Darkness.

SECTION I.—THE AGONY.

SECTION II.—THE APPREHENSION.

SECTION III.—THE CONDEMNATION.

PART II.

The Day of Sorrows.

SECTION I.—THE HALL OF JUDGMENT.

SECTION II.—THE CRUCIFIXION.

SECTION III.—THE SEPULTURE.

ERRATA.

Page 202, line 17, *for* for great, *read* to great.

    203, — 2, *for* and it was stated, *read* it was stated also.

    203, — 18, *read thus:* but still keep their vices; and who con-
        tinue.

    211, — 8 from bottom, *for indeed he, read* indeed " *he.*

    219, — 4, *for* blessed, *read* Most Holy.

    223, note 2, *read thus:* St. Ambrose translates St. Matthew's ex-
        pression *chlamydem* coccineam; and paraphrases St. Mark's,
        &c.

INTRODUCTION.

Our Blessed Lord took apart His three favoured disciples, that they alone might witness His agony by a closer and more intimate approach: it might, therefore, seem a hazardous presumption for us to venture near, and gaze upon His most sacred sorrows. But if we might be allowed to do so, He seems to teach us that it must be to watch and pray with Him the while. If these indeed were the only ones privileged to behold Him in His humiliations, we might indeed draw back with fear. But even the heathen Pilate was moved to awe at the sight of Him in His crown of thorns. Even the Roman centurion, from standing at the foot of His Cross, was led to confession: and the thief on the Cross, from beholding Him more nearly in His afflictions, had his soul healed. But it may be said, these approached His adorable person in ignorance of His Divine Majesty, and in unbelief; and from beholding Him, learned something of godly fear; or by their own sufferings were made partakers of His Cross; and, so far as they knew of His inconceivable greatness, they reverenced and adored. Be it so: we therefore may draw near to Him, if it be but in fear; and every school of severe visitation affords the privilege to behold Him, and to be with Him. Not the beloved Disciple only, and His blessed Mother, were allowed to approach to the foot of the Cross; and to receive His last gracious commands. The penitent Mary Magdalene and the other faithful Mary found a place there for a while: and others also, those Galilean women, had it granted them to be spectators of that sad scene; when they stood, beholding from afar off, and beating their breasts, returned. And a little before the Crucifixion itself, those poor women of Jerusalem that followed Him, bewailing and lamenting Him, along the way of sorrow and shame, were admitted to receive His sacred words and admonitions, although before the Chief Priests, Pilate, and the wicked Herod, He had observed that judicial and awful silence. And His words intimated that those who would weep with Him may indeed do so: but it is for themselves they are to weep. Let us, therefore, accompany Him, and if we be allowed to weep over guilty Jerusalem, together with Him, yet let it be for ourselves that we mourn.

Let it be with becoming thoughts of self-abasement and humiliation that we draw near to the city of His sorrows. When He came nigh unto Jerusalem He wept over it, at the thoughts of those calamities it was to endure. Far greater cause have we to weep on approaching the same, when we look back on the sufferings He there endured. Let us lay aside the luxuries of life, and all that ministers to human pride, while we approach it; and partake in the feelings of those holy pilgrims whom the Poet describes:

> " To that delight which their first sight did breed,
>   That pleased so the secret of their thought,
>   A deep repentance did forthwith succeed,
>   That reverend fear and trembling with it brought:
> Scantly they durst their feeble eyes dispreed
>   Upon that town, where Christ was sold and bought;
>   Where for our sins He faultless suffered pain,
>   There where He died, and where He lived again.

" Their naked feet trod on the dusty way,
   Following th' ensample of their zealous guide ;
Their scarfs, their crests, their plumes, and feathers gay,
   They quickly doft, and willing laid aside ;
Their moulten hearts their wonted pride allay ;
   Along their watery cheeks warm tears down slide ;
     And then such secret speech as this they used,
     While to himself each one himself accused.

" Flower of Goodness, Root of lasting Bliss,
   Thou Well of Life, whose streams were purple blood
That flowed here, to cleanse the soul amiss
   Of sinful man, behold this brinish flood,
That from my melting heart distilled is,
   Receive in gree these tears, O Lord so good ;
     For never wretch with sin so overgone,
     Had fitter time, or greater cause to moan."

    Tasso, Jer. Deliv. Fairfax's Trans. b. iii. stanz. 5. 7, 8.

PART I.

THE HOUR OF DARKNESS.

SECTION I.—THE AGONY.

" He shall see of the travail of His soul, and shall be satisfied."

GETHSEMANE.

OUR Lord had now gone forth from the city, wherein, according to the law, He had eaten the Paschal supper, and passed *" over the brook Cedron"* (John); that stream over which King David had before passed together with his companions in sorrow [1]. Proceeding over this mountain brook, and up the foot of the hill, He arrived at the spot where it appears to have been usual with Him to retire to prayer. *" Then cometh Jesus together with them,"* says St. Matthew: or, *" they come,"* says St. Mark, *" to a place which is called Gethsemane"* (Matt. Mark); *" where there was a garden,"* says St. John, *" into which He entered, and His disciples."* We know that, on other occasions, it was our Lord's custom to spend the night in prayer, apparently in open and exposed places. But it does not appear very evident why at this time He should have passed the night together with His disciples in the open air, for we know that the night " was cold." It may have been usual with them on account of their

---

[1] 2 Sam. xv. 23.

B

great poverty, for we know that the Son of Man had not where to lay His head; and perhaps the house at Bethany was not sufficient to afford them its friendly shelter, for the concourse at Jerusalem was of course now very great.

"This place, Gethsemane, in which He prayed, is shown even to this day," says Bede, "at the foot of the Mount of Olives." The word Gethsemane is by interpretation the "olive-press:" and who does not perceive the name itself to be replete with something of a divine significancy? For the Olive is the emblem of Christ Himself, and of His Church, and of the Christian; and the Oil in Holy Scripture ever denotes the Spirit of God, and His sanctifying gifts. And how strongly does the olive-press, from which this holy oil of Divine charity is obtained, set forth in expressive figure the Passion of our blessed Lord!

St. Jerome, however, interprets the word Gethsemane as implying a luxuriant garden, "the valley of fatness;" as if from the very richness of the garden it was calculated to bring forth more abundantly those thorns of which Adam sowed the seed. "It was in this, the valley of fatness," says he, "that the fat bulls of Basan closed Him in on every side." It is in the rank and rich ground of human prosperity that evil spirits have, as it were, most power against Christ in all ages of the world.

It is remarkable that both the Passion and the Grave of Christ were in a garden. As St. John expressly states of our Lord's agony, it was "a garden into which He entered," and it has been ever since known as "the garden of Gethsemane;" so does St. John also expressly mention of our Lord's burial, that "there was a garden, and in the garden a new tomb, in which no one had been

yet laid." As in all other matters respecting our blessed
Lord, so in this also there appears to have been some
peculiar adaptation and providential fitness. In a garden the powers of evil overcame the first man ; and in
a garden they were overcome by the second : and as it
was in a garden that Adam sinned, so was it ordained
that in a garden should be both the agony and also the
tomb of Christ. In a garden the first Adam ate of the
pleasant fruit : and in a garden the Second Adam resigned Himself to drink the bitter cup. In a garden the
old serpent beguiled Eve : and in a garden the powers
of darkness were let loose against Him who was born of
woman, and in Him against His Church, who is " the
mother of all living," but found nothing in Him. The
garden in which Adam was placed brought forth to him
all abundance without the sweat of his brow : but this
garden into which the Son of Man was cast, was not
only watered by the sweat of His brow, which was the
curse of Adam, but with His sweat of blood. And
therefore as in the former case Eden became a wilderness
of thorns ; so this became the rich garden, the valley of
fatness, being rich in the graces and charities of Christ.
Again, it was in a garden that the sentence of death was
passed on all mankind because of sin : and in a garden
the Second Man voluntarily submitted to endure the
full weight of that penalty. The voice was heard of the
Lord God " walking in the garden in the cool of the
day," when the excuses of the first Adam took place :
and in the cool of the day in a garden the Second Adam
laid Himself down in stillness and silence to take the
doom pronounced on the first Adam. It was as he left
the garden that the first Adam had the sentence pronounced against him, that the earth should bring forth
thorns : and it was when in death He entered the garden

to be laid in the tomb, that the Second Adam was divested of the crown of thorns that He had worn.

Nor does the subject stop here: for as it was in a garden that Christ yielded up Himself to drink of the cup of sorrow and to lie in the grave; so also in a garden did He overcome death and the grave by His Resurrection. And indeed in a garden itself there is something emblematic and suitable, where nature dies, and is again renewed; where the seed perishes, and is quickened and brings forth an hundred-fold. And this may be the reason why through the book of Canticles, in the mystical accounts of our Lord's burial and resurrection, the figures are so much taken from a garden. "Thou that dwellest in the gardens, the companions hearken to Thy voice: cause me to hear it [2]." Thus also is it with ourselves, that the place where we die to the world is the place where we rise again to God; in whatsoever man humbles himself, in the same is he exalted. In like manner St. Jerome says of our Lord's apprehension in the Mount of Olives, "from whence also He ascended into the Heavens, that we may know that from that place, where we watch, and pray, and are bound, and resist not, we also ascend unto Heaven."

It seems therefore, that as in Christ mankind, who are exiled from Paradise, again return to Paradise: so also in dim figure mankind, who were exiled from the garden, again in Christ return thither. Christ restores to us that which we had lost, but sanctified by His gift and blessed by His own adoption of the same. We have lost our Paradise, our first and happy estate; we have lost the childhood of our years; but in Christ we must return to that Paradise we have lost, we must return once more to

---

[2] Song of Solomon, viii. 13.

lost childhood, and become again as little children in Him.   But this Paradise to which we return in Christ is not an Eden of delights, as it was to the first Adam ; but a garden of suffering and expiation, where we must watch and pray with the Second Adam.   But it is a pledge of a better Paradise hereafter.   And so likewise the second childhood, unto which we are restored in Christ, is a state of mortification and suffering ; but a pledge of a new birth hereafter, when they that are found worthy shall be made sons of God, and the children of the Resurrection, being equal to the angels. It is to His own childhood that Christ brings us back : and His childhood is marked by circumcision.   But the day of His Circumcision is the day of His Resurrection also,—the eighth day.   The eighth day with regard to what is past ; the first day with regard to what is to come ; the day of our new year in Christ ; the first day of the new creation ; the coming in of the new Heavens and the new Earth, wherein dwelleth righteousness.   It is the Circumcision and the Resurrection, both of them the first day and the last day of the week ; for Christ Himself is the First and the Last, the Beginning and the Ending, the Alpha and Omega.   It is the new creation and the new childhood, but marked with the Circumcision ; which implies mortification in the flesh, but in the spirit a new creature.   And such is this garden into which we are admitted with Christ ; it is truly our Paradise, for there is no other place on earth, of which it may be so truly said for us His fallen creatures, that "it is good for us to be here."   Adam was alone in Paradise, but he said it is not good to be alone, and the mother of all living was admitted to be with him. And even in this dark garden of sadness, Christ, in unspeakable condescension, seems to say, it is not good for Him to be alone, but takes the Church to be the partner of His sorrows, saying, Come ye apart, and watch with Me.

"Master, it is good for us to be here:" and may we without irreverence apply the whole of St. Peter's memorable words, "it is good for us to be here, and let us make here three tents, one for Thee, one for Moses, and one for Elias." For it is not the Christian Church only, but the Law and the Prophets also, who must be here present with Christ. For they are witnesses of the crimes of mankind, and must be of their penalty; for of both do they speak. Moses and Elias are both witnesses of the garden of human wickedness. Moses, who hath recorded the garden of Eden, and the sin of Adam. Elias, who met Ahab taking possession of the garden of blood, the vineyard of Naboth. Both are witnesses also of hope and pardon held out, for Christ's sake, to the penitent. Moses, who testifies of the promise made to Adam; and Elias, who bore to Ahab the respite of his sentence. All mankind, whether living before or after, are taken to be with Christ the witnesses of His Passion. Nay, He takes us not only with Him to Gethsemane, but He also takes us back with Him to the Paradise of Adam, to the vineyard of Ahab: He takes us back to the places and seasons of our own crimes, that He may show us how He has to wash that ground, which is stained with the blood of souls.

THE THREE DISCIPLES APART WITH CHRIST.

"*And when He was at the place, He said unto them, Pray ye, that ye may not enter into temptation*" (Luke). As He had been all the evening preparing them for this their danger, so now for the last time does He exhort them to put on that spiritual armour which can alone defend them against the powers of darkness. For now they had nothing else to do but to pray. "*And He saith unto His disciples, Sit ye here while I go and pray* (Matt. Mark) *yonder*" (Matt.); leaving them probably at the entrance of the garden; as if it had been His custom so to retire from them with that purpose, praying without ostentation, and without over-studied concealment. "*And He took with Him Peter* (Matt. Mark) *and the two sons of Zebedee* (Matt.), *James and John together with Him* (Mark), *and He began to be exceedingly amazed* (Mark), *and sorrowful* (Matt.), *and very heavy* (Matt. Mark). *And then He saith unto them, My soul is exceeding sorrowful, even unto death; stay ye here, and watch* (Matt. Mark) *with Me*" (Matt.).

We may ask what the watching with Him means; was it against His treacherous friend, and for his approach? Or was it for those enemies of darkness, of which He spake in saying, " The prince of this world cometh, and hath nothing in Me?" Whatever it might have signified to them, to us doubtless it means that we must watch by good works, in order that we may pray; and must pray in order that we may watch with Him. It is to be observed, that although our Lord intercedes for them, yet it is necessary that they too should pray together with Him. Thus also now He intercedes in Heaven, but is likewise, by His Providence, ever arousing us to pray with Him. But there may be also in this action of our Lord's something of human tenderness and affection, which in times of extreme distress looks to the presence of friends for alleviation, and which thus gives and receives the strongest tokens of human friend-. ship. " He would not go far from them," says Origen, " as wishing to be with them;" leaning upon them, as it were, for support and sympathy, and having selected them from the others, as able to watch with Him; and thus does He draw us all near to Him in His agony, by partaking of our human affections and afflictions, drawing us unto Him with " the cords of a man." Those that were less strong He left apart, saving them from the severe trial of witnessing His agony; but to be allowed to draw near unto Christ is to partake of affliction; and blessed are they who by so doing are led to watch and pray with Him, and from the example of the Son of Man are led to pray. These three disciples were indeed united to their blessed Lord by a more intimate union and sympathy; and by this distinction He hallows our human affections, which draw to us some in closer union than others. But doubtless in our adorable Example such partial affection and choice was founded on that Divine love, which loves most of all those who are most conformable unto the will of God; and which, even in making a distinction, does so for the good both of those that are brought more near, and those who are left at the entrance of the garden. For even in Heaven stars differ from one another in brightness, according to a difference of light within them, or in their degrees of nearness to that Sun, from whence they derive their lustre. Moreover, it was perhaps fitting that those three who had witnessed our Lord's manifestation of Himself in glory on the Mount of Transfiguration, and in power on the raising of Jairus's daughter from the dead, should witness also the agonies of His Passion. And greatly as this added to the trial of the disciples, whose whole strength depended on a sense of our Lord's Divinity; yet to St. Peter himself, who had been elated with self-confidence, such a lesson was at this moment most seasonable,—the lesson which was set before him in Christ's extreme humiliation and affliction.

Of the disciples thus in their several places abiding with Christ, Origen beautifully says, " Wherefore let us abide where Jesus hath commanded, and according to what the Apostle also enjoins, let every one in the vocation wherein he hath been called, therein abide with God[3]! let us do all things, that we may watch with Him, the Keeper of Israel, who neither slumbers nor sleeps.   For this purpose also He took them with Him, and especially Peter, who had great confidence in himself, that they might see and hear where the power of man is, and how it is obtained. That they might see Him falling on His face, and hear Him saying, If it be possible, let this cup pass from Me. And might learn not to think highly, but lowly to esteem themselves ; not to be swift to promise, but anxious to pray[4]!" The same writer says, " These He wishes to watch and pray, that they enter not into temptation, because he who is more spiritual ought to be the more anxious, lest the great good that he doth should suffer the more grievous downfal."

It was from this circumstance of our Lord's withdrawing from some of His disciples, that the custom obtained in the early Churches of making distinctions of place in their assemblies of prayer. Not that they would say as the Pharisee to the Publican, " Stand apart, for I am holier than thou ;" but a little leaven leaveneth the whole, and open sin must break all that sympathy and union which is the pledge of Christ's presence in worship. Add to which, such retirement

---

[3] 1 Cor. vii. 20.   [4] In Matt. Lat. Com. 91.

from the world is the dictate of natural modesty and
piety. At such times by withdrawing from man we
may draw more near unto God. But our blessed
Lord's example furnishes us with the rule and the
qualifications of it. And thus as in that celestial
Paradise where Christ will take mankind to dwell
with Him hereafter, there are "many mansions;" so
also in this garden of His suffering below there are
many mansions or places of abode for His disciples,
in which, in various degrees of nearness, they may be
allowed to watch with Him.

CHRIST WITHDRAWS FROM THE THREE DISCIPLES.

"*And having gone a little further*" (Matt. Mark),
or, as St. Luke says, speaking apparently of this occasion, "*and He was withdrawn from them about a stone's
cast.*" But the word *withdrawn* is much stronger in
the Greek ($\dot{\alpha}\pi\epsilon\sigma\pi\dot{\alpha}\sigma\theta\eta$), and also in the Latin version
(avulsus est), and perhaps implies some involuntary
impulse of extreme grief; as on our Lord's former
temptation after His Baptism, St. Mark says, "the
Spirit driveth Him into the wilderness." And here
"*He fell* (Matt. Mark) *on His face* (Matt.), *upon the
earth, and prayed that if it were possible, the hour might
pass from Him* (Mark). *And He said, Abba, Father,*
(Mar), *My Father, if it be possible* (Matt.), *all things
are possible unto Thee* (Mark), *take away this cup*
(Mark), *let this cup pass* (Matt.) *from Me* (Matt.
Mark). *But not as I will, but as Thou*" (Matt. Mark).

Such is the account which the two first Evangelists
give of this passage. But it is not very evident of which
of the three occasions, when our Lord prayed, St. Luke
speaks, as he does not mention them separately. It

might indeed be supposed that it was not the first time when "He fell on His face;" for St. Luke says, "and having knelt down," He prayed. Of course it might have been the case that He first "knelt down," and afterwards at the same time "fell on His face;" and the words of our Lord's prayer are very much the same as those recorded on the first occasion. But still, as our Lord prayed three times, using the same words, it might have been at the other times of which St. Luke speaks. His words are, "*And having knelt down, He prayed, Father, if Thou wilt, take this cup from Me. Let not My will, but Thine be done.*" And he proceeds to mention the appearance of the angel, which one would suppose to have occurred later.

The variations in the accounts are but slight; but even a slight discrepancy in inspired words may contain great and Divine significancy. Thus St. Matthew records the words "My Father," where the term "My" appears to have a very strong and peculiar import, being the highest and most prevailing name which our Lord could use to the Father, as the "Firstborn" and "Only-begotten," and appealing, therefore, to the Father, in a manner that no other could do, as His own Father. And so also the expression which St. Mark alone introduces, combining the Hebrew "Abba" with the Greek term of "Father," has been supposed to have its peculiar meaning. Perhaps the Lord, says Augustin [5], hath used both terms on account of some Sacramental import; wishing to show that He had taken upon Himself that sorrow in the Person of His own Body, that is, of His Church, to which He is made the Corner-Stone, and which Church cometh unto Him, partly from

[5] De Consens. Evan. lib. iii. c. iv.

the Hebrews, unto whom the word "Abba" appertains, and partly from the Gentiles, unto whom appertains the word "Father." And it may further be observed, that when our Lord, in the person of sinful mankind, complains of utter dereliction on the Cross, He does not use this term, "My Father," implying nearness, but that of "My God," signifying awe and reverence, as from one who, on the Cross, "was made a curse for us." We may also conclude, in like manner, that the term "the Cup," by which our Lord is pleased to designate His sufferings, is replete with great meaning. The expression is, we know, often used in the Scriptures concerning the wrath of God: in the Old Testament it is spoken with reference to the temporal calamities; and in the Book of the Revelation, to the eternal punishment of the wicked. Thus in the prophet Jeremiah we read, "take the wine cup of this fury at My hand[6];" and in Isaiah it is "the cup of fury," and "the cup of trembling[7];" and in Job we read of "drinking the wrath of the Almighty[8]." It therefore seems to signify that our blessed Lord was taking upon Himself the wrath of God and punishment of the wicked. But the expression seems also to have a higher and Sacramental import, and to have some connexion with, and an allusion to the Cup of the Eucharist, by which the Church is made the partaker of our Lord's Blood and His life-giving Passion. And this is the more evident from this circumstance, that on another occasion, when our Lord speaks of suffering under this same term of "the Cup," He speaks of His own disciples partaking of it, in some sense, although not fully in the same sense that He did; and also connects it with an expression relative to the

---

[6] Ch. xxv. 15.   [7] Ch. li. 17.   [8] Ch. xxii. 20.

other Sacrament, " Are ye able to drink of the Cup that I shall drink of, and to be baptized with the Baptism that I am baptized with[9]?" And indeed as all suffering receives the blessing of the Gospel, as bringing us more near to the Cross and Passion of Christ, it may seem to partake of something like a Sacramental efficacy, on account of some secret connexion with our Lord's sufferings. For it is not humanity only which in Christ is brought into life-giving union with the Godhead, but especially suffering humanity.

THE CUP OF AGONY.

Now as our Lord drew near unto Him His disciples in His agony, therefore we may be allowed to approach Him: but as it was only the favoured three, it shows the danger of our presuming to draw near to Him in His sorrows without suitable feeling of awe and humiliation. May we reverently venture to ask, what might have been the cause of this His agony of mind, and the cup which He desired might pass from Him? May it have been that as our Lord was to exhibit the most exquisite of bodily sufferings, so was He also to suffer the most exquisite of mental agonies; whereby it was shown that not in His body alone, but also in soul, He was perfect man? And that as He came to bear our sorrows, may it have been that He was to bear the heaviest of all, the indefinable depression of mental anguish and despondency? Or may it have been from the approach of the powers of darkness, for this was their hour: and that they were now permitted to afflict His pure and righteous Soul, as on the following day His pure and righteous Body: and that with this bitter cup all that was human

[9] **Matt. xx. 22. See Vol. Min. 3rd Year, p. 473.**

in Him was thus overwhelmed?　Or it may have been that dread of death which is inherent in our human nature, and of which the Psalmist speaks as the greatest of terrors which our nature is capable of?　And it is apparently in the person of Christ that he is thus speaking, when he says, " My heart is disquieted within me : and the fear of death is fallen upon me.　Fearfulness and trembling are come upon me : and an horrible dread hath overwhelmed me [10]."　And " the snares of death compassed me round about [11]."　Thus St. Jerome speaks of it as an expression of humanity, for we naturally love life, and shrink from death.　And Gregory [12] says that " at the approach of death He expressed in Himself the struggle of our mind, who suffer strong terror and dread, when by the dissolution of the flesh we approach the eternal judgment."　Or of course it may have been a combination of these three things we have mentioned, an indefinable mental agony, and the operation of evil spirits, and that horror of death which is natural to man : and indeed all these may be but different modes of explaining, or different ways of viewing but one and the same effect—that conflict so terrible to humanity with the King of Terrors.

On a subject so awfully mysterious and inscrutable it were, perhaps, better to leave it thus ; and such simplicity is often our best wisdom.　But there are some considerations which prevent our acquiescing in the above view as a satisfactory explanation ; for on the other side it may be said that the Epistle to the Hebrews, apparently with a reference to this occasion, says, that " He was heard in that He feared ;" but as He was not delivered from death, therefore death itself was not the

---

[10] Ps. lv. 4, 5.　　[11] Ps. cxvi. 3.　　[12] xxiv. Moral. cap. xvii.

object of His deprecation or apprehensions. Besides which, when St. Peter exclaimed against our Lord suffering a painful and ignominious death, he was strongly rebuked by our Saviour for so doing, in words that implied that to offer any suggestion of shrinking from that death was acting the part of Satan. Add to which it may be said, that as Christ in His own martyrs and saints has overcome the dread of death, and even heathen heroes have done so; to attribute our Lord's agony to the fear of death, might appear to derogate from His inconceivable fortitude and majesty. He at all times exhorts us not to fear man, nor that death which man can inflict, but above all things to fear God and His wrath. He was suffering, therefore, under this wrath for our sins. As St. Hilary says [1], " I ask whether it is consistent with reason to suppose that He should have feared to die, who expelling from His disciples all fear of death, exhorted them to the glory of martyrdom; for what sorrow could He Himself be supposed to have felt in the sacrament of death, who gives life to them who die for Him ?" It would seem, therefore, to be a more worthy mode of explanation, to infer that it was not the natural fear of death with which our Lord was thus overwhelmed, but something more peculiarly connected with His meritorious and expiatory sacrifice, and perhaps the effect of His divine charity. It may have been the sins of us all, the weight and penalty of which was upon his soul, and the foreknowledge and recollection of which weighed Him down to the earth. It may have been, also, the thought of the impenitent world, and especially of those His own people, the Jews, who should have a hand in His death; and of His own

---

[1] De Trin. lib. x. 10.

disciple Judas that should betray Him ; and of those also hereafter who should crucify afresh the Lord of Life, and to whom the Cross should be a rock of offence, and on whom He who was the Corner-stone should fall, and grind them to powder. The thoughts of all these, who should have no benefit in His Passion, may have been the bitter cup which He would have had removed. And we shall find, moreover, that the sorrows of His Saints and Prophets, and especially of Jeremiah, that Prophet who was the representative of His own sorrows, was attributed to this cause. "When I would comfort myself against sorrow, my heart is faint in me. For the hurt of the daughter of my people am I hurt ; I am black ; astonishment hath taken hold on me. Oh that my head were waters, and mine eyes a fountain of tears [2] !" It seems moreover natural, on such a subject, to look to signs and expressions of grief, which on other occasions escaped from our blessed Lord. And we shall find that in all instances it was for the sake of others, and on account of others, and not for Himself, that He was affected with grief. When "He sighed," or "was troubled," it was when about to speak of Judas ; and when He "wept," it was at the grave of Lazarus ; and when He gave vent to passionate lamentations and tears, it was over guilty Jerusalem. The expressions connected with His sorrow, on all these occasions, imply that it is for others, and not for Himself, that He is afflicted. Thus St. Hilary says, "Our Lord had before warned them that they should all be offended, and that Peter should thrice deny Him : and it is when He took with Him Peter, and James, and John, that He began to be troubled ; as if it was for those He had taken with Him He was troubled."

[2] Jer. vii. 18. 21 ; ix. 1.

Not that St. Hilary would confine it to this view; for he says[3], "All His fear was for those who should suffer, and He prays for those who should suffer after Him, that the cup should be drunk by others, as it is by Him, without distrust of hope, without sense of pain, without fear of death. And by the expression, 'if it be possible,' He implies that such suffering was naturally a terror to flesh and blood. Whereas according to the Will of the Father, it was necessary for the devil to be overcome, not alone through Christ, but also through His disciples." St. Hilary would, in this place, seem to attribute it to those natural pains which our Lord sustained in the person of mankind. And St. Jerome says, "The Lord was sorrowful, not from the fear of suffering, for He came to suffer, and He had convicted Peter of temerity, but on account of the most unhappy Judas, and the offence of all the Apostles, and the rejection or reprobation of the people of the Jews[4]." Why indeed should we not suppose that it was for the danger of the twelve, and of all His ministers, and of all His Church, and of all the perils, and sins, and disobedience of us all to the end of the world, the denyings of St. Peter, the betrayals of all the Judases that should hereafter arise? Origen again and others, who adopt something like this mode of explaining it, especially apply it to the reprobation of the Jewish people. Origen says, "There is another interpretation of this passage to this effect, that, as the Son of God's love, according to His foreknowledge indeed, He loved those who should believe in Him from the Gentiles; but the Jews He loved as branches of the good olive, as the seed of the holy Fathers, whose was the adoption, and the glory, and the covenant, and

---

[3] Can. xxxi. in Matt. aur. cat.   [4] In Matt. ad loc.

C

the promises. And loving them, He saw what they would suffer who were seeking Him unto death and choosing Barabbas unto life ; therefore, sorrowing for them, He said, ' Father, if it be possible, let this cup pass from Me.' Again, recalling that desire, and seeing how great the advantage to the whole world which would arise through His passion, He said, ' But not as I will, but as Thou wilt.' He saw already, that on account of that cup of His passion, Judas, who was one of the twelve, would be ' the son of perdition.' Again, He understood that through that cup of His passion principalities and powers would be triumphed over in His Body. On account of these, therefore, who He was unwilling should perish in His passion, He said, ' Father, if it be possible, let this cup pass from Me.' But on account of the salvation of all mankind, which through His death would be purchased unto God, as if on a second thought, He said, ' Yet not as I will, but as Thou ;'—that is, if it be possible, that without My passion all those benefits might be allowed, which will be derived through My passion ; let this passion depart from Me, that both the world may be saved, and the Jews may not perish in My passion." We shall see, further, what Origen says on this subject, when we come to speak of our Lord's agony on the Cross. Theophylact alludes to this notion of the rejection of the Jews as a known opinion, saying [5], " Some have understood this as if He said, ' I am sorsowful, not because I am to die, but because the Israelites, who are My kindred, are to crucify Me, and through Me to be excluded from the kingdom of God.' " And St. Jerome seems to take the same view ; in one place he suggests this explanation, that " if Nineveh,

<hr>

[5] Comm. in Marc. aur. cat.

that is, the people of the Gentiles, cannot otherwise be saved unless the gourd be dried up, that is, Judea, let the will of His Father be done, which is not contrary to the will of the Son, as He Himself says through His Prophet [6], ' My will is to do Thy will, O My God.'"   The same writer says, " He requires that if it were possible the cup of His passion might pass from Him, not from fear of suffering, but from compassion for His former people, that He might not receive from their hands the cup He had to drink.   He therefore says expressly, not the cup, but ' this cup,' i. e. that of the people of the Jews, who could have no excuse for their ignorance in slaying Me, who have the Law and the Prophets daily to foretel Me.   But returning to Himself, that which He had tremblingly put from Him in the person of man, in that of God and the Son He accepts, ' But not My will, but Thine, be done.   Let not this be,' He says, ' which I speak out of human affection, but that on account of which I descended to earth at Thy will [7].' "

St. Ambrose also speaks much to this purpose : " Nor is it far from the truth, if He was sad for His persecutors, who He knew would suffer punishment for that enormous sacrilege.   And therefore He said, ' remove this cup from Me,' not because the Son of God feared death, but because He was unwilling that even the bad should perish.   At last He saith, ' Lord, lay not this sin to their charge,' that His passion might be salutary to all [8]."   The same writer also mentioning that some wished to explain away this expression of our Lord's desire to put away His cup, says very beautifully, " But I am so far from considering it a thing to

[6] Ps. xl. 10.   [7] In Matt. lib. iv. c. 26.   [8] Expos. in Luc. lib. x. 62.

be excused, that I do never more exceedingly admire His piety and majesty; for He would have conferred less on me, if He had not undertaken my affections. Therefore for me He grieved Who had for Himself nothing for which to grieve; and having put away the blessedness of eternal Divinity, is affected with the heaviness of my infirmity. For He undertook my sorrow, that on me He might bestow His joy; and by our footsteps descended even to the sadness of death, that by His footsteps He might recall us unto life. With confidence, therefore, I speak of His sadness; because I preach His Cross. For He took upon Him not the semblance of our incarnation, but the reality[o]."

St. Chrysostom also mentions it as an instance of our Lord setting before us by His own example, what He taught us when He told us to pray, that we be not led into temptation. But the whole subject as much transcends our thoughts as the ineffable union of God with man, and the prayer He addressed unto His Father must necessarily surpass all our imagination. In this, the mysterious nature of our Lord and God, we rejoice and tremble, and may say, " I will give thanks unto Thee, for Thou art fearfully and wonderfully made." It, however, serves to indicate, as the ancients observe, the reality of this our Lord's union with our nature, incredible as it might have seemed to be. " First of all," says Chrysostom, " He sent prophets to announce it, afterwards He Himself comes clothed with flesh; and so that you could not suppose it a mere phantom, He permits His flesh to endure natural wants, to hunger, to thirst, to sleep, to labour, to be affected and distressed; on this account He refuses not death, showing His true human nature."

[o] Expos. Luc. lib. x. 56.

From the very variety of opinions expressed on this subject, we may see the force of the term by which our Lord's agony is expressed in the ancient Greek Liturgies, as ἄγνωστα παθήματα, or His unknown sufferings. It was the hour of the powers of darkness, and we know nothing of spiritual agencies. Even of the mental sufferings of each other, it is said, "The heart knoweth its own bitterness." But thus much we may see, that our Lord's obedience would not have been so perfect if His human soul had not shrunk back from that act by which His obedience was perfected: and, as the Son of Man, He not only grew "in wisdom and stature," but also "learned obedience by the things which He suffered."

But it must be observed, that as our Lord's death was perfectly voluntary, so also was this the fear and agony of His Passion, such as He might have set aside if He had pleased. Of which St. Austin says [1], "that He took upon Him these things in His human soul at His own will, as at His own will He was made Man. We indeed have affections of this kind from the infirmity of our human condition: but not so the Lord Jesus, Whose infirmity was from His own power." And Damascenus also [2]:—"Nothing in Christ is to be considered as by compulsion, but all things were by His own will. He willingly hungered, He willingly feared, and was sorrowful." "As man," says Ambrose, "fearing death; as God, adhering to His purpose."

THE BLOODY SWEAT AND THE ANGEL.

St. Luke, perhaps, as writing from St. Paul, who derived his Gospel by immediate revelation from God,

[1] De Civ. Dei, lib. xiv. c. ix.   [2] In lib. iii. c. xx. aur. cat.

here relates two circumstances, which are more removed from human testimony; that "an Angel was seen by Him," and that His sweat was as it were "drops of blood;" and St. Paul himself, in his Epistle to the Hebrews, mentions another circumstance of "strong crying and tears," with which our Lord's prayer was accompanied; and also of His prayer being heard, which may perhaps have reference to the Angel St. Luke speaks of. For to this occasion St. Paul seems to allude in saying, "that in the days of His flesh He offered up prayers and supplications unto Him that was able to save Him from death, and was heard on account of His reverence," or godly fear, or, as it might mean, was heard and saved from the object of His terror [3]; as in the expression, "Thou hast heard me also from among the horns of the unicorns."

St. Luke's account is,—"*And there was seen by Him an Angel from Heaven, strengthening Him: and being in an agony He prayed more earnestly: and His sweat was as it were great drops of blood falling down to the ground.*" As on His former temptation, when He had overcome the tempter, "Angels came and ministered unto Him," so now when He overcame, in His dismal conflict with the powers of darkness, one good Angel appeared strengthening the Son of Man. In such infinite condescension did He deign as man to suffer agony, and in that suffering to receive support from one of His own creatures, who was made and who lived by the breath of His mouth. This Angel has been supposed to have been the Angel Gabriel, which signifies the strength of God; and it is observable, that on another occasion, when St. Luke records the appearing of this Angel, it was under circumstances in some de-

[3] Heb. v. 7, ἀπὸ τῆς εὐλαβείας, conf. xii. 28.

gree analogous.   It was to the priest Zacharias in the holy place apart, and by the altar of incense [4]; so now was it to our merciful High Priest, apart with God, interceding for us, and, as it were, engaged in the great sacrifice of Himself, and especially in the oblation of Himself in prayer, as an incense most pleasing to God.   There is also another occasion in Holy Scripture of the appearance of an Angel, which bears some similarity to it, as supporting a servant of Christ, and granting the lives of others to His intercessions.   We read in the Acts of the Apostles,—" After long abstinence Paul stood forth and said,—There stood by me this night the Angel of God, saying, Fear not, Paul; thou must be brought before Cæsar: and, lo, God hath given thee all them that sail with thee [5]." If, without irreverence, we might mention together things so infinitely distant, the very words might be applied to this occasion ;—" Fear not, for Thou must be brought before Pilate; but God hath answered Thy request, and given Thee all those that sail with Thee through the stormy and dark voyage of mortality." It is important to observe resemblances of this kind, as tending to furnish us with some glimpses of a great principle, the connexion of every blessing with the sacrifice of Christ.   The consolations derived from prayer are known to men by experience, but all such effects may derive their strength from some resemblance to Christ, and secret connexion with His prayer and passion.   Theophylact says, that the Angel is here recorded as appearing for our sakes, that we may be taught the sure efficacy of prayer; if, therefore, there can be a resemblance in our prayers, and a sure efficacy in them, this efficacy must consist in that resemblance.

[4] Luke i. 11.   [5] Ch. xxvii. 23, 24.

But here by the Angel we behold such effects in a living and sensible manner; and it is remarkable how often what we consider mere spiritual effects of certain causes, are in Scripture attributed to living agents; and on this occasion we might have been told that our Lord was strengthened, without our being allowed to behold the Angel. Nor is there any thing in this appearance unworthy of the Son of Man; for if He prayed, and was afflicted and overwhelmed, there is no reason why His wants may not have been supplied by means of one of His creatures.

From the mode in which it is mentioned in St. Luke, it might appear as if the most earnest prayer and the sweat of blood followed the appearance of the Angel, but one would have supposed it was otherwise. Some have thought that it is not meant that His sweat was literally of blood, but that this was a proverbial expression for the vehement profusion and intensity of it. And indeed Theophylact mentions this interpretation. But it appears better to take it literally, especially as cases are recorded of persons having been known to sweat blood from intense mental agony, as Dr. Jackson mentions[6]; and also Maldonatus[7]. In this our blessed Lord's sweat, "falling upon the ground," we can perceive that He bore in its fulness the curse laid on Adam, that in the sweat of his brow he should till the ground, as on the following day He bore the thorns it was to produce. In both cases did the Second Man bear the curse, not figuratively only, but also literally; and that too in a fuller sense than any other child of Adam. For those thorns it produced actually pierced His bleeding temples;

<hr>

[6] Vol. ii. p. 818. [7] Comm. in Matt.

and the sweat which He shed was no other than the blood of His agonized heart, which fell upon the ground that had been cursed for Adam's transgression.

OUR LORD RETURNING TO HIS THREE DISCIPLES.

"*And he cometh* (Matt. Mark) *to His disciples* (Matt.), *and findeth them sleeping, and saith unto Peter.*" (Matt. Mark.)   And here the Gospel of St. Matthew alone would leave us to ask why it is said that our Lord addresses St. Peter; for what He says is in the plural number, as if spoken to them all alike: "*Thus have ye not been able for one hour to watch with Me?*" (Matt.) But St. Mark, or St. Peter by this Evangelist, could not forget or omit that particular warning which magnified his own transgression, and adds the words first addressed to St. Peter himself, "*Simon, sleepest thou?*" thou who hast spoken such great things, thou who art so ready to die for thy Lord : "*hast thou not been able to watch for one hour?*" (Mark.)   And then to them all, "*Watch ye, and pray that ye may not enter into temptation : the spirit is ready, but the flesh is weak.*" (Matt. Mark.) As St. Peter had especially asserted his fidelity, he is more especially addressed; but as they all likewise maintained the same, they are all likewise included in our Lord's admonition.

And here it is not quite evident whether it is to this or to the second occasion of our Lord's coming to them, that the account of St. Luke applies; but the words spoken are chiefly the same as those mentioned by the others. "*And when He rose up from prayer, and had come to His disciples, He found them sleeping for sorrow; and He said unto them, Why sleep ye? rise and pray, that ye enter not into temptation.*" (Luke.)   It is to be observed that St. Luke, the Evangelist of compassion, alone mentions this charitable explanation for their sleep, saying that it was "for sorrow," but not either of the disciples themselves. St. Chrysostom says, "The eyes of the disciples were oppressed with distress, and their sleep was not that of indifference but of grief." The circumstance of their thus sleeping might also lead one to think that it was customary for them thus to sleep in the open air, and may in some slight degree support the supposition that the Transfiguration also occurred by night; but St. Chrysostom mentions that it was not so[8].

"As long as Jesus was with His disciples," says Origen, "they slept not: but when He went but a little from them they could not watch even for one hour, when He was away. Wherefore let us pray that not even for a little while Jesus should depart from us, but should fulfil what He promised us, in saying, 'Lo, I am with you alway, unto the end of the world[9].' For so shall we watch when He shaketh off sleep from our soul, without which it were not possible to fulfil the command which saith, 'Give not sleep to thine eyes, nor slumber to thine eyelids;' 'Deliver thyself as a roe from the hand of the hunter, and as a bird from the hand of the fowler[1].'"

But it may be asked, what is the full meaning of this word "watching?" Origen says, "He watches who does good works; he watches who is anxious for the truth of the faith." Gregory says, "He watches who holdeth his eyes open to the aspect of the true light." The present passage seems to explain itself, as containing both these senses, that it is a shaking off of sleep in order to pray. And this word "sleep" may be taken

---

[8] Vol. Min. 3rd Y. 107.   [9] Matt. xxviii. 20.   [1] Prov. vi. 4, 5.

in a further sense for any thing that keeps the soul from a right estimation of its true condition: all sin is in this sense a sleep of the soul; all forgetfulness of God, and unconsciousness of His presence is so. Sleep and night are in this sense the representatives of evil: and perhaps the alternations of night and day represent "the spirit ready, and the flesh weak," which is the state of the natural man, in contradistinction from that state of perfection where there is no night, and the Lamb is the light thereof. "For these contend with each other," says Origen[2], "in the imperfect; but in the perfect the flesh no longer opposeth, but is mortified. But concerning this weakness the Lord speaketh to the Apostle, 'that strength is perfected in weakness[3].'"

"*Again He departed* (Matt. Mark) *a second time* (Matt.), *and prayed, saying* (Matt. Mark) *the same words* (Mark), *My Father, if this cup cannot pass from Me except I drink it, Thy will be done.*" (Matt.) But, although this was the same prayer as the first, yet it may be observed that there is a slight difference in the meaning and effect of it: for the first prayer was, that if it were possible (*i. e.* possible to the Divine justice, not to the Divine Power, for to that of course all things are possible)—that, if it were possible, "the cup might pass" from Him. But the second implies not only the same perfect resignation, but even in some degree, as Origen observes, a desire to drink it; "If this cup cannot pass from me except I drink it, let Thy will be done." There is not in this even a request to be released from it; for the prayer on the former occasion was, That, if possible, the cup might pass; the prayer now is, That the will of God be done. If we might compare our poor

---

[2] In Matt. Lat. Com. 94.　　　　[3] 2 Cor. xii. 9.

desires with any thing so transcendently and supremely good, we might say it is but that change to higher and still higher resignation, which is ever found in continued prayer.

RETURNING THE SECOND TIME.

"*And he returned* (Mark), *and He came* (Matt.), *and found them sleeping again; for their eyes were heavy.*" (Matt. Mark.) And St. Mark, perhaps writing from St. Peter, gives a more exact description of the state of their feelings, and adds, "*and they knew not what to answer Him.*" (Mark.) The expression is similar to that of the same Evangelist at the Transfiguration, where he states that Peter "knew not what to say, for they were exceedingly afraid." "*And leaving them, He departed again, and prayed the third time, saying the same words.*" (Matt.) "Thus," as St. Jerome says, "did our Lord not only suffer alone for all, but prays also alone for all:" "and the object of His prayer was," says Bede, "that the disciples might obtain leave to repent." But St. Chrysostom notices on this occasion that very remarkable circumstance, which we find so often in Holy Scripture, of the repetition of an act implying confirmation. "By praying a second and a third time," he says, "He certifies that He is truly made man, from that affection of human infirmity by which He feared death. For any thing taking place a second or third time greatly demonstrates certainty in the Scriptures, as Joseph said to Pharaoh; 'for that the dream was doubled unto Pharaoh twice, it is because the thing is established by God.'"

Throughout the account it may be observed that St. Mark follows, step by step, with St. Matthew to detail all that related to our Lord's humanity; St. Luke, all that related to our merciful High Priest, which may afford consolation to a suffering penitent. St. John omits all mention of our Lord's temptation before, and of His sufferings now: dwelling entirely on His Godhead, which was of course incapable of temptation or of suffering: whereas the other three both mention His temptation before and His desire now to put away the Cup, which, as the Fathers mention, was the proof of His true humanity.

It is in this latter point of view that our Lord throughout His mysterious sorrows affords us His most perfect example; and so far as we approach Him in following it, we shall partake of the efficacy of His Passion. In this, as in all other matters, did He who said, "Learn of Me, for I am meek and lowly," humble Himself to the lowest of all humiliations; for what posture of prayer could be more low than that of prostration on the ground? From the efficacy of these His humiliations it has passed into an eternal law, that he who humbles himself shall be exalted. And when He thus resigned Himself to the will of His Father, far greater doubtless was His resignation, on this very account, that human nature shrunk in agony from the Cup, than if His Divine Power had mitigated the bitterness of His suffering humanity. Again, teaching us, in the severest of our own trials, to be ever mindful of others, in the midst of His agonies our Lord returns from His devotions, being ever mindful of His disciples more than of Himself in His Divine love; and teaching us to combine our prayers for others with kind offices to them. Again, He returns to prayer, teaching us by His own example what He had so often taught by precept and parable, "that we faint not in prayer, but continue in the very word of prayer, until we obtain what we have begun to demand[4]." Having enjoined us to seek retirement in prayer, this also He teaches us, by Himself on each occasion going apart: and here again, by His own example also, as well as by the examples of others whose entreaties He answered, He instructs to say the same words, though we use not vain repetitions.

It is in this manner that ancient writers are ever watchful to observe how replete with stores of Divine instruction is every part of our Lord's human example. Thus Gregory Nyssen speaks of our Lord's posture in devotion : " He who carried our infirmities, through the manhood which He assumed, bends His knees in prayer, teaching by the sanction of His example that we behave not proudly in the time of prayer, but by all things conform ourselves to humility; for ' God resisteth the proud, and giveth grace unto the humble[5].' " And St. Cyril, of our Lord's retirement in prayer, says, " Here you will find Him retiring apart in prayer, that you may learn, that with attentive mind and quiet heart we must converse with the lofty God. But it was not as needing the assistance of another, that He continued in prayers, Who is the most Almighty Power of the Father; but that we may learn that we must not sleep in temptation, but persevere the more in prayer." St. Chrysostom also speaks of our Lord's retiring to pray, as our example : " It was His custom to pray without the disciples; and this He did, instructing us that in our supplications we should compose ourselves to quiet, and seek solitude."

[4] Origen. in Matt. 95.   [5] 1 Pet. v. 8.

OUR LORD'S LAST RETURN.

" *Then* (Matt.) *He cometh* (Matt. Mark) *the third time* (Mark) *to His disciples* (Matt.), *and saith unto them, Sleep on now for the future, and take your rest.*" (Matt. Mark.) As if He had said, "I asked you to watch and pray with Me one hour, but that hour is now past: that opportunity for watching and praying with Me is now over; the time for putting on your spiritual armour is past." " *It is enough* (Mark); *behold* (Matt.) *the hour* (Matt. Mark) *hath come* (Mark), *or is at hand.*" (Matt.) My need of your watching with Me is now over, " it is enough," or it is all over, you now can do no more. " *Behold* (Mark) *the Son of Man is betrayed into the hands of sinners. Arise, let us depart. Behold, He that betrayeth Me is at hand.*" (Matt. Mark.) "For in the Spirit," says Origen, "He beheld Judas drawing near to betray Him, when he was not yet seen by His disciples."

There is an apparent discrepancy in our Lord's words, for He first tells them to " sleep on," and afterwards to " arise." St. Austin suggests that our Lord was silent after speaking the first words, and, after a short interval, added the latter sentence. But the more obvious way of understanding it seems to be to suppose our Lord's first words are meant as a gentle reproof, and, as Theophylact expresses it, are spoken ironically, if we may venture to apply such a term to our Lord's words. And this is confirmed by finding that our Lord does so speak by His Prophets, when something else is implied besides that which the words, taken literally, would signify.

It seems natural to suppose that circumstances, so momentous and awful as are here described, may contain some great mystical references, that look both before and after. That such a supposition is not unnatural would appear from this, that something of the kind suggests itself to ancient writers. Thus St. Jerome says, that this circumstance of the disciples sleeping three times, signifies the three whom our Lord raised from the dead; the first in the house, the second near the sepulchre, the third from the sepulchre. And St. Hilary suggests a future reference [6], that " on His return to them, and finding them asleep, on His first coming He reproves them, on the second He is silent, on the third He bids them rest." And this He applies to our Lord's visitations after His Resurrection, " when first of all finding them dispersed, distrustful, and alarmed, He reproves them. At the second time He visited them by sending them His Spirit, the Comforter, when their eyes were heavy to behold the liberty of the Gospel; for they were for some time detained in their love of the law, and possessed as it were by a sleep of faith. But at the third time, that is, on the return of His brightness, He will restore them to security and to rest." Such observations of the Fathers are at all events sufficient to show that it is not unnatural to suppose, that these circumstances, in themselves so important, might also furnish analogies with respect to the Christian Church, fulfilled in various ways and directing the thoughts to higher developments. For of course three occasions of raising the dead; three returns of our Lord to awaken His disciples; three times of retiring to prayer, may also have a reference to some dealings of Christ with mankind in the Christian dis-

---

[6] Com. in Matt. xxxi. 11.

pensation. For very mysterious as the government of God is, yet we may observe throughout, that His providences have a tendency to unfold themselves again and again under analogous circumstances, and in similar results ; and all these going on to further developments in that which is infinite. In like manner as in things natural the course of time developes itself in a recurrence of similar nights and days, and of similar seasons, again and again appearing in like manner. And all these but shadows of greater things hereafter, the morning of the Resurrection, and the great New Year and restoration of all things.

If therefore such a prophetic reference is not unreasonable; and we may suppose that our Lord's visitations of His Church may in some degree partake of a resemblance to these His returns to His disciples, on that night of their watching; we may perhaps venture to suggest one point of analogy in all visitations of God, and especially in the descriptions which are given of His last and final return ;—which is the following.

Independently of the deeply solemn interest of this scene to every child of Adam ; there is something very remarkable in the awful stillness wherein our Lord visits His disciples : which seems to bear a great analogy to that of His last coming. It is midnight, and silence, and darkness. And notwithstanding the occasion is one of such momentous concern and consequence, the disciples were weighed down heavily with sleep and sorrow, and the arts of the tempter. There is something in it similar to that of His awakening His disciples at the Transfiguration, when in like manner they were heavy with sleep, and awakened by His Divine touch and voice. And as that scene of the Transfiguration appears to represent the great and general Resurrection : so this also carries on our thoughts to that time, which is so often described as our Lord's coming at midnight, and finding mankind asleep in the dead stillness of night. His last Advent is especially likened to the coming of a thief, which is closely and literally applicable to this approach of Judas. And when our Lord now comes to His disciples with His warning voice, the agonies of that night appear to be over, and succeeded by a calm. So is it supposed that the distress and tumult of the last age will be over, and men shall say, " Peace, and all things are safe," when in the night of Antichrist and of darkness He will be at hand. In the mean time the Spirit of Christ in His Church, who intercedeth for us and in us "with groanings that cannot be uttered," is ever calling on His disciples to watch and pray with Him. He it is in His Church, the great Keeper, who neither slumbers nor sleeps, who is represented as perceiving the approach of the Judge, who is drawing near as a thief in the night; before a sight or a sound of His presence is heard by the slumbering world. It is He who gives the midnight cry, " Behold, the Bridegroom cometh." And is ever ready for His coming, saying at the end of His revelation, " even so come." And His Church also awakened by Him, will be able to " lift up her head," and behold that her " Redemption draweth nigh;" and, before its actual appearance, to discern that the time is at hand.

It will be observed that there is something in many of the descriptions of our Lord's return which partake of this very awful and quiet stillness which characterizes this scene that precedes the coming of Judas, and is to the disciples our Lord's warning and visitation. Let us take for instance the parable of the Ten Virgins, which being put in the persons of virgins, seems to represent the state of God's elect, in His visible Church. It is the dead of night, when all expectation of Christ's return seems to have ceased: so still and quiet, that not only the unfaithful servants, but even the good and faithful are slumbering, for it is expressly said, "while the Bridegroom tarried they all slumbered and slept." There is no sound without, and no thought within, that arouses them up, as if they heard a step approaching— the well-known step of their Lord returning—the sound of the thief in the night—the movement of the angelic armies. But it is all dead stillness and sleep when— the midnight cry is heard;—and that so deep and awful, that it has been thought to be but the summons of the conscience awakening within; or the whisper of an angel, or of One greater than an angel. At the same time there is already present One who bears "the keys of David," "the keys of death and of hell." The voice that awakened them seemed to say, "Could ye not have watched with Me one hour?" They are awakened from sleep, and the door is closed! Something of the same kind is the case with other events that typify or prefigure this great coming of God. Thus in the taking of Babylon, that city which so often is the representative of the world, it is at midnight, and if not actually in a state of sleep, for they are eating and drinking at a feast, yet it is in that spiritual slumber which Scripture describes. But what is to be observed is, that the same still and awful quietness pervades this visitation of God, and the warning that announces His coming. Not a voice is heard; nor a form seen: but a hand is perceived quietly writing in fiery letters on the wall, to tell them that their time of trial is over and finished: they had been already weighed in the balance and found wanting. He whom Christ had "called by name" and appointed to save His people was already at the gate. The same was the case also in Egypt: it was there also at the very dead of the night, the Angel passed by with an unerring but noiseless step, and suddenly, at midnight, a cry was heard! Whilst Israel, as it were Christ in type, of whom it was said, "Out of Egypt have I called My Son," was waiting in quietness, with loins girded, with shoes on his feet, ready to depart when the summons came—to pass through the Red Sea of blood to the heavenly land, and saying, as Christ to His own, "Come, let us go hence." There was much of the same kind in the destruction of Sodom, and in the account of God's coming to it on the previous night. There is something tremendously awful in the calm and momentous tranquillity that attended the coming of the Angels to that city, as it must have appeared to Abraham. The sun set as usual—there was Lot sitting at the gate, and the apparently houseless strangers quietly approaching—the Angel seized Lot by the hand, warned and aroused him three times while he lingered, and said, "Escape for thy life!"—Early the next morning Abraham looked to the place where the city stood, and, lo, the smoke went up as the smoke of a furnace.

The same deep and solemn calm attended also our Lord's first coming. It was in the stillness of night. There is no reason to suppose that there was any thing more than usual in that night, or any awakened expectation; the shepherds were watching their sheep in the field when the Heavens were opened upon them. "The glory of the Lord shone round about them." "And suddenly there was with the angel a multitude of the heavenly host, praising God." At our Lord's rising also from the grave, it was the dead stillness of night. Among the many thousand children of Adam that covered the globe, no one heard a sound, no thought occurred to any one respecting that great event, which lifted up all the earth nearer Heaven.

Thus the visitations of God we ever naturally connect with solitude and stillness, and expect them in the noiseless step of an angel, or a spirit, or a shadow, or a dream; modes in which they have been usually vouchsafed. And all these His visitations are but forerunners of His great and last. The throne of God is sometimes represented to us as borne on living wheels, but these wheels sound not perceptibly to human ear, though the Spirit of Christ in His Church is capable of discerning them. And the reason of all this may be on account of the unalterable and deep stillness in which the throne of God is, of which all things partake that are connected with it. It is represented to us here below, by the calm stillness of the Heavens, beyond the reach of our earthly clouds: and the still watches of the stars, which are like the outposts of that dread tranquillity.

As this is the case in the last and great visitation of God, and in many things in Scripture which shadow forth that event; and as it is the case in the sensible instances of His interference, so is it also in those circumstances which, spiritually and figuratively, we are in the habit of calling visitations of God. His comings and goings are such as cannot be discerned: His ways are in silence and solitude, so are all His visitations of the soul. There is something of awfulness in the stillness and quiet in which they come and go. Men love ever to be in excitement, in agitation, business, noise, or company; endeavouring thereby to flee from God, who dwells in unspeakable calm. But in the intervals of these, in awful and dead stillness, God visits. This is the case with that greatest of visitations, which is death. There is nothing in death so striking, so overpowering to survivors, as that dreadful and unearthly stillness with which it is accompanied: profound, and deep, and still! In strange contrast to the agitation and feverish stir of life. The same is the case whenever God visits; all things that trouble or excite the mind must be set aside, and we must meet our God in silence and stillness, in order that we may hear that still and small voice in which God is. In stillness and solitude God is apt to commune with the good, and to awaken the consciences of the wicked. All these seem but tokens and preparations for that scene which is on the other side of the grave: when all the noise of the world will be set far away; and all its concerns unheard and forgotten; and we shall stand alone with God: in that awful world where God is: where there are no wars nor rumours of wars: no buying and selling: no planting and building: no marrying or giving in marriage: no change of seasons: no noise of days, and months, and years, but the calm stillness of eternity, in which the sinner will have to stand alone with his God.

What wonder, therefore, if all things of awful moment, when the Judge stands by our side, should partake of this calm—when the earthquake and the whirlwind have gone by, and nothing is heard but the still and small voice of Christ, awakening the disciples? Such is the scene which now comes before us—deep and dreadful is the calm, while the Judge is standing by, in the dark and profound quiet of the garden of Gethsemane; where the disciples are unable to keep themselves awake, and the gracious hand and voice of their Lord is in vain attempting to arouse them. And now He has come to them with the intelligence that all is over.

SECTION II.—THE APPREHENSION.

" He laid his hands upon such as be at peace with him, and he brake his covenant."

THE APPROACH OF JUDAS.

SOME time had now elapsed since Judas had left the room of the Last Supper, and many circumstances had since taken place; the cup of the Eucharist, perhaps, and our Lord's parting discourse in the house, and the hour of His agony in the garden; during which time the traitor had to go to the Chief Priests, to inform them that a favourable opportunity had now arrived for the execution of their purpose, to collect the officers, and then, perhaps, to wait for that dead hour of night, which would most suit the execution of his diabolical design. The very spot he had selected for this purpose was remarkable; St. John shortly mentions it in these words, " *and Judas also, which betrayed Him, knew the place: for Jesus ofttimes resorted thither with His disciples.*" It is evident he was aware our Lord was not to be found in a house, but in this secret and retired resort of private friendship, which he knew from being one of His friends ;—the circumstance of which the Psalmist complains,—it was not Mine adversary, " for then peradventure I would have hid Myself from him [7]." The spot indeed was so familiar to him as the place where our Lord usually resorted with His disciples, that he might cal-

[7] Ps. lv. 13.

culate on finding Him there. St. Luke had said, when speaking of our Lord's teaching in the temple during this week, that " He went forth and stayed the night at the Mount of Olives;" and this evening also he says, on their coming to the garden, that " He went forth, as His custom was, to the Mount of Olives[8]," which seems to indicate that in the former expression He spoke of this place to which He resorted every night. It seems probable that not only during the week of our Lord's Passion, but at other times, this had been the place of their resort; for it is said, He " oftentimes resorted thither:" and on another occasion, at the Feast of Tabernacles, St. John speaks of His retiring from the temple to the Mount of Olives[9]. The Fathers, too, as Origen, Chrysostom, and Theophylact, observe, that it was our Lord's custom to withdraw into mountains and gardens and solitary places, to converse with His disciples on the sublimer mysteries of the faith; and especially, says the last-mentioned writer, at festivals. Here therefore the traitor had oft resorted with Him, had witnessed His prayers, and heard His discourses, and here he knew He was now engaged in prayer. No spot, one would have thought, could have been more hallowed than this spot, a more unapproachable sanctuary, fit only for the haunt of good angels; but as the powers of darkness had now intruded there, so also had their earthly minister. And how remarkable does it seem, that the spirits of darkness have no power unless they get mankind to co-operate and conspire with them: in like manner, as the Chief Priests and Pharisees had no power until they get one of Christ's chosen disciples to co-operate in league with them.

8 Ch. xxi. 37. xxii. 39.   9 Ch. viii. 1.

Our Lord at the moment had gone, as we observed, to His disciples, from the place where He had been praying, to arouse them and said, "Behold, he that betrayeth Me is at hand." "*And immediately* (Mark), *while He was yet speaking*" (Matt. Mark, Luke), there appeared through the dark olive garden a mingled troop, hastening forwards towards them, with torches and arms. It is mentioned that there was a great crowd of them, consisting of soldiers and servants. And Judas himself, who is emphatically called by three of the Evangelists "one of the twelve," was distinctly seen; for he was the first of the band, and leading the way, as St. Luke informs us. "*Behold* (Matt.), *there cometh forward*" (Mark), or "*came*" (Matt.), "*Judas, one of the twelve, and with him a great multitude with swords and staves, from the Chief Priests* (Matt. Mark), *and the Scribes* (Mark), *and the Elders* (Matt. Mark) *of the people.*" (Matt.) St. John mentions more distinctly who they were; "*Judas therefore having received a band and servants from the Chief Priests and Pharisees, cometh there with torches, and lanterns and weapons.*" And St. Luke describes the guidance and advance of the traitor: "*Behold the multitude, and he that is called Judas, one of the twelve, went before them.*" That the three Evangelists allude to the great guilt of the traitor by merely adding the words, "being one of the twelve," is noticed by St. Chrysostom and others; and this expressive simplicity partakes of that peculiar severity and sanctity with which Holy Scripture often alludes to crimes; as indeed do men of humble and holy heart, under the teaching of the Spirit. And now, as Judas was seen leading the band, so he advances a little before them, and approaches our Lord; and here it may be necessary to pause, and consider the order of events that ensue.

In proceeding thus we arrange the accounts rather differently from some modern harmonists (such as Archbishop Newcome), who would suppose that our Lord first goes forth to meet them, as St. John records; and that afterwards Judas comes forth from among them to kiss Him, according to the other accounts. The reason for preferring the mode here adopted is this, that it seems more natural to suppose that the sign of recognition would take place before our Lord declared to them all who He was, than afterwards; and that Judas is mentioned in the Gospels as advancing before the others, which our method supposes him to do, and because it is said, " Immediately when he came he went up to Him." It is supposed that the traitor came not only preceding, but almost as one detached from the crowd, as if from another quarter; so that our Lord's allusion to His betrayal has been considered as of itself an act of His Divine foreknowledge, which it could not have been if the traitor had been already standing with the armed company. And we have the sanction of St. Augustin for this arrangement, for he says [1], "The Lord, when He is betrayed, first said what Luke mentions, ' Judas, with a kiss betrayest thou the Son of Man ?' Next what Matthew says, ' Friend, wherefore art thou come ?' and, lastly, what John records, ' Whom seek ye ?' "

As it might be expected that our Lord Himself would not be discernible from the rest of His disciples, especially at night, and to a mixed multitude of men who

---

[1] De Consens. Evang. lib. iii. c. 5.

had perhaps never seen Him, the traitor had agreed on a signal; "*Now he that betrayed Him had given them a sign, saying, Whomsoever I shall kiss the same is He; hold him fast*" (Matt. Mark); to which St. Mark emphatically adds, "*and lead Him away safely*" (Mark). The traitor added this from an apprehension, we may suppose, that our Lord might escape, as He had often done, from the very hands of His enemies. St. Luke mentions one instance of this kind, when they took Him to the brow of the hill at Nazareth[2]; and St. John more than once speaks of it at Jerusalem[3]. "*Immediately when He came*" (Matt. Mark), say two of the Evangelists, "*he came up to Him (Mark), to Jesus (Matt.), and said, Hail (Matt.), Master*" (Matt.), or, in emphatic agitation, "*Master, Master (Mark), and kissed Him* (Matt. Mark). *Jesus*," addressing him by name, "*said unto him, Judas! with a kiss betrayest thou the Son of Man?*" (Luke.) And adds, according to St. Matthew, as if in further words of kind remonstrance, and perhaps looking to the armed crowd that accompanied him, who were now coming up to him, "*Friend, for what purpose art thou come?*" Then, with calm self-possession, as if in full consciousness of all things that were coming upon Him, He went forth, as St. John tells us, to meet His enemies; and said, as if to show there was no occasion for this signal of the traitor, "*Whom seek ye? They answered Him, Jesus the Nazarene. Jesus saith unto them, I am He*" (or I am). And Judas, who had now stepped back from our Saviour's presence, stood among the foremost of the crowd by the side.

Here we have a remarkable instance of the mode in which one Gospel comes in to explain another; for

---

[2] Ch. iv. 30.   [3] As ch. viii. 20. 59. x. 39. vii. 30.

St. Luke mentions his coming with a kiss, and also our Lord's reply, but he does not mention what the others record, the circumstance of his having agreed upon this signal with his companions. So wonderful is the manner in which God is pleased to supply us with knowledge, not in one place and at one time, but so as that it may be collected from different sources, as if the more to awaken our interest and to claim our pains and attention. And by adjusting the different accounts, and putting the Evangelists together, we obtain a more varied, a more lively and full description of our Lord as perfect God and perfect Man, than any one continued narrative could have afforded.

THE KISS OF JUDAS.

The very nature of the signal which Judas had agreed upon is remarkable, and worthy of deep contemplation, as setting before us the conduct of our adorable Lord and God, manifest in the flesh. In the first place, it is like all such minute circumstances, in itself interesting, as disclosing to us the demeanour of our blessed Lord to His own disciples : for it is supposed that the kiss of charity in the early Church took its rise from this circumstance ; the custom to which St. Paul alludes in saying, " Greet one another with an holy kiss." But it is much to be noticed on the present occasion, as indicating the very affectionate and friendly footing with which our Lord was wont to receive this wicked man ; and is of the same character as that of His eating at supper out of the same dish with him, and washing his feet on this very night. Such a token of love and gentleness, habitually afforded to so evil a man, can only be equalled by that forbearance and goodness which the same Divine Master ever shows in His natural providence, whereby He maketh His sun to rise on the evil and on the good, and continues to benefit the unthankful. This is the conduct He has held forth to us as our pattern of love, telling us that our perfection consists in being merciful as our Heavenly Father is merciful. But this should render us careful not to presume on that kindness, as if it afforded any intimation that we were pleasing Him now, or should be finally accepted of Him. For this His mercy is full of mystery, and therefore a reason why, as the Psalmist says, He should be feared. But though the case of Judas might have appeared to all human eyes as incurable, yet the Divine Physician does not give up His care of him in the depth of his misery. Our Lord's answer on this occasion contains the last of those touching and solemn appeals to him, of which so many are recorded. By his name He addressed the traitor, which, as St. Chrysostom observes, was like one that was grieved and would recall him, not an expression of provocation or anger. And St. Ambrose says, it was to arrest the traitor by so affectionate an appeal. "How great," exclaims Theophylact, with wonder, " was the patience and long-suffering of the Lord, that He should even kiss the traitor, and address him with friendly words! For He did not say, O wicked wretch, O most wicked traitor, is this the return thou makest for all My benefits? but 'Judas!' which is rather the voice of pity than of anger."

Then adds our Lord yet more touchingly, "with *a kiss* betrayest thou?" for these are the first and emphatic words in the original Greek. And if the term, " betrayest thou," was a proof of Divine knowledge which ought to have struck him with awe and apprehension, the expression of " the Son of Man " that followed, was surely enough to move him to affection. It is not

' thy master,' nor ' thy benefactor,' nor ' thy friend,' it is
by a term more condescending and endearing than any of
these that our Lord designates Himself, as one that had
come down from the right hand of God to save him,
" the Son of Man."　Thus St. Ambrose considers that
He discloses as God His knowledge of the betrayal, and
still does not withhold His long-suffering.　By manifesting things hidden He shows that it is God whom he betrays, while He meekly calls Himself the Son of Man.

In words still more expressive of affectionate grief
and surprise, " Friend, wherefore art thou come ?"　The
very appellation at once brings before us the prophecy,
" Yea, My own familiar friend whom I trusted, who did
also eat of My bread, hath laid great wait for Me[4]."
Origen, indeed, remarks of this word " friend," we know
no one in the Scriptures thus addressed in honour; but
to the bad man not clothed in the wedding-garment it is
said, " Friend, wherefore camest thou in hither ?"　And
in the parable of the labourers in the vineyard, the bad
man is addressed with " Friend, I do thee no wrong[5]."
This observation is very remarkable, that the term should
be thus used on occasions of evil; yet it is, notwithstanding, in itself expressive of affection.　Nor is it
without authority that we consider our Lord's conduct
to Judas on this occasion as that of great kindness and
affectionate admonition.　St. Chrysostom mentions it as
a proof how deaf to all warnings is the soul which is given
up to any sin.　And yet he says,—" that after the example of Christ, we must not cease from admonishing our
brother, although nothing is effected by our words, for
rivulets continue to flow on still, though no one draws
from them; and if perhaps you shall not have persuaded

---

[4] Ps. xli. 9.　　　　　[5] Comm. in Matt. xx. 13.

to-day, you may be able to do so to-morrow. For the fisherman, after drawing his empty nets all the day, may take a fish towards the evening.—Hence our Lord, though He knew that Judas would not be converted, yet He ceased not to do all that lay in His part." And St. Ambrose, as we observed, mentions our Lord's receiving him with a kiss, and thus addressing him, as an effort to move him by affection. "Our Lord kissed him," he says, "not that He would teach us to feign affection, but both that He might not seem to shrink from being betrayed, and that He might the more move the betrayer by not denying him the offices of love."

The token of betrayal, and the place of betraying, were both of them very astonishing certainly. It would appear, from the signal, that Judas had thus kept up to the last, and still desired to keep up, the external show of friendship; which seems to indicate more strongly, that our Lord's words to him, in declaring his intention, were a proof of Divine knowledge ; and, like the subsequent manifestation of His power, an indication to them that if He was taken it was as a willing captive. Kindness therefore, and reproof, friendly intimacy, and Divine omniscience, were all shown in those few short words; and patience, more than human, under outrage most surpassing and most trying of all, that of a treacherous friend. But it moves him not, for he was as one spell-bound by evil purpose, or, as our blessed Saviour has told us, by the indwelling of Satan. And thus it ever is that wicked men, blinded by their crimes, and indeed all of us, as far as we are under the dominion of evil, act as if God were blind also. Nor is there any thing in the world more wonderful and mysterious than this blindness; so much so, that the accounts of it would appear incredible in reasoning beings, did not experience daily set cases of it before us. He is passed, in one short hour, from the presence of Light at the Supper of the Lamb into outer darkness : from the Apostleship of Christ into the ministry of Satan ; has become a servant of the Chief Priests, and is depending on their aid, and a band of armed men, and yet knows not what he had so often witnessed, that by a word, or the mere act of His will, Christ might overcome them all, and scatter them as the chaff before the wind. And yet even this knowledge of Christ's power seems involuntarily to drop from him, when he says, " Hold Him fast, and lead Him away safely." But thus it is, as St. Jerome observes,—he who despairs of the assistance of God leans on the power of the world. Indeed this transaction is but a type of those who do so, and of the broken reed that pierces them.

But the depth of his wickedness, and the extraordinary blindness of eyes, and dulness of ears, and slowness of understanding, which characterize his whole conduct, seem to indicate that he was now sealed up in the power of the evil one. And indeed our Lord's words of gracious warning, that failed to stop his headlong career, were not more remarkable than the minute descriptions of him in the Psalms. In two distinct Psalms is he set forth as the " friend " and " companion ;" and the very kiss of his treason is described, " he laid his hands upon such as be at peace with him ; and he brake his covenant. The words of his mouth were softer than butter, having war in his heart[6]." It is indeed greatly to be observed how much there is in the Psalms respecting Judas throughout; partly, we may suppose, from his being so prominent in the his-

---

⁶ Ps. lv. 22.

tory of the Lord, and partly from his becoming, from that very circumstance, in some manner the great type of the wicked; and therefore it is that what is said of him is also in some degree true of the Jews, and a type that is still further developed in bad Christians, and last of all, and chiefly, in Antichrist. Of whose forerunners it is expressly said, " Beware of them; for they come to you in sheep's clothing, but inwardly they are ravening wolves;" and of Antichrist, " that he sitteth in the temple of God;" and of Satan, that he is " transformed into an Angel of Light." For who can be more properly described as the wolf in sheep's clothing, than he who came to take the Lamb of God, and to scatter the sheep of the good Shepherd? He sat indeed in the temple of God, as he sat in Christ's nearer and visible presence; of whom Christ says, " We walked in the house of God as friends." He sat in the temple of God as one of those twelve to whom He had appointed twelve thrones in His kingdom: and he was indeed transformed into an Angel of Light, for even the eleven Apostles suspected him not. Well, therefore, might he serve for a type of those awful things to be more fully manifested in the Wicked one hereafter.

Perhaps too in the very kiss of Judas there may be a sign of some great principle in apostasy. " But I suppose," says Origen, " that all betrayers of the truth feign love for the truth, and use the sign of the kiss, in token of affection, when they betray the Word of God to His enemies[7];" and this he applies to the case of heretics, and says, that " to all of them Jesus replies in the same peaceful manner." It may be the same principle which Bishop Butler alludes to, when he says—

---

[7] In Matt. tom. iv. 100.

that no evil is carried on in a public way, but under the specious name of virtue.   For this is in fact to betray the Son of Man with a token of affection; this is practising wickedness while sitting in the temple of God.

It is further to be noted, that the sin which thus blinded the eyes of Judas was that to which "deceivableness" is especially attributed, and which was the source of evil in the other false pretenders, or prophets, as Balaam and Simon Magus, and those of the last days, of whom the Apostle speaks, who make a trade of godliness.   There is no reason to doubt but that if this vice had been removed, he would have seen, equally as clearly as the other Apostles, "the things that belonged unto his peace."   Probably even in their case it was all a matter of degrees, according to their freedom from earthly vices, that they apprehended Christ and His words and actions.   As it is, he seems as one under an enchantment.   The prophecies were being fulfilled, one by one, in every event and expression that arose, but he saw not.   Our Lord had been long manifesting a miraculous power before his eyes, but he saw not.   He had also all his own designs shown to him, which fully proved a Divine presence, but he saw not.   Very much the same was the case with the Jews.   Even, in some degree, was there something of this human blindness and dulness in the Apostles; but this was in their case very partial, and neither inveterate nor continuous. Was it not nine times that they were told of the Crucifixion? but they understood it not.   St. Peter had confessed our Lord to be the Son of God, but now he seems to have forgotten it, or he would have seen the mountain encompassed "with chariots of fire and horses of fire."   Although his denial was so often foretold, yet he knows it not till it is passed.   And all this is probably a picture or emblematic representation of human nature, as it will appear when all things are revealed hereafter, and life is over. But now Scripture strongly pourtrays it as " having eyes " and " seeing not."

It may be further observed, that the aggravations of Judas's crime, the mode, the place, the accompanying circumstances, the Person, are all connected with the exceeding greatness of his privileges. Perhaps, indeed, it was the greatness of these advantages vouchsafed to him, that occasioned the abandoned and desperate character of his irreclaimable course : for, as Quesnel well observes, "the higher from whence we fall, the less hope is there of recovery," For his case is something like that which the Epistle to the Hebrews describes of " those who have once tasted of the heavenly gift " and have fallen away, "whom it is impossible to renew again unto repentance." In the case of the Holy David, it is mentioned by St. Chrysostom as a proof of his extraordinary piety and goodness of heart, that he should have been able to repent after so great a fall as his was, from so great a height of holiness. For recovery in such a case is in the highest degree remarkable and extraordinary ; and partly perhaps on that account causes a movement and a stir among the blessed societies of Heaven, who rejoice over one sinner that repents.

THE MULTITUDE STRUCK TO THE GROUND.

It does not appear evident why so large a body of men, and those armed, should have come. It was probably from fear of the multitude : or it might possibly be also, as Origen remarks, from a sort of indescribable dread of our Lord's power, whether they attributed it to magical arts or the agency of Beelzebub, or merely felt that indefinable and mysterious awe which He shed around Him when seemingly defenceless and in their power. Therefore they wished perhaps to support each other, as men do when half afraid, by a show of strength. "But there hath come down to us a tradition of this kind," says Origen, "concerning Him, that not only were there two forms in Him, one indeed according to which all beheld Him, the other according to that to which He was transfigured in the presence of His disciples on the Mount, when His countenance shined as the sun; but also He appeared to each according as he was worthy. And though it was He Himself, yet it was not so that He appeared unto all; like as is written of the manna, when God sent bread from Heaven to the children of Israel, which adapted itself unto every taste[8]." And something of this kind must of necessity have been the case, for they who, like St. John, saw God manifested in Jesus Christ, beheld a very different person from what they did, who, like Judas, beheld only a despised man. There must, therefore, have been communicated from one to another an unconscious fear respecting Him.

There is a simple and Divine majesty in the beloved Disciple's words, as he proceeds to record it: "*Jesus therefore, knowing all things that were coming upon Him, went forth and said unto them, Whom seek ye?*" This going forth to meet them seems to imply that readiness to be offered up which He had so often evinced. Thus, when advancing to Jerusalem for the last time, it is said that "He went before them," with such stedfastness setting His face toward Jerusalem, that "they were amazed and alarmed in following Him[9]." And

[8] In Matt. Com. tom. iv. 400.   [9] Mark x. 32.

afterwards when His human nature recoiled from the conflict, if we may so speak of Him, He seemed to stir up His soul within Him to meet the hour by saying, "Father, glorify Thy Name!" Again to the traitor He said, " What thou doest, do quickly ;" and when He was leaving the supper table, as St. John says, He arose from it as if with earnestness, and said, " Arise, let us go hence;" and just before the approach of Judas He repeats the words, "Arise, let us be going." So now, in accordance with all this, He goes forth to meet them, in calm and heavenly meekness indeed, as a lamb to the slaughter, but with a more than martyr's courage. So wonderfully do the two circumstances seem to coincide and run parallel together through-out, that of our Lord's freely and spontaneously sub-mitting Himself to death, as the Great High Priest who offered up Himself as a perfect sacrifice ; and that of His enemies, all taking a part in His death, and laying their hands as it were on the head of the victim.

To His question, "Whom seek ye ?" they reply, "*Jesus of Nazareth. Jesus saith unto them, I am He (or I am). And Judas, who betrayed Him, stood among them. When therefore He said unto them, I am He, they went backward and fell to the ground.*" They spoke of Him by that most blessed but most dreadful Name, at which " every knee shall bow, of things in Heaven, and things in earth." The prophet and the historian describe our Lord's enemies, and His own resignation and courage, in much the same characters. " When the wicked, even Mine enemies and My foes came upon Me to eat up My flesh, they stumbled and fell. Though an host of men were led against Me, yet shall not My heart be afraid." By this circumstance they might have perceived that they had no power to apprehend

Him, if He were not a willing captive; for even when
He was present before their eyes, they could not know
nor acknowledge Him. As St. Chrysostom observes,
" He first sets before them every thing that might be
the means of reclaiming them, that it might not be
supposed that He tempted them on to His destruction."
And this is but a visible type of what He does daily in
His moral providence with us; He warns, and shows
indications of His power, but leaves men to their own
free will. Nay, by His inscrutable and adorable mercy,
He casts men to the ground; but they acknowledge
Him not in His judgments, and attribute their fall to
accident and not to His invisible power, and arise and
proceed with their designs against Him. In another
sense also is it symbolical, for that which was then
fulfilled in the letter is fulfilled in the figure also; for
from that hour to this our Lord by His Gospel seems
to be saying to the Jews, "*I am He*." "But," adds St.
Austin, "Antichrist is expected by the Jews, so that
they go backward and fall to the ground, for they
are deserting things heavenly, and desiring things
earthly[1]." St. Cyril of Alexandria observes the same
mystical figure. "What here happens in part," he
says[2], "to those who came for His apprehension, is a
sign of the fall of the whole Jewish nation. Whence
the Prophet Jeremiah laments the Jews, saying, 'The
house of Israel hath fallen, who shall raise it up?'"
The occurrence also may be an image of a necessary
consequence; for it teaches the utter and entire fall and
prostration of those who meditate evil against Christ.

Our Lord a second time advanced towards them with
the same question,—"*Again therefore He asked them.
Whom seek ye? And they said, Jesus of Nazareth.*

---

[1] In Joan. Tract. cxii. 3.   [2] In Joan. l. xi. 6.

Jesus answered, I said unto you that I am He" (or I am).
(John.)   Thus does our Lord twice come forth to the
Jews, who are seeking Him in the dark night with lanterns and torches, though it be the full Paschal moon.
What He does twice He will do a third time also, as
twice He drove them from His temple in typical anticipation of His "coming to His temple" the third time;
so now also, a little while, and He will come forth to
the Jews, His enemies, and say, "Whom seek ye?"
and by His wounds, and the sign of the Son of Man,
He will say to their inquiries, "I am He;" so that they
shall fall to the ground before Him.   Not only so, but
"shall say to the mountains, Fall on us; and to the hills,
Cover us ³;" for if one gentle expression had such power,
what must it be to hear from Him "one rough word ⁴?"

OUR LORD INTERCEDES FOR HIS DISCIPLES.

It may be asked what apparent reason was there for
our Lord's thus exercising His divine power, as He
afterwards consigned Himself as a voluntary captive
into their hands; and they do not appear to have been
moved or bettered by this event? A part of His address
to them, and the circumstances that follow, will perhaps
explain the cause.   For as our blessed Lord thus presented Himself as a willing victim to meet the danger, so
were His thoughts still directed, as they were before in
the hour of His agony, to the protection of His disciples.
"*If therefore,*" He said, "*ye seek Me, let these go
their way:*" hereby fulfilling first of all that which He
was going to fulfil to the uttermost, the sign of the good
Shepherd, that He, "layeth down His life for the sheep,"
and that He "loved them even unto the end;" and

³ Luke xxiii. 30.   ⁴ Wisdom xii. 9.

that prophecy concerning Himself, " I have trodden the wine-press alone, and of the people there was none with Me[s]."   This exercise of Divine power in going forth and striking His enemies to the ground, may have been in order that He might rescue His disciples. The circumstance appears to have been one of the many instances wherein the Jews were made, even while putting Him to death, involuntarily to acknowledge His Kingly authority, in that they not only fall before Him, but obey His word, that His friends should depart unhurt: for no power is more Kingly than this, that He should have no occasion to fight against His enemies, but that without force when He speaks they should obey Him. But how gentle and sweet is even this exercise of His Kingly power over His deadly enemies: for He shows them His omnipotent power, but withal in a manner so tender that not a hair of their heads is hurt! Hereby also, in obtaining the release of His disciples, our Lord accomplished in one sense what He had this night declared in His solemn address to the Father; for St. John adds, " *That the saying might be fulfilled which He spake, Of those whom Thou hast given Me, have I lost none.*" The beloved disciple mentions it as if he had himself noticed this fulfilment of his Lord's words; but in his charity he does not repeat all the declaration which our Lord had pronounced that evening; the dreadful part of which was now also fulfilled; as if leaving to the awful reflections of those that hear it the concluding words of the sentence, which could not but suggest themselves to himself and others on this occasion, "and none of them is lost, but the son of perdition, that the Scripture might be fulfilled."

But there is some question respecting the application

<hr>

[s] Isaiah lxiii.

of these words of our Lord's, that "none of them were lost," whether they speak of their rescue at this time from bodily danger, or of their spiritual salvation. For certainly they seem on this occasion to refer to their temporal escape from apprehension: but if we look to the passage where they were used by our Lord Himself in the previous chapter, they clearly can indicate nothing less than their spiritual and eternal salvation. And commentators seem to take its application on this occasion in the same sense; thus Dr. Thomas Jackson says, "St. John (to my apprehension) intimates, if they had been put unto the same fiery trial unto which He Himself was exposed, they had denied Him and their former faith. Therefore He commanded His apprehenders to let them go their way, that the saying might be fulfilled which He spake [6]," &c. St Augustin also takes it in the same sense, for he says, "If they were to die hereafter, how would He lose them by their dying now, but that they did not as yet so believe in Him, as those must do who perish not [7]?" But St. Chrysostom does not appear to take it exactly in this sense: "The perdition of which He had spoken was not that of death, but that which is eternal; but the Evangelist hath taken it also of present death [8]." But may not both of these interpretations be true, according to the analogy of Scripture? May not the Evangelist have observed and intimated that our Lord's words were fulfilled: first, in their rescue from the impending danger and their bodily safety, of which also our Lord always showed a natural and tender regard, as partaking of all human sympathies: and secondly, that this their temporal safety

---

[6] B. viii. s. iv. c. 4.   [7] In Joan. Tr. cxii.
[8] In Joan. Hom. lxxxiii. 1.

was a pledge and earnest, and also a means of their
eternal salvation ? The trial, perhaps, would have been
too great for them, especially at this time before they
were confirmed by the Holy Spirit; and thus therefore
as in the days of Antichrist, the time will be shortened
for the sake of the elect, so likewise was their trial
now diminished according to their weakness. However, as in the Sacred prophecies there is generally a
prior and inferior fulfilment; so it seems their temporal preservation, of which the Evangelist speaks, was
their pledge of our Lord's promise, "that none of them
should perish," and "that no one shall pluck them out
of His hand." Since writing the above, I find that St.
Cyril of Alexandria applies to it this mode of interpretation, considering that even the Evangelist also himself had this in his mind. "The wise Evangelist," he
says, "produces this which then took place to a separate
and peculiar part, as a palpable indication of the mercy
He would extend to all who came to Him by faith."
"And this particular fact is to be received," he adds,
"as an image of the more general redemption*." Thomas
Aquinas also takes it in this sense, that the Evangelist
extends to their bodily safety what had been said of
the body and soul. And Quesnel says, "This saying,
which has two proper and literal meanings, the one
relating to temporal, the other to eternal life, plainly
shows the copiousness of the word of God." So sweetly
and tenderly does the Almighty Disposer of our lives
blend with our temporal deliverances, with our release
from danger, and with the signs of His present protection, hopes and pledges, and assurances of His care
for our eternal salvation.

* In Joan. l. xi. 7.

ST. PETER USING THE SWORD.

And now from this circumstance, recorded by St. John alone, we proceed with the united accounts of the four Evangelists, as one comes in to bear on and fill up the other, and they all combine to furnish us with a close account of all that took place. " *Then they came up* (Matt.) and *laid their hands* (Matt. Mark), *on Jesus* (Matt.) *and took Him*" (Matt. Mark), seizing with rude hands the adorable Son of the Most High, who is blessed for evermore, in whose sight the angels tremble. "*But when they which were about Him*" (Luke), (for probably the whole of the eleven disciples were now assembling around our Lord) "*saw what was about to take place, they said unto Him, Lord, shall we smite with the sword?*" (Luke.) They had forgotten the admonition which our Lord had given them, when James and John wished to call down fire on the Samaritan city, and the reproof of St. Peter, when he attempted to deprecate the Cross of his Lord. At all events "one of them," in the momentary delay that intervened between their asking and our Lord's reply, in the eagerness of his defence had struck the blow. "*And behold* (Matt.) *one of them* (Luke), *one of those who stood by* (Mark), *who were with Jesus* (Matt.), *stretched forth his hand* (Matt.) *and drew his sword* (Matt. Mark), *and struck the servant of the High Priest* (Matt. Mark, Luke, John), *and cut off his right* (Luke, John) *ear*" (Matt. Mark, Luke, John). St John, who wrote so long after the event, and the whole generation had passed away, inasmuch as nothing could be apprehended from the persons being known, and probably also for higher mysterious reasons, mentions to us who it was that struck the blow, and who the servant was that was wounded. "*Simon Peter having a sword drew it.*" We might have anticipated that it was Peter, being ever foremost in his zeal and earnestness for his Master, and too impatient to wait for His reply. And St. John further adds, "*the servant's name was Malchus;*"—he might have been personally known to this disciple from his acquaintance with the High Priest. The very action itself, as St. Chrysostom observes, showed the vehemence of St. Peter, from his striking at the head of the man; and perhaps this person, from his being a servant of the High Priest's, was himself the foremost in the attack. "*Then Jesus,*" turning instantly to Peter, who had struck the blow, "*saith unto him, Put up again thy sword into its place, for all they that take the sword shall perish with the sword.*" (Matt.) Not only preventing any further mischief, but so exceedingly watchful was our Lord, even at this moment, to add to the occasion some kind and memorable admonition for good and perhaps replete also with deep prophecy. But at the same moment our Lord had again to intercede for His disciples, who were much endangered by this circumstance, and, "*Jesus answering said, Suffer ye thus far*" (Luke); requesting, or rather, we might say, by His secret royal authority requiring this of His enemies, however enraged they might have been. But St. Luke, who is so unwilling to pass over any incidental miracle of mercy, mentions, that, turning to the man who was hurt, "*and touching his ear, He healed him.*" After the healing of this His enemy, we may well suppose, it was that our Lord turned again to St. Peter, to console and support him at this trying and perplexing moment, especially after an expression of something like reproof which He had just spoken to him. "*Jesus therefore said unto Peter, Put thy sword into its sheath. The cup that my Father hath given Me, shall I not drink it ?"* (John.) In these most gracious words, expressing His own most perfect and even glad resignation to the drinking of that cup, from which, ere while, His human nature had shrunk; and also perhaps at the same time speaking that same lesson to St. Peter, which He had formerly expressed when He told him, that His deprecation of evil and suffering savoured "not the things that are of God, but those that are of men [1]." And indeed St. Chrysostom thus considers these words as intended for consolation, after the others of rebuke ;—"He not only restrained him with threats," as Matthew relates, "but also comforts him by saying, 'The cup that My Father hath given Me, shall I not drink it ?' showing that the things that were happening were not owing to their power, but of His own concession, and that He was not contrary to God, but obedient even unto death [2]." And now we may suppose it was that He added the words of St. Matthew, "*Thinkest thou not that I am able to ask My Father, and He shall set by Me more than twelve legions of Angels ?"* And returning again to the same point which He was constantly reminding them of, to show the immediate ordering and control of God, He adds, "*but how then shall the Scriptures be fulfilled, that thus it must be ?"* (Matt.) So exceedingly important was it that it should be kept strongly in mind, that God was present in these things, for His own word in the Scriptures had spoken it. It was the cup that God Himself gave, and which must be taken cheerfully as from His hand. When prophecy speaks, it proves that it is His will, and therefore there is every reason for

---

[1] St. Matt. xvi. 23.   [2] In Joan. Hom. lxxxiii. 2.

resignation and perfect stillness. "The Lord is in His holy temple, let all the earth keep silence before Him." "Be still, and know that I am God."

But the expression, "I can ask My Father, and He shall afford Me more than twelve legions of Angels," is certainly remarkable. This form of expression is not unlike that in the Psalms[3], "The Angel of the Lord encampeth around those that fear Him, and delivereth them;" for encamping implies an army, like legions in the way of battle. But it occurs to one that it may contain some allusion to His second coming, when the Son of Man shall return "in the glory of His Father and with all the holy Angels." And here it may be asked, why it is said, "twelve legions?" The number "twelve" may, perhaps, signify a great and perfect company; according to the use of the number twelve, both in nature and in Scripture, to denote fulness or completeness[4]. Thus twelve hours constitute the day; twelve months make up the year; twelve signs the zodiac; twelve tribes the Church; twelve disciples the Apostolic choir; why, therefore, may not twelve legions, or something corresponding to it, make up the Angelic Host? Or it might be, as St. Jerome takes, an allusion to the number of the Apostles;—"I need not the assistance of you twelve Apostles, though you were all to defend Me, when I am able to have twelve legions of an Angelic army." Remigius supposes that this mention of twelve legions may have some reference to the Roman armies under Titus and Vespasian, who should destroy Jerusalem and avenge the death of Christ. If so, this allusion of our Lord's would be in effect not very unlike that action of Elisha under similar circumstances, when to prove that they who were with him

<hr>

[3] xxxiv. 7.   [4] See Vol. Min. pp. 55, 56.

were more than they who were against him, he showed his servant the Angelic hosts under the appearance "of chariots and horses of fire," inasmuch as in this sense the Roman armies would represent Angelic hosts. This opinion too of Remigius will bear on the suggestion above, that the expression may contain an allusion to the day of Judgment, and the Son of Man then appearing with twelve legions of Angels; for if that day had a typical and symbolical counterpart throughout in the destruction of Jerusalem, it might have been that this circumstance also contained the double allusion—to the Roman armies at Jerusalem, and the Angelic armies at the end of the world. The word *legion* is, I believe, peculiar to the Romans; for it does not appear that the army of any other nation was composed of legions.

But there is something to be observed in this miracle in itself of a peculiar character: "it is the only miracle of healing," as Quesnel well notices, "that does not appear to have been asked for." In all other miracles faith seems to have been the essential requisite in those who required for others or themselves, and received the benefit. But this appears to have been performed in favour of an enemy, in whom therefore we should not look for such faith, and as a pure act of our Lord's charity and forgiveness. And indeed St. Chrysostom seems rather to enhance the action, on the ground that he was the servant of our Lord's chief enemy; and that this servant was afterwards the one that struck Him before the Chief Priest. But this latter does not appear to have been supported by any adequate authority; and one cannot but suppose that there might have been secretly some good in him known to our Lord, which rendered him meet for this mercy being vouchsafed to him. One might, indeed, be curious to know what effect so wonderful a cure and miracle might have had at such an awful time; possibly in the heat of the moment the man neither noticed the wound nor the miraculous cure; but still it may have had the effect of ultimately reclaiming him, and withdrawing him from that service; and with the deeper penitence, if, as St. Chrysostom suggests, he continued for that night to use his Benefactor with insult and cruelty.

Another question is asked, how St. Peter himself came to be thus armed in company with such a Master? It was perhaps owing to our Lord's having spoken of the sword at supper time; but this does not explain it. St. Cyril of Alexandria supposes that he was thus armed for self-defence according to the Law, which allowed of retaliation; or that it was on account of their spending the night in the open air, for that Judea abounded with wild beasts. But St. Chrysostom seems to think, that it was either the knife they had used for the sacrifice of the Lamb; or that St. Peter, from fear of the Jews against his Master, had for some time thought it necessary to be thus armed. However, it is interesting and curious to observe, that the action itself which is thus minutely recorded, is supposed by the Fathers, generally, if not universally, to contain within it some figurative or mystical allusion. They suggest that this servant of the Chief Priest's, who lost the right ear by the sword of St. Peter, indicated the Jewish people, in that they would not hear, or heard wrongly, the Scriptures, in the letter and not in the spirit, which letter they say is the right ear, or right mode of hearing. And as they thus interpret the wound given, they apply, of course, the same mode of interpretation to the healing also; which perhaps we cannot better express than in

the words of that very patristic French writer Quesnel.
"The right ear," he says, "is an emblem of docility,
obedience, and a true understanding of the Scriptures,
which will not be found any more, either in the priests
or people of the Jews, until Christ shall one day restore
these to them by His grace[5]." Much the same interpretation is expressed by Theophylact, both of the
wound and of its restoration, that—the cutting off the
right ear of the servant of the Chief of the Priests may
be a sign of that deafness, which was most inveterate in
the Chief Priests ; and that the restoration of the ear
afterwards may signify the ultimate renovation of their
understanding in the Israelites on the coming of Elias.
Some meaning of this kind is also inferred by Thomas
Aquinas, Ven. Bede, Titus, Isidorus, Cyril of Alexandria, Jerome, Hilary, Augustin, Ambrose, Origen ;
which will be enough to show that such a suggestion is
not the mere fancy of an individual ; but such a consent
of opinion either implies something of a Catholic traditionary interpretation, or, if derived from one individual's suggestion, that it was such as readily recom-
mended itself as probable.   We find also in the Levitical law especial mention is made of " the right ear[6]"
being touched with the blood of the Sacrifice ; a circumstance evidently containing some latent meaning. Our
attention too is arrested to something remarkable, by
the fact that the circumstance is recorded by all the
four Evangelists, and that each of them expressly mentions that it was "the servant of the High Priest," and
all of them record the very particulars of the injury,
saying, " And cut off his ear !" and St. Luke and St.
John " his right ear." Add to which, that when St.
John repeats or mentions such incidents, they are gene-

[5] On St. John, ch. xviii. 10.

[6] Lev. viii. 22.

rally supposed to contain mysterious wisdom; for whenever he speaks, his thoughts seem to have gone beyond earth, and to be dwelling on things heavenly, which he sees reflected in them; and all human events seem to him to be, but mirrors and semblances, wherein he sees, though it be but in a glass darkly, the image of the Divine Lord, and His purposes with regard to His Church. We might almost say, that even in the simple narrative of the Gospel he sees the Apocalyptic vision, and the sea of glass which is before the throne of God; sees all things symbolical of what is to be in Christ's kingdom, and conceives them to have a sacramental import, though he knows not what it is.

ST. PETER AND ST. JOHN.

We naturally feel some interest to know what were the respective feelings of St. John and St. Peter at this very critical and awful moment. If we may suppose St. John's account to partake, as it seems to do, of the character of his own mind, and his peculiar impressions at the time, we shall be furnished with some marks of the difference between himself and St. Peter, which may account for the difference in their subsequent conduct. St. John, supported with a calm sense of our Lord's mysterious power and Godhead, seems to have noticed in Him at this time those things that indicated a supernatural or Divine Presence; reclining, as it were, at all times on the breast of His mysterious Godhead, and drinking from His mouth heavenly wisdom, and a courageous repose of mind and overflowing charity. Thus he alone records that manifestation of a Divine strength in His weakness, and at this dark hour; for such was His going forth to meet His enemies; and this he introduces with an allusion to His Divine dignity. It may further be observed, that whenever about to mention any act of humiliation, St. John divinely prefaces the account, by coming down from above, and speaking, first of all, of Him, " Who, being in the form of God, thought it not robbery to be equal with God;" he then proceeds to speak of His taking upon Him " the form of a servant," and, being so found, of His humbling Himself still more. He presumes not to think of Him as Man without a previous adoration of His Godhead. Thus, in the commencement of his Gospel, he speaks first of His Eternal Godhead, before he ventures to speak of His appearing as Man ; and at the Last Supper, before his account of His girding Himself as a slave and washing their feet, he says, first, " Jesus, knowing that His Father had given all things into His hands, and that He was come from God and went to God; He riseth from supper and layeth aside His garment." So now, also,—as if he observed something about His Lord's demeanour that evinced His perfect omniscience, and saw the striking effect produced on His adversaries,—he adds, "Jesus, therefore, knowing all things that were coming upon Him, went forth and said." And we cannot but notice the very expression with which He went forth ; for although it may be taken as merely an answer to their question, implying that He was the man they sought, yet it was that which also denotes His own eternal existence and Godhead ; it was the hidden Name of God, " I am," at which they fell to the earth. This awful and incommunicable Name, whose hidden power here overcomes His enemies, we observe, on another occasion, sustains His disciples. It is the same Divine appellation by which He stills their fears in the storm, " I am," as three Evangelists record; for when they were greatly troubled, " immediately He talked with them," and said, " Be of

good cheer; I am He;" or "I am; be not afraid[7]."
For it was, as St. Augustin beautifully expresses it,
"the Everlasting Day lying hid in mortal limbs, for
which they were seeking with lanterns and torches."
And yet, perhaps, we need not suppose that even on this
occasion there was any thing like an unusual or overwhelming display of Divine power to a casual observer;
for we find something of the same kind, on many occasions, when they came to take Him. Even the officers
from the Chief Priests confessed that they were unable
to do so, not only because, as is sometimes said, His
hour was not yet come, but also on account of something awful, and more than human in His words[8]. "The
officers answered, 'Never man spake like this man.'"
But at all events the circumstance itself, like many
others, indicated that our Lord was a willing victim;
and it is possible that St. John may have noticed this
in his watchful adoration of his Lord. And probably it
was the case, to those who had faith to discern it, that
during our Lord's apprehension there were many indications of His Divine strength, bursting forth, as it
were, like rays of glory from His secret Majesty. Of
these several are noticed. Perhaps His knowledge of the
traitor Judas, and of his design, might be considered as
one. Another was, that after Judas had betrayed Him
with a kiss, yet they could not perceive Him, nor know
Him; as if to indicate to them the futility of the traitor's signal, if Christ had wished to avoid the being
taken by them. Thirdly, His paralyzing His armed adversaries, so that they fell to the ground at His presence. In the fourth place, we may mention His healing
the ear of Malchus. And in the fifth, as St. Austin
remarks[9], "that His word was so full of efficacy, that

[7] Vol. Min. p. 384.   [8] John vii. 46.   [9] In Joan. Tr. cxii.

they could lay no hands on His disciples, not even on Peter, when He required that they should depart." Perhaps too, one reason for the Evangelist mentioning the young man who escaped, was in order to show His miraculous deliverance of the Apostle from a crowd so incensed. And it may be noticed, that most of these instances are mentioned by St. John. On every occasion whatever, on which our Lord's conduct is devoutly watched, it will be seen that His Human nature was ever radiant with His Divine, the cloud was kindled up by the sun, the covering of flesh was as a veil over His Godhead, but a veil transparent to the eyes of faith. When apparently most helpless, His Divine power was most effectual; as an infant He exerted Kingly sway on the hearts of the Magi; when on the Cross, a Divine power on the heart of the thief; when before Pilate, He struck His judge with awe: when the Chief Priest and Jews seemed most wanton and triumphant, they were fulfilling His prophetic word; and thus every part of our Lord's life, that is contemplated, will appear like the heavens at night, at first dark and starless, but as soon as we gaze, star after star comes forth. So is it in His capture now. Such are the points which St. John seems to notice.

But the act of St Peter, though indicating his zeal and fidelity, yet seems to imply a sort of forgetfulness of what He had confessed, of our Lord's power and Godhead, as if He could have needed such aid as the sword of man. And the expressions of our Lord to him, which were so calculated to support and strengthen him, yet convey also, as we have said, some little of gentle reproof for his having forgotten this;—"Thinkest thou not but that My Father would at My request give Me twelve legions of Angels?" And here again, in this expression, it must be observed that our Lord, in condescension to him, speaks as Son of Man, for as God He had no need to ask the aid of Angels. This Origen remarks,—"He speaks not this as needing the succour of Angels, but according to the conception of Peter, who was desirous to succour Him. For Angels needed more the succour of the Only-begotten Son of God than He of them." And on this account also it is written, " He shall give His Angels charge over Thee, to keep Thee in all Thy ways [10]." Which of course is not to be understood as spoken of the Only-begotten Son of God; but either in the person of Christ of every Christian; or of Christ according to His human nature [1]. What our Lord therefore says to St. Peter implied, in fact, but the first article of the Creed, the power of faith in God the Father, which ought to suppress all desire either to take the sword or to shrink from the cross. And indeed it is in like manner of expression that our Lord speaks on other occasions of Angels, when He speaks of Himself as the Son of Man; as when He describes His coming on the day of Judgment, as the Son of Man, to judge mankind in His Father's glory, and with the holy Angels. It is therefore in condescension to the weakness of St. Peter's faith that our Lord here speaks of Himself as the Son of Man rather than as the Son of God. And indeed St. Chrysostom, though not alluding to this distinction, yet well remarks the condescension and gentleness of our Lord in using this mode of speech; as if the very poetical form, if we may say it, of the language He adopts, was such as was peculiarly adapted to lay hold of and support their weak minds. " On account of this fear," he says, " and weakness, he puts His speech into a figure, for indeed they were dead with fear."

The history of St. Peter's state of mind during this

---

[10] Ps. xci. 11.   [1] In Matt. Lat. Comm. 102.

night appears to have been this. First of all, when our Lord speaks of one betraying Him, he evinces an intense anxiety and secret distrust of himself; when relieved of this apprehension, he is overflowing with love to his Lord and confident assurance; doubtless he felt, and felt truly, that he would gladly have died as a brave Galilæan soldier in the rescue of his Lord, or by His side in battle. In this zealous self-confidence he slept rather than prayed: and now the hour seemed to have arrived to put his love and zeal to the test, and he was eager to make good his promise of dying with his Lord. But, as is usual with us, the temptation of Satan, who desired to have him, was from a very different and an unexpected quarter. For all this was, in fact, not the highest degree of faith; it had in it too much of what is human.

Had St. Peter, if we may so speak of so holy an Apostle—had St. Peter preserved, throughout his trial that was to ensue, a right faith in our Lord's Divinity, he would not have failed in that temptation; so closely connected is right conduct with sound belief in that doctrine; not only in that keeping the commandments opens the heart to receive that great truth, but that stedfastly believing that truth enables us to keep the commandments, especially on occasions the most trying and severe. The difference, therefore, may be shown by the figure used by our blessed Lord Himself; " When the floods arise and the winds blow upon the house;" that is, when violent persecutions of men and of evil spirits arise in the day of temptation; then he will stand who is built on the Rock, but he that is not built on the Rock will not stand. The Rock indeed we all know is Christ, but more especially the confession of His Divinity; for on this Rock, right faith in His Divinity, our Lord said that He would build His Church. When the floods arose and the winds blew, St. Peter began to sink, being, notwithstanding his ardent affection for his Lord, not sufficiently established in a firm sense of His Almighty Godhead.

But the answer of our Lord to St. Peter, that "all they who take the sword shall perish with the sword," seems not only to imply the gentle Christian principle of forbearance and a promise that meekness, to which the inheritance of the earth is given, shall in the long-run be more powerful than the sword; but may also contain a prophetic reference and bearing to that Church which has attached to itself so much the name of St. Peter, which has allied itself with temporal power, and taken the sword in defence of what it considers the faith; and, may it be added, that God has indeed healed, and will heal the wounds of those afflicted by it! Indeed, if there be any truth in the observations we have before made on the connexion of what is said to St. Peter, or recorded of him, with the history of his Church, (which, like St. Peter among Apostles, takes, whether rightly or not, the pre-cedence among Churches,) the parallel may be further drawn even in this manner. What we wonder at in St. Peter is, that after such a confession as he had made of our Lord's Divinity, and after asserting so earnestly his maintenance of the right faith, he should be so forgetful of our Lord's Divine power and of this faith, as to use such human means in its support; without sufficiently relying on His own intrinsic and essential Divine strength however oppressed. Now all this in St. Peter seems connected, as has been observed, if we may venture to say so, with some degree of presumption, and putting of himself before his brother Apostles: "Though all shall be offended, yet will not I." And if this figure is still to hold in the Church of Rome, it may go on even to the denial of Him, if it has not already done so, in finding itself disappointed in using worldly arms of defence. Yet still, should this be the case, then of course this very history of their apostle would suggest a hope that they may be restored, and may come forth strengthened and purified out of the fire. This is a better hope than that after this he should be "beating his fellow-servants," and that his Lord should "cut him asunder" from His Church, which is suggested by the answer to St. Peter in St. Matthew's Gospel (xxiv. 51).

But the question may be reverently asked, "Why was not this action of St. Peter's prevented by our Lord?" Indeed, it may have been occasioned by a misunderstanding respecting our Lord's meaning, when He had spoken to them this very night of preparing a sword. And St. Luke says that they had asked, "Master, shall we smite with the sword?" as if it were not perfectly evident to them that such means would have been disapproved. Now it will be sufficient to observe that this difficulty, as far as it goes, is only that very ordinary case of persons mistaking the words of God in Holy Scripture, and afterwards not with sufficient patience perhaps waiting for His direction, but proceeding to wrong action. Yet was the action in itself not only overruled for good at the time by the work of mercy, and by a touching example of the duty of doing good to our enemies; but it has had the effect of teaching St. Peter, and in him all Christians unto the end, that this kind of zeal and earnestness, even to drawing the sword in our Lord's defence, was not that in which true faith and courage consisted; for these qualities were soon after to be tried and found wanting. The history of St. Peter's subsequent fall would have lost much of its instructive character, had it not been combined with this proof of the more heroic virtue; which thus is found not to be of any true service in the day of trial. For it may be observed that the act of St. Peter, however wanting in Christian meekness and perfection, yet was of the most excellent heroic kind of virtue: it was no less than incurring the danger of one's life in defending one's friend and master. It was not in his own defence that he drew the sword, but in that of his Lord. And, indeed, Augustine does not seem to think that there is any reproof in our Lord's words to His disciples, but only a deprecation against further defence of Him, which he considers the words " suffer ye thus far," to express, as if spoken, not as we have supposed, to our Lord's enemies, but to His disciples.

OUR LORD EXPOSTULATES.

It was " in that hour," says St. Matthew, and therefore probably soon after what had taken place, and before the disciples had left Him, that our Lord expostulated with them. "*In that hour* (Matt.) *Jesus answered and said* (Matt., Mark) *unto them* (Mark) ;" "*unto the crowds*," says St. Matthew; and St. Luke, "*Jesus spake unto them that had come against Him, Chief Priests, and captains of the temple and the elders.*" From this expression of St. Luke's it would appear that there must have been these persons of higher rank blended with the crowd who came to apprehend our Lord, or else the words must have been spoken later than this time of His immediate apprehension. There appears to have been something very emphatic and significative in these words, which are recorded by the three Evangelists; and the more so because the full force and meaning of so solemn an appeal is not obvious. "*Have ye come out as against a thief, with swords and staves* (Matt., Mark, Luke), *to take Me ?* (Matt., Mark.) *Day by day, I was* (or *sat*, Matt.) *with you in the temple* (Matt., Mark, Luke), *teaching, and ye seized Me not* (Matt., Mark), *nor stretched forth your hands against Me*" (Luke). An expression something similar is recorded soon after before the High Priest : " I ever spake openly to the world, I have taught in the temple where the Jews always resort, and in secret have I said nothing." Perhaps the meaning of the passage may be thus explained : " Why should I be treated as a robber, and seized by night with these arms and instruments of violence ? there has been nothing in my conduct towards you which could require any thing of this character ; I have ever been meek and gentle among you ; I have ever taught openly before you." Origen [2] interprets the passage in a manner much like this. Or might it be that our Lord meant to mark the circumstance of His humiliation, that He was treated (now and afterwards) as a thief, and " numbered with transgressors ;" He who thought it not robbery to be equal with God, treated as a thief by man, and thus led " as a sheep to the slaughter ?" Or perhaps it was to draw their attention to the occasion : He who had taught publicly, and whom they were not able to take because He was protected by an overruling power, and because His hour (as is often recorded) " had not yet come [3] ;" now yielded Himself because the hour was come, the powers of evil were let loose : " *But this,*" He added, according to St Luke, "*is your hour and the power of darkness.*" " It is foolish," says St. Jerome, " to be seeking with swords and staves for Him who spontaneously delivers Himself into your hands, and to be searching by means of a betrayer, and

[2] In Matt. xv. 103.　　　　[3] John viii. 20 ; vii. 8. 30. 44.

by night, as if for a person concealing himself, when
He teaches daily in the temple. But the reason why
you are gathered against Me in darkness is because
your power is in darkness." Or it might be, like every
thing else, to mark our Lord's free will and voluntary
offering of Himself; for indeed every thing throughout
is of this character. Thus, as St. Cyril says, "He
refutes those who might rashly suppose that they had
seized Him against His will. 'You could not have
taken Me before when I was among you, when I willed
it not, nor could you now, unless I submitted to your
hands.' Hence follows, 'but this is your hour;' that
is, there is but a short time allowed you for exercising your pride against Me. 'But this,' He adds,
'is the power given to darkness;' that is, to the devil
and the Jews." St. Chrysostom says, to the same
effect, that "they had not seized Him in the temple,
for they had not dared to do so on account of the multitudes; wherefore the Lord went out, in order that by
time and place He might afford them an opportunity
of taking Him. By which He teaches them, that unless He of His own accord had permitted it, they would
not have been able to take Him." And Theophylact
also says, "This circumstance showed His Divinity,
for when He taught in the temple they could not take
Him, although He was in their hands, for the time of
His passion had not arrived; but when He Himself
willed, then He delivered up Himself, that the Scriptures might be fulfilled, 'that He was led as a lamb to
the slaughter, not crying nor lifting up His voice, but
voluntarily suffering.'" This interpretation of the
words appears far preferable to the other, as affording
an explanation very great and worthy of that occasion,
when we look for something mysteriously significant in

our Lord's breaking silence; and because it perfectly harmonizes with many other actions of our Lord at this time, which manifested His perfect Godhead and voluntary oblation of Himself, in the season of His apparent weakness: indications of Himself which were not indeed palpable to the crowd, but sufficient for a watchful faith.

But with regard to the words recorded by St. Luke —"but this is your hour, and the power of darkness"—our Lord seems often to make use of this kind of expression; as if alluding thereby to the emblematical meaning of night and day, as representing the two kingdoms of good and evil, whose reign here on earth is blended. Thus when His disciples expressed surprise, that He should venture back to Jerusalem, He said, "if any man walk in the day he stumbleth not, because he seeth the light of this world; but if a man walk in the night, he stumbleth, because there is no light in him;" and so on this occasion He drew their attention to the fact that it was night, and wished them to understand the figure. And indeed it may be observed that the symbolical meanings of these expressions pervade the Scriptures throughout. We are quite familiar with such common instances as these, that Christ is the "true light," and Christians are "the children of the light," and "the lights of the world," and their works are "light shining before men," and their spiritual strength is "the armour of light," and Heaven is "the kingdom of light," and "God is light, and in Him is no darkness at all;" so also the reign of Satan is "the kingdom of darkness," and his works are "works of darkness," and his influence is "the light within being darkened," and his kingdom is "outer darkness," and he is "the power of darkness." Thus it is said of the wicked; "they are of those that rebel against the light; they know not the ways thereof, nor abide in the paths thereof," and "the morning is to them even as the shadow of death[4]." Thus did our Lord by a few words allude to that "mystery of iniquity" which is represented by "the darkness of this world." And this expression also, "this is your hour," may serve for the consolation of us all in times of great persecution. "This is your hour," but the day cometh—the everlasting day and blessed light, and that will be Christ's hour, and the hour of those who will continue faithful with Him.

"*But all this happened,*" St. Matthew adds, "*that the Scriptures of the Prophets might be fulfilled,*" where it appears to be the observation of the Evangelist himself. But as it occurs in St. Mark, it would almost appear as if they were a part of the words which our Lord was speaking: "*But that the Scriptures might be fulfilled.*" At all events our Lord had just made a similar remark to His disciples, as St. Matthew records. And it is not, it may be observed, one Prophet or Prophecy, but the Prophets generally and throughout, who had spoken. It is not merely to show the fulfilment of prophecy that this remark is made; but the fact that all these things had been prophetically spoken, is a proof for a good man to rest on, that all these were under a Divine superintendence[5]. The Almighty and All-creating Word had spoken, and the events must follow, for they are His will: hence the law of perfect resignation. It seems as if Scripture was always more bent on declaring God's foreknowledge than man's free will. It is true, as St. Athanasius observes, that " God's foreknowledge was not the cause of Judas's betrayal, or of Peter's denial; for the same is the case in the creation of the devil and the first man. The foresight and foreknowledge of

<hr>

[4] Job xxiv. 13. 17.   [5] See Vol. Res. 176—180.

God is not the cause of future events; but the future events of that foreknowledge." But the subject is so infinitely beyond us, that perhaps we are nearest the truth when we say least about it, but think of it reverently with awe and wonder. Perhaps more has been said to explain these very frequent expressions of Holy Scripture than need have been done: they are explained until they are almost explained away: and yet doubtless the constant repetition of them is intended to inculcate on us some impression which, by always explaining and qualifying them, we are likely to lose.

THE DISCIPLES FLEE.

And now "*all* (Mark) *the disciples*" (Matt.) we are told by two Evangelists, "*forsook Him and fled*" (Matt., Mark). "It was," says St. Chrysostom, "when He had spoken these words to the crowd, and they perceived that there was no further hope, for that He voluntarily yielded Himself, then they forsook Him and fled[6]." The disciples were of course blameable for so doing, for it is spoken of as their being offended, " All ye shall be offended in Me this night," and yet perhaps it was in some degree excusable, for our Lord had obtained leave for them to depart unhurt. Origen well and charitably says, " For they had not yet the Spirit, because Jesus was not yet glorified[7]; neither the Spirit of Power nor of love. For if they had, they would not have been thus powerless, nor done any thing contrary to Divine love."—"They all forsook Him and fled." As no exception is made, we may conclude that St. John and St. Peter were in the number, although they afterwards returned. Herein was fulfilled the prediction of our Lord, that this very

---

[6] Hom. lxxxiv.   [7] John vii. 39.

night all should be offended at Him, when they saw Him thus apparently powerless; that the prophecy of Zechariah should be fulfilled,—the Shepherd smitten, and the sheep scattered abroad;—that "they should be scattered every man unto his own, and leave" Him "alone." Other prophecies also were now fulfilled, such as "Thou hast hid Mine acquaintance out of My sight, and made Me to be abhorred of them." "I am so fast in prison that I cannot get forth." "I looked for some to have pity on Me, but there was no man; neither found I any to comfort Me."

Our Lord indeed had interceded for them that they should be allowed to escape with impunity, and they were granted to His request[8], but yet danger might naturally be apprehended from so violent a crowd. And a circumstance occurred, which showed that our Lord's care of them was not without being needed. For a young man who, perhaps, awakened by the noise, had rushed in the hurry from his sleep, half clothed with a linen garment about his naked body, was seized by the attendants, and fled away, leaving his garment with them. Theophylact suggests that this person came from the house where they had eaten the Passover, and mentions that some said it was St. James the Just, our Lord's brother. Epiphanius, and I think St. Jerome[9], mention the same opinion. But was he not too old at this time to be called "a certain young man?" St. Ambrose[1], Gregory[2], and Bede, suggest that it may have been St. John, who was a young man at that time, and that he afterwards returned, having recovered his clothing, and blending with the crowd entered the palace; but neither of these opinions is maintained with any confidence or

<hr>

[8] John xvii. 8, 9.   [9] Or the Author, on Psalm xxxvi.
[1] Ambrose, Psalm i. 30.   [2] Gregory, Moral. lib. xiv. c. 23.

on any adequate authority. It has also been supposed to have been St. Mark himself; and in the absence of any sufficient proof it seems natural to acquiesce in this last supposition. For he alone records the circumstance, without any adequate reason being quite apparent for his doing so: and it has been thought, without reference to this circumstance, that it was his house where they had been received for the Last Supper, which would so far fall in with Theophylact's opinion. This would also suggest an explanation why St. John may have been mentioned, and the ambiguity may have arisen from this, that both of those names are found in the same person, in "John, whose surname was Mark;" at whose house indeed they are soon afterwards collected[3]. For this conclusion would then take in the various accounts, that it was one from whose house they came, that this house was Mark's, that the person here recorded was Mark, who was also named John; and that the same may have been this Evangelist who records it. To this it may be further added, that it would certainly appear from the account that it was not one of the Twelve, for they "all" had already "fled[4]." Besides which they appear to have been sleeping in the open air; and therefore would not have been so thinly clad. There appears no reason for supposing it the beloved disciple, but his youth, which is a very slight reason. Nor is the action characterized by the calm love and majesty which marks St. John throughout. But, as Maldonatus well observes, whoever he was, he was zealous in the cause of Christ, for it is said that he followed Him, and not the crowd; and they attacked him as being a friend and defender of Christ.

[3] See Acts xii. 12.

[4] Mark xiv. 50.

REFLECTIONS ON OUR LORD'S EXAMPLE.

We now leave in silence the great truths of Doctrine and Divinity, which may be mysteriously implied in all these circumstances of our Lord's capture, and contemplate Him as the Son of Man. The practical example which it affords us is in the highest degree interesting and important; and all of us are liable to have our courage and charity tried on occasions, wherein the touching character of our Lord's example will do more to secure our presence of mind than any precept. But the most perfect charity, combined with the most perfect courage which is evinced throughout, is rather a subject for adoration and worship than for human scrutiny. For the deepest veneration and awe is necessary when we speak of Christ; and the more so, because He deigned to appear as one of us. This very example itself is infinitely more conforming and converting, when we consider Him not as an example alone, but therein adore Him as our God; for then Divinity goeth forth from Him, and makes His very human actions powerful to mould us to them. It was in an act of love and mercy to His disciples, even in the midst of His agony, that our Lord was engaged when the traitor came: it was with a kiss, the sign of friendly good-will and gentleness, that He was betrayed, such as He allowed from the worst of enemies. His words to him were those even now of gentle expostulation and winning reproof, as if not giving over every effort to recall him even yet. Then He went forth to meet them with a Divine Majesty blended with courage; showing that though He, like Elijah of old, had power to destroy His enemies without their approaching Him, yet He only showed His power, but exerted it not. He showed it to work on them, if possible, for good, and to indicate that it was His own acquiescence, or that they could not take Him. In this critical moment His thoughts were engaged only for their good ; every word, and every action was for the benefit of friend and foe. He thinks only of others, and not of Himself ; when He shows His power, and yet yields Himself as their victim, it is for His disciples He exerts it, and to give force to His intercession for them, that they may be allowed to depart unharmed. And when on His enemies laying hands on Him Peter used the sword, He prays for them that they may be suffered thus far, and is apprehended in the act of kindly healing His enemy, and turning from them mildly to console and comfort Peter His friend ; reminding him of His great power, and of His Father's will. He was fulfilling all His own precepts of love and forgiveness. And now He turns meekly to expostulate against these signs of violence towards one so meek and unresisting as He had always been among them. 'You see I have not fled from you away, for I was with you daily.' He quotes the Scriptures also, and to these He constantly refers, to support St. Peter, as if to point out to him that it is all according to the Divine superintendence and orderings of God, and that He must needs wish to drink of that cup which His Father had given Him to drink ; for if an earthly father gives nothing but what is good to his children, how much more a heavenly ! And when they all forsook Him and fled, He had prepared their minds beforehand for this the greatest of trials that could befall Him, the dereliction and desertion of His disciples, in words that had evinced His own perfect resignation even to this, "ye shall be scattered every one to his own, and shall leave Me alone;" to which He added, as if to deprecate any thought of impatience or complaint, "And yet I am not alone, for the Father is with Me." Such are the reflections which occur to one, when allowed to approach our Lord by that term with which, in unspeakable condescension, He delighteth to designate Himself, inviting us to Him by that engaging appellation of "the Son of Man."

But when the consideration of our Lord's Divinity is seriously reflected on by us, the whole narrative becomes so deeply mysterious that we cannot wonder for it to have been, and always to be, a stumbling-block. It is, therefore, very important to observe, that it is precisely in the same manner that Christ still acts, and always has done, in His moral government of the world, the circumstance which is the great stumbling-block to those who want faith to discern Him. Wicked men are allowed to go on until their wickedness is matured and developed in action; they lay their designs as if God knew them not; the difficulties to their execution vanish before them, and they succeed. Christ, in the mean while, is "as a man who hath no strength;" And He is, if we may so speak, as one bound captive in their hands. The power of good is overcome by them; they seem to themselves and to the world as those who have the upper hand, and are successful. Yet to those, who, like St. John, have eyes to watch and see the course of events, all the while there is present a Divine power, which, it may be, incidentally manifests itself, making them to fall to the ground before Him, yet does not interfere to stop the course of things by exerting itself, but submits to be put in bonds. And, moreover, as prophecy was so much introduced on this occasion to show the Divine superintendence, so also the course of events in the world, to him that watches with Scripture, are but the fulfilment of what Scripture describes. It is also observable, in like manner, that while the wicked are thus allowed to go on, yet the Almighty ceases not throughout to warn them, though they are incapable of attending to His warning while bent on the attainment of their object! and He ceases not to do them good in His natural providence, to heal them, and afford them protection. It is likewise according to the same analogy that the good also, notwithstanding the protection and approbation of Christ in general, are yet allowed to sleep, although warned not to do so, to mistake the commands of God, and to err, but still are, on the whole, cherished, watched over, and supported; so that, of those whom God hath given to Christ, not one shall be lost, and not a hair of their head shall fall unnoticed to the ground. And as the dealings of Christ are still very similar to what they were in those days of His incarnation: so also is the difference with which Christ is viewed, according to the diversities of moral characters, very similar to what was then manifested; I mean, there is the same discrepancy in the ways in which persons read and speak of the sacred history. Some, it is to be hoped, there may be, who are, as if, with St. John, they calmly and deeply adored, and worshipped, and saw nothing in all things but indications of Divinity; some, as if, with St. Peter, they loved, but with too weak, low, and human affections, being as yet more ardent than firm, and depending therefore too much on human things: some, as if they could lay hold with rude and constraining hands, like the Jews, on the Lord of life; neither knowing, nor fearing, nor loving Him: some, as if they would betray Him for a little money, like Judas; and that with a kiss or expressions of attachment. But all these things carry on the thoughts of a Christian to the contemplation of those higher doctrines of Christ throughout all the world suffering in His members. It is this circumstance of the analogy and sameness with which He is seen in His manifestations, under variety of circumstances, that renders those prophetical descriptions of these things respecting Christ throughout the Psalms so descriptive of the condition, the trials, the enemies, the support of Christians at all times; and perhaps explains why those prophecies respecting Christ are often expressive of infirmities, sins, and complaints, which find not a place in Himself, as suffering in the flesh, but in His members.

As the sun in the Heavens develops his similitude and image in the broad mirror of ocean, and yet at the same time also casts an unbroken reflection of himself, in equal distinctness and perfection, in numberless waves, and the smallest drop of water; so likewise the true Sun of Righteousness in Heaven, in all His earthly providences, towards Churches and individuals, is again and again set forth in characters so similar and coincident, that, from being used to these resemblances and shadows of Him, we cannot fail to recognize Him when we behold Himself manifested before us. Though we dare not gaze upon Him, and our eyes are dazzled at the light of His unapproachable holiness; still we see enough to know that He is but one and the same, whose image we are used to contemplate in the things that are daily brought before us in His providence. It is probable that the more we come to the mind of the Spirit, the more shall we detect this resemblance to Christ manifest in the flesh, in all His dealings with mankind; and the more again from these His dealings with mankind shall we acknowledge Christ also when manifested before us in the person of man. We shall perceive in both those features, and that expression of the features, which we are wont to dwell on in that countenance which we adore and love. And this we may conclude to be the mind of the Spirit, inasmuch as we find throughout the Scriptures expressions which are evidently closely applicable to Christ; and yet it might be doubted whether they were expressly spoken of Christ or not, were it not for this mysterious analogy between Himself, as seen visibly in the Son of Man, and in His providences. Thus, for instance, the Psalmist bursts into passionate deprecations on beholding the heavy sufferings of good men :—"Up, Lord, and let not man have the upper hand! Put them in fear, O Lord, that the heathen may know themselves to be but men[5]." This is spoken of a case than which there is none more ordinary in the world, of good men overcome by the wicked, *i. e.* of God being apparently bound in His servants: but no words could express more closely our feelings at beholding the captivity of Christ, now put in bonds. Again, the following words of the Prophet would be equally descriptive of both; " O the Hope of Israel, the Saviour thereof in time of trouble, why shouldest thou be as a stranger in the land, and as a wayfaring man that turneth aside to tarry for a night ? Why shouldest thou be as a man astonied, as a mighty man that cannot save ? yet Thou, O Lord, art in the midst of us[6]." And so much was this noticed among the affairs of men, that in the book of Wisdom the wise man endeavours to explain the cause of this wonderful forbearance of God[7]. " But Thou, mastering Thy power, judgest with equity, and orderest us with great favour: for Thou mayest use power when Thou wilt. But by such works Thou taughtest Thy people that the

---

[5] Ps. ix. 19, 20.   [6] Jer. xiv. 8, 9.   [7] Ch. xii. 18.

just man should be merciful; and hast made Thy children to be of a good hope that Thou givest repentance
for sins[8]."

SECTION III.—THE CONDEMNATION.

" I have heard the blasphemy of the multitude, and fear is on
every side, while they conspire together against Me, and take
their counsel to take away My life."

THE HOUSE OF ANNAS.

" *Then the band, and the captain, and the officers of
the Jews, took Jesus and bound Him* (John): *and led
Him,*" St. Mark says, " *to the High Priest;*" and St.
Matthew adds, " *to Caiaphas the High Priest;*" and
St. Luke, " *having seized Him, they led Him away, and
took Him unto the house of the High Priest.*"   But St.
John says, they " *led Him first of all to Annas, for he
was the father-in-law of Caiaphas, who was High Priest
that same year.*"   From this, and a subsequent mention
of Annas by St. John, has arisen a question, whether
part of the ensuing narrative respecting the ill usage of
our Lord and the fall of St. Peter took place in the house
of Annas or of Caiaphas.   On comparing together the
Evangelical accounts, it certainly does appear beyond all
doubt that the whole occurred in the house of Caiaphas.
For St. Matthew says, that the High Priest to whom
they went was Caiaphas; and St. Luke mentions, that
it was " the house of the High Priest " to which they

---

[8] See all these observations exemplified in the Services of our
Church for King Charles the Martyr.

went: and St. John says, that it was the High Priest to whom he was known, and into whose house he obtained access: and, moreover, the mention of Annas in this place appears incidentally introduced by St. John; for it is of Caiaphas that he immediately proceeds to speak. It is of course allowed that Annas is also spoken of in Scripture as High Priest; as where, in the beginning of St. Luke's Gospel, he is coupled with Caiaphas, in the same manner as Zadok and Abiathar are in the Old Testament: and also in the Acts of the Apostles we read of "Annas the High Priest and Caiaphas." But all this only goes to prove that Annas was also invested with some authority, which of course the present narrative indicates by the fact of our Lord being first taken to him. It appears notwithstanding that by the High Priest, in this account, Caiaphas is meant, and that it is of his palace the Evangelists proceed to speak.

But the difficulty on this subject mainly arises from one of so great authority as St. Augustin supposing that the circumstances respecting the denials of St. Peter, which now ensue, took place in the house of Annas. However, on the one hand Origen, St. Chrysostom, St. Cyril, Theophylact, and others, consider them to have occurred in that of Caiaphas; and on the other it is evident that this apparently erroneous supposition of Augustin is to himself a source of great difficulty in the general interpretation, especially in making out the narrative of St. John. His misapprehension seems to have arisen from St. John afterwards introducing the mention of Annas, when he says, " Now Annas had sent him bound unto Caiaphas;" which words do not appear at all to imply that at that period of the narrative He was sent there, but that their introduction in that part is parenthetical, and it admits of an easy explanation. And, indeed, it must be allowed that St. Chrysostom and Theophylact, though they do not suppose that the denials of St. Peter were in the house of Annas, yet fall into the same opinion from St. John's words, that the narrative, up to the point where St. John speaks of his being bound by Annas, contains what passed in the house of Annas. So also does our own Bishop Andrews, who thus arranges it in his Devotions; where, before his enumeration of the indignities offered to our Lord in the palace of Caiaphas, he speaks of His being struck by the attendant before Annas: and Bishop Taylor, in his Life of Christ, does likewise the same. But these great names do not carry the authority on this subject which they otherwise would, as they are not critically harmonizing and arranging the narrative, but merely dwelling on the circumstances as the mention of them occurs in the Gospels, as subjects of practical or devotional contemplation. Whereas St. John, speaking more at length of Caiaphas, and then of the introduction of St. Peter into the hall, of himself clearly indicates that he is then speaking of the hall of Caiaphas.

But if the whole account is thus to be confined to the house of Caiaphas, the question arises, What could have been the purpose in going to the house of Annas? The explanation about to be given of this point will, I think, account for the mention of it by St. John, and also afford a satisfactory reason for our Lord being taken there. The reasons which have hitherto been alleged, however true in themselves, do not appear sufficient to explain it. St. Augustin[9] suggests that it might have been from the desire of Caiaphas, or that the house of Annas was by the way as they passed: St. Chry-

---

[9] In Joan. Tract. c. xiii. 5.

sostom, that it was from a feeling of triumphant malice, and as a sort of wanton display of their victim. Our own Ven. Bede expresses a sentiment which is thankfully accepted in confirmation of this view, that thus Annas became in some degree accessory to the crime of our Lord's death; and that it was thus divinely ordered, so that he who was the kinsman of the High Priest in blood became partaker of his crime also. We may gladly allow of this inference, as intimating the indications of a mysterious Divine superintendence, by which every part of the Jewish nation had, as we shall afterwards have occasion to see, a part in our Lord's death. For Annas was evidently one in authority, and therefore a representative of the nation; and, as we shall show, made himself in an important respect guilty of His condemnation. But these reflections on the subject do not in fact explain it; for they still leave quite untouched the former question which was at issue, viz., What were, humanly speaking, the reasons and the motives in the agents that induced them first of all to take our Lord, on His apprehension, to the house of Annas? We may, I think, see a reason for it, which will in no way contravene those purposes which St. Augustin and St. Chrysostom suggest, nor yet the reflection of Bede, by merely considering what was the state of feeling in our Lord's enemies at the time. The great object which they had in view, throughout the whole of our Lord's apprehension, was either to avoid the knowledge of the people, or to apprehend Him in spite of them. This was the reason for their taking Him by night; it was from their fear of the people that they were accompanied with a band so numerous and strongly armed: and the admonition of Judas, that they should hold Him fast and lead Him away safely, indicates some fear of His escape. While therefore they were, as was evidently the case, in this state of apprehension, it is natural to suppose that they should first of all take Him to a private house, where they might put Him more securely in bonds, and so prevent any rescue on the part of our Lord's disciples or followers, before they took Him to the more public hall of the High Priest; where the Sanhedrim were used to meet, and other people of various sorts assembled.   Now in confirmation of this view, we find, I think, that there is but one circumstance mentioned with reference to our Lord's being taken there; and this both fully agrees with the supposition above given, and indeed requires it for its explanation; for St. John introduces by the way, and out of the thread of his narrative, the mention of Annas, as explaining and aggravating the circumstance he was speaking of, viz. that when our Lord was struck as he described, He was already in bonds; for that He had been bound at the house of Annas, "now Annas had sent Him bound to Caiaphas the High Priest [1]."   It is probable that this circumstance of our Lord being taken first of all to the house of Annas was not in any other way material on account of any thing that occurred there; so that the other Evangelists entirely omit the mention of it: but St. John records it partly perhaps in a natural way, as he was probably now following the crowd, and waiting whilst our Lord was detained there; and partly from some Divine purpose, which he often indicates in matters apparently trivial.

There is also another circumstance to be considered with regard to putting our Lord in bonds; that subsequently in the account it is stated [2], that the Sanhedrim bound Him after they had condemned Him to death,

---

[1] Ch. xviii. 24.　　　　　　　[2] See p. 166.

and before taking Him to Pilate. And thence a difficulty arises, how they can be said to put Him into bonds at that time, if He was already bound in the house of Annas. But if we suppose that at the house of Annas He was merely put in bonds for the sake of security, and afterwards into the chains of a criminal condemned to death, in order that He might be delivered in that manner to the governor, this will satisfactorily explain the difficulty. "It was the custom of the Jews," says Bede, "that when they had condemned any one to death, they delivered him bound to the governor, that the governor, by seeing him bound, might understand that he was condemned to death." Thus, therefore, was our Blessed Lord led to the house of Annas, according to the human motives of the agents, in order to secure Him more safely as a prisoner: with regard to our Blessed Lord Himself as a voluntary Victim, it was adding to His humiliations to be led, at will and in sport, from place to place. But according to the Divine superintendence, which regulated every circumstance with respect to Christ, even in the conduct of wicked men, it was in order that every part of that guilty nation might have a share in His innocent blood, the blood of the Victim slain by all and for all; and that as a nation all might suffer the penalty of the crime.

CHRIST IN BONDS.

Now therefore we come to this amazing scene, to contemplate our Lord as led away captive! Surely if St. Paul could say, "remember my bonds," how much more does Christ call upon us to remember His bonds?

He is in bonds, but it is altogether for our sakes: those bonds were due to us for our manifold misdeeds, but Christ is bound that we may go free. Seeing us tied and bound with the chain of our sins, Christ is bound with galling and severe cords of oppression, but it is because He was bound also with the stronger cords of love. "Could He not set Himself free," says St. Cyril[3], "who freed Lazarus from the bonds of death after four days, and loosed Peter from the iron bands of his prison? Angels stood around Him ready, saying, 'let us burst their bands in sunder;' but they held back, because their Lord was pleased to undergo it."

From henceforth, as every other evil of life is sanctified by His sufferings, so captivity also is rendered a blessing, and even sweet and profitable for the love of Christ[4]. From hence arise those interesting accounts of suffering saints who have spoken of captivity as being replete with blessed fruits; sufferings which are, as St. Paul says of his own bonds, to "the furtherance of the Gospel," and in which "the Gospel is not bound." Christ is in bonds, but it is altogether for our sakes: Quesnel has well said, "the binding of Christ is the effect, the punishment, and the remedy of the ill use which we make of our liberty." And as it is the punishment of our earthly liberty, so is it the purchase of our heavenly liberty, of that which is called "perfect freedom" and "the glorious liberty of the children of God."

As this His captivity and the effects of it are developed in His children till the end of the world: so also it is prefigured in those that went before. "Here," as St. Jerome says, "is the true Joseph, sold by his brethren, so that the iron entered into his soul." Here, we may add, is Samson, the true Nazarite, in the hands

---

[3] Lect. xiii. 12.

[4] μένει τὸ θεῖον δουλίῳ περ ἐν ζυγῷ. Æsch. Ag. But the contrary occurs in a poet of our own: "Patience itself is meanness in a slave."

of his enemies. Here is the obedient Isaac, bound by his Father. Here is Jeremiah, the man of sorrows, put in bonds for his testimony to the truth of God. Here is Judah, whom his " brethren shall praise," led captive to Babylon; taking our sins upon Him, as if they were His own, and saying, " the yoke of my transgression is bound by his hand: they are wreathed and come up upon My neck: He hath made My strength to fall; the Lord hath delivered Me into their hands [5]." " He hath hedged Me about, that I cannot get out: He hath made My chain heavy [6]." And the disciples might take up their lamentation, and say, " they hunt our steps that we cannot go in our streets: our end is near;" " the breath of our nostrils, the Anointed of the Lord, is taken in their pits, of Whom we said, Under His shadow we shall live [7]." But what tongue shall worthily declare the sufferings of the Son of Man! for if His " knees were weak through fasting," and the chains were on His weak frame, how much more keen and heavy was that iron which, in the language of Holy Scripture, entered into His soul! Betrayed by one friend, denied by another, deserted by all, and soon,—as it might appear from our Lord's bitter cry upon the Cross,—to be forsaken of God! And even now was He suffering under the weight of His unknown heavy agony, and with the drops of that bloody sweat still fresh upon His sacred Body. Well, therefore, in the 109th Psalm, which describes Judas as taking Him, is He spoken of as " the poor and helpless man who was vexed at the heart," as one " helpless and poor," whose " heart was wounded " within Him. Who indeed but His own Psalmist, the man after His own heart, could rightly speak of His sorrows? " I go hence,

[5] Lam. i. 14.   [6] Ch. iii. 7.   [7] Ch. iv. 20.

like the shadow that departeth,"—" He brought down My strength in My journey, and shortened My days."

And now having followed our Lord through the scene of His betrayal and capture throughout the Psalms, and especially the 109th Psalm, we come to the concluding verse of the scene, where we have the assurance that " God will stand by Him, and save Him, and deliver His soul from unrighteous judges."   In what way He will deliver Him is here left in mysterious silence; but in the following Psalm, the 110th, there opens a new scene in Heavenly places, wherein " the Lord said to My Lord, Sit Thou on My right hand, until I make Thine enemies Thy footstool."   For thus we may suppose that our Lord, with the Psalms in His mind, as they seem to have been throughout, now arrives at that scene in the Hall of Caiaphas, where the remarkable testimony to which He bears witness is the great truth contained in the 110th Psalm.

THE PALACE OF CAIAPHAS.

From the house of Annas our Lord was led very shortly after to the palace of the High Priest; not, however, as a criminal before a just judge, for the determination of the High Priest had been already made, and St. John, in mentioning him on this occasion, adds, *" now it was Caiaphas who had given counsel to the Jews, that it was expedient for one man to die for the people."* We learn further from Josephus, that he had obtained the Pontificate for the year from the Romans, for money; and was inclined to exercise that office in their favour.   Naturally, then, he would exercise unjustly that which he had unjustly obtained.   Yet even this injustice, as we are told on that occasion, was full of

Divine prophecy, " for such," says St. Chrysostom, " is the superabundance of truth, that even its enemies speak the same." · But in thus speaking divinely, and truly, though he meant it wickedly and in a worldly sense, he afforded but one instance, among many, in all that took place on this momentous scene, whereby the purpose of God, together with the free will of man, is discernible throughout in every part; the overruling control of· God commanding, but the madness of men executing His commands, even in their own disobedience and rebellion against Him.

The High Priest was now up, in his hall, and " *all the Chief Priests* (Mark) *and the Elders and the scribes* (Matt. Mark) *were collected* " (Matt.), or at least were now " *collecting with him* " (Mark) and awaiting the return of their emissaries with the prisoner. It is mentioned on another occasion that the palace of the High Priest was the usual place of their assembling [8], but it does not appear that this was yet the formal meeting of the Sanhedrim, for that seems to have taken place later in the morning; but that merely on account of their animosity, and their wish to support with their advice, and to know the intentions of Caiaphas, they were already assembling around him. " The scribes and Elders," says St. Chrysostom, " were collected together, that they might do all things according to the mind of the Chief Priest: for Caiaphas was the High Priest. And thus they spent their night, and continued in watching, and without sleep, for this purpose." —" For they were exceedingly enraged; and after so many vain attempts to kill Him, having now unexpectedly taken Him, they neglected even the Passover to

---

[8] Matt. xxvi. 3.

H

gratify their murderous intent." Our blessed Lord was now set before them bound; and their enmity and hatred, which had been so long increasing, was turning to exultation at the sight of their victim, apparently helpless, before them, and in their power. And the High Priest began to question Him. Scripture had before described it. "The rulers take counsel together against the Lord, and against His Anointed." "They cast their heads together with one consent; and are confederate against" Him. "They spake against Him with false tongues, and compassed Him about with words of hatred." "They took this counsel together, saying, God hath forsaken Him: persecute Him and take Him, for there is none to deliver Him."

In the mean time St. Peter and St. John were following the crowd. "*But Simon Peter followed Jesus, and that other disciple*," says St. John. The other Evangelists make no mention of this other disciple, but only say expressly, that "*Peter afar off followed* (Matt. Mark, Luke) *Him*" (Matt. Mark). His following at all when the other disciples had fled, evinces, of course, that zeal and great fervour by which he was made meet to become the first of Apostles; but at the same time, if his following testified his zeal and love, yet the expression "afar off," may serve to signify his fear. As he looked before him, and watched the crowd, and saw his Lord violently dragged along as a powerless captive, the faith of his great Confession began to give way. This his following from afar has been thought to represent the Church afar off following her Lord; as St. Paul speaks of "her filling up that which is behind of the sufferings of Christ[9]," and "even unto this present hour, we both hunger, and thirst, and

[9] Col. i. 24.

are naked, and are buffeted, and have no certain
dwelling place[10]," after the pattern of her Lord. He
followed as we must follow, but it was "afar off," for
indeed if any one follows Christ it must be "afar off."
Origen, St. Augustin[11], and St Chrysostom[12] all allow
that "the other disciple" was St. John himself. The
latter says, "why did he conceal his name? As he had
lain on Jesus's breast he naturally conceals himself."
This indeed accounts for the humility inseparable from
good men; approaching nearer to the light of God's
presence, they see their own nothingness, and wish to
be hid, so that the words expressive of the highest
Divine affection are, "Thou art a place to hide me in."
Such is indeed especially the case in deep contemplative affection, such as St. John's was. And observe,
that while He introduces himself into the narrative in
the simplicity of Divine love, yet he would lead us to
infer what doubtless he himself felt, that his knowledge of the High Priest made it not so great an act of
courage on his part as it was in his beloved friend, St.
Peter. "*Now that other disciple was known unto the
High Priest, and*" on that account obtaining admission, "*he entered together with Jesus into the hall of
the High Priest. But Peter stood without, at the
door. The other disciple, therefore, who was known to
the High Priest, went out and spake to the woman that
kept the door, and brought in Peter*" (John).

The denials of St. Peter do not appear to have preceded the examination and ill-treatment of our Lord,
but to have taken place about the same time, and perhaps, for the most part, while our Lord was being
buffeted by the servants after His having been questioned by the Chief Priest. For the times of St. Peter's

---

[10] 1 Cor. iv. 11.   [11] Tr. cxiii.   [12] Hom. lxxxiii.

last and first denials were distinctly marked by the two crowings of the cock. " Concerning the temptation of St. Peter," says Augustin, " which took place between these insults of our Lord, all do not relate in the same order : for Matthew and Mark first mention the latter, and afterwards the temptation of Peter. But Luke first unfolds the temptation of Peter, and then these insults of the Lord." The state of the case is here clearly mentioned, excepting that the difference which St. Augustin remarks between the first two Evangelists and St. Luke may be this, that the examination of which St. Luke speaks, is not that before Caiaphas, which the other two record, but that before the Sanhedrim, later in the morning, and after the ill-treatment of the servants. And to this account of the other Evangelists it is to be added, that St. John interweaves and blends the denials of St. Peter with the narrative concerning our Lord, which account appears to be precisely as the circumstances took place; we may therefore, in considering the arrangement of the incidents, adhere to the order of his narrative, although, for the sake of convenience, we proceed first of all to give the account of St. Peter's denials. St. John mentions what took place with regard to the one, and then passes to speak of what was taking place with regard to the other. This sets before us the whole account, and naturally indicates, I think, that it was coincident, not only with regard to time, but also with regard to place ; and that St. Peter was in the same hall with our Lord, although in a different part of it. St. Augustin, indeed, and some others, have supposed that our Lord's examination before Caiaphas was taking place in a different room. To support this, St. Augustin is obliged to suppose that our Lord's looking on St.

Peter is to be explained mystically, and not literally; but one cannot think that the letter is ever set aside by the spiritual interpretation. Again, Dr. Townson suggests that our Lord, after being questioned by the Chief Priest, was removed, and put out into the place where the servants were, while Caiaphas consulted with the Elders concerning Him; and that He was there being insulted by them, at the time when He looked on St. Peter; and that afterwards, when the Sanhedrim had assembled on the morning, He was led again to their council-chamber, as the Evangelists mention. This may have been the case; the supposition falls in, for the most part, with the different accounts, and is of itself natural and easy. But notwithstanding, as there is nothing in the sacred narratives that alludes to this having been the case, and no early writers that mention it as traditional; and since the accounts of the two orders of circumstances with respect to our Lord and St. Peter run so simultaneously in St. John, as to lead one naturally to infer it was in the same place; and as there is no difficulty whatever in supposing it to be all in one large room, it seems safer to adhere to this arrangement. And, first of all, with regard to the whole case of St. Peter.

THE DENIALS OF ST. PETER.

The place into which they were admitted seems probably to have been a large kind of hall, such as we are familiar with in public buildings and colleges, in the upper, and probably raised, part of which the Chief Priests were assembling, and the High Priest was interrogating the Ever Blessed Jesus. In the lower part of this hall were the attendants and servants, and into this place, among them, it was that St. Peter was admitted.

The very variety and discrepancy of the expressions with which it is described, will tend, if put together, to afford the best description we can have of the place. St. Matthew, in speaking of our blessed Lord, mentions where St. Peter was, as his being "in the hall without," and St. Mark, "in the hall below," or as the Vulgate translation has it (*in atrio deorsum*), in the hall towards the lower part, or down below; and yet, though it appears an outer and lower part, yet we may infer that it was in the same room, for our Lord turned and looked on Peter. Besides which St. Mark also speaks of it as "within the hall[1];" and St. Luke mentions the fire, where St. Peter was, as being "in the midst of the hall." Such, therefore, was the place into which they had all now come; St. Peter and the attendants were within the hall; but our Lord was at the further end, in an upper and interior raised part, in the sight of those who were in the lower part of the hall.

It was now dark and about midnight, being nearly twelve o'clock, and probably this lower or outer part of the hall was dark, excepting for the light of the fire in one part, around which a mingled group of persons were collecting on account of the cold. For St. John says, "*the servants and attendants had made a fire, for it was cold.*" And St. Luke, "*now when they had kindled a fire in the midst of the hall, and while they sat together, Peter sat in the midst of them;*" perhaps sitting in the midst to avoid observation. "*He sat there together with the attendants,*" says St. Matthew and St. Mark, "*to see the end* (Matt.); *and*" St. Mark adds, "*was warming himself towards the light.*" These conderations will account for the circumstances which gave rise to the first accusation and denial. On the first

[1] xiv. 54. ἠκολούθησεν αὐτῷ ἕως ἔσω εἰς τὴν αὐλήν.

occasion, all the accounts agree in saying, that the person who first charged him was a woman; and St. John adds, that this woman was the door-keeper who had admitted him. It is probable, therefore, that the first thing which attracted her attention to him was connected with her office; that the light which she had in her hand fell upon him as she admitted him in the dark; and that as a person in such a place of responsible trust she was more observant. But it was not on his admission that she charged him, but afterwards, as he was by the fire. Then " *cometh one of the maids of the Chief Priest* (Mark); *there came up to him a maid* (Matt.); *a certain damsel* (Luke), *and beheld Peter warming himself*" (Mark). St. Mark expressly adds, " *looking upon him;*" and St. Luke, " *when she saw him sitting towards the light, and earnestly gazed upon him.*" It is remarkable that three Evangelists speak expressly of the fire, as if this circumstance was intimately connected with the recognition of him in that dark hall; and their very words imply that he became distinctly visible from that circumstance as he sat turned "towards the light[2]." And all the Evangelists likewise mention, on this occasion the maid-servant, who we find was the person that had admitted him, as if this circumstance, also, was connected with his detection. " *She said,*" St. Luke tells us, as if addressing the bystanders, "*This man was with Him;*" and then she says to St. Peter, " *Thou also wast with Jesus* (Matt. Mark) *the Galilean* (Matt.) *of Nazareth* (Mark). *Art not thou also one of this man's disciples? He saith, I am not* (John), *woman, I do not know Him* (Luke); *I do not understand what thou meanest* (Matt. Mark);*" and thus " *he denied* (Matt. Mark, Luke) *Him* (Luke) *before them all*" (Matt.).

[2] πρὸς τὸ φῶς.

But St. Peter, being now in great uneasiness and alarm, and the more so when he had thus lost his self-possession and conscious fidelity, would no doubt be glad to escape from the crowd, as soon as he could do so without attracting notice, and especially to retire from the glare of the fire by which he had been detected; and he got up "*and went out into the vestibule*" (Mark), and while he was there, St. Mark. adds, "*the cock crew.*" But he was so absorbed in mind with his own fears, and the fate of his Master on this eventful night, and under circumstances so strange and mysterious, that he probably noticed not, at the moment, the fulfilment of his Master's declaration. " the cock crew," says St. Chrysostom, " showing that it neither prevented him from denying, nor recalled his promise to his memory."

But after he had once arrested attention, his retiring from the hall would not have lessened the suspicion, especially as the woman who had the charge of the door had been the person to observe him. "*The maid a second time,*" St. Mark says, and we should suppose it means the same maid. And also "*another maid,*" St. Matthew says, who combined with her in the charge, as he was going out again remarked it, and drew attention to him. It was not to himself that she observes it, for he had now "*gone out,*" or was going out, "*into the porch* (Matt.), but *to those who were there* (Matt.), *the standers by*" (Mark). The former of these women saying, "*that this man also is one of them*" (Mark), and the other maid, "*and this man also was with Jesus of Nazareth*" (Matt.). And probably after he had been out, (for it was " *a little while after*," St. Luke says,) he returned, and did not sit, as before, among those at the fire, but, being in great uneasiness and alarm, "stood:"

"*now Peter was among them standing and warming himself*" (John). And St. John afterwards returning to the narrative from which he had digressed, speaks of this attitude, saying, "*now Simon Peter was standing and warming himself.*" They, therefore, to whom the damsel that kept the door, and her companion, had perseveringly repeated the charge, now attacked him again. They all, according to St. John, addressed him; but as in many pressing a charge, there must be one more particularly who speaks, St. Luke mentions it in the singular number; "*And after a little while another person saw him, and said, And thou also art one of them*" (Luke). "*They said therefore to him, And art not thou also one of His disciples?*" (John.) "*He again* (Matt. Mark) *denied it*" (Matt. Mark, John), addressing the man who spoke, "*Man* (Luke), *I am not*" (Luke, John). And St. Matthew says, that he added an adjuration, "*again denying,*" as if to them all together, "*with an oath, I know not the man.*" The discrepancies of the four Evangelists can thus be easily reconciled on this occasion, although in the mention of the persons who charged him, St. Matthew says, "another maid" noticed him; St. Mark, "the maid seeing him again;" St. Luke, "another man;" and St. John, "they at the fire." For the two first who speak of the women do not say that they charged him, but that they spoke; St. Matthew says, "*to those who were there;*" St. Mark, "*to those who stood by.*" To them, therefore, the woman appeals; it was they therefore who, according to St. John, spoke to St. Peter; and as they could not all speak at once, one of them, according to St. Luke's account, addressed him more particularly; to whom he replied, "O man," in the singular number. And with regard to the same or a different woman, as St. Matthew and St. Mark relate it variously, it may be one and the same action of both observing at the same time.

But not only is there no necessary contradiction, nor even discrepancy, in the mention of the same maid, and also of another maid, for both might be true, and even that simultaneously; but it should be observed that this tends, like all the apparent discrepancies, to render the account more graphic, and sets it in a more lively manner before the eyes; for we seem, in comparing the accounts, to behold the scene, as it breaks more and more distinctly upon us; it manifests the interest and eagerness of the parties, the maid who kept the door, and her companion too, with rival zeal, charging him, and then all present, interested and excited with one movement respecting him, while he secretly shrunk from them in trembling agitation, and then one of them, more eager than the rest, seeing and questioning him.

St. Augustin confirms this view, excepting that he considers it to be at the house of Annas. "We find," he says, "from St. John that it was not before the door, but at the fire-place, that Peter denied the second time, and therefore he had then returned; for it was not after he had gone out and was without, that the maid saw him; but as he went out, *i. e.* as he had risen to go out, she perceived him, and spoke to those who were there at the fire-place in the hall. But he, when he heard it, returned to clear himself: or, what is more probable, he did not hear as he was going what was said of him: and it was after he returned that the maid, and that other one whom Luke mentions, said unto him, 'Thou also art one of this man's disciples;' and as the person whom Luke mentions insisted more vehemently and said, and 'Thou also art one of them,' Peter says to him, 'Man, I am not[3].'"

[3] De Cons. Evan. lib. iii. 24.

Origen also takes it the same way, that it was not after he had gone out, but as he was going out the second time, "not when he was outside the door, 'without,' but wishing to go out, though not yet having gone forth [4]." But St. Augustin does not seem to think that there were two different maids spoken of by St. Matthew and St. Mark, but that both expressions allude to the same person. And yet the expression "the maid" in St. Mark would seem to imply "the same maid" he had spoken of the first time, viz. the maid who kept the door; whereas St. Matthew clearly says "another maid" on this second charge.

But here it is worthy of notice, that the women introduced on this occasion are the only women that are mentioned as taking part with the enemies of our Lord: and even they are not concerned in bringing about His condemnation, nor any further than to detect St. Peter. It is remarkable that no woman is mentioned throughout as speaking against our Lord in His life, or having a share in his death. On the contrary He is anointed by a woman for His burial, women are the last at His grave, the first at His resurrection; to a woman He first appeared; women ministered to His wants from Galilee; women bewailed and lamented Him; a heathen woman interceded for His life with her husband the Governor; and above all, He was born of a woman. So that as woman was most conspicuous in the first transgression, and doomed to subjection and pain of child-birth; so she is not conspicuous in the second great crime of the children of Adam. It may be because she had more particularly to partake of suffering and bear the Cross: and women and children were perhaps most noticed by Christ on account of their

[4] Lat. Comm. in Matt. 114.

natural infirmity. For the same reason that the poor are the objects of the benediction, the afflicted of the consolations of the Gospel; and " God hath chosen the weak things of the world to confound the strong." Before our Lord's birth He selected women here and there singly ; and eminent types of Christ were born of women that were barren, or beyond the natural age of child-bearing, as setting forth our Lord's supernatural birth of a virgin, and showing that when most weak, they were in Him most strong. But since His birth He has dispensed His sanctifying afflictions and graces, not by partial choice to a few women, the mothers of saints, who were singly to represent our Lord's Virgin Mother: but has diffused throughout all the sex His strength. By choosing woman for His super-human birth, and submitting to childhood, He has drawn women and children more especially to Himself in the endearments of His Gospel, affording them the measures of His grace, according to the measure of their infirmities and needs.

We must now endeavour to enter into the feelings of St. Peter, and consider the situation in which he was placed. He was necessarily in a state of great agitation and alarm ; it was a large dark hall ; he was in the midst of enemies; had already been twice on the very point of complete detection ; and he could scarcely be otherwise than conscious of what was now going on at the upper part of the hall, although our Saviour's back was probably turned towards him: and great must have been his consternation and amazement, that He, whom he had believed and confessed to be no less than the Son of God, was there being shamefully entreated and spit on, and authoritatively denounced by the Elders. Thus a cloud was coming over his mind by the arts of the tempter. As he had now been betrayed by the light, for on both occasions he was close to the fire, he would naturally withdraw into the dark parts of the hall where he could escape observation. But it is in vain to avoid external occasions of temptation, while the liability to fall arises from within; and whenever we are ready to deny Christ, the occasion for doing so will seldom be wanting. Nay, the very means we take to avoid detection will be the occasions and means of detecting us, as it was with St. Peter; for He who is about our path will make our very darkness to be light, nor is there any hiding place from His power. The Master hath not lost sight of His disciple; the sinner shall not escape the watchfulness of his God. He who appears to have His back turned to us, and not to notice or regard us, has all the while His ear open to our words, and His eye within our hearts, watching every movement of our thoughts. The supposition that St. Peter had now retired from the light, appears in itself quite natural and probable; and also serves to explain the circumstances mentioned of the third denial; for as three Evangelists had before spoken of the fire, or the light, when the Apostle was first detected, so they now concur in stating that on this occasion it was his speech that betrayed him. St. Matthew says,—"*A little while after, they that stood by came up to Peter and said, Truly thou art one of them, for thy speech maketh thee manifest.*" We might have been at a loss to apprehend how his speech could have afforded such strong evidence to convict him, were it not for the words of St. Luke and St. Mark. St. Luke says, that "*after the interval of about an hour some one else confidently affirmed, saying, Of a truth this man also was with Him, for he is a Galilean:*" and St. Mark, that "*a little while after, they that stood by again said to Peter, Of a truth thou art of them, for thou art a Gali-*

lean, and thy speech agreeth thereto."   Some time had now elapsed since the former charge had been made : St. Matthew and St. Mark say, " a little while after," implying that it was not immediately on the former occasion, but after some time had intervened; and St. Luke says it was " about an hour " after.   So that St. Peter was now sitting a little removed from the immediate glare of the light, and was beginning to feel himself safe, and becoming by degrees a little relieved from his apprehensions, after such an interval of time, and was venturing perhaps to converse again with the bystanders ; not thinking of another mode of recognition, which would arise from the strong dialect of that distant province of Galilee.   And St. Matthew, by using the words, " they who stood by came up to him," seems to indicate that his position had been changed, and that he had retired from that place where he had been on the previous occasion, sitting or standing with the crowd. St. Matthew and St. Mark here speak of their charging him in the plural number, as if there was something of a stir among them.   But St. Luke mentions that there was one more particularly that affirmed it—" some one else."   And St. John mentions of this person, who probably was known to him from his acquaintance with the High Priest, and also from his being now present at the circumstance, that it was " a servant of the High Priest's," a relative of him whom Peter had this very night attacked and wounded.   Or perhaps this was not the individual whom St. Luke is speaking of, but another bystander, who hearing the commotion about St. Peter, and the charge made against him, and in the twilight gazing on the accused person with a determination to convict him, seconded and supported the asseveration of the first; for the account of the first two Evangelists

would lead one to suppose that certainly more than one
person was engaged in drawing notice to St. Peter. And
St. John's account is more like that of a person second-
ing the accusation of another than making it himself.
"*One of the servants of the Chief Priest, being kinsman
of him whose ear Peter cut off, saith, Did I not see thee
in the garden with Him?*" To this St. John meekly adds,
in the gentle simplicity of his narrative, "*Peter therefore
again denied.*" St. Luke records his words, "*Peter
said, Man, I know not what thou sayest.*" But St. Matthew and St. Mark record the circumstances in a manner
very characteristic indeed of St. Peter's earnest vehemence of temper, but a lamentable instance of the grow-
ing power of guilt and temptation, when it has once been
yielded to. "*Then* (Matt.) *he began to curse and to
swear,*" saying, "*I know not the Man* (Matt. Mark)
of whom ye speak" (Matt.).   It has been simply, but
well noticed [5], "how St. Peter's denial increases more
and more vehemently, from his first of all saying, I
know not what thou sayest, and secondly his denying
with an oath, and thirdly that he began to curse and
to swear that he knew not the Man. For to persevere
in sin gives increase unto crime, and he who despises
least things falls into greater."

This is the great and good St. Peter, the Chief of
Apostles, and declared by Christ Himself to be
"blessed." So very different are the same persons
under different circumstances and in different companies. And perhaps the shame, as well as the danger,
of being connected with so mean a prisoner, led him
at this time quite to forget his Master in the thoughts
of himself. Independently of other reasons why this
circumstance should be so minutely recorded at this

[5] Rabanus Maurus. Aur. Cat.

time, one thing may have been, that it so forcibly sets before us, as a warning, the want of stedfastness which is often found even in the better sort of persons, such as have much energy and zeal, which promises great things, but have not yet attained to that stedfastness which will enable them to perform them. For although the account of so wonderful a change of mind, in so few hours, seems at first almost incredible, yet, when considered in all its circumstances, it will be found an exact picture and description of the declarations and resolutions, which men make when alone with God at their prayers, as contrasted with their conduct a few hours afterwards, when the season of temptation shall have overtaken them. And surely it is a matter worthy of the deepest consideration, that not only is so very little told us of the Saints of God, but what is recorded is for the most part to their prejudice. And this is the case even with regard to those who approached most nearly to the Person of our blessed Lord, and might be supposed to partake of the radiance that went forth from Him. Even they are not allowed to exalt themselves, nor glory in His presence; nay, indeed, were perhaps on that very account the more signally abased before all men, that none might presume. Of our Lord alone it is said, "The prince of this world cometh, and hath nothing in Me[6]."

But yet there is much to be said in excuse for St. Peter, which cannot be said for us, who have received the Spirit. For, as the Fathers observe, St. Peter had not yet the Spirit, as He was afterwards bestowed. "No one," as Origen says, "can say that Jesus is the Lord, excepting by the Holy Spirit[7]. But the Spirit was

---

[6] John xiv. 30.   [7] 1 Cor. xii. 3.

not yet among men, because Jesus was not yet glorified, as St. John says [8]. But we shall have no excuse if we shall deny Him, since the Spirit of the Father is mighty to speak in us, and it is in our power to give place to the Holy Spirit, or to the devil [9]." And as St. Jerome says, " Without the Spirit Peter trembled at the voice of a maid-servant, with the Spirit he withstood princes and kings." And St. Cyril of Alexandria particularly dwells on this, that the Spirit was not yet given; and that Peter was afterwards capable of enduring the greatest trials. But at the same time he says, that this instance of infirmity and pardon was allowed to happen for our consolation.

Indeed, we may humbly venture to think that this melancholy failure in one so eminent and favoured, was permitted to occur, to afford us encouragement and hope in similar derelictions and temptations. And that as our Lord could not afford us an instance of human infirmity in Himself, He has given it to us in the person of the most exalted of His pastors: that all may fear, and none may presume, and all may hope. " On this account," says Leo, " as it appears, he was allowed to waver that the remedy of repentance might be laid up in a chief of the Church, that no one should dare to trust in his own goodness, since even the blessed Peter could not escape the danger of mutability [10]." And Theophylact says, that our Lord " allowed him to suffer from a Providential dispensation, that he might not exalt himself; and at the same time that His own pitifulness might be shown in one who was instructed by Himself, of the issue of human infirmity." We may indeed consider

---

[8] John vii. 39.   [9] In Matt. Lat. Com. 114.
[10] In Serm. de Pass. Dom.

I

it as one of those emanations of exceeding compassionateness which gather around the Cross of Christ, like the acceptance of the penitent thief, and our Lord's prayer for His murderers. They are like objects of mercy kneeling around the Cross of Christ, from whose reception every sincere penitent may find consolation unto the end of the world. The last-mentioned writer well says, "Tears brought Peter to Christ through repentance. Let those Novatians therefore be confounded who affirm that he who sins after the reception of Baptism is not admitted for his sins to be forgiven. For behold Peter, who had received the Body and Blood of Christ, is admitted through repentance. But the failings of the Saints are written on this account, that we also, if we should have fallen through carelessness, might have the means of retracing our steps by their examples, and might hope through repentance to be relieved." Much to the same effect is Nicetus; "The evil," he says, "arose from human cowardice; and that the disciple was condemned by his own conscience, his lamentation itself would at once teach us, and the tears of his remorse. And, when converted, he failed not of the mark: for he continued, what he was, a genuine disciple; and richly obtained the remission of his offence. But this we say, that the failings of the Saints we learn from the Holy Scriptures themselves, that we may become imitators of their repentance. For the mercy-loving God hath devised repentance, as a saving remedy for those who are on earth, which they endeavour to destroy, who say that they are pure; not perceiving that to have such an estimation of themselves is replete with all uncleanness, for, as it is written, 'no one is clean from pollution.' For let them not forget this also, that before Christ had been taken, and Peter had denied Him, he had been

partaker of the Body of Christ, and His precious Blood,
and thus he slipped, and by repentance procured remission.   Let them therefore not accuse the calm patience
of God, remembering how distinctly He says, ' As for
the wickedness of the wicked he shall not fall thereby,
in the day that he turneth from his wickedness [11].' "

THE LORD LOOKING ON ST. PETER.

But though St. Peter had forgotten his Lord and
Master, his Lord had not forgotten him.   For we read
that "*immediately* (Matt. Luke, John) *while he was
yet speaking*" (Luke) in this strong manner, "*the cock
crew* (Matt. Mark, Luke, John) *a second time* (Mark).
And*" at the sound, "*the Lord turned and looked on
Peter*" (Luke). Although Peter had secluded himself
in the dark, and thought that as he sat there no eye
beheld him, yet there was One in the light to whom his
eyes could not but unconsciously turn; Who in His
Divine Spirit and affectionate care still saw and heard
him, though afar off: and Whom, as He stood in the
light at the upper end of the hall, a prisoner bound and
beaten among His enemies, Peter, as he sat below, could
not but distinctly behold, though at a distance.   What
was expressed in that look of our blessed Saviour,
thought of man cannot conceive, and words cannot utter.
That it spoke of all that had passed in our Lord's long
intimacy with St. Peter, and especially the conversation
of that night, and that it derived a peculiar force and
meaning from the indignities which our Lord was suffering; and that at such a time His own favoured disciple
should deny Him; that it seemed to say to him, "all this

---

[11] Ezek. xxxiii. 12.

ignominy and oppression I could have endured, and do endure in silent patience, but this hath grieved Me more than they:" that it implied something of this we may well suppose, but what more we cannot tell. The conciseness and sublimity with which it is mentioned, resembles the account in Genesis of His Word being spoken, at which the world was created. The Lord looked—the spell of Satan was dissolved. The Lord looked—and he wept bitterly. The Lord looked—and the darkness of death was fled, and light filled his mind. The thought of our Lord's Divinity, which he had believed, but had forgotten, now rushed afresh on St. Peter's mind. "*And Peter remembered the word* (Matt. Mark, Luke) *of the Lord* (Luke), *which Jesus had spoken unto him* (Matt. Mark), *how He said unto him* (Luke), *Before the cock crow thou shalt deny Me thrice* (Matt. Mark, Luke). *And Peter*" (Luke) immediately rose up and "*went out* (Matt. Luke), *and when he thought thereon* (Mark), *he wept* (Matt. Mark, Luke) *bitterly*" (Matt. Luke). In the darkness and silence of the night his eyes were opened to all that had passed, and "he wept bitterly." They were partly perhaps human tears, for having deserted the Friend he loved; and partly those of a still deeper remorse for having offended his God. Here is the beginning of repentance as a pattern to us all, and to be continually renewed; to behold Christ's eye upon us, to retire from the occasions of sin, in solitude and stillness of night, to weep, and to think over and remember Christ's words. It is reported, though I know not on what authority, but said to be that of Clemens Romanus, that St. Peter so deeply repented, that all his life long, whenever he heard the cock crow, he fell on his knees and wept, and prayed for pardon.

The Lord looked on Peter, and he repented: herein

is showed that man, even in his best estate, is altogether vanity, that none doeth good, no, not one; for Satan had desired to have them all, and he had gotten the chief of Apostles into his net, and was weaving his meshes more and more around his victim: as far as human nature went, he was utterly overtaken and fallen. "But I have prayed for thee," said our Lord; and this His prayer broke the bonds of the enemy, and let the captive go free. It was that prayer of Christ, and the efficacy of that prayer, which was shown in this look. It was not Peter, but the look and prayer of Christ which overcame. It was not their own arm that helped them, "but the light of Thy countenance, because Thou hadst a favour unto them."

"And Peter remembered the word of the Lord." Here we have a strong instance of the purpose of prophecy, that it is not for us to notice the fulfilment of it beforehand, but that when it is fulfilled it may be to us an indication and assurance of God—when the cock crew then the Lord turned and looked on Peter;— when it comes to pass then we notice the eye and the hand of God.

The Lord's turning and looking on St. Peter, upon the perpetration of his crime, is also analogous to His usual dealings with mankind. Inasmuch as He is the "Light that lighteth every one," this might be expected: it is not under the influence of temptation, of passion, or fear, but when the evil is done, that the eye of God breaks upon the soul. Not only with the wicked but with good men this is the case: their want of faith then appears when they have denied their Lord, and this it is that recalls them to God and themselves: whether it is the eye of Christ, or His supporting hand, which in like manner, on another occasion when Peter began to sink, seized hold of and supported him, saying, " O thou of little faith, wherefore didst thou doubt ?" Often, too, thus it is in some trifling external circumstance that we see Christ's eye upon us, and repent. The Lord could now no more speak to Him by His encouraging and divinely consoling voice as He had done in the garden, but " His look," as St. Chrysostom says, " was now instead of His voice :"—thus ever, in His mindful and watchful compassion, does He find some way to speak to us. At one time His voice, at another His look, at another His hand, supports His failing Church, when slumbering in temptation, or sore beset by her foes, or walking on the sea of danger. Happy he who is recalled to Christ, and to himself, and immediately retires from the world to weep and pray.

Here moreover, in the case of St. Peter, we have a remarkable instance of what Scripture mentions, a state of mind in which the ears cannot hear, nor the heart understand. For the memory of our Lord's prediction seems quite to have passed from St. Peter's mind, nor did he notice the cock-crowing which he heard. The light within him had for a time become darkened. It was the hour of darkness in more senses than one: the powers of darkness were let loose, and like clouds they had obscured his soul, till the countenance of our Lord, like the sun, dissipated those clouds, or made them to fall in tears of repentance, and the light was again rekindled within him.

"Behold," says St. Austin, " the prediction of the Physician is fulfilled, the presumption of the sick man convicted. It is not as he said, I will lay down my life for Thee ; but it is as the other had foretold, Thou shalt deny Me thrice." "Admire," says St. Chrysostom, "the care of the Master, in that when He was bound, He was so mindful of His disciple, and by beckoning to him brought him to tears." "For Him to look," says Bede, "is to have pity, for the mercy of God is not only necessary upon repentance, but in order that repentance may take place." "But his tears," adds St. Chrysostom, "were not on account of himself, but because he had denied Him whom he loved, which to him was more painful than any punishment." "Happy, O holy Apostle," exclaims St. Leo, "were thy tears, which had the power of holy Baptism to wash away the guilt of thy denial. For the right hand of the Lord Jesus Christ was present with thee, which checked thee in falling before thou wast deceived, and in the very crisis of thy fall thou receivedst firmness to stand. Soon therefore did Peter return to his stability as one receiving courage, that he who had been so terrified then in the time of Christ's passion, in his own sufferings hereafter might not fear, but stedfastly endure [12]." And St. Ambrose, "Blessed the tears which wash away guilt! They at length mourn on whom Jesus looks. Peter denied the first time, and wept not, because the Lord looked not on him. He denied a second time, and wept not, for as yet the Lord had not looked on him. He denied also a third time, Jesus looked on him, and he wept most bitterly. Lord Jesu, look on us, that we may know how to weep for our sin, and wash out the guilt! Hence also the failing of the Saints is profitable. The denial of Peter hath not at all injured me: his repentance hath profited me [1]."

"O Jesus, look upon me with the same eye of compassion, whenever I shall do amiss, that I may see my fault, and forthwith return to my duty:—let this instance

---

[12] Serm. de Pass.   [1] Exp. in Luc. x. 89.

of Thy mercy be our comfort, since so great and repeated a crime did not exclude this penitent from Thy
mercy ; but let not this make us fearless of offending
Thee, lest we never repent [2]."

THE COCK-CROWING.

But in the circumstances of the cock-crowing there is
another remarkable discrepancy in the accounts. St.
Mark mentions that after the first denial, " the cock
crew," and after the third time, that " the cock crew
twice," or a second time; and that this had been the
expression of our Lord, " Before the cock crow twice,
thou shalt deny Me thrice." Whereas St. Matthew and
St. Luke both say, " Before the cock crow thou shalt
deny Me thrice." We must reverently suppose that
both statements were made by our Lord, and that one
referred to that watch of the night which was usually
known by the name of " the cock-crowing," such as St.
Mark speaks of on another occasion when he mentions
the four watches of the night [3], which comprehends the
space of time from twelve o'clock till three; and the
expression might have referred more particularly to
the more distinct crowing of the cock, which takes
place at about three o'clock. It appears to be usual for
the cock to crow, repeatedly and consecutively, at one
period of the night. and then to be silent, till another
period ensues, when it crows again in a different and more
distinct manner. And this circumstance will explain
the expression of St. Mark, as applying to the natural
crowing of the cock at these two periods, rather than to
the civil term of " the cock-crowing," and that which was

[2] Bp. Wilson.   [3] Ch. xiii. 35.

more distinctly and decidedly the crowing of the cock
at the later hour of the morning. This particularity partakes of the characteristic minuteness and accuracy of
detail in St. Mark; and as the companion of St. Peter,
and writing from him, he mentions more particularly,
the actual crowing of the cock: "It is his own disciple
St. Mark," St. Chrysostom says, " that mentions this
aggravating circumstance, that already after one denial
he received this gracious warning in vain." Probably,
on reverting in memory to the whole transaction, St.
Peter remembered that the cock did crow after the first
denial; and that on recollection it occurred to him, that
our Lord had used that very expression on the preceding evening, "Before the cock crow twice." He
ventures therefore on both occasions to differ from St.
Matthew, in order to record the very minuteness of the
prediction and its fulfilment; but neither of these occasions of the cock-crowing, seems to have arrested his
attention till our Lord looked on him: as we may have
often occasion to observe, that St. Mark mentions circumstances disparaging to St. Peter, or such as would
to St. Peter's own mind have been remembered as aggravating, and for which he severely judged himself;
" for if we judge ourselves we shall not be judged of the
Lord." Thus we had occasion to remark that he speaks
of the appeal being made more particularly to St. Peter
on this night, "Simon, sleepest thou? couldest thou not
have watched one hour?" and here he only mentions
"when he thought thereon he wept," (or, as St. Augustin translates it, "he began to weep;" as others
render it, " he covered his face and wept,") and does
not add as the other Evangelists record, " he went out
and wept bitterly." As judging himself he dwells most
strongly on his warnings, least strongly on his tempt-

ations, and lessens the account of his repentance. But it is his friend St. John, who seems to mention most what may lessen the fault of his brother Apostle and companion: he simply states on each occasion, that he denied, as marking the fulfilment of his Lord's prediction, but says nothing of his protestations or oaths: and he mentions all the company that was there, "servants and officers," and speaks in the plural number of their accusing, and not as St. Mark "another maid;" and on the last occasion, he mentions that one of the accusers was a kinsman of that very Malchus whom he had wounded, as showing how very sorely his friend was tried by those who must have been his most formidable enemies[4]. It may further be observed, that the account which St. Luke gives of our Lord looking on St. Peter, is highly characteristic of St. Luke, writing of our merciful High Priest whose compassions fail not; and in other respects it is a circumstance which he, who was accounted a painter, would delight to record for its exquisitely touching beauty. For our Lord's looking on St. Peter, of itself, speaks to the heart more than volumes of teaching.

But still one is led to think, that we know very little of the reasons why this account of St. Peter's previous assurance, his subsequent temptation, and his fall, should be so particularly dwelt upon by all the Evangelists: it seems as if there might be contained in it some great principle or prophetic history, and perhaps both: some great principle to be developed in the future history of the Church, or of St. Peter's Church; and one is the more inclined to think so from St. John, the Evangelist of divine and mysterious wisdom,

---

[4] See Plain Sermons, vol. ii. p. 290. Serm. lxxi.

thinking it necessary to give a detailed account of it, in addition to the other Evangelists, who had so fully recorded it before.

The cock which was thus introduced into the most momentous and memorable scene, has not been forgotten by the Fathers: nor the sacred part which was assigned to that bird in this transaction. It has been treasured by them in affectionate memory, and considered the watch-bird of piety, recalling seasons of devotion and repentance. "Who is the cock, the bird of light," says St. Jerome, "but the Holy Spirit, by Whose voice in Prophecy and in Apostles, we from our threefold denial are aroused to most bitter weeping after falling; for having thought evil of God, and spoken evil to our neighbours, and done evil to ourselves." And St. Ambrose in his account of this bird, in his work on the Six days of Creation, dwells on the present history: and also in his beautiful Hymn on the crowing of the cock:

> " The Church, our Rock, the warning hears,
>   Again to wash her fault with tears."

And afterwards :—

> " The slumbering soul his larums chide,
>   The cock reproves him that denied.

> " Jesu, look on us when we fall,
>   And by Thy look to Thee recall;
>   Strength at Thy look returns again,
>   And tears wash out the guilty stain."

And Prudentius has a long Hymn on the same subject, with similar spiritual applications :

> " The voice of birds, that singing stand
>   Beneath our roof at morn,
>   Prefigures our great Judge at hand,
>   And Day-spring onward borne."

And again : —

> " 'Tis said that Satan's evil flock,
> Which wander forth at night,
> Start at the crowing of the cock,
> And vanish with affright.
>
> " The power of this the warning bird
> Is shown in Christ's own word :
> ' Thrice, Peter, ere the cock is heard,
> Shalt thou deny thy Lord.
>
> " For sin is pass'd with shades of night,
> And standing by the door,
> The herald of approaching Light
> Doth bid us sin no more."

Our venerable Bede, too, after the same mode of interpretation, says, " I think this cock is to be mystically understood as some one of the doctors, who chides those that are lying down and asleep, by saying, ' Awake to righteousness, and sin not.' " And probably the allusion comes through Origen : " Perhaps all men," he says, " when they deny Jesus, so that their denial of Him is capable of medicine, seem to deny Him before the crowing of the cock, before the Sun of Righteousness hath as yet risen, or His rising hath drawn near unto them. But after the rising of this Sun hath taken place in our minds,—if we shall have sinned willingly, after we have received the knowledge of the truth, there is now left no more sacrifice for sin, but terrible judgment, and a consuming fire, which shall destroy the adversaries [5]." In a word, the cock seems to represent the external warning, whatever it may be, that comes to us in God's Providence. This we learn is of no avail till Christ turns on us the light of His countenance, and

[5] Comm. in Matt. 114.

then His Holy Spirit from within also gives ears to hear, and a heart to understand; and when He thus gives us spiritual ears to hear, we perceive that the warning voice from without was no other than His own gracious call; His call from without and His call from within respond to one another; and all is His,— it is His work: "Be still, and know that I am God."

OUR LORD BEFORE CAIAPHAS.

In the mean while, or rather before these circumstances had occurred with regard to St. Peter, Christ was standing before the High Priest. While those who belonged to the Council, and were to take part with Caiaphas in this business, were assembling, or sent for to assemble, he himself proceeded at once to question the Lord. "*The High Priest therefore questioned Jesus concerning His disciples, and concerning His doctrine*" (John). He did this in his judicial character apparently, as if to learn and ascertain the truth; but as he had already determined, from motives of popular expediency, that our Lord should die, he could of course, in these inquiries, have had no intention of learning any thing; they must have been either for the purpose of ensnaring Christ by some admission that he might take hold of, or else have been merely carried on out of a certain show of justice. Our Lord, wishing perhaps quietly to show him the self-deceit and hypocrisy of such conduct, reminds him, as He had done before those who came to take Him (which the other three Evangelists record), that the very mode of His teaching would not allow of such a construction, as that He had taught any thing that would be disloyal, or injurious, to the Jewish religion, or the Roman state; that He had ever spoken openly to the world. St. Chrysostom says, "as they could bring no charge against Him, therefore they asked Him concerning His disciples, perhaps, who they were, or for what reason He had collected them; and this with the desire of convicting Him as a seditious person, and one having revolutionary designs, and as if none but His disciples attended to Him[6]." And then they proceeded to question Him concerning His doctrine, wishing to convict Him of teaching against the Law of Moses, and so to condemn Him of blasphemy; or else of sedition, so as to give Him up to the Roman Governor. But to this our Lord answers, with Divine wisdom, "in such a manner as not to appear wanting in the defence of the truth," says Theophylact, "and yet at the same time not as desiring to defend Himself." *"Jesus answered him, I spake openly to the world; I ever taught in the Synagogue and in the Temple, whither the Jews alway resort, and in secret have I said nothing"* (John). The places of His teaching were those most publicly frequented, for they were the Synagogues in the country villages and the Temple at Jerusalem; and He had said nothing in secret, *i. e.* nothing of a secret, insidious character. His mode of expounding mysteries to His disciples, as a religious rule of distinction, was of course nothing to the world, —nothing that it alluded to or understood. "A question has arisen," says St. Augustin, "how He spake openly to the world, if even to the disciples themselves He did not speak openly, but promised them a time when He would speak openly; and, moreover, to the disciples themselves He spake much more plainly when He was with them removed from the crowds, when He opened the parables which He brought forth

[6] In Joan. Hom. lxxxiii. 3.

unexplained to the multitude. But by His saying that He taught openly to the world, He meant that many heard Him, for no one teaches in secret who teaches before so many: and even that which was of a secret character, which was taught to the disciples, was hereafter, through them, to be made known to the world." And St. Chrysostom, also, "He spoke indeed in secret, but not in the manner that they intended, as one in fear and causing sedition, but where the things that He spake were above the comprehension of the many. But wishing abundantly to bring forward testimony worthy of credit, He appeals to those who heard Him, even to His enemies who were lying in wait for Him. For this is an incontestable demonstration of truth, when a person adduces his enemies as witnesses." But, what is very wonderful to observe, our Lord's words themselves are still replete with mysterious wisdom, and mark the Son of God. For His very expression is taken from the Prophet, where He Himself, Who made the worlds, deigns in unspeakable condescension to speak His own defence, and declare His own cause before the Jews: "Thus saith the Lord that created the Heavens, God Himself that formed the earth—I have not spoken in secret, in a dark place of the earth: I said not unto the seed of Jacob, Seek ye Me in vain: I the Lord speak righteously. I declare things that are right[7]." Wonderful mystery! surely it is God Himself, now speaking before them in the very words by which He pleaded His cause to them of old. But they knew it not.

To these inquiries thus put to Him by the High Priest, He was as it were bound to answer, from the

---

[7] Isa. xlv. 18, 19.

same meekness which led Him afterwards to be silent; for otherwise it might have appeared an ungracious sullenness. And to Caiaphas's repeated inquiries He replies, that those persons who had openly heard Him might testify: there could be no difficulty in the matter, if He really were suspected of any dangerous teaching, *"Why askest thou Me? ask those who heard Me what I said unto them. Behold, they know what I said"* (John). Thus were His words graciously calculated, like all others which He spake on this night, to show to His enemies their own selves, their own wicked purposes, in case they should not be too hardened to learn; they were indeed replete with truth, wisdom, and charity. But as, nevertheless, however wisely and meekly intended, they could not but have the effect, as before, when He spake in the Temple, of showing His great superiority to His adversaries, and putting them to silence; as not a word could He utter, but from the secret weight of ineffable holiness and purity, it must have been such that authority must stand abashed and confounded before Him:—*"When He had said these things, one of the attendants of the High Priest,"* feeling for the shame with which our Lord's words must overwhelm his master, *"as he stood by, struck Jesus with the palm of his hand, saying, "Answerest Thou the High Priest so?"* (John.) It has been reported that this servant was that very Malchus whose ear our Lord had restored this very night, and that he was an Idumean slave [8]. And certainly it is not improbable that the first of that band in violence should be one of the chief attendants about the person of the High Priest. But as our Lord's silent acquiescence in this

[8] See Bp. Taylor's Life of Christ, who quotes from Vida the line, —"Malchus Idumæis missus captivus ab oris."

blow would have given the impression that He had indeed acted wrongly, that the substance of what He said, or His manner of speaking to the High Priest, had merited the blow, He therefore expostulates with the man who strikes Him. "*Jesus answered him, If I have spoken evil, bear witness of the evil, but if well, why smitest thou Me?*"(John.) And this wanton blow was the more cruel and unjustifiable, as He was already, the Evangelist observes, in bonds at the time. "*Now Annas had sent him bound to Caiaphas the High Priest*" (John). And here again, in the causeless outrage of this servant, there is a fresh subject for wonder and adoration at the unfailing testimony of Scripture; for as our Lord's words were mysteriously a secret appeal to the Prophet's testimony, when He had before spoken to them to the same effect, pleading His cause as God; so now also the wanton action of this servant is but fulfilling the Divine word, according to the prophetic declaration, "I gave My back to the smiters, and My cheek to them that plucked off the hair[9]." And as every thing respecting our Divine Lord is the fulfilment of foregoing prophecy, so also every action of His is the fulfilment of His own precepts : not indeed in the letter, but in that manner in which He would have us to fulfil them, in the spirit. For hypocrisy often fulfils the commandment in the letter, but true love only in the spirit and intention ; and our Lord now was in the highest degree acting up to the principle of His own command, to offer the other cheek unto him that smites[10].

St. Augustin remarks of this conduct of our Lord, that it was a comment upon His own great precept of patience ; " showing, as it was necessary to be shown,

<hr>

[9] Isa. l. 6 ; Lam. iii. 29.   [10] Luke vi. 29.

that those commands were to be kept, not by bodily. display, but by a preparation of the heart. For ostensibly an angry man might offer the other cheek. How much better does the truly meek man answer to the truth, while in mind prepared to bear heavier things! By His true, and gentle, and just answer, not only did He offer the other cheek to the smiter, but prepare His whole body to be transfixed on the Cross[11]." And indeed His gentle answer was more difficult to true patience, than it would have been literally to have turned the other cheek; and it was also more kind. Surely no other than the highest love could have dictated our Lord's conduct to this man, for whom He was desirous to die. As St. Augustin observes, " He that made the world by a word of His mouth, could, if He had wished, have overwhelmed him with lightning from heaven, or earthquake from below, or have given him over to the power of evil spirits, or to any punishment worse than these." And we indeed, under the feelings of our nature, "when we consider who He was who received the blow, could have wished," says St. Austin, "that the man might have been thus punished. But, instead of so doing, He preferred to teach us that patience by which the world is overcome." St. Cyril of Alexandria in like manner speaks of this action of our Lord's[1]: " We may observe what an incomparable and transcendent image of the most perfect patience the Saviour hath pourtrayed to us in these things; and in what relates to Himself, has delineated the most exalted form of meekness. For being able to destroy all the Jews utterly by one only nod, He is smitten like a slave, nor does He avenge Himself. Being not like us, of a weak mind, or tyran-

---

[11] In Joan. Tract. cxiii. 4.   [1] Comm. in Joan. lib. xi. 13.

nized over by anger or pain, or overcome by the weight
of ambition, He meekly reproves His assailant, saying
that he ought not to strike Him who had done no wrong.
The Lord Jesus Christ, though He is the true God, the
Lord of earth and heaven, endures to be smitten on the
cheek. But we wretched men, who are but dust and
ashes, mean and poor, who are likened unto the grass of
the field, and to the flower, if any of our brethren fail in
a word against us, are embittered against him, like dragons; nor look to the Author and Founder of our faith,
even Jesus;—who being Lord of all, hath set before us
such a pattern of inexpressible patience, and for this
cause hath said unto us, 'The disciple is not above his
master, nor the servant above his Lord.'"

But these words of the blessed Jesus were not only
calculated to be to us, to the end of the world, our wisdom and our hope; but such also as were best suited
both to bring this man to a better mind, and to convey
the highest instruction and warning to the High Priest,
and to all that were concerned with him in this wicked
transaction. For if there really was any evil, or any
cause of death, let the testimony be brought, and, if guilt
is found, let the guilty be condemned; but if not, why
should He be stricken? Throughout it may be observed
that He appeals to them all, as the witnesses of His innocence. This seems to be implied in every expression
that our Lord had spoken, first of all to those who came
to take Him, "I sat daily with you teaching in the temple, and ye laid no hands upon Me;" and secondly, "Ask
those who heard Me what I said unto them;" and now,
" If I have done evil, bear witness of the evil." This
appeal too may have some secret reference to the Day of
Judgment, when all shall be made to declare the righteousness of God, and every mouth shall be stopped and

found guilty before God.   And, beside this ulterior and final import, we may well suppose that such words of our Lord are full of deep intent and application, respecting Himself and His true followers in all ages.   It is, He has expressly declared, essential to those who truly follow Him, that they should be hated by the world: it is intimated, that they shall have all manner of evil spoken of them falsely for His sake.   For this hatred of the good shows itself most especially in calumnious falsehoods and misrepresentations.   This was the case even among the heathens, as Socrates said at his trial, that he should have nothing to apprehend from distinct testimony brought against him, but that it was impossible for him to do away with the weight of those calumnies, which were propagated falsely against him.   It was in a similar mode of appeal that the Apostle St. Paul says, they cannot "prove the things whereof they now accuse me."   "If I have done any thing worthy of death, I refuse not to die."   This has been the declaration of martyrs of all ages, and of suffering Christians, " If I have done evil, bear witness of the evil, but if well, why smitest thou Me?"   But in a sense infinitely higher than to any of sinful mankind, was testimony now called to the perfect innocence of Christ.   In unspeakable condescension He comes down from the throne of His judgment, to be judged by His creatures, saying, " O my people, what have I done unto thee ? and wherein have I wearied thee ? testify against Me[2]."   " What iniquity have your fathers found in me[3]?"   But as His Prophets had declared Him spotless, so do His enemies.   Pilate the judge declared, " I find no fault in this Man."   To all wicked men and wicked spirits Christ says,

<hr>

[2] Micah vi. 3.   [3] Jerem. ii. 5.

"Which of you convinceth Me of sin?" and "If I have done evil, bear witness of the evil:" but even the devil had already confessed Him to be "the Holy One of God."

O gracious and Divine Saviour, write this Thy adorable pattern of meekness in the hearts of us all, who are the least and the lowest of Thy servants, who are not meet to be called Thy servants, or in any sense Thine; for we have done very wickedly, and in the worst evils that can befall us, we receive but the due reward of our deeds, but Thou hast done nothing amiss. So deeply engrave this lesson in us, that "when we judge" our brethren we may "carefully think of Thy goodness; and when we ourselves are judged, we may look for mercy [4]."

THE FALSE WITNESSES.

And now "*the Chief Priests* (Matt., Mark) *and the Elders* (Matt.) *and the whole council*" (Matt., Mark) were collecting with the High Priest. In the eye of Holy Scripture "they were gathered together against the Lord and His Christ—For to do whatsoever Thy hand and Thy counsel determined before to be done [5]:" For God had regulated all things, even to the very ordering and appointing of every circumstance as it arose. But as it appeared to human eyes, they were doing as they did afterwards in the case of St. Stephen; they "*were seeking false* (Matt.) *witness against Jesus*" (Matt., Mark) in order to execute what they had already resolved to do, viz. "*to put Him to death*" (Matt., Mark). It is called false witness; for that is false testimony which gives a false sense, drift, or colouring even to the words that were truly used in another sense; and much more when

----

[4] Wisd. xii. 22.　　　　[5] Acts iv. 26. 28.

the words themselves are slightly perverted, as in this case, to effect that purpose. And in thus seeking false witness, they were doing as they ever did with the words of God, laying hold of the letter, and slightly perverting it in order to compass evil; in this manner did they deprive parents of their due, and devour widows' houses, and fast in order to smite with the fist of wickedness. We have no mention of what these charges generally were, but that they refuted each other, and their testimony agreed not with itself: although many came forward, yet they could substantiate no charge "*And they found none. And though many false witnesses came, yet they found none* (Matt., Mark). *For their testimonies did not agree together* (Mark), *until afterwards two false witnesses came forward* (Matt.); *certain persons rose up and bore witness against Him, saying, We ourselves have heard Him*" (Mark). The accusation was one which it was very natural for them to bring, for it was founded on a slight alteration of words which were really spoken; and it was on the subject of the Temple, that charge which of all others they thought the most serious, as appears in the case of St. Stephen and St. Paul. And this they did, although the Prophet had expressly warned them against a religion which consisted in the cry of "The temple of the Lord, the temple of the Lord[6]." But although this charge was, humanly speaking, so natural, yet it was of all others the most singular and astonishing, as showing at this time the mighty power and superintendence of God, Who, even in their tumult and rage against Him, had His "hook in their nose and His bridle in their lips[7]," and made them, like the wicked Balaam of old, to prophesy to themselves and others

---

[6] Jerem. vii. 4.   [7] Isa. xxxvii. 29.

His own great purposes. Our Lord had uttered the prediction, on which their charge was founded, three years before, on His first taking upon Him at that Passover His public teaching and authority. It was the great object of His coming into the world; that one thing, which He wished most deeply to fix in their minds. But how was this to be done? the prediction had been spoken long since, and might have been forgotten. As their wickedness would fufil the deed in destroying Him, so their falsehood and malice in the very act of so doing would bring out the prophecy, and write it up as in fiery characters on the wall, so that he who runs may read it. Even running in the haste of their passion, with feet swift to shed blood, their eyes might be arrested by the words of His accusation, written up by themselves, while they were fulfilling it according to His word. Not only in the good deeds of the righteous, but even in the wickedness of the unrighteous, is God's hand awfully present: in heaven He is present in mercy, in hell He is present in judgment: If I go down to hell, says the Psalmist, Thou art there also. They had indeed now gone to hell in their wickedness; but in their darkness was His light seen, and even there also did His hand lead them, and His right hand held them. Not the good only, but the wicked also shall confess Him and do Him honour. Not only "fruitful trees and all cedars," but the bramble also and the thistle bear the marks of His hand. "Beasts of the forest also," "the lion roaring after his prey," these all wait upon God, and fulfil the voice of His word. Not only do Saints bow before Him, and Angels bear Him in their hands, but He shall "go upon the lion and adder, the young lion and the dragon shall He tread under His feet." Good and evil shall both work His inscrutable counsels.

And now they might have brought some other charge, like that of His breaking the Sabbath, and the like: but if there was any prophecy which we may suppose our Lord would have wished to bring forward, and fix on the attention of these deluded Jews at this time, it was the very one which He and they too were now in the act of fulfilling. Nor is this all; but by the very alteration which they made in our Lord's expression, in order to substantiate their false accusation, they used words which were true in a higher sense, and divinely significant; they gave utterance to a great truth, which our Lord was especially desirous to teach them with regard to these events, Their falsehood became divine truth, and their wickedness was but subservient to God's glory. So inconceivably mysterious and gracious are God's ways, as much surpassing ours, according to His own declaration, as Heaven is above earth. Even the " cloud " of man's transgression is made " bright " by His light, and "is turned round about by His counsels: that they may do whatsoever He commandeth them upon the face of the world." " Therefore am I troubled at His presence; when I consider, I am afraid of Him [8]."

For the case was in fact this, that our Lord had said three years before, "Destroy ye," or "Ye shall destroy this Temple, and in three days I will raise it up." But in order to suit their own purposes, they alter, and give a false colouring to these words, as if our Lord had declared that He was able to destroy it, or would destroy it. Their charge was, " *This fellow said, I am able to destroy the Temple of God and to build it in three days*" (Matt.); or as St. Mark says, perhaps recording the still

---

[8] Job xxxvii. 12, and xxiii. 15.

more remarkable words of the other false witness, "*We heard Him say, I will destroy this temple made with hands, and in three days I will build another made without hands*" (Mark). Our Lord's own words had been different; He had prophesied of their conduct, and what they were now bent on doing. But this expression of theirs sets forth that very thing, which He was so desirous to instil into them, of which He had so often reminded His disciples. He said to these very Jews, as Joseph, His type, had said before, in charity to his brethren, that it was not they but the overruling Hand of God. "Be not grieved, nor angry with yourselves, that ye sold me hither; for God did send me to preserve life." For though indeed they were guilty of His death, and it is often spoken of as their doing, yet throughout it is also often spoken of as not being their doing, but the gracious will of Christ Himself. Like the concave and convex of a circle, in itself one and the same line, so the same act is their voluntary wickedness and Christ's voluntary suffering. Thus it is said indeed that Judas delivered up our Lord to the Jews; and the Jews delivered Him up to the Gentiles; and the Gentiles delivered Him up to be crucified. And yet it is said in another sense, that God delivered Him up for us all: that He delivered up Himself as a ransom for many. This was the great truth, which their own words unconsciously and unwillingly testified, that, although they took away His life as they thought, yet it was He who was their willing victim. "I have power to lay it down, and I have power to take it again." "No man taketh it from Me." Thus one false witness bears testimony to His power, "I *am able* to destroy, and I *am able* to rebuild." And the other false witness, in his falsehood bears witness to His will, "I *will* destroy." This was the great truth that His actions and His words were intended to teach them, and this He now speaks by the voice of their own witnesses. This great work was God's work, though men and evil spirits were the agents: "all men shall say, This hath God done, for they shall perceive that it is His work." They were now destroying that temple, as He had said they should do; but while they were doing it, the very words out of their own mouth declared that it was God and Christ that gave them licence. "Shall there be evil in a city and the Lord hath not done it[9]?"

Nor is this all, for there is also something very remarkable in the addition, which is made to the words by one of the false witnesses. Whether our Lord had used the expression, although the Evangelist has not recorded it, or that it was merely the invention of the false witnesses, it is equally replete with a Divine import. For the false witness in St. Mark says, that our Lord stated that the temple He should destroy was "made with hands," and the one He would build was "not made with hands." Now in whatever way we explain our Lord's prediction which he alluded to, for it seems to be capable of more than one interpretation, yet these words seem strongly to describe the fulfilment of it, in whatever sense it was fulfilled. For the words, "made with hands," seem to describe most fully our Lord's natural Body, which was made of the earth earthy. As it was said in the beginning, of Adam, that "God formed him of the dust of the ground[10]." And the words, "not made with hands," describe that spiritual Body, with which He arose from the dead, and which was Heavenly. For the second Man is "the Lord from Heaven."

---

[9] Amos iii. 6. [10] Gen. ii. 7.

The words also, as they now used them, describe in the same closeness of signification that Jewish Temple, which these disobedient Jews, and our Saviour, in His just judgment, was on the point of destroying, which was " made with hands:" and that Christian temple which our Lord was now about to re-establish in its place, and which had been described by Daniel, as the stone cut out of the mountain " without hands [11];" and which St. Paul speaks of as the " house not made with hands, eternal in the Heavens [12]." Thus indeed the temple they destroyed was His own Body, for it needs must become a sacrifice for sin; but this Body He will raise again, and will raise His Church, and establish a glorious temple, " not made with hands [12];" His own spiritual Body, His Church, which by His resurrection He will build up: by anticipation on earth, for in Him we are already risen again; and in fulness on the last day, for He is the Resurrection.

But even still in this charge, although it was founded on a fact, yet there was a discrepancy in their statements; " *not even thus*," says St. Mark, "*did their testimony agree together*." For indeed were it only this, that one said, " I am able to destroy," and the other, " I will destroy," in such a case, " I am able," and " I will destroy," were, humanly speaking, important differences; though, in a Divine sense, both mysteriously true. Thus, " *Though many false witnesses came, yet found they none* " (Matt.). For so was it divinely ordered, that all things should declare Him innocent; that "He had done no wrong, neither was guile found in His mouth [1]." " Many, and bad, and crafty as they were," says Origen, " they could find no likelihood of fault in

---

[11] Dan. ii. 45.   [12] 2 Cor. v. 1.   [1] 1 Pet. ii. 22.

Him; so blamelessly had He spoken and done all things[2]." In another point also, beside those two which we have mentioned, was their testimony untrue; for, as St. Jerome observes[3], "our Lord's expression had been 'I will raise it up;' that is, a living and breathing temple. To build is one thing, to raise another."

Again let us stop to dwell on this: how all things conspire and combine to testify to our Lord's immaculate purity, that snow-like garment of celestial whiteness with which His manhood was clothed. "Such is the Divine innocency," says Quesnel, "that falsehood itself cannot invent any thing which is capable of tarnishing it." It is, indeed, His raiment like the light, for like the light of the Sun it shineth in the midst of all things, however foul, and exposeth them, but is incapable of being stained by them, or losing aught of its brightness.

THE ADJURATION OF THE CHIEF PRIEST.

"*And now*," upon this, "*the High Priest*" (Matt., Mark), perhaps impatient at being thus thwarted by the contradiction of the false witnesses, and at our Lord's meek silence, "*arose up* (Matt., Mark), *and stood in the midst*" (Mark), as in a solemn authoritative manner, or, as St. Jerome says, "from anger and impatience," "*and asked Jesus, saying* (Mark), *Answerest thou nothing? what is it that these witness against Thee?*" (Matt., Mark.) "Wishing thereby," says St. Chrysostom, "to elicit some reply, that by it they might lay hold of Him." But all reply, in His own justification, would have been useless, as there was none who would listen to Him. "*But Jesus was silent* (Matt.); *He was silent and*

---

[2] In Matt. tom. v. 107. [3] In Matt. lib. iv. 26.

answered nothing " (Mark).   And this silence, we are
told by the Prophet, was in meekness and patient forbearance, for it was "as a sheep before his shearers is
dumb, even so He opened not His mouth."   "The
silence of Christ," says St. Jerome, "expiated the defence, or excuses, of Adam."   And as Quesnel seems to
carry on the same reflection, "the silence of the eternal
Word confounds the pride of the sons of Adam, who are
always eager to justify themselves."   Origen likewise,
more than once, speaks of this conduct of our Lord as
the example we are to follow, when slanderously accused; so much so, that in the opening of his Treatise
against Celsus, he thinks it necessary to prove, that in
writing that defence he was not acting against the spirit
of this our Lord's example of silence.   And of course
one cannot but remember how frequently and emphatically the Prophets notice this silence of Christ's, "I
will keep My mouth, as it were, with a bridle, while the
ungodly is in My sight; I held My tongue, and spake
nothing; I kept silence, yea, even from good words:
but it was pain and grief to Me[4]."   The ungodly man
of whom the Prophet speaks, is Caiaphas, says Origen.
And no less evidently does the previous Psalm speak
of Christ, "They also, that sought after My life, laid
snares for Me:"—"as for Me I was like a deaf man,
and heard not: and as one that is dumb, who doth not
open his mouth.   I became even as a man that heareth
not, and in whose mouth are no reproofs.   For in Thee,
O Lord, have I put my trust; Thou shalt answer
for Me, O Lord My God[5]."   This silence, whereby He
committed Himself unto Him that judgeth righteously,
does also, as by a figure, represent to us the manner

---

[4] Ps. xxxix. 2, 3.   [5] Ps. xxxviii. 15.

in which we are to rest in quietness and confidence, and leave the issue of things in God's hands, engaging Him, thereby, to execute His own great purposes, without their being marred by our interference. For herein human nature meekly yielded itself, in order that God might take His own cause in hand, and obtain His own victory over the power of darkness. It is analogous to the case of the Israelites by the Red Sea, when it shut them in before and behind. "And Moses said unto the peole, Fear ye not; stand still, and see the salvation of the Lord, which He will show to you to-day. The Lord shall fight for you, and ye shall hold your peace [6]."

The High Priest being still frustrated of his purpose, and, as St. Jerome says,—becoming the more enraged from our Lord's silence to the false witnesses and wicked Priests,—now challenges Him to reply, in order that by His answer some occasion might be given for a charge against Him. Again he asks Him, and puts his demand with a solemn adjuration of the Name of the Living God, to which our Lord must needs reply. It is remarkable, that in this his adjuration he does not demand the truth of the allegations that had been made, "whether," as Maldonatus says [7], "He had raised commotions, or taught false doctrine, or threatened the destruction of the temple." He comes at once to the great and solemn charge, whether He was the Son of God; secretly knowing that our Lord, although He did not openly allege it, yet had given His followers to understand this, and that He would on no occasion deny that He was indeed the Son of God. "*The High Priest* (Matt., Mark) *again* (Mark) *answered and said unto*

---

[6] Exod. xiv. 13, 14.   [7] Com. in Marc.

Him, I adjure Thee by the living God that Thou tell us (Matt.) *if Thou be the Christ* (Matt., Mark); *the Son of the Blessed* (Mark); *the Son of God* (Matt.). *Jesus saith unto him, Thou hast said* (Matt.) *I am* " (Mark). The expression, "Thou hast said," is the same reply which our Lord makes to Pilate; and Origen and Jerome understand it, not as simply stating the fact of Himself, but as confirming the High Priest's assertion and adjuration: " He did not deny," says Origen, "that He was the Christ, the Son of God, nor yet openly confess it, but takes, as it were, the testimony of him that adjured Him, saying, ' Thou hast said [8].' " But St. Augustin seems to understand the expression as simply equivalent to that of St. Mark, " I am [9]." Such Divine words, probably, contain some mysterious signification, and are more than human words; as the expression, " I am," is a declaration of His eternal Godhead; so that of " Thou hast said," seems to allude to the truth, that " every tongue shall confess Him;" that He maketh His enemies, even in their mockery and malice, and even evil spirits also, to acknowledge Him.

But in addition to this, and beyond what was required of Him, our Lord Himself now speaks, and in solemn silence we must listen for His words, and thoughtfully weigh their vast import. It is observable that in His great, and momentous, and final teaching in the Temple, when they had ceased from tempting, He Himself spake to them by an interrogation; and on both occasions, as well now as then, it is to the same great truth that He alludes, then by referring to the Psalm that announced it [10], and therefore darkly, and as it were by parable: now, by His own most open and therefore dreadful asse-

----

[8] In Matt. 110.   [9] De Cons. Ev. iii. 20.   [10] Ps. cx.

veration, "*But I say unto you,*" it is the solemn declaration of Him who is the Truth itself; whose Word is more durable than the Heavens and the earth; and that too in answer to the adjuration of God's Name. "*But I say unto you, Hereafter* (Matt.) *ye shall see the Son of Man sitting on the right hand of Power, and coming with* (Mark, or *on*, Matt.) *the clouds of Heaven*" (Matt., Mark). Humanly speaking, and as addressed to those Jews, the words may imply,—"You think this indeed incredible, that the apparently mean man who stands before you is the great Messiah, and the Son of the Blessed; but His great triumphal advent, of which the Prophecies speak, is to be fulfilled by His second coming hereafter; then you shall see Him in all that glory in which you expect Him; then you shall all stand before Him to be judged, as He now stands before you. The scene will be soon reversed. This is the solution of all your Scriptures; this is the Lord of whom David spake; Jesus Christ sitting within the veil on the right hand of God, until His enemies be made His footstool. If you will understand this, you will understand the Scriptures concerning Me." It may be observed, that our Lord's extreme humiliation and His glory are usually combined together; when suffering as a criminal, He is exerting throughout a Divine power over and in His enemies, making them to speak as He had foretold they should, and the like. And now, at the same moment of His suffering the extreme of indignities and condemnation, here is His testimony of Himself, as of One sitting on the right hand of God, and coming in the clouds of Heaven. In like manner, in the Prophecies His glory is ever combined with His humiliations: as, for instance (which Origen notices), in that remarkable passage of the 50th chapter of Isaiah, He is described as the

Almighty and terrible Judge, "Have I no power to deliver? Behold, at My rebuke I dry up the sea. I clothe the Heavens with blackness, and I make sackcloth their covering." And this it is that commences the description of His humiliating sufferings: "I was not rebellious, neither turned away back. I gave My back to the smiters, and My cheeks to them that plucked off the hair. I hid not My face from shame and spitting."

It may be observed, that the High Priest, and also the Sanhedrim, afterwards speak of the Son of God; and our Lord acknowledges Himself as such, but meekly proceeds on both occasions to speak of Himself as the Son of Man. The Son of Man indeed implies the Son of God; but as the Son of Man does He humbly reveal Himself to us: as the Son of Man is He now standing to be judged: as the Son of Man will He come to judge us: as the Son of Man does He sit as our Friend on the right hand of power: it is the Son of Man that shall henceforth be thus exalted, and of whose kingdom our Lord proceeds to speak; for the Son of God was from everlasting equal to the Father; but of course as God also, united with man, never to be divided.

This declaration of our Lord, respecting the dispensation of the Son of Man, appears to be twofold. And this twofold interpretation is suggested by the very ambiguity of the expression; for our Lord combines in the very expression the mention of two different actions; He speaks of His sitting in Heaven, and also of His coming in the clouds. The word "sitting" seems to indicate continuance and stability; the word "coming" expresses motion and activity. And they seem to refer to two events; the former to His sitting now in Heaven, and the latter to His coming again at the last Day. Yet each of the expressions is also in itself twofold, in that each is alike applicable to both events : for the last Advent is expressed by our Lord's coming to judge, and also by His sitting to judge. And also the present dispensation is the time of our Lord's sitting in the kingdom of Heaven; and besides, is the time of His coming in His kingdom. It is, too, in perfect accordance with the analogy of Scripture, thus to consider our Lord's words; for it may be observed that it is usual throughout the Scriptures to combine the two events together; our Lord's first and second coming are spoken of at the same time, and sometimes with the same expressions. This may be shown throughout all parts of the present declaration of our Lord; first of all, it must be observed that the word translated "hereafter" means "from this time," or "from henceforth:" and in the similar passage in St. Luke it is "from this time." For it was from this period, the season of our Lord's humiliation, that God had said, "Sit Thou on My right hand till I make Thy foes Thy footstool." It applies therefore to the Christian dispensation, in the course of which all wicked men shall be put under His footstool. Nor will it be less applicable to His last Advent also, which is always spoken of as coming so speedily, as to be almost already come : " the hour cometh, and now is, when they that are in their graves shall hear the voice of the Son of God." So also the expression of their "seeing the Son of Man sitting at the Right Hand of Power," will bear likewise this twofold sense. For doubtless, in some very high and full signification, it will be fulfilled in the consummation of all things, that His enemies shall behold Him ; and that in some manner visibly beyond all present thought, " Every eye shall see Him, and they also which pierced Him ;" that the just shall " see Him as He is," that "all flesh shall see His salvation;" that,

as Job says, "In my flesh shall I see God, whom I shall
see for myself, and mine eyes shall behold, and not
another." Thus St. Stephen and St. John saw visibly
and recognized the Son of Man, the earnest of their
seeing Him in that great manifestation. Yet these
words will also fully bear the previous and lower interpretation, as applied to the kingdom which He has
taken possession of from that very period, so as to have
been sensibly discerned by those whom He addressed.
For His enemies have in some sense even beheld Him
sitting at the Right Hand of Power: inasmuch as,
however contemptible He then appeared to them, He
has ever since visibly exerted such power throughout
the world, that even Jews and unbelievers,—although
they cannot discern His secret sitting in His kingdom
of Heaven, and in the hearts of believers,—yet have
beheld that power of His displayed in the establishing
of His kingdom, in which as in a dim shadow and figure
they already behold that which will be fulfilled, when
they shall behold Him in judgment. And even now do
they behold Him also coming in clouds; whether we
understand the clouds as signifying that mystery and
darkness which He throws about all His comings and
goings ; or, as the Fathers understand the term in Scripture, as signifying the Prophets, and Apostles, who are
now heralding and attending, as it were, His coming in
the hearts of men : of which it is said, "He maketh the
clouds His chariot." -Whereby His kingdom already
shows forth, as in dim vision, His coming with "so
great a cloud of witnesses," i. e. the companies of Angels and Saints on the last day. Thus the Psalmist
speaks of Him, "He sitteth in the Heavens over all
from the beginning. Lo, He doth send out His voice,

yea, and that a mighty voice: ascribe ye the power to God over Israel: His worship and strength is in the clouds [11]."

We have the sanction of Origen in thus interpreting it. He considers that this sitting of the Son of Man implies a certain kingly stability, as of Him Who alone is Power; Who is fixed on the right hand; Who hath received all power from the Father, both which is in Heaven and which is in earth; and that a time will be when even His adversaries shall behold this His firm sitting. "And this," he says, "may be considered to have been fulfilled from the time of the Christian dispensation. For the disciples beheld Him rising from the dead, and thus beheld Him seated at the Right Hand of Power. Or else it may be, that according to that duration, which is with everlasting God, the interval from the foundation of the world even unto the end is but one day." And therefore he thinks that this "henceforth," which the Saviour here speaks of, may imply the very short space which is to intervene before the end. And of our Lord's coming in the clouds of Heaven, he says, "These clouds are the Prophets and Apostles of Christ, heirs of God and joint-heirs with Christ, who will reign together with Him [1]." St. Jerome, though rather differently, yet virtually to the same effect, says, that His sitting on the Right Hand of Power implies His reigning in eternal life, and with Divine power. And of His coming with clouds, he says, on a cloud He ascended, with a cloud shall He return; that is to say, with His Body alone, which He received of a Virgin, He ascended; and with a manifold Church, which is His Body and the fulness thereof, He will come to judgment.

[11] Ps. lxviii. 34.   [1] Com. in Matt. ad loc.

THE HIGH PRIEST RENDING HIS GARMENTS.

" *Then*," (Matt.) on this reply of our blessed Lord, "*the High Priest rent his clothes, and said* (Matt., Mark), *He hath blasphemed*" (Matt.). "He did this," says St. Chrysostom, "in order that by so doing he might aggravate the offence, and add weight to his words of condemnation." And therefore, of course, if he knew that the condemnation was false, the passion he evinced was feigned, and false also. He did this as acting a part, and hypocritically: but it is awful to think that God fulfils in earnest what men do against Him fictitiously and in mockery; thus he rent his clothes for a light purpose, but God rent them for him in very deed and truth. They arrayed Christ in royal robes, and a crown, and a sceptre, and proclaimed Him King of the Jews, in mockery; but God made Him all these in a Divine reality, and in a manner infinitely substantial. As Caiaphas prophesied, though he knew it not; and the false witnesses, though they knew it not, in lying spake truth; so now the High Priest, in rending his garments, acted a real and deep tragedy for himself, for he thus declared that the order of Levi, the Jewish Priesthood, was rent, and even now no more.

The garment seems especially to denote the external ordinance and institution of the Church: as the robe of our blessed Lord, which in mysterious contrast with this rended garment of the High Priest, not even His enemies could rend asunder, signified the union of His own Church. So, too, in the parable of the new cloth on the old garment, the garment represents the Jewish Church, and the new cloth the Christian institutions and ordinances. The figure was used with a similar signification in the Old Testament, when God took away the kingdom from Saul. "As Samuel turned about to go away, he laid hold on the skirt of his mantle, and it rent. And Samuel said unto Him, The Lord hath rent the kingdom of Israel from thee this day[2]." In like manner the Prophet "Ahijah caught the new garment that was on Jeroboam, and rent it in twelve pieces," and explained it by saying, that the kingdom of Israel was rent, and ten of the twelve tribes were given him[3]. But the garment of the High Priest implied, of course, rather the Priesthood than the kingdom: it was that garment, respecting the fashion, and colour, and ornaments of which such minute directions were given by God Himself, inasmuch as it contained within it great and Divine significations and figures of things heavenly; this garment it was which was now to be torn and rent, and scattered to the four winds. This was the garment of the Levitical Priesthood; whereas the garment of our Lord was that of a better Priesthood, even that after the order of Melchizedec, which is indissoluble, and abideth for ever, without end of days. But afterwards, when they put on Him the royal robe of Herod, and that also of the Roman soldiers, it implied that He was invested with the kingdom also, that of the Jews and that of the Gentiles. In the instances above quoted from the Old Testament, the garment is rent by the Prophet of God; whereas here the High Priest is made to rend his own garments, inasmuch as that Priesthood is its own destruction. And the words of the Priest, that accompanied this act, were by themselves destructive of His Priesthood, for as he rent his garment he declared that Christ, the Holy One of God, had blasphemed. And as this rended

---

[2] 1 Sam. xv. 27, 28.　　　　　[3] 1 Kings xi. 30.

garment stands in contrast with our Lord's imperishable robe, so does it also present itself in comparison and contrast with the rended veil of the temple. For the Priest's garment was rent by his own hands: the veil of the temple was rent by supernatural and Divine means, at our Lord's death, and the hearing of His dying voice. For the opening of the sanctuary of God, the rending of the veil into the Holy of Holies, was the doing of God alone; no man had a share in this: man may rend and destroy; he cannot restore, nor open Heaven.

This mode of interpreting this mysterious action is supported by ancient interpreters. "This took place with a deeper mystery," says Ven. Bede [4], "that in the Passion of the Lord the Chief Priest should himself rend his own garments, when the vesture of the Lord could not be rent, even by the soldiers themselves who crucified Him. For this showed by figure that the Priesthood of the Jews was to be rent asunder, for the wickedness of their Priests. But the solidity of the Church, which is wont to be called the vesture of the Redeemer, can never be torn in twain." And again, "he rent his garments," says Origen [5], "disclosing the turpitude and nakedness of his soul, and manifesting, in mystery, that the ancient Priesthood and the robe of office were rent asunder." "By this," St. Jerome observes, "he showed that the Jews had lost the glory of the Priesthood, and that the seat of the Chief Priest was void." Indeed, in that declaration of his the Levitical Priesthood had ceased; in that confession of our Lord's, a Priest for ever after the order of Melchizedec, had appeared. And well might that Priesthood be at an end which had declared Christ

<hr>

[4] Aur. Cat. in Marc.   [5] In Matt. tom. v. 112.

guilty of blasphemy. " From that time," says Theophylact, " their Priesthood was rent from them, when they condemned Christ as guilty of death."

" Yet a little while, and the ungodly shall be clean gone; thou shalt look after his place, and he shall be away[6]." Ever since that hour the House of Christ has been gradually filling the earth, and also the Heavens. That of Caiaphas and his Priesthood has vanished. " The house of Caiaphas," says St. Cyril[7], " shows by its present desolation the power of Him who was judged there."

> " Low lies thine house, blaspheming Caiaphas,
>   Wherein Christ's holy face was struck with blows:
>   Such end awaits the sinners;—soon o'erwhelm'd
>   In ruin'd heaps their life for ever lies."
>
> PRUDENTIUS, ENCHIRIDION, XL.

THE CONDEMNATION.

As he rent his clothes, the High Priest said that Christ had blasphemed: " *What think ye ?* (Matt.) or *What does it appear to you ?* (Mark) *and they all* (Mark) *answered and said* (Matt.), *or condemned Him* (Mark), *that He is guilty of death*" (Matt., Mark). And what was this alleged blasphemy but that He had interpreted that question which He had Himself, in the Temple, asked them to interpret, while in mercy He withheld the full disclosure of His dreadful Divinity; the question, namely, of whom it was that David spoke when he said, " The Lord said unto my Lord, Sit Thou on My right hand till I make Thy foes Thy footstool." How vast was the guilt of this Chief Priest, who denounced as worthy of death the very Principle and Fount of Life; Him from whom life and

[6] Ps. xxxvii. 10.   [7] Lect. xiii.

immortality flows to them who rise again; nay, Him who alone is Himself Life and Resurrection, and in Himself hath life! How little did he know of the unspeakable weight and consequence of his crime! Oh, amazing and stupendous extent of man's guilt and blind folly, that he should come to this! Surely, as our blessed Lord said of them, in ineffable charity, they knew not what they did. No doubt our Lord would teach us in this, that if we persecute the innocent, we know not what we do. It is Christ in them. It is we know not what. But now from greatest evil comes, by God's mercy, greatest good to His distressed creatures; they condemned Him to be guilty of death, but the condemnation of Him who was guiltless has released us, who were worthy of death, from condemnation.

But how awful are the effects in this disclosure which Christ makes of Himself on that wicked company! "From this," says Theophylact, "it is evident that the disobedient derive no benefit from the more secret things of God being revealed to them; but acquire greater punishment, because such things ought to be concealed from them." St. Ambrose also says, "the Lord chose to prove Himself King rather than to say that He was so, that they might not have cause for condemnation." And Quesnel observes, "To ask what truth is with a double heart, or with no sincere desire to know or follow it, blinds the eyes and hardens the heart." "We ought to be very reserved," says the same writer, speaking of our Lord's silence at His trial, "in the discovery of truths when men are not well disposed to hear them, that we may prevent their being condemned." But, it may be asked, if this awful declaration of our Lord's Divinity was of so terrible a nature, being "a savour unto death" to the unworthy, why did He in His meekness break His merciful silence? It may be observed, that the oath put on Him by the Chief Priest bound Him to do so. For it is written in the Law[8], that if a soul is thus adjured to bear his testimony, and "do not utter it, then he shall bear his iniquity." And this seems to have been the reason of the Chief Priest's adjuration; that if He was silent, He might be condemned as guilty of breaking the Law; if He confessed Himself the Christ, He might be guilty of blasphemy. And as every thing else, in this most awful and momentous of all occasions, seems to have been provided for in the Divine counsels, so does this also. For the ruin of the wicked, and the just judgment of God, which took place on account of this solemn appeal to the Almighty God, and the victory of the Righteous over all His enemies, seem to have been prophetically intimated in the prayer of Solomon[9]; "If any man trespass against his neighbour, and an oath be laid upon him to cause him to swear, and the oath come before Thine Altar in this house, then hear Thou in Heaven and do, and judge Thy servants, condemning the wicked, to bring his way upon his head: and justifying the righteous, to give him according to his righteousness."

Indeed, throughout the whole scene, the Hand of God is very wonderful, and so distinct as to be almost visible from behind the veil. Our Lord has no specific charge brought against Him, but that of His own prophetic declaration respecting the Temple, delivered three years before; and which, whether we take it literally of the restoration of His human Body from the grave, or of His raising up His own Christian Church on the ruins of the Jewish Temple, has, of all

<hr>

[8] Lev. v. 1.   [9] 1 Kings viii. 31, 32.

things that could have been adduced, the most signal bearing on what was now doing, and to be done. In the next place, He is put to death after all, on no other charge but that of His own declaration of His own Godhead. With regard to ourselves there is also another consideration connected with this point. It is His eternal and awful Godhead which is the thing put forth, as the cardinal point on which all our considerations of His Death and Passion turn; which the Church indicates by the selection of her Epistle for Good Friday. Nor is it His Godhead only which is thus brought forth; for it is worthy of great attention to observe how all things are constrained to bear witness to the manifold character of Christ. His own sufferings throughout indicate Him to be very Man; His own declaration, and the fulfilment of all Prophecy, pronounce Him very God. All persons, however unwillingly and unconsciously, confess Him the King of the Jews; all things declare Him perfectly innocent, as the Lamb without spot; all things declare the free agency and sin of the Jews; all things prove the Hand of God, and His will, in the accidents of casual occurrence, or the passions of men.

CHRIST ABUSED.

It is not improbable that the High Priest, and the Council that attended, may at this time have withdrawn, and left Christ in the custody of the guard and attendants who now began to abuse His most sacred Person. *"And the men who held Jesus mocked and beat Him,"* says St. Luke: *"some began to spit on Him* (Mark), *and spat on His face"* (Matt.), which was not only in itself an action expressive of abhorrence and loathing, and the highest of all natural

indignities, but legally also marked as the most ignominious of inflictions, as in the case of an undutiful
brother[1]. And "*they covered* (Mark, Luke) *His face*"
(Mark) by way of mockery, and they "*beat Him on
the face* (Luke) *and began to* (Mark) *buffet Him*
(Matt., Mark), *and others struck Him with the palms
of their hands*" or with staves (Matt.). And St. Mark
tells us that it was *the attendants* who *struck Him with*
these *blows;* from which one might be led to think
that it was with their official staves, which this word
imports ($\dot{\rho}\alpha\pi\acute{\iota}\sigma\mu\alpha\tau\alpha$). This they did after they had
concealed His face, in a way that they might not be
seen, out of mockery; "*and they asked Him, saying*
(Luke), *Prophesy* (Matt., Mark, Luke) *unto us, Thou
Christ*" (Matt.), Thou great Anointed Prophet, "*who
is it that struck Thee?*" (Matt., Luke.) These things,
which the inspired writers have mentioned, are not
intended for a full account of these indignities, but
only as a specimen of them; for to this account St.
Luke adds, "*And many other things they spoke unto
Him, blaspheming.*" It seems not improbable that
many particulars of our Lord's sufferings throughout,
certainly the fuller description of many, might be
gathered from the Prophets, in points which the Evangelists have not recorded. Thus we are told, what we
might reasonably conclude was the case, from the
bruises and blows, that "His visage was so marred
more than any man, and His form more than the sons
of men;" so that "many were astonished[2]:" and in
another place, in addition to His giving "His back to
the smiters," and that "He hid not His face from shame
and spitting," it is also said, that He gave His "cheeks
to them that plucked off the hair[3]," which might have

---

[1] Deut. xxv. 9.   [2] Isa. lii. 14.   [3] Isa. l. 6.

been either now, or when they put on the crown of thorns: and also that the blood with which He was covered, probably when His robe was put on after the scourging, " stained all His raiment[1]." There are many such particulars in the Old Testament, as that of the Psalmist, that his " knees were weak through fasting."

Thus was our Lord and Master silent, and "as a sheep before her shearers is dumb, so He opened not His mouth:" but in this unspeakable silence, His Divine charity was not silent, for it was about this time that He turned to look on St. Peter, who had reason to say with the Psalmist, " Thou turnedst Thy face from me, and I was troubled;" "lift up the light of Thy countenance upon me." By this His silence also, as by a Divine eloquence, He was teaching His Church, and speaking more strongly than words could express, the lesson which He had taught, " learn of Me, for I am meek and lowly." They spit over His sacred countenance, that we may think no more of beauty of countenance, but lament the guilt to which it has led us : they beat Him with the palms of their hands, that false human honour may be at an end, and that we may be ashamed of avenging our dishonours; they beat Him with the fist, that our bruises may be light to us, and that we may not dare to maltreat our brother, who is to us in Christ's stead. They covered His face in order to mock and strike Him, that He might expiate our many slanders of our neighbour ; and that we may not be grieved to be ourselves calumniated. So perfect an example to us in all things is the adorable Son of Man. St. Chrysostom observes, that " the Evangelist with the greatest care mentions those things which appear most opprobrious, concealing nothing, and ashamed

---

[1] Isa. lxiii. 3.

of nothing, but esteeming it the greatest glory, that the Lord of the world should sustain such things for us." "This let us read continually, this let us inscribe on our hearts, and in these things let us glory [5]." And St. Basil also [6] : "Here Christ hath afforded us an example of longsuffering and patience, in bearing the injuries of the Jews : who, when heaping insults upon insults they loaded Him with contumelies, yet accused them in nothing, that they should desist from their malice and wickedness : and was so far from avenging Himself, that He did not in the slightest degree contradict or resist them. On the contrary, He laboured to repay their inhuman cruelty with benefits. By the abundant bestowing of blessings He requites their wickedness ; and at last sustained the Cross, for the sake of them who were crucifying Him."

But as to His wretched persecutors, how little did they conceive what they were doing ! hiding His face, as if He were some ignominious and wretched man unfit to look on, in a sort of perhaps drunken frolic : hiding that face which is the light of heaven, and from which angelic creations drink ineffable bliss and hope. Surely it was of this the Prophet spake, when he said, "Be astonished, O ye heavens, at this, and be horribly afraid : be ye very desolate, saith the Lord [7]." But even now in their wanton folly, they are constrained by a mysterious providence to acknowledge Him the Christ, although in mockery ; and to personate by their mad actions the very history of their own condemnation and judgment. Thus did they hide His face from them ; and yet if He lifted not up the light of His countenance upon them, and they did not behold His glory, the glory as of the only begotten Son of God, it would have been well for

---

[5] Hom. lxxxvi.   [6] De Patientia Christi.   [7] Jer. ii. 12.

them never to have been born. Yet it was not that He hid His face from them, but that they, by their foolish and careless and cruel mockeries of justice and truth, by their thorough want of seriousness, had shut up and blinded their own eyes; so that they could not behold Him. And when they, by their evil deeds, had persuaded themselves that the face of God was hidden and covered, when they thought that they could insult and beat Him with impunity, and be not at all the worse for it. This is the very description of the wicked in all ages: they say, " He hideth His face, and will never see it." " The Lord doth not see, neither doth the God of Jacob regard it [8]." Thus as the High Priest when he rent his clothes, so these now in their wickedness, did that which was Divinely significant of themselves, of their own conduct and fate. It was not that He, like Moses, put a veil over His face, that they might not behold His glory; but they themselves veiled His face in their wickedness. This would exactly describe the manifestation of Christ among the Jews; this would describe their case unto this day; the veil is on their heart, and placed by them on His countenance. So is it with all unbelievers. It would seem as if all this wonderful scene was intended to set before us a description of all folly and wickedness of men at all times: for in their sins they must be in the sight of good Angels like these men, and sin itself is an insult in the presence of the most High, and a denial of His adorable Majesty. But may God grant that we all, even in these His humiliations, " with open face beholding as in a glass the glory of the Lord, may be changed into the same image from glory, to glory, even as by the Spirit of the Lord [9]!"

[8] Ps. x. 12; xciv. 7.   [9] 2 Cor. iii. 18.

From the Divine superintendence and the agency of wicked men, we may observe something of another who was most active in this scene; one more wicked and more crafty than men; and doubtless never was all his craft and all his power more exerted than on this occasion. And it may be seen, that with those who hold with him, and give themselves up to act his part, he prevails more and more, and gains an ascendency over them, as in the case of Judas and Caiaphas.   But all his arts against our Lord and His faithful followers are made to recoil on his own head, and work the good he intended not. He was allowed to afflict Christ and to oppress Him with a weight of agony; but it only serves to make His resignation more perfect, and His prayer more earnest, and His sacrifice more meritorious.   Then he instigates His disciple to deny Him, and seems to prevail; but in the moment of his victory Christ brings His disciple back to Himself and to repentance, and thereby opens His arms of mercy to all penitents : and on this temper of penitence, as on a rock, His Church is founded, being more rich in penitent sinners, than in righteous persons. And now when he excites these bad men to rival each other in cruelty against Him, not only does Christ quench all the fiery darts of the wicked one by the shield of invincible patience, but by a Divine and overflowing charity and serene fearlessness of death, overcomes and tramples under His feet all the power of the enemy.

THE MEETING OF THE SANHEDRIM.

We come next to a point in the narrative which admits of some considerable doubt and difficulty; for St. Luke's account of our Lord's Confession and Condemnation so much resembles that of the other two Evangelists, that some have supposed it to be the same circumstance. By omitting, however, any reference to it in the foregoing arrangement, and placing it here, it is of course considered as a different transaction. And I proceed to mention on what grounds. We may observe that the first two Evangelists mention the ill treatment of our Lord, by the servants, as occurring after He was condemned by the High Priest; but St. Luke mentions it as occurring before this meeting on the morning. It was from the hands of those in whose custody our Lord was: "*Now they that held Jesus mocked Him.*" Add to this, that St. Matthew and St. Mark, when they come to speak of the morning, which was of course after the cock-crowing and the denials of St. Peter, speak of a council taking place. "*And straightway when it was morning*" (Mark), or "*When it was now morning* (Matt.), all* (Matt.) *the Chief Priests* (Matt. Mark) *and Elders of the people*" (Matt.), or "*with the Elders and Scribes and the whole Sanhedrim* (Mark), *took counsel together*" (Matt. Mark), or called a formal assembly, "*against Jesus to put Him to death*" (Matt.). This expression, "when it was morning," and also that of St. Luke, that "when it was day" they took Him to their Council, clearly denotes the order of time, and marks this assembly as evidently distinct from our Lord's examination in the night by the Chief Priest and his assessors. It is also intimated, that it was a necessary circumstance in order to their accomplishment of His death. But the first two Evangelists make no mention of what took place at that assembly, which they speak of as being convened at this time; and this is the account which St. Luke supplies. Indeed the assembly of which St. Luke gives the account, is not only at the same time as that spoken of thus by the other two, but is also introduced by him with the mention of their leading Jesus "into their council" from the place where the servants were abusing Him. Add to this, that to make both condemnations one and the same, would be to consider the High Priest as president of the Sanhedrim, which it does not appear that he was. They met indeed in his house, for at the meeting on the Wednesday, when Judas betrayed Him, it is said [10], "Then assembled together the chief priests, and the scribes, and the elders of the people, unto the palace of the High Priest, which was called Caiaphas." And here on this night they appear to have been collecting around the High Priest, before the meeting of their own court. But a formal act of their own body might have been necessary on a capital charge, in their own council-chamber. And yet this meeting of their Council might be no more than merely a formal act, inasmuch as the real power devolved on the High Priest, from his unjust connexion with the Romans. At all events, the express mention of them "all" distinctly, and "their whole Council," is very remarkable.: such words are not without a purpose. Dr. Lightfoot, who understood the Jewish customs, arranges it in his harmony as a separate circumstance, as it is here done, without apparently considering the point open to question. We may conclude, therefore, that what St. Luke relates took place at this council, after what had passed before the High Priest, and his sentence.

There still remains this difficulty; how the circumstances are so similar with regard both to the question and the reply that is made to it. We may account for this by supposing that they, having known and witnessed by what means the High Priest had at last succeeded in condemning our blessed Lord, put the same questions

---

[10] Matt. xxvi. 3.

themselves in order to elicit the same answers. And this is confirmed by our noticing that they afterwards put distinctly a question, which the High Priest had not put, but to which they had now learned that our Lord would make a full confession, viz. " Art Thou the Son of God?" Moreover, although the circumstances are similar, yet, it may be observed, they are not the same; and indeed even the words of our Lord's declaration are not the same. For before the High Priest our Lord says, " Ye shall see the Son of Man;" but in St. Luke it is, " From this time the Son of Man shall be." And although in both He speaks of His " sitting on the right hand of Power," yet in St. Luke He adds nothing of His " coming in the clouds of Heaven " as Judge. The statement in St. Luke is as follows: " *And when it was day, the Presbytery of the People, and the Chief Priests and Scribes came together, and led Him into their council, saying, Art Thou the Christ? tell us. And He said unto them, If I tell you, ye will not believe : and if I also ask you, ye will not answer Me, nor let Me go.*" This passage, in confirmation of what has been said, might be explained thus; that they, in order to elicit the same answer which the High Priest had done for His condemnation, say unto Him, " Art Thou the Christ?" Our Lord answered to the effect, that He did not wish to avoid answering, if they really had any desire to know; but the fact was, if He told them, they would not believe it; and if He were to ask them questions, such as must necessarily lead them to a conviction and confession of the truth, as He had asked them in the Temple, they would not consider the subject: they would not give Him any answer; nor if He were to ask them would they acquit Him, and let Him go; there was therefore no good to be done by His speaking. He therefore simply states to

M 2

them, what moreover He had called their attention to in the Temple, the declaration which He knew they were now desirous to obtain from Him,—solemnly adding, "*From henceforth shall the Son of Man be sitting on the right hand of the power of God.*" They, knowing the statement He had made before the High Priest, immediately took up the words, and "*All of them said, Art Thou then the Son of God? He said unto them,*" answering their formal judicial question put by all, "As ye say, even so I am," or "*Ye say that I am. They then said,*" (as the High Priest had done before,) "being enraged," says Chrysostom, "and assuming an expression of disgust;" "*what further need have we of testimony? for we have heard it from His own mouth.*" If this be the mode of explaining the words, then they would contain the formal condemnation of the Sanhedrim, in addition to that of the High Priest; so that three parties, Annas, Caiaphas, and the Sanhedrim, would each by a distinct act have had a share in His death.

Some suppose that our Lord's answer is intended to convey to them a warning and denunciation of the day of Judgment; "as if He had said," Theophylact observes, "hereafter it is not a time for discourses for you, but from henceforth it shall be a time for judgment, when ye shall see Me sitting on the right hand of Power." But we should rather take it with Quesnel,—not as any thing that implied a threat to His judges, though doubtless containing that awful truth,—but a calm declaration "of the power of that state in which His Resurrection would place Him;—that, instead of the mortal life they were going to take from Him, He shall receive a new one full of power and glory."

Nor is the repetition of this declaration any sufficient argument against the present arrangement; we know from many instances in the Gospels, that it was our Lord's custom to repeat the same declarations on different occasions: and we have before had to remark, that the Almighty throughout the Scriptures does repeat His assertion a second, and a third time, when the matter is very important, and strongly established with God. For, the same reason which Joseph mentions to Pharaoh may be applied to this subject, where he says that the dream was repeated "because the thing is established by God, and God will shortly bring it to pass [1]." In like manner, when Abraham had offered up his son, it is not once only that his acceptance is declared of God, but twice. "And the Angel of the Lord called unto Abraham out of Heaven the second time, and said, By Myself have I sworn, said the Lord [2]."

[1] Gen. xli. 32.   [2] Gen. xxii. 15.

On further consideration, the writer is more inclined to think that St. Luke is but recording the same transaction as the two former Evangelists. There is a difference of precisely the same kind in the two accounts of the centurion at Capernaum, as given by St. Matthew viii. 5—10, and St. Luke vii. 1—10, where the latter is evidently detailing the same incidents, but more circumstantially, and, therefore, with diversity in particulars. We find also in the Acts of the Apostles the High Priest acting in like manner in Council with the Elders, as ch. iv. 5, 6, and v. 17. 41.

Third Edition.

PART II.

THE DAY OF SORROWS.

SECTION I.—THE HALL OF JUDGMENT.

" Lord, how are they increased that trouble Me! many are they that rise against Me."

CHRIST LED TO PILATE.

IT was probably at the meeting of the Sanhedrim they considered over what to do to the Lord; they might have kept Him till after the Feast, as Herod afterwards did St. Peter, but that would not have been a safe procedure, and their passions were too inflamed; so that they adopted this expedient of giving Him up to Pilate, thinking that he would put Him to death without hesitation or inquiry. And now *"the whole multitude of them,"* that is, the whole body of the Sanhedrim, *" arose "* (Luke), and *" having bound* (Matt. Mark) *Jesus "*(Mark), as one condemned to death,—for indeed He had been bound as a prisoner in the house of Annas,—*" they led Him away "* (Matt. Mark, Luke, John), as it has been recorded [1], with a halter or cord around His neck, *"from the palace of Caiaphas,"* in which the Council of the Seventy had their assembly, *" to the Prætorium "* (John), or place of the Roman Governor : *" and delivered Him up to Pontius* (Matt.) *Pilate* (Matt. Mark) *the*

----

[1] See Bishop Taylor's Life of Christ.

Governor" (Matt.). Now this they did, either because they had not the power of putting any one to death by a judicial sentence; or because it was "not lawful" for them to do so at the time of their Feast. "As they wished to put Him to death," says St. Chrysostom, "and were themselves unable to do it on account of the Feast, they led Him to the Governor. And consider how this was brought about, that it should be at the Feast, for so it had been prefigured from above." Thus did God overrule their previous intention, which was, that it should not be at the Feast; and fulfilled the prophecies, that our Lord should be delivered up to the Gentiles, and crucified. Their own motive might have been, that the execution of a Roman Governor would take place in spite of any opposition from the people; and they might have preferred this mode of gratifying their revenge, in order to expose Him, in the sight of His followers, to the humiliations of the worst of public executions. But, whatever it was, what was intended by malice as the greatest evil, became the greatest good, by the manifestation of Christ crucified.

Here we cannot but again pause to observe, that as the author of evil has had throughout the evil which he intended recoil upon himself, and as the weapon he framed is turned against him, so also is it the case with the human instruments he uses. For here again, as in every act of their wanton wickedness, the Jews are personating, as in type, their own judicial punishment, which was to be delivered up to the Romans. As of old, wicked Haman died on the gallows which he had prepared for Mordecai, thus Judas brings on himself that death which he prepared for Christ; thus Caiaphas, to save his nation from the Romans, gives up Christ to them, and thereby Christ and His true followers escape death, but the nation is left in their hands; thus the High Priest, in his zealous care that the Temple be not evil spoken of, destroys it; and pretending a keen sense of blasphemy, the hearing of which polluted his pontifical robes, rends the Priesthood, and unsanctifies it for ever. They accuse Christ of blasphemy, but are themselves, by the same words, blaspheming. They bring Him to Pilate from a mysterious fear of shedding innocent blood, in order to throw the guilt on another; but thereby they made it more signally their own act, than they could otherwise have done; with one voice taking the blood on themselves, and exculpating Pilate. Again, Pilate sacrifices Christ for fear of the Romans, and in order to gratify the people, and the people afterwards complain of him to the Romans, and he is in consequence deposed, and falls into the fate which he desired to avoid. Instances of this kind are so numerous, as to indicate some mysterious principle of the Divine dealings, in all the operations of Christ's enemies, whether spiritual or human. To this the Psalmist so often alludes, they "are sunk down in the pit that they made; in the same net which they hid privily is their foot taken [2]:" he "is fallen himself into the destruction that he made for other; for his travail shall come upon his own head [3]:" "Let them be taken in the crafty wiliness that they have imagined [4]:" "Let his net, that he hath hid privily, catch himself, that he may fall into his own mischief [5]:" "He shall recompense them their own wickedness, and destroy them in their own malice [6]:" "Let the ungodly fall into their own nets together, and let me ever escape them [7]." And many are the instances of the same kind in the other Scriptures. St. Cyril says, "This their impiety was not unknown to the Prophets, for the blessed Isaiah saith, in a certain place concern-

[2] ix.   [3] vii.   [4] x.   [5] xxxv.   [6] xciv.   [7] cxli.

ing them, 'Woe unto the wicked, for the reward of his hands shall be given him [8].' And Ezekiel, 'I will recompense their ways upon their own heads, saith the Lord God [9].' For as they gave up Christ, the Saviour of all, to the soldiers of the Romans, so shall they, in just requital, be given up to the Roman power, and be consumed by their hand."

There is something very awful in this mysterious overruling of God; and yet, at the same time, there is something consolatory in this very mysteriousness, as being indicative of infinite power. It is as Job expresses of the Divine presence, " Behold, I go forward, but He is not there; and backward, but I cannot perceive Him. On the left hand where He doth work, but I cannot behold Him; He hideth Himself on the right hand that I cannot see Him: but He knoweth the way that I take [10]." The very feeling of want, because we are not able sensibly to perceive His presence, arises from the stronger sense we spiritually entertain of it: we feel after a presence of which we entertain a vivid mental apprehension: it was a strong spiritual discernment of God's presence, that made Moses to ask for a visible manifestation of God.

JUDAS RESTORING THE MONEY.

It is not clear at what period of time Judas repented and restored the money; for the word "then" ($\tau\acute{o}\tau\epsilon$), with which St. Matthew introduces the account, does not, with this Evangelist, imply immediate continuance in point of time. But as every other arrangement must depend on mere vague supposition, it seems better to adhere to the order of the inspired narrative; as if by a speedy judgment he actually preceded Christ

---

[8] Isa. iii. 11.   [9] Ezek. xi. 21.   [10] Ch. xxiii. 8—10.

in his death. Perhaps immediately on the perpetration of his crime, he had been half conscience-stricken, and waited, in fearful suspense, for the issue; and, while so doing, now saw our blessed Saviour dragged through the streets, as a criminal condemned to death: "*Then Judas, who had betrayed Him, when he saw that He was condemned, repented himself, and brought again the thirty pieces of silver to the Chief Priests and Elders, saying, I have sinned in that I have betrayed the innocent blood*" (Matt.). Here it may be noticed, that Judas only speaks of our Lord as "the innocent blood:" nor is there ever any allusion to his knowledge of our Lord's Divine nature: and this agrees with what we have so often observed, that the knowledge of our Lord's Divinity was an especial gift of faith, even to those who were most near His sacred Person; for that a knowledge of His Divine greatness and power was imparted to all, in various degrees, according to their religious attention.

But on reading of his repentance, the thought may occur, why the traitor should have repented at this time, when he found that our Saviour was condemned; for this he might have reasonably expected, when he betrayed Him into their hands. Nor would it lessen the difficulty to suppose, that he expected our Lord would have delivered Himself by some great exertion, or manifestation of His supernatural power; for this would render it more unaccountable that he should have been faithless to Him, or betrayed Him, as it would have afforded him less prospect of impunity. But it may be very easily accounted for, on considering the usual effects of sin, and the mode in which the devil exercises his temptation; as soon as the sin is committed, then he gives up the sinner to the knowledge, and often to the full weight of his guilt, " Perfecto demum scelere, magnitudo ejus intellecta.est," as the philosophical Roman historian says of the greatest of Nero's crimes. " Observe," says St. Chrysostom, " that he repents when the sin is completed and brought to its termination. For the devil does not permit those, who do not watch, to see their sin, till they have perpetrated the evil."

The motive of this wretched man appears clearly, from the consent of all, to have been covetousness: this was the vice to which he was addicted; nor does any other appear as the prevailing principle on which he acted. But to this main spring of action others would be subordinate; and by it many other passions would be called into operation. Deceit and dishonesty would become the means he would habitually take for the attainment of his ends; and the more malicious passions would be excited when his governing temper was counteracted. And so it appears to have been now: for we cannot but suppose that feelings of revenge and ill will had some share in instigating him to these means of attaining the objects of his avarice. This indeed is apparent from the occasion, on which his purpose is first formed, namely, on his being thwarted and disappointed respecting the money spent on the ointment; and that disappointment was accompanied with something of a reproof from our Lord, when He prevented his purpose. Now all these bad passions would suddenly give way, when he perceived the victim of his malice overcome by his successful treachery; and his avarice had been satisfied on receiving the money. Then on a sudden, in the calm that succeeds on the gratification of excited passion, all the circumstances of his guilt would rush to his mind; and the devil would throw no impediment in the way of their doing so: our Saviour's many kindnesses, and long forbearance, and repeated warnings, His spotless life, and ineffable goodness, would appear strongly before him as for the first time. And though it is said that he repented, yet the Greek term (μεταμεληθείς) rather signifies that he was stricken with remorse, or repented in the way that we use the word for regret. The devil who, we read, had taken possession of him, now filled him with such horror at what he had done, as to instigate him onward to a fresh crime. For what we humanly describe as the known effects, and the usual operations, of passion, Holy Scripture speaks of as the agency of the evil spirit. Indeed Origen very admirably writes to this effect: "Perhaps Satan, who after the sop entered into Judas, after he had done what he wished, retired from him. And as the devil was retiring he understood and perceived, that in betraying the innocent blood, he was condemned of God: and his mind being now left to itself, and not having the devil working in him, was able to comprehend. He was able, therefore, to repent, as the devil was departing from him, and to restore the thirty pieces of silver to those who had given them: and he could say, that which before his departing he could not say, 'I have sinned in betraying the innocent blood.' Not that the devil, in departing from such a one, ceases to lie in wait for him; but he observes his time: and when a person has come to the knowledge of his second sin, the devil watches for another occasion to deceive him." Origen then proceeds to show, that "it was thus in the case of the incestuous Corinthian, who after the devil had tempted him to crime, sorrowed unto repentance; yet St. Paul urged the Corinthians to restore him, lest being swallowed up with overmuch sorrow, Satan should gain an advantage; 'for we are not ignorant,' he says, 'of his devices[1].'"

But little commiseration for sorrow and repentance is to be found among companions in crime. In the Temple he makes his confession, and offers restitution, but they in the Temple, who ought to receive the penitent, are the partners of his guilt. "*They said unto him, What is that to us? see thou to that*" (Matt.), in scorn at his relenting, when they themselves were hardened, and wished to harden themselves more against the voice of conscience: "What is that to us?" this will express the difference at all times between the fellow-feelings of the unbeliever and the faithful. No burden that our brother can bear is nothing to us; his burden is our burden, as our burden is the burden of our and his merciful Saviour: how much more when it is under the weight of our own common guilt that he labours! To sympathize with his repentance, may be the means which God has provided to bring us to a sense of our own sin. But here, on the contrary, we have the voice of the children of Cain, "What is that to us?" Am I my brother's keeper? And happy he who seeks that mercy from God, which he cannot find in man. It was not so with Judas: for now he felt the full weight of the curse of Cain, "My punishment is greater than I can bear. Behold, Thou hast driven me out this day from the face of the earth; and from Thy face shall I be hid[2]." "*And casting down the money in the temple, he departed, and went and hanged himself*" (Matt.); or as St. Luke records in the Acts of the Apostles[3], "*falling headlong he burst asunder in the midst, and all his bowels gushed*

---

[1] 2 Cor. ii. 11.   Orig. in Matt. 117.   [2] Gen. iv.   [3] Ch. i. 18.

out." We may suppose, that frustrated in the attempt to hang himself, he afterwards accomplished his evil purpose in the other way; or rather, that having hanged himself, he fell down from the place over the precipice. Some suppose, that the word translated " hanged himself" might mean, that he was overwhelmed with grief and suffocation, and so died; but there appears no adequate authority for this interpretation; and Origen, Chrysostom, and others mention that he hanged himself.

The question may be asked, whether the repentance of Judas would have been available at this time, if he had sincerely repented? And from the unbounded nature of Scripture promises, we cannot but suppose that he would have been received even now, if he had truly repented. " For if," says Origen, " after he had restored the money, and confessed his crime, in betraying the innocent blood, he had not gone and hanged himself, but had sought place for repentance, he could perhaps have found Him who hath said, ' As I live, I will not the death of a sinner, but his repentance'.'"

Throughout the dispensation of the Gospel covenant, the door of mercy is open to the last hour to the true penitent; no sin is beyond the power of Christ's blood to wash out; every sin against the Son of Man may be forgiven; true repentance on the part of man is indissolubly united with the forgiveness of sins on the part of God. But it appears equally clear from the whole analogy of Scripture, that true repentance becomes more and more difficult, according to the degrees of grace rejected, and after a certain point impossible. The heathen moralists describe this to be the case in the ultimate progress of vice : and the state of nature is herein a shadow of the spiritual probation in the state

[†] Ezek. xxxiii. 11.

of grace. Thus it may be observed, that St. Paul never intimated that repentance is in any case unavailable; or that the door of pardon is closed against those who are "renewed unto repentance." But he does say, in his Epistle to the Hebrews, that it is "impossible to renew them unto repentance," who have grievously fallen away after great privileges. So that if the words, "though your sins be as scarlet, they shall be as white as snow: though they be red like crimson, they shall be as wool[5]," describe the unbounded extent of God's mercies in the Gospel covenant; yet, notwithstanding this, the state of probation under the Gospel is described in a certain sense by those other words, "Can the Ethiopian change his skin, or the leopard his spots? then may ye also do good, that are accustomed to do evil[6]:" and, "He which is filthy, let him be filthy still[7]."

Numerous as those expressions are which describe the mercy promised to repentance, yet not less numerous are those which speak of repentance becoming more and more difficult, and at length impossible after the rejection of grace given. As for instance in the expressions, of God Himself hardening the heart, and blinding the eyes, so that they cannot believe; of His sending a strong delusion on those that have pleasure in unrighteousness; of the light within being darkened; of the things belonging unto their peace being hidden from their eyes; of quenching the Spirit; of sin against the Holy Ghost, which is unpardonable; of sin unto death beyond the power of prayer; of seven other spirits taking possession of the soul worse than the first; of finding no place for repentance though sought carefully with tears. There may of course be a

---

[5] Isa. i. 18.   [6] Jer. xiii. 23.   [7] Rev. xxii. 11.

case worse than that of Judas, inasmuch as that plea is perhaps to be extended to him, which is pleaded for all the disciples; that the Holy Spirit was not yet given. Yet St. Ambrose speaks of his crime, as if it was sinning against the Holy Spirit, and that therefore repentance was vain [8]. His case was doubtless highly aggravated by the greatness of his privileges, and the strange enormity in the nature of his crime. What other example could profit him who had experienced so long Christ's endearing charities, had witnessed the holiness of His life, and beheld the evidences of His power? great and irreparable must have been the fall from that heavenly height of Divine favour. Nor was this crime merely a single act under the influence of passion; but apparently the result and termination of a course of wickedness: for it appears that he was in the habit of stealing out of the common stock of that poor and little company; and this, notwithstanding his being at the same time in the hearing of our Lord's daily discourses, of faith and heavenly mindedness, " of temperance and judgment to come;" and that on the occasion on which he was provoked, he actually had designed to steal what was given for the poor. It appears from an expression of our Lord's a whole year before this time, that he was even then under the influence of the evil spirit [9]. Indeed, when God allows men to fall into great crimes, it has the effect of showing to them, in sensible external action and palpable effect, what was secretly going on in their own heart. And this sight is too much for them to bear. This case also seems to bring out, and put in a strong point of view, the many passages that speak either by precept, parable, or incident, of the sin

<hr>

[8] Expos. in Luc. lib. x. 94.   [9] John vi. 70.

of covetousness, especially in our Lord's discourses.
There must have been something exceedingly subtle and
powerful in that influence, which could have rendered a
man so blind, as to have been incapable of perceiving
Christ in all that He did: and it is very evident from
numerous cases in the Gospels, that such a sin as this
does thoroughly prevent a person from believing in
Christ, or understanding His words. Yet at the same
time our Lord's careful warnings of Judas to the last,
teach us that no one is to be given up by others as
irreclaimable; but that in his own case, each has to fear
a state of impenitence and irrecoverable hardness of
heart, and to take care that the eye of the soul be ever
kept open and watchful, lest of a sudden it should open
on the knowledge of guilt for the first time, when faith
and hope are gone.

On these various derelictions of God, Damascenus
has the following striking passage. " Of derelictions,
one is in order to the manifestation of some hidden
virtue, as was that of Job; another for the avoidance
of pride, as was that of Paul; a third for the correction
of another person, as in the case of Lazarus and the
rich man, for we are naturally chastened by the sight of
suffering; a fourth for the glory of another, as he who
was blind from his birth was so for Christ's glory; a
fifth to provoke to emulation, as in the case of martyrdom. But simply there are but two kinds of dereliction; of which the one is by dispensation and for discipline, the other entire and to reprobation. That which
is by dispensation and for discipline, tends either to
correction and salvation, and the glory of the sufferer;
or else to the emulation and imitation of others, or to
the glory of God. But that which is entire dereliction
is, when God hath done every thing that can be done

for salvation; and yet a man still continues to the last incurable, on account of his own determined bent of mind; for he is given up to destruction as Judas was."

THE POTTER'S FIELD.

The circumstance which follows respecting the Chief Priests is remarkable, as one among the many instances which they showed at this time of extraordinary superstition; that is to say, of great wickedness combined with religious scruples. It was as our Lord said of them, they "strained at a gnat and swallowed a camel." " *The Chief Priests took the pieces of silver, and said, It is not lawful to put them into the treasury, because it is the price of blood*" (Matt.).   These are the same persons who deprived parents of filial support, because they said the money was set apart for this same treasury of God; and who probably took from the treasury this very money, to purchase the betrayal of innocent blood. But even now, as ever, in their superstitions and crimes, they were but fulfilling the great purposes and prophecies of God. "*And they took counsel,*" it is said, they probably held a meeting of their Sanhedrim for the purpose, "*and bought with them the potter's field, to bury strangers in,*" so that "*on that account the field was called the field of blood unto this day*" (Matt.). "*And it was known to all that dwell in Jerusalem*" (Acts).   And here their very religious scruples themselves were overruled to bear testimony against them.   For, as St. Chrysostom observes, their not putting the money into the treasury was because their own consciences condemned them, that they had thereby purchased blood; and the very name of the field continued an indelible testimony against them; "for," says he, "louder than any trumpet it proclaimed their thirst of blood." Whereas, if they had put the money into the treasury, nothing might have been heard of the circumstance. And as no word of Scripture is without its depth of meaning, their "taking counsel" to do so also bears again on the wonderful economy of their *all* sharing the guilt of His blood. "They not only do thus," says St. Chrysostom, "but by taking counsel; and so it is in every way that no one should be guiltless, but all accountable for that deed." There is a discrepancy here between St. Matthew and the Acts; in the latter, it is said that Judas "purchased the field." It may therefore be, that they completed the purchase which he had commenced, by giving his money for it, or it might be called his purchase as being bought by his money, though he had no hand in the contract. In the account given in the Acts of the Apostles, it would almost seem as if it was in this field that he destroyed himself, but from thence fell down by a precipice;—as if that sacred field, purchased with that Holy Blood, was no place for him; so that, even though hanged there, he fell down from thence. It was to be "a field to bury strangers in," the proselytes perhaps who came to Jerusalem to worship. And who can hear the words without seeing in them great and Divine import? For the price of Christ's blood was not to enrich the Temple of the Jews, but to supply a resting-place for the Gentiles; to receive their bodies till the general Resurrection. St. Jerome, who had been at the place, mentions that they showed this field in his time, that it lay at the south of Mount Sion, and that they buried there the poorest and meanest of the people.

And the prophecy, which is referred to, is very mysterious as bearing upon this subject: or it may be not prophecy, but prophecies from two distinct prophets, from two different points, throwing together their light on this one transaction, and forming together one spiritual lesson concerning it.   The very obscurity which hangs about it, would lead one to suppose, that there was far more in the matter than appears on the surface; for in the Inspired Records there is not even apparent mistake or accident without a Divine purport.   "*Then was fulfilled that which was spoken by Jeremy the prophet, saying, And they took the pieces of silver, the price of Him that was valued, whom they of the children of Israel did value, and gave them for the potter's field, as the Lord appointed me*" (Matt.).   Now these words are not found in the prophet Jeremiah.   But in Zechariah [1] we read, "they weighed for My price thirty pieces of silver: and the Lord said unto me, Cast it unto the the potter: a goodly price that I was prized at of them.   And I took the thirty pieces of silver, and cast them to the potter in the house of the Lord."   The last remarkable words "in the house of the Lord," are not mentioned by St. Matthew, nor some other striking points which are found in Zechariah.   But it will be seen that some of the words which are used by St. Matthew, as a quotation, are not here found in this Prophet; "whom they of the children of Israel did value, and gave them for the potter's field, as the Lord appointed me."   For the purchase of "the field" therefore, we have to look elsewhere to some other prophecy.   St. Augustin mentions that some MSS. have only "by the Prophet," omitting the word Jeremiah, but not sufficient to be of any authority.   And some explain the circumstance by a similarity, which the Jews suppose to exist, between the prophets Jeremiah and Zechariah; and that this

---

[1] Ch. xi. 12, 13.

passage in Zechariah is taken from some fuller prophecy in Jeremiah which is lost. But however that may be, it seems, like some other quotations in the New Testament, to combine an allusion to two prophecies. For besides this prophecy in Zechariah, which appears very distinct and remarkable, one cannot but suppose some reference contained in it to that solemn transaction of Jeremiah, in purchasing the field as the Lord appointed him, the evidences of which purchase were to be "put in an earthen vessel, that they may continue many days [2]." This field was to be to them a pledge and assurance that the captives should return, "that houses and fields and vineyards shall be again possessed in this land." The whole passage, therefore, taken with that prophecy would come to this meaning,—that we captives have in our own land a field, which is a pledge that we shall return thither. We, that are strangers and captives in this Babylon of the world, being buried with Christ in Baptism, have a place of rest in our own land, a burying-place in Christ, purchased by His blood. In the land of promise, given to Abraham, we strangers and proselytes have but one field, and that is the field purchased for us by Christ's blood. As Abraham of old said unto the sons of Heth, "I am a stranger and a sojourner with you; give me a possession of a burying-place with you [3]." And as Jacob, at his death in Egypt, spoke so earnestly of that field and burying-place which Abraham had purchased in Canaan; so may we in our captivity in this world, which is our Egypt and house of bondage, look to that field of rest purchased for us. We have no spot to call our own on earth but our burying-place, and that is purchased by Christ for us, that

---

[2] Ch. xxxii. 14.   [3] Gen. xxiii. 4.

we may rest in peace; for the Evangelist says, "It is called the field of blood unto this day." And it is the "sons of the stranger" who take hold of His Covenant, whom God has promised to bring to His "holy mountain [4]."

It is something in this manner that St. Augustin takes it; "a burying-place of strangers, as if it were for a stay and resting-place for those who, being strangers in this world, are buried together with Christ through Baptism; for those strangers, who, without home and country, are tossed about the whole world as exiles, for whom rest is provided by the blood of Christ." And St. Ambrose not only thus interprets it, but confirms this reference to Jeremiah's prophecy, and says that "herein is fulfilled the oracle of prophecy, and the mystery is revealed of the rising Church." Explaining the field as the world, and the Creator as the Potter, "by whose mercy, although dead in sins, we are again formed anew [5]." "This field, the world, is bought by the blood of Christ. He reserves therein those who are buried with Him in Baptism, and dead together with Christ, unto the grace of immortality." And "a burial is there for those who, being once strangers and foreigners, are now made fellow-citizens with the Saints, and of the household of God." But Origen interprets it quite differently, applying it to the strangers who die by casualties abroad, and come not into the sepulchres of their fathers. He takes them spiritually to represent those who are "strangers from the covenant of promise," "who being strangers from Christ to the end, and aliens from God, are not buried with Christ in the Rock, but are buried in the potter's field, which is the field of blood [6]."

[4] Isa. lvi. 6, 7. [5] Expos. in Luc. x. 95.
[6] Comm. in Matt. 117.

THE JEWS FEARING DEFILEMENT.

At this period of the narrative, the Gospel of St. John comes in to explain incidentally many things which would have given rise to great difficulty were it not for his circumstantial account. He now tells us, that the Jews themselves would not enter into the governor's house, but that the examination was carried on by Pilate coming out to them, and then returning to his prisoner within. "*And they themselves entered not into the prætorium,*" or judgment-hall, "*lest they should be defiled, but that they might eat the Passover*" (John). These words, spoken in simplicity by the Evangelist, cannot be read without a feeling of astonishment, at the greatness of their hypocrisy and self-deceit. They could not enter into an heathen house lest they should be defiled, but they feared not the defilement of slaying an innocent man : it was not lawful for them to put any one to death at the time of the Festival, but they had no hesitation in procuring the death of another at such a time, by means the most unjust and unmerciful. So wonderful is the mystery of iniquity : they unconsciously revered the shadow, while they trampled under foot the reality. As St. Cyril of Alexandria says, " What is more strange than all, they keep themselves pure in order to slay the lamb, which lamb signified nothing else but the shadow of the mystery of Christ. They do honour to the type, while dishonouring the very truth represented by it : and, while feigning purity for the sake of the figure, pollute themselves with the murder of Christ. Well therefore did Christ call them whited sepulchres." And this the consummation of their extraordinary hypocrisy, would have been prevented, had they afforded any attention to our Lord's frequent and constant expostulations with them against this vice. The warnings of our Lord, and those of Scripture in general, when unheeded, assume in some sense the character of prophecy, as directed by Him who knows the human heart, and the events to which it is tending. They derive an awful force from their consummation, as in the case of those Scriptural warnings against the love of riches, when viewed in the consummation to which it tends in the parable of the Rich man in the other world. For it will be observed, that to this one point all our Lord's admonitions to the Pharisees were directed; all of them especially warned them to look to charity and the keeping of the heart, instead of cloaking their wickedness by external washings and observances [7]. And indeed He had by His prophets been particularly explicit on this subject, and by His herald and forerunner, the Baptist; who had commenced his preaching by telling them,—not to depend on their being outwardly the children of Abraham, but to repent; this was the general character of his admonitions.

That the warnings and commands of Holy Writ do become in this manner prophetic, seems alluded to by Origen. "I suppose," says he, "that it is on account of that festival in which Barabbas was chosen unto life, and Christ set aside, that the Lord says by the Prophet, 'Your new moons and your appointed feasts My soul hateth [8];' and because they preferred to keep their solemn festival with the robber who was released rather than with Jesus. For if they had observed that solemnity rightly, as Josiah, or such as he, would have done, and then had the liberty of making such a request, they would doubtless have demanded Jesus, and

____

[7] See Vol. Min. 3rd Year, p. 4—10.   [8] Isa. i. 14.

condemned Barabbas." This thought of Origen's is confirmed by the words that follow in the Prophet to whom he refers, viz. that God will not hear their prayers, because, notwithstanding this show of religion, their "hands are full of blood." St. Cyril also remarks, that if they had attended to their Prophets, they would have escaped such wickedness; "Behold," he says, "although the Prophet Jeremiah says, 'O Jerusalem, wash thy heart from wickedness, that thou mayest be saved[9],' they utterly set at nought all internal holiness, and that of the heart, and in bringing Christ to Pilate, avoid places as impure, and bodies of the uncircumcised; while as long as they do not commit the crime with their own hands but make Pilate the minister of their cruelty, they suppose in their folly that they shall be free from guilt[1]."

The hypocrisy doubtless is very common in all ages whereby something else is substituted for the keeping of the heart: and the greatest crimes even in a Christian land have been committed under this cloak. But the particular shape which it hath assumed at this time among the Jews was peculiar, and perhaps was owing to a strong reaction that had taken place in consequence of the Captivity which they underwent for not keeping to the law; so much so, that the non-observance of their Sabbaths determined the very period of their captivity, the seventy years for which "the land should enjoy her" neglected "Sabbaths." It may be expected therefore, that this hypocrisy will usually assume its peculiar form and complexion from the spirit of the age, and that perhaps regulated by strong external reactions; whereby "the form of godliness" may be kept up while "the power" is denied.

<hr>

[9] Ch. iv. 14.　　　　　　　　　　[1] In Joan. lib. xii.

THE CHARGE OF SEDITION.

The Jews had now delivered our Lord unto Pilate as one worthy of death, and were very clamorous against Him. But in all this the Governor could not see any clear charge distinctly brought forward concerning His guilt, and seems at a loss to understand it. "*Pilate therefore went forth, and said, What accusation bring ye against this man? 'They answered and said unto him, If He were not a malefactor, we would not have delivered Him up unto thee*" (John), "As if," says St. Augustin, "he would yield to their authority, without further inquiry into the nature of the charge." And here we find that the Gentile comes forth from the judgment-hall to them, and shows a regard and reverence to their laws; but they who should be the light of the heathen, and who boast themselves of the knowledge of God, only lead him to partake in their guilt. The very appeal he makes to them serves to show, as St. Cyril observes, the greatness of their injustice in contrast with the Gentile, who was used to judge a criminal according to justice, so that their wickedness seems to astonish him. But the greater the injustice, the more does it tend to show our blessed Lord as the most perfect pattern of patience; and the more does it sanctify to His followers every case of the most cruel oppression. As they could find no definite accusation that could fix itself on His most spotless life, they call Him a malefactor;—Him, who alone of all that are born of women, was perfectly innocent, and without blemish. But so did He offer Himself, and was accepted of God as a malefactor, or in place of malefactors: as for our sakes, and for their sakes, He was as a malefactor, "bearing the sins of many;" as one who took upon

Himself every evil that had been committed, though Himself innocent. The very term malefactor comes forth with a Divine emphasis. As all things proclaim Him "without sin :" so do they with equal pointedness mark Him out as bearing condemnation, and "numbered with transgressors."

This vain declaration, however, is not sufficient to satisfy the Roman judge ; but the matter appeared to be one with respect to themselves and their own religion, for the protection of which and their temple the Romans allowed them soldiers and a court of Judicature. "*Pilate therefore said unto them, Take ye Him and judge Him according to your law*" (John); which words from a Roman governor seem to imply that they had the power. "*But the Jews said unto him, It is not lawful for us to put any one to death*" (John) ; *i. e.* as St. Chrysostom, St. Augustin, and St. Cyril of Alexandria, take it, it was not lawful for them to put any one to death at this time, during the Festival. For this is the only point on such a subject in which he could need information from them ; and otherwise we find them too ready, as in the case of our Lord at other times, of the woman taken in adultery, and of St. Stephen, to execute their vengeance by instant death.

And here, lest our minds should be taken up in the narrative of secondary causes, so as to forget God's hand and overruling presence in them, the Evangelist, after the example of his Lord, seems to pause at every step, to point out to us that in all this it was Christ freely offering up Himself, according to the will of God. This he does by showing that this happened in the fulfilment of our Lord's declaration ; "*that the word of Jesus might be fulfilled which He spake signifying by what kind of death He should die*" (John). For these are the very

words which St. John had before applied to a saying of
our Lord's, when in coming up to this feast He had said,
"If I be lifted up from the earth, I will draw all men
unto Me." "This He said," adds the Evangelist, "signifying what death He should die [2]." And the other
Evangelists mention our Lord's frequent intimation that
He should be delivered up to the Gentiles, and crucified [3]. It would appear, therefore, that this could only
have taken place by the concurrence of so peculiar an
occasion. Thus did our Saviour die the most humiliating
and painful of all deaths; and thus also was it provided
that these Jews, who had all the accumulated guilt of
His death, yet were not allowed to lay hands on, and
touch His most sacred Body in death.

The other Gospels are here necessary to carry on the
narrative of St. John: for in this Evangelist we find
Pilate returning to our Lord with questions, which he
does not account for, but St. Luke does. For finding
that Pilate required a specific charge which appertained
to him as Roman governor, as we learn from St. Luke,
then "*they began to accuse Him, saying, We found this
man perverting the nation, and forbidding to give tribute
unto Cæsar, saying, that He Himself was Christ a king*
(Luke). It was hearing this charge therefore that, as
St. John mentions, "*Pilate entered again into the judgment hall, and called Jesus*" (John); and as a prisoner
obeying his command, "*Jesus stood before the governor*"
(Matt.). The charge of forbidding to give tribute unto
Cæsar was, we know, an untruth; for they had in vain
endeavoured, in conjunction with the Herodians, to obtain grounds for it; but that of His being a King was a
new charge, though a subject which of all others most

[2] Ch. xii. 33.   [3] Vol. Min. 3rd Year, p. 470.

concerned the Roman governor, an account of the suspicious cruelty of the Emperor Tiberius. And the more so because, as St. Cyril notices, the Romans were particularly severe with the Jews in such cases, on account of their seditious character.

Here we stop to contemplate the adorable Son of God at the beck of a heathen Prefect, set as a criminal before him. " He that is appointed by the Father the Judge of all creation," says Origen, " see how He hath humbled Himself, to submit to stand before the judge of the land of Judæa, and to be asked any question which Pilate pleased to put to Him in derision or in doubt."

" *And the governor* (Matt.) *asked Him* (Matt. Mark), *saying, Art Thou the King of the Jews ?* " (Matt. Mark, Luke, John.) And now, if it were not for the more circumstantial account, which St. John has given us, of Pilate's conversation with our Lord that ensued, we might have been in great perplexity ; for the other three Evangelists mention that " *Jesus* (Matt.) *answered and said, Thou sayest* " (Matt., Mark, Luke), confessing to the charge. On which St. Luke informs us, that Pilate went out and declared to the Jews, that " he found no fault in Him ;" when from that confession we should have expected an opposite judgment, viz. that the prisoner acknowledged the truth of their accusation. But St. John, by giving us the account of the conversation which intervened with our blessed Lord, renders the whole circumstance perfectly clear ; and explains how it is that our Lord's acquittal takes place on the part of Pilate, and not His condemnation, on His pleading guilty to the charge of His being a King.

THE CHARGE OF BEING A KING.

Here, therefore, comes forth a fresh and remarkable circumstance, the charge of our Lord being a King. For in like manner, as before, when they falsely called Him a malefactor, that appellation was in one sense Providentially and Divinely true, in that He stood before His Father in the place of transgressors,—so also was this title, now used, of His making Himself a King. For He had indeed desired, and sought for Himself, a kingdom more extensive than Cæsar's; for God had said, "Desire of Me, and I shall give Thee the heathen for thine inheritance, and the utmost parts of the earth for Thy possession [4]." The Jews delivered Him to the Gentiles as their King, whom they rejected; the Gentiles received Him and bowed the knee.

But further:—the circumstance of the Jews entirely altering the nature of their accusation, is a proof that all that had passed before the High Priest and the Council, the High Priest rending his garments, and the sentence of the Sanhedrim, was nothing more than an hypocritical pretence; for now they are equally vehement in prosecuting a perfectly different charge. And this accusation on which so much of the wonderful circumstances that ensue depends, arises as it were by accident. It is one of the many instances of that striking truth, which we must keep in mind, and ever return to, throughout this history: that every incident arising out of the passions, the caprice, the malice of men, or the most trifling apparent contingency, invariably turns out to be of Divine intention, and weighed long before in the counsels of the Almighty. Such are

[4] Ps. ii. 8.

like things apparently trivial, and having a relation to passing events, in the Ceremonial Law, which are found replete with representations of Christ's kingdom, being according to the pattern showed in the Mount. The obedience of Moses was his blessing; and the disobedience of Pharaoh was his curse; but both alike worked the glory of God. It is with the events themselves, as with the narrative that records them. In the inspired accounts of the Gospels respecting our blessed Lord, we believe that every thing is full of a Divine purpose, and that points, which appear to worldly critics but the inaccuracy, or accidental repetition, or omission of an Evangelist, are regulated by a Divine superintendence: wherein we lose the person of the human writer, and see but a Hand without a body, that writes supernaturally on the wall. So in the course of events that minister to Him, we believe that, like words and syllables, they fall into a Divine order to do Him honour, and to speak His language. The accusation to Pilate, of His being a King, is of this character. It does not appear that our Lord ever before declared Himself a King; but that the circumstance of His being the Christ necessarily implied it. Hence, from this accusation arises our Lord's own declaration, that He was a King. Hence the remarkable fact takes place, of His being put to death on the two distinct charges which He admitted in courts of justice; in the first, that He was the Son of God, and in the latter, that He was a King. In both our Lord sanctions and does honour to earthly courts of judicature, by making them ministers and instruments of His own testimony. From an occasion equally trifling arises apparently the subsequent inscription of Pilate on the Cross. And even more than this;—by the same kind of accident, as it were, it comes to pass that He has the inscription written up in Hebrew, and Greek, and Latin. This he does merely for the more effectual expression of his contempt; but it becomes, beyond this, Divinely significant, as implying that to all nations, of every tongue, He was also King of the Jews. And it is to be observed that they are Gentiles, both at first and at last, who declare Him so; for they were the Wise Men from the East who then, at His birth, came asking for Him, "Where is He that is King of the Jews?" And now Pilate answers that inquiry to all nations, saying in reply, "This is the King of the Jews." Moreover, at our Lord's birth it was the Roman Emperor, who was made by Providence to point out to all the world the King and the Son of David, by causing Him, through the taxation, to be born at Bethlehem. And it is the Roman Emperor, the lord of this world, who is made again to do the same by Pilate his Governor. Then Herod, too, acknowledges Him as the King of the Jews, although it is only to slay Him: and now also the Jews acknowledge Him King in this charge, although it is only to slay Him. By a similar kind of apparent accident the Jews unconsciously acknowledge our Lord under both titles; for in mockery and insult in the palace of the High Priest they acknowledge Him, addressing Him as Christ the Prophet; and before Herod they arrayed Him, and knelt before Him as the King. And the soldiers of Pilate afterwards did the same, so that He is now also acknowledged by Jew and Gentile: in like manner as He was at His birth.

To the question of Pilate, which he asked of Christ on returning to the Judgment-hall, whether He was "the King of the Jews?" our Lord makes no direct reply; but He Himself, first of all, makes an inquiry of

Pilate. "*Jesus answered him, Sayest thou this of thyself, or did others tell it thee of Me? Pilate*"—irritated at the bare supposition that he should feel any concern in such a matter, as if he were a contemptible Jew—"*replied, Am I a Jew? Thine own nation and the Chief Priests have delivered Thee unto me,*" and have preferred this charge. What is the reason of all this? I do not understand it. "*What hast Thou done?*" (John.)

And now may we reverently inquire, what our Lord intended by thus interrogating Pilate, as if He needed information? For at first sight it may excite surprise, to judge humanly, that our Lord should have to ask questions at all; as He knew all things, and His especial attribute is to know the thoughts of the heart; and therefore, as the disciples said, He "needed not that any one should ask" Him. For among mankind the reason why questions are asked is from a desire to know that of which we are ignorant. Nor is this by any means a solitary instance; on many occasions we find our all-knowing Lord asking questions, as man of man; and even when raised from the Dead, when with His new and spiritual body He joined His disciples going to Emmaus, He asked the subject of their conversation, and they replied as to one ignorant of the circumstances concerning which He inquired.

Now one point which may be observed with regard to this subject is this,—that this conduct of our Lord, in the days of His walking in the flesh, is in perfect analogy with what we read of Him in the Old Testament, when He speaks as God to man. Thus for instance it is, that Almighty God questions Adam, and makes inquiries of him, as man would of man, respecting what he had done; and also of Cain, saying, "Where is thy brother?" And the same may be also found throughout the Prophets;

as in that saying, " Come, now, and let us reason together, saith the Lord⁵." That our Lord should thus
speak, when He condescended to take on Himself human
infirmities and natural weakness, is not so surprising as
the wonderful harmony which it preserves with the conduct of God through the Old Testament. For it seems
as if in all these things, which are there spoken of God,
there may be some mysterious allusion to the Incarnation; to God conversing with us as man with man; and
also to His judging and questioning man on the Day of
Judgment, as " the Son of Man." This is indeed a subject
on which we might probably see a great deal more by a
devout attention, viz. that the actions of our Lord in
the days of His flesh were prefigured by all His previous
dealings with mankind, whereby He revealed unto us
the Almighty Father. It seems not unreasonable to
suppose, that all human parts and passions attributed to
the Almighty, and all manifestations of Himself to mankind, had some reference to His appearing as Man.

But, however, the point to be at present noticed is
this,—the fact of our Lord's asking a question should
arrest and rivet our attention to it, and the purpose of it; for as He cannot ask from any desire to
know, it must be that by His inquiry, and the reply to
be given and recorded, He may best inform us of something we ought to know. As our Lord said on another
occasion, when He prayed aloud to His Father, that it
was for the sake of others He did it⁶: so are His inquiries for the purpose of drawing out, in definite act or
words, the thoughts of the heart; or of thereby putting
forth some fact more strongly to our notice. And to
this effect is the remark of St. Austin; " The Lord,

-----

⁵ Isa. i. 18.   ⁶ John xi. 42.

forsooth, knew both that which He Himself asked, and what the other would answer, but yet He wished it to be said, not that He Himself might know, but that that should be written which He wished to be known."

If it might be allowed in reverence to paraphrase our Lord's words, we might humbly venture to suppose that He intended something of this kind. ' Had you really any desire of yourself to know whether I am the King of the Jews, then of course I would tell you. But, I know, you of yourself consider such a charge very unreasonable: but who is it that has told you so? They are Mine own nation, and the Chief Priests of that nation; thus you here solemnly pronounce to Me, as judge to a prisoner, the cause on which he stands accused; and this declaration of yours must be made known unto all the world, that it is on this charge, made by the Jews, that I am brought before you, and on which I die. Let them not say, therefore, that all their prophecies of a promised King are not fulfilled, for I come as their King; and as the babes in the Temple acknowledged Me in Hosannahs, so do these in reproaches. And you ask Me " what hast Thou done?"—What have I done to prove Me this promised King? Ask the sick, the lame, the blind, the paralytic, the lepers, the demoniacs: ask of the hungry I whom have fed; of the dead whom I have raised; ask of those who have heard My doctrine, if ever there was a King more worthy of the name, than the long promised King of the Jews: the King they now acknowledge to you. But as far as regards the charge, and the grounds upon which they allege it to you, in order that I should be put to death, as one dangerous to worldly authority, the charge is perfectly groundless. " *Jesus answered, My kingdom is not of this world*" (John). This I declare to you and to them, to Gentiles and Jews both alike, that My kingdom is not of this world.'

This mode in which we have ventured to explain our Lord's intention, is confirmed by a few words of St. Augustin. "He asks him in return," says he, "whether he said this of himself, or had heard it from others, wishing to show by his (Pilate's) reply, that this was the crime objected to Him by the Jews; laying open to us the thoughts of men which He Himself knew, that they are but vain. And to them, after the answer of Pilate, to both Jews and Gentiles, now inquiring, He answers, the more seasonably and suitably, My kingdom is not of this world."

"*If My kingdom were of this world*," our blessed Saviour continued, "*then would My servants fight for Me, that I should not be delivered to the Jews*" (John). For they who in this world wish to obtain or preserve a Kingdom, use a sword in their defence, and have recourse to means of this kind; but the Kingdom of Heaven is obtained and preserved by the opposite means. The first declaration which our Lord had made respecting this His kingdom, was that it belonged to "the poor in spirit." And this the nature of His kingdom our Lord had Himself pointed out to those who came with arms to apprehend Him; saying, that there was no occasion for swords and staves, against one who had sat so peaceably in the midst of them in the Temple. "*But now is My kingdom*," added our Lord, "*not from hence*" (John). That His kingdom was not of the world, is what our Lord had before declared to all His disciples, "ye are not of the world, as I am not of the world; but because I have chosen you out of the world, therefore the world hateth you." His kingdom is not of the world, nor is it from the world, but out of Heaven;

for it is no other than that Holy City, which St. John saw "coming down out of Heaven," "the tabernacle of God," to be "with men." If it had been an earthly Kingdom, it would have needed the help of armies and men; but a Heavenly Kingdom is sufficient in itself, and needs not these, but arms of a more ethereal temper. It is indeed in the world, but not of the world, nor from the world, but from Heaven. Its ministers, its Sacraments, are of Divine appointment. The graces of all its members are from above, not from hence. It has indeed established itself in the midst of the kingdom of Satan in order to overthrow it, to take from it the armour wherein it trusted; but it is not from hence, nor of human means.

But though the Governor understood not the full purport of our Lord's words, yet on hearing Him speaking of His kingdom, the words arrested his ear: "*Pilate therefore said to Him, Art Thou a King then?*" (John) as if this declaration in some way accounted for the charge of the Jews. And perhaps at this time repeating the question more distinctly, "*Pilate* (Mark, Luke), *the Governor* (Matt.), *asked Him, saying, Art Thou the King of the Jews?* (Matt. Mark, Luke.) *He answered,*" in the words of that solemn attestation recorded in all the Gospels, "*Thou sayest*" (Matt. Mark, Luke, John). So important was this declaration which is here judicially made and repeated, that God had fulfilled His promise by all the Prophets, and had set His King on His holy hill of Sion. "*Thou sayest,*" St. John continues, "*that I am a King. I was born for this purpose, and for this purpose came I into the world, that I should bear witness unto the truth*" (John).

This attestation of our blessed Lord's is the very pattern for all martyrdom, as St. Paul implies, for he speaks of it as of His " witnessing before Pontius Pilate a good confession." And here Christ declares that which was His own great office, viz. to bear witness; and in union with Himself, that of the Holy Spirit also, Who is " the faithful Witness." In this as in all other things, our Lord is pleased to admit His apostles to partake in some sense in His own office, saying to them, " ye also shall bear witness," and His Church, which is to be a " witness unto all nations :" for it is He in it, and He in them, and therefore as He is the Witness, they also are witnesses. He is essential Truth in some substantial, ineffable, and ever enduring manner, in distinction from which " all men are liars." It is therefore as if He had said, all the world lies in falsehood and vanity, and they, who follow any of its ways, will so far find at last " a lie in their right hand;" the kings of the world, and all pertaining to them, are but shadows and vanity. I alone am the true King; Mine alone is the true Kingdom; I alone have the true riches, true power, true life, true light. " *Every one,*" continues our blessed Lord, " *who is of the truth, heareth My voice.*" The very test and proof of the character of each, of the mode in which he has been dealing with himself, of the life he has led, of the duties he has fulfilled, of the disposition he has attained unto, of the degree in which he loves God, and loves his neighbour, the very test and proof of all this is, whether he hears the voice of Christ. He has Himself declared that His sheep know His voice; that they who hear Him not, are not of God. He who believes in Christ fulfils all righteousness, he who believes Him not, is in sin.

Pilate, on hearing these words, was probably struck at the Divine authority and superhuman wisdom of our Lord's mode of speaking. He for a moment forgets his office as judge, and becomes His disciple. "*Pilate saith unto Him, What is truth?*" What is that on which you speak in such awful terms? "Thus," St. Chrysostom says, "by saying these things He attracts and persuades him to listen to His discourse; and therefore at last led him on to ask Him this question, 'What is truth?'" "He not only liberates him from his fears," says St. Cyril, "but engages him to lofty thoughts concerning Himself." And what was the truth to which He had . come to bear testimony but this, that of His kingdom? "For this end," says St. Chrysostom, "was I born, to persuade men of this truth." And the same writer observes, that He shows His humility in that, "when accused of being a malefactor He bore it in silence; but when interrogated concerning His kingdom, then He spake to Pilate, instructing him, and leading him on to higher things'." Nor can we wonder that He who took such pains even with Judas, would do all to recover an ignorant Gentile. Besides this, it seems to represent, in mystery, the Gentiles, who seem to have been asking so long of nature and philosophy, "What is truth?" and now He has come Who can alone answer them, if they will patiently listen to His voice.

But after asking this question, Pilate suddenly recollecting himself and the business he was about, saw clearly that the charge of the Jews was a frivolous and vain one; and therefore rushed out without waiting for an answer. St. Austin [8] thinks that the reason of this abruptness was, that Pilate now perceived that it was envy on the part of the Chief Priests, and that therefore the thought suddenly occurred to him, of his being able to make an appeal to the people, and to release a

[7] In Joan. Hom. lxxxiii.   [8] In Joan. Tr. cxv.

prisoner on the occasion of the Festival. And the account in St. John, taken by itself alone, would very well have borne out this supposition. But it appears from St. Luke, and indeed from the general narrative, that the sending to Herod must have intervened, which would quite do away with that suggestion of St. Austin's. But if we agree with St. Austin on this point, then we must explain it thus, that all this charge of our Lord being a King, was subsequent to his sending Him to Herod; and that before that time the charge only was of His "stirring up," and "perverting the people" in a general way.

Pilate, "*when he had said this, went out again to the Jews, and saith unto them, I find no fault in Him* (John), *Pilate said to the Chief Priests and the crowd,*" says St. Luke, "*I find no fault in this man.*" At this time it probably is that St. Matthew and St. Mark speak of their becoming so clamorous, and of our Lord's remarkable silence. "*And when* (Matt.) *the Chief Priests* (Matt. Mark) *and the Elders* (Matt.) *accused Him* (Matt. Mark) *of many things* (Mark), *He answered nothing*" (Matt.). Making no defence or denial, as a prisoner naturally would against false charges, when Pilate returned to Him from the Chief Priests to mention the accusations, or had brought Him forth to confront them. "It is evident," says Origen, "that Pilate was kindly disposed towards Christ, but yet he had no settled judgment, and was wavering, and when inclining to the worse opinion, the Lord answered him nothing." "*Pilate again asked Him, saying, Answerest Thou nothing?* (Mark.) *Hearest Thou not* (Matt.) *how many things they testify against Thee? But He (Jesus still,* Mark) *answered not* (Matt. Mark) *even a single word*" (Matt.). As if to say, that if by accusations

which they knew to be false, they wished to take away
His life, He offered Himself up a voluntary Victim to
them. "*So that Pilate* (Mark), *the Governor*" (Matt.),
thinking how easily our Lord might refute such charges,
"*marvelled* (Matt. Mark) *greatly*" (Matt.). "He marvelled," says Theophylact, " that being a teacher of the
Law, powerful and eloquent, He did not by His answers
refute their charges, but rather manfully sustained
them." We may also suppose that there was something
in our Lord's manner and words, so different from what
is usual in a criminal, that the Judge felt something of
awe and wonder before Him. " The expression," says
Origen, "not only that Pilate marvelled, but that he
marvelled greatly, moves me to think, that it appeared
to him a great miracle, that when brought forward on
a capital charge, Christ should continue undisturbed,
and stand before death, which among all men is esteemed
terrible[9]." Nothing would have moved a Roman so
much as fearlessness of death ; it was therefore perhaps
so ordained, that the Roman should witness this quality
of intrepidity in Christ ; and that God should appeal to
him through that virtue, for the shadow of which he was
himself so eminent. Quesnel speaks of this silence as
something more wonderful even than miracles, from its
evident effect on the Governor. In another point of
view perhaps the silence of Christ may represent us, who
before our Judge must put our hand upon our mouth,
and be silent, as guilty sinners ; for Christ's readiness
to die implied that He was, in our place, bearing sin.

Now from St. Matthew and St. Mark we have found
them accusing our Lord of many things, but the charges
are not recorded, as being unimportant ; but one thing

[9] Comm. in Matt. 119.

they now mentioned arrested the Governor's attention. For on his saying that he could find no fault substantiated, "*they were urgent, and said, He stirreth up the people, teaching throughout all Judea, beginning from Galilee to this place. Pilate, when he heard of Galilee, inquired if the man were a Galilean.*" It occurred to to him that he might get rid of the question, and also further ends of his own, in effecting a reconciliation with Herod by this mark of deference. Half conscience-stricken, half moved by self-interest, he was like that other Governor, Felix, before St. Paul, who trembled at " temperance and judgment to come," and yet soon after endeavoured to obtain a bribe from him. "*And when he knew that He was of Herod's jurisdiction, he sent Him to Herod, who also was himself at Jerusalem in these days*" (Luke). And here again, as in every step, the malice of the Jews is overruled for great and Divine purposes, for by mentioning Galilee, they thought more to excite the attention of the Governor; for that people, as Theophylact observes, was then given to insurrections. Judas, who is mentioned in the Acts of the Apostles, was of Galilee; and the blood of those Galileans which " Pilate mingled with their sacrifices," was shed on account of some sedition. But it was thus ordained that wicked Herod also should have a hand in His death, after having slain His herald and Prophet.

CHRIST SENT TO HEROD.

This Herod Antipas, to whom our Saviour was sent, was the same who had heard John the Baptist "gladly," and had done " many things because of him ;" and had afterwards imprisoned him, and put him to death ; and when he had heard of the miracles of Christ, he thought it was the Baptist, whom he had beheaded, risen from the grave; and it was stated at that time that he was " desirous to see Him [10]."   His character is given by our Lord Himself, Who spoke of him as "that fox [11]." *" But Herod, when he saw Jesus "* thus brought before him, *" was exceeding glad: for he had been for a long time desirous to see Him, for he had heard many things of Him; and he hoped to see some miracle done by Him "* (Luke). Not only must he have heard much, as being the governor of Galilee, but even the wife of his own steward was one of our Lord's devoted followers; so that from those about him, he would have heard of some of our Lord's most remarkable miracles, and from persons who would have narrated them with much interest. One would apprehend he was in that most fearful state into which persons sometimes fall, when they have had their feelings once excited on the subject of religion, but still kept their vices; and who still continue to entertain an interest and curiosity in matters of religion, having lost godly fear.   For he actually wished to see a sign, as if from curiosity, without any apprehension of the power of God, which such a sign would indicate. Not stern and cruel as his father had been, but wily, having first deceived himself, and then deceiving others; and from thence led on to suppose that he could deceive God. "Not," says Theophylact, "as likely to derive any advantage from beholding Him, but from the desire of novelty, to see a stranger of whose wisdom and miracles he had heard : and curious to hear what He had to say, by questioning Him in derision and mockery."   But what strange wickedness of every kind is here brought out.   Pilate knows Him to be innocent, but has not

---

[10] Vol. Min. p. 341.   [11] Vol. Min. 3rd Year, p. 321.

courage to acquit Him, and for a political friendship will sacrifice Him: Herod, by wishing to see a miracle done by Him, acknowledges His being a teacher from God, with power of miracles, but only to mock Him.

To one in such a state we need not wonder that our Lord had nothing to say; Herod "*questioned Him in many words, but He answered him nothing*" (Luke): still observing that most remarkable silence which He had maintained before the High Priest and before Pilate. And surely no state can be so awful as that in which men no longer hear the voice of God speaking to them. Throughout His trial indeed occasionally He spake, as if to prevent any appearance of sullen reserve, or to communicate some great truth in charity, but for the most part was silent. So that of this His silence, St. Chrysostom observes, that it was indeed fulfilling the expression of Solomon, that "there is a time to keep silence, and a time to speak [1]." This silence and speech, so wonderfully adapted in Divine wisdom, are both described by the Psalmist,—"I kept silence, yea, even from good words;" and also, "I will open my mouth in parables;" and at another time, "My tongue is the pen of a ready writer." Thus, as Theophylact observes, "Jesus, Who did all things by reason, and, as David says, directed His words in wisdom, thought it pious in such things to keep silence. For speech put forth to him whom it profits not, is cause of his condemnation." "He was silent," says St. Ambrose, "and did nothing; for they deserved not to hear Divine things; and the Lord avoided display. And perhaps typically in Herod all the wicked are represented, who, if they believed not the Law and the Prophets, could not behold the wonderful works of Christ

---

[1] Eccles. iii. 7.

in the Gospel." And Gregory[2] says, that from "these
things we ought to learn, that whenever our hearers wish
to hear what we have to say, in order to praise, and not
to amend what is wrong, we should be altogether silent.
For there are many things which destroy the soul of the
hearers, especially if our hearers praise what they hear,
and do not follow what they praise."

But "*the Chief Priests and the Scribes*" would of
course have accompanied Christ to Herod through the
streets of the city, as they had before dragged Him from
the palace of Caiaphas to Pilate, and were now, we may
suppose, become more vehement from the impediment
they had met with in Pilate. They "*stood and vehemently accused Him*" (Luke). But here again they do
not seem to have succeeded in establishing any charge
against Him, which Herod could take hold of, as a
just pretext for putting Him to death. Herod was not
himself a person to take the lead in an open and bold
crime : and possibly the circumstance of the Feast might
have prevented him also from gratifying the Jews by
shedding blood. For we find in the Acts of the Apostles
that his nephew Herod Agrippa put Peter in prison,
keeping him through the days of unleavened bread, "in-
tending after Easter to bring him forth to the people[3]."
"*But Herod*," partly instigated by the violence of the
Chief Priests, and partly by being disappointed in the
object of his curiosity, and from that wanton hatred of
goodness which bad men entertain, "*set Him at nought
with his men of war, and mocked Him, having put on Him
a white shining robe*" (Luke); such as Eastern kings
wear, whence "the glory of Solomon" is compared for its
whiteness to "the lilies of the field[4]." They therefore

---

[2] Moral. xxii. 11.   [3] Ch. xii. 4.   [4] St. Matt. vi. 29.

unwittingly acknowledge Him as King, and array Him unconsciously in the kingly robe of innocence, after a faint similitude of that His own raiment, white as snow and glistering, with which He was invested at His Transfiguration.

"It was not without a meaning," says St. Ambrose, " that He was clothed in a white robe by Herod, giving tokens of His spotless Passion; in that the Lamb of God without spot, with His glory took upon Him the sins of the world⁵." And as Theophylact observes,— " The very derision which the devil heaped upon Him, and the white robe with which He was clothed in mockery, were involuntary declarations of His innocence; inasmuch as if there had been any fault in Him, their reproaches would have assumed the shape of some allusion to it." But, with regard to the mystery contained in this transaction, perhaps in this case, as well as in the mockery of Pilate's soldiers, the investing of our Lord with these mock-kingly robes, might indicate that the Kingdoms had gone from Herod, and from Cæsar, unto Himself: that of the Jews and the Gentiles He was from henceforth to be Himself the King. Thus, though they meant it not, and knew it not, yet do the Jews and Herod act the part of the Egyptians and Pharaoh, while our Lord is seen in the great type of Joseph. "And Pharaoh said unto Joseph, Thou shalt be over my house, and according unto thy word shall all my people be ruled . . . . And Pharaoh said unto Joseph, See, I have set thee over all the land of Egypt. And Pharaoh arrayed him in vesture of fine linen . . . . And they cried before him, Bow the knee⁶." But Pharaoh and the Egyptians were far better, for they did it in

⁵ Exp. in Luc. x. 103.   ⁶ Gen. xli. 39—43.

good will to the type only of all goodness, But Herod and the Jews in mockery and malice to goodness itself.

And now, after they had vented their malice in reproaches and insult, Herod "*sent Him back to Pilate*" uncondemned. And here it must be again remarked how it was ordered and brought about, by the mysterious providence of God, that all things should combine to speak aloud His innocence. Before the High Priest the witnesses could not agree, and could prove nothing: Judas himself declared that he had betrayed the innocent blood: Pilate repeatedly declared that he could find no fault in Him: nor yet Herod, the Jews accused Him before him, but in vain. There were two charges only that could be put forth against Him, and those were His own declarations: the first, that He was the Son of God, and the last, that He was the King of the Jews. So shall it be at the day of Judgment, the perfect justice of God shall be acknowledged by every tongue: every mouth shall be stopped: God shall be true, and every man a liar:—"That Thou mightest be justified when Thou speakest, and be clear when Thou judgest[7]."

Observe also, that as our Lord had spared no pains to bring Judas to a sense of his crime, so does He appear throughout to have done every thing for the Jews, to bring them to repentance. Such was His expostulation on first being taken; such His speech to the Council; such the death and declaration of Judas; such the remonstrances of Pilate, and his washing his hands, and such the very mockeries of Herod. Perhaps in this manner, in His moral providence, warnings are always given to persons in the course of sin, but they have no eyes to see, nor ears to hear. And when sinners are by any

[7] Ps. li. 4.

means suddenly awakened to a sense of their condition, they come to an instinctive consciousness of this; so much so, that when their minds are as yet ill-regulated, they fancy they hear supernatural voices, and see sights of warning; whereas, long before, the voice of God was in fact speaking to them in all things, though they observed it not; now they know it, but in alarm know not where to look for it. Under such circumstances, the light that falls on the path of duty is our only protection; the warnings it shows us on all sides are doubtless from God, and sent to us in His mercy.

Observe also how all things combine to speak the need of a sacrifice, and the great corruption of our nature: the covetousness and malice of Judas, the expediency and anger of Caiaphas, the policy and cowardice of Pilate, the scorn and mockery of Herod, the envy or Pharisees, the cruelty of soldiers, the madness of the multitude, nay, even we may add the unfaithfulness or St. Peter, and weakness of all the disciples;—all show the power of the Evil one, which our Lord overcame in this conflict.

And now the sacred Evangelist, in recording our blessed Lord's being brought back to Pilate, adds, that *" Pilate and Herod were made friends on the same day with each other, for they had been before at enmity between themselves "* (Luke). The less important this incident may appear towards the unfolding of the momentous narrative of our Lord's death, the more is one inclined to look for some great principle or mysterious prophetic intimation contained in it. St. Ambrose suggests that this may relate prophetically to the ultimate reconciliation between the Gentile and the Jew. The same thought is pursued by Quesnel, who says,—" In a very little time, O Jesus, Thy death will reconcile and unite together, not only a Gentile and a Jew, but Jews and Gentiles, by one and the same faith, in one and the same Body, and under one and the same Head[8]." This interpretation is a charitable one: but does it not seem a friendship of worldly persons formed at the expense of Christ; and are there not other indications of the same thing in Pharisees, and Herodians, and Sadducees, combining together, who "before were at enmity between themselves," in a common alliance against Christ? May it not allude to some great and universal principle, that worldly persons of all parties will drop their mutual enmities in order to combine against Christ and His truth, whenever it is to be found among mankind? This sentiment of old writers is found in the Ven. Bede, who says that the alliance of Herod and of Pilate signifies that Gentiles and Jews, persons differing in race, and religion, and mind, agree together in persecuting Christians.

But the wanton cruelty and enmity of so many parties against the adorable Son of God, if merely considered as directed towards an innocent and helpless person of great holiness, is worthy of deep reflection, as indicative of something in the corrupt nature of us all. For it can scarcely be supposed that the circumstances, openly alleged against our Lord, were of themselves sufficient to account for the enmity and ill-treatment He met with: one would be disposed to think that the circumstances alleged were rather the symptoms than the causes of that enmity. Origen, on the Psalms[9], has the following striking passage: "He who is bent to think and to act aright hath many adversaries. For there are both men and devils full of envy, who are grieved at the good of those who act aright. Perceiving this, the Prophet

---

[8] On St. Luke, ch. xxiii.   [9] Selecta in Psalmos, v. 8.

attributeth not to himself the power to contend against his enemies; but hath besought God to stretch forth His hand over him to shelter him, and keep him unhurt from enemies so many, and so great, saying, Lord, lead me in Thy righteousness, for thus only can my ways be rightly directed in Thy sight!" The sentiment, which is contained in this passage, will perhaps serve better to account for the hatred which our blessed Lord and good men have met with, than any attempting to explain it from secondary causes. For it is often spoken of, as a great invariable maxim, that they who would live godly in Christ Jesus must suffer persecution. The same principle, considering the agency of evil spirits as well as evil men in this matter, will be the best key to other events of the like kind in history. And there appears to be much thought in what Origen says here of the motive of their persecution,—that it is envy. For perhaps this word will best express it both in evil spirits and evil men. For out of envy of the devil sin entered into the world; and the violence of the Pharisees is here expressly attributed to envy : and envy is frequently mentioned in the Acts, as the instigating cause against Christianity.

Throughout the whole of these circumstances, at every step we are obliged to pause with wonder, as we observe the development of the two great mysteries,—the mystery of godliness, and the mystery of iniquity. Here they both come forth in their great consummation, and appear throughout doubly mysterious. And they are both in the strongest sense mysteries ; for they both mark the active presence of agents spiritual. Almighty God overruling for good ; Satan working evil. Satan displaying wickedness so great as to be almost incomprehensible ; Almighty God in every case converting evil into good.

CHRIST REJECTED BY THE PEOPLE.

On the return from Herod, "*Pilate called together the Chief Priests and the Rulers*" of the Sanhedrim, "*and the people, and said unto them, Ye have brought this man unto me, as one that perverteth the people: and behold, I have examined Him before you, and have found no fault in this man, concerning those matters of which ye accuse Him*" (Luke). As I stated this to some of you before, so I now repeat it in presence of you all here assembled. And in addition to my own judgment in this matter, there is now also that of Herod. "*Nor yet hath Herod*" found any fault in Him; "*for I sent you to him, and lo, nothing worthy of death is done unto Him;*" which proves that neither before him have ye been able to substantiate any thing. "*I will therefore chastise Him, and release Him*" (Luke).

It is evident that this would not satisfy the Priests and Elders, and perhaps from knowing this, Pilate had on this occasion summoned the people together with them. But "*the multitude*" now assembled had their thoughts full of another matter, and "*crying out to him began to demand of him that he would do as he was always wont at the Feast*" (Mark). For "*at the Feast he was always wont to release one prisoner* (Matt. Mark) *to the multitude, whom they would*" (Matt.), or "*whomsoever they demanded* (Mark); *indeed he was under a necessity of releasing unto them one at the Feast*" (Luke), as a privilege granted them by the Romans; and their minds were then fully bent on one whom they desired to release, for "*they had then a notorious prisoner, named Barabbas*" (Matt.). But Pilate having now clearly perceived the nature of the case; "*for he observed that they* (*i. e. the Chief Priests,* Mark) *had*

delivered Him up from envy " (Matt., Mark) thought
of the expediency of referring the matter to the people,
which this occasion furnished him with the opportunity
of doing. He therefore came forth and said unto them,
" *Ye have a custom that I release unto you one at the
Passover* (John), *are ye willing therefore that I release
unto you the King of the Jews ?* " (Mark, John.)   It
may be observed that he keeps continually repeating
this term, " the King of the Jews," which he does as
an expression of his contempt for so unreasonable a
charge, though his tongue was governed therein by a
mysterious Providence. He then formally put the
question to the people, giving out the names of both;
" *Whom will ye that I release unto you, Barabbas ? or
Jesus who is called Christ ?* " (Matt.)

Now considering how the people had publicly received Christ on the preceding Sunday, being touched
with the gracious miracles He had wrought, especially
that of raising Lazarus to life; and how on the following days in the Temple they had " hung upon " His
most awful but not less gracious words, so that the
Chief Priests did not dare to apprehend Him : it might
have been thought that they would now have required
His release. But those who were really deeply moved
by His doctrine would have been the least loud and
prominent in such a multitude, being more in secret :
and in large bodies of men and popular assemblies good
is smothered, the bad predominant : good principle is
despised by the wicked, and the weak are ashamed of
it : moreover, on this subject of Barabbas, they were
seditiously excited, and perhaps nationally. " *The Chief
Priests* " (Matt. Mark), therefore, " *and the Elders*
(Matt.) *stirred up* " (Mark) and " *persuaded* (Matt.)
the multitude (Matt. Mark), *that they should ask for*

Barabbas (Matt.), *that he would release Barabbas unto them* (Mark), *and should destroy Jesus"* (Matt.). The circumstances might be very well accounted for by the change of impulse to which the popular voice is subject; and indeed it is a true, but sad, picture of the changes in the hearts of individuals at all times; our feelings are often such that they would join in Hosannas to-day, and to-morrow, in the time of visitation, cry out, "Crucify Him." To this our blessed Lord often alluded in His teaching, saying to these same Jews, "If ye abide in My Word, then are ye my disciples indeed."

This appeal of Pilate to the multitude is an appeal to "the many," and the many are they who walk, as Origen here observes, the broad way to destruction. The voice of the many must, it may be supposed, be in general against Christ. And here is strongly marked the difference between a popular appeal—an appeal to what is popular—and that Universal Consent which has been considered in all ages the test of truth. Such was it esteemed to be among heathen philosophers of old, and God has made it to be so in an especial manner in His Church. For by an universal consent of all parties, against their own private passions, prejudices, and wishes, Christ was declared innocent; by the false witnesses, who could prove nothing, by Judas's confession, by Pilate, by Herod, by the thief on the cross, by the conduct of the Chief Priests. At the same time, by the popular voice He is condemned to death.

It may be also an extensive maxim, that the Church will be sacrificed by worldly-minded Rulers to the popular voice, as in the case of Saul, who was perhaps a type of the Cæsars of the world, "because" he "feared the people and obeyed their voice[1]." Yet, at the same time perhaps, under a pretext of good, for

[1] 1 Sam. xv. 24. and 20.

Saul first said unto Samuel, "I have obeyed the voice of the Lord."

This privilege of releasing one at the Feast was not, as Theophylact observes, a Roman practice in itself, but a privilege which the Romans granted, in compliance with a Jewish custom. Origen mentions that this was a part of Roman policy towards their subjugated states, in order to rivet more closely their chains, and that the practice had formerly existed among the Jews. Both of these writers mention the instance of the people begging of Saul the life of Jonathan. And what does this signify but that at this great Festival, the true Passover, we, to whom death is due, are let go free? Christ is taken, we, who are guilty, like Barabbas, escape.

Pilate, after a short interval, came forward to demand a reply to his formal proposition. "*The Governor answered and said unto them, Which of the two will ye that I release unto you? But they said, Barabbas*" (Matt.). And as Pilate, either by expression or manner, suggested to them Jesus, who was probably standing bound before them, "*They all, with the whole multitude, cried out, saying, Away with this man, and release unto us Barabbas*" (Luke). Upon this "*Pilate wishing to satisfy the people*," "that is," says Theophylact, "to do their will, and not that which was pleasing to justice and to God"—wishing to satisfy the people, he "*releases Barabbas unto them*" (Mark). "*Now Barabbas*," says St. John, "*was a robber;*" and St. Luke, that "*he had been cast into prison on account of some insurrection which had happened in the city, and for murder.*" And St. Peter describes it thus, "*ye denied the Holy One and the Just, and desired a murderer to be granted unto you*[2]." And St. Mark says, that "*he was bound together with his fellow conspirators, who had committed murder in the insurrection.*" Wherein it may be further noticed, that the contrast between Barabbas and Christ is not simply in his being a murderer, preferred to the Prince of Life, but also a seditious person; one who, like Satan himself, stirs up others to crimes and death. St. Chrysostom says of him, that he was a notorious person, "notorious for many murders." And, in fact, their demanding the acquittal of a murderer is but the parallel to their requiring the death of an innocent person, as St. Ambrose observes;—for it is but the very same law of iniquity, that they which hate innocence should love crime. They rejected therefore the Prince of Heaven, and chose a robber, and a murderer, and an insurrectionist, and they received the object of their choice; so was it given them, for insurrections and murders did not fail them till the last, when their city was destroyed in the midst of murders and insurrections, which they now demanded of the Roman Governor. Ancient writers notice that Barabbas is, by interpretation, "the son of a father," and with this mysterious import our blessed Lord had said, "Ye are of your father the devil, who was a murderer from the beginning," "and the lusts of your father ye will do." "At the exhortation of the Priests," says St. Hilary, "the people chose Barabbas, which is, by interpretation, the son of a father; in which is set forth the secret of their infidelity in preferring Antichrist, the son of sin, to Christ [3]." And St. Ambrose speaks to the same effect [4].

There is another allusion that suggests itself to one, not contrary to, nor superseding this, but additional to it. As Jonathan was demanded of Saul, his father,

[3] Com. in Matt. xxxiii. 2.   [4] In Lucam, lib. xi.

by the people; so Barabbas, the son of a father, is demanded by the people of Cæsar; and Cæsar is now to them as Saul was, as being the King which they chose in preference to God. And the king of Rome is the king of that city which represents the world, and wars and murders. Of this their. king therefore they demanded the son of a father, *i. e.* Barabbas. Barabbas therefore is as the son of the ruler of this world, is as the son of their own Cæsar, their chosen king, although he be himself a Jew. For the same reasons also, and in the same manner, we must consider Barabbas as the son of their father, the devil, who is the spiritual ruler of this world. They choose therefore the son of the temporal, and the son of the spiritual ruler of this world, which lieth in wickedness, and is at enmity with God. And in all these points Barabbas may be considered as a type of Antichrist. It has been supposed that Antichrist also will be a Jew, and that he will come forth from Rome; he will doubtless be in an especial manner the son of his father the devil, and preferred before the Prince of Life.

From this time we hear no more expressions concerning Barabbas from the crowd, and therefore we conclude that Barabbas was at this time given unto them; and, receiving a murderer, they become the more bent on murder and bloodshed: but it is possible that the formal release of Barabbas might have been later. The Evangelists here introduce it, "*And Pilate decided that their request should be granted* (Luke), *and he released unto them* (Matt. Mark, Luke) *Barabbas* (Matt. Mark), *him that on account of sedition and murder had been cast into prison, whom they desired*" (Luke).

"*But Pilate, wishing to release Jesus,*" and for this purpose wishing to inspire them with shame. says Origen.

and also to mark the measure of their impiety,—"*again addressed them aloud* (Luke), *What therefore shall I do* (Matt.), *would ye that I should do* (Mark), *with Jesus who is called Christ?* (Matt.) *Him whom ye call the King of the Jews* (Mark). *They all say unto him, Let Him be crucified* (Matt.): *they again cried out, Crucify Him"* (Mark), and continued "*exclaiming, Crucify Him, crucify Him"* (Luke). Not merely requiring the release of a guilty person and a murderer, but a good man's death, and that, too, most stedfastly. After this Pilate again came forward, "*and said unto them a third time* (Luke), *Why, what evil hath He done?* (Matt. Mark, Luke.) *But they cried out the more vehemently* (Matt. Mark), *Crucify Him* (Mark); *let Him be crucified"* (Matt.). But Pilate proceeded, "*I have found no cause of death in Him"* (Luke). And then, returning to the intention he had expressed, before he had appealed to the people's choice, and they had demanded Barabbas, he repeats his former words, "*I shall therefore chastise Him and release Him"* (Luke xxiii. 16 and 22). He then proceeds to put his purpose into execution.

He had in this made two separate appeals to the people, one in offering our blessed Lord instead of Barabbas; and when they chose Barabbas, he seems to have given them a new and unusual offer of sparing Christ also. "When they asked for the robber," says St. Chrysostom, "he said, ' What then shall I do with Jesus, who is called Christ?' wishing to commit the matter to their authority, in order that from very shame and vanity they might ask Him off. For to reason with them, only rendered them the more contentious; but to commit His preservation to their humanity was the strongest means of persuasion. But even then they cried out, ' Let Him be crucified.' " The same writer says, "petition for the condemned is usually the part of the people, and concession that of the Prince : but here it is the reverse ; the Governor makes the petition, the people are rendered the more fierce."

And then arose their fearful cries. Thrice did Pilate appeal to them, and thrice did they demand His terrible death.   The whole multitude, and with one voice, and that by a threefold repetition, adding confirmation to their choice.   "It was," says Theophylact, "by this threefold voice that they might approve of the murder of Christ, which they had demanded and extorted." This, their tremendous and fierce cry, St. Cyril considers to be that roar of the lion which the Prophet speaks of: "I have given the dearly beloved of my soul into the hand of her enemies. Mine heritage is unto Me as a lion in the forest, it crieth out against Me[5]." And he thus describes this figure, which is so strongly expressive of their fierceness[6]: "It may be well to mention what the lion does in the forest. For they say that when he wishes to hunt down any creature in the woods, that this great and most terrible beast, raising himself on some promontory in the mountains, roars in a loud and horrible manner; and creates so great a shudder in those that hear it, that, unable to withstand the threatening and fearful sound, they immediately fall, whether man or any other animal, and drop to the ground at the mere voice alone of the beast; which God confirms in a manner, by His Prophet, 'the lion hath roared, who will not fear[7]?'" Thus were they, as the Psalmist says, "like a lion that is greedy of his prey;" but the lion's voice itself is feeble, indeed, to express this most terrible and hideous cry of mankind: "I have

---

[5] Jer. xii. 7, 8.   [6] Joan. lib. xii. 40.   [7] Amos iii. 8.

heard the blasphemy of the multitude; and fear is on every side, while they conspire together against Me, and take their counsel to take away My life[8]."

THE SCOURGING.

On this subject, of the scourging of our blessed Lord, there are two points which require to be mentioned. First of all, that this is not that infliction which usually preceded crucifixion, and was considered to form a part of that punishment, but independent of it, and brought out into a more distinct and separate act by greater severity. Secondly, that there appears no reason to believe that it was afterwards repeated, as some have supposed; a repetition which probably no sufferer would have been capable of sustaining. Our Lord's prophetic declaration, that the Gentiles should "scourge Him and crucify Him;" by the two expressions, of both "scourging and crucifying," seems to indicate these two separate circumstances; and that "the scourging," here alluded to, was distinct from the tortures accompanying the crucifixion, of a nature so terrible as to be thus strongly recorded with it. And St. Matthew and St. Mark mention that Pilate delivered Him up to be crucified, having first "scourged Him," using the Roman word for that punishment[9]. And it may be observed, that since Pilate had this intention, after the return from Herod, his words are not that he "found no fault," as he had said before[1], but "nothing worthy of death[2]:" indicating that he would consent to the lighter infliction. His reason might have been, that it would be unworthy of a Roman Governor to put to death without cause; but like Lysias, the chief captain, in the Acts[3], he had

[8] Ps. xxxi. 15.　[9] φραγελλώσας.　[1] Luke xxiii. 4. John xviii. 38.
[2] Luke xxiii. 15 and 22.　　　　[3] xxii. 24.

no hesitation to inflict scourging without any offence being proved or apparent. His motive was, that he thought the spectacle of so terrible an infliction as that of scourging, would move them to commiseration.

It is very clear that this is the scourging and mockery which St. John records, for it appears from this account that Pilate had not at that time determined on crucifying Him, for this the Chief Priests then demanded, and after that Pilate "sought to release Him." And although the account of the scourging in St. Matthew and St. Mark may appear to speak of a different period, yet unless we suppose that the circumstances of the mockery, the crown of thorns, and the purple robe, were all twice repeated, which seems quite incredible, we must conclude that they are describing the same occurrence as this in St. John, and that it took place as he states, before our Lord was condemned to be crucified. The account is indeed introduced in St. Matthew by the word "then," as if immediately following on His condemnation to death: but we have often occasion to show that the particle "then," in the Gospels, and especially in St. Matthew's Gospel, is not determinate of time. The account therefore is simply this, that Pilate first appeals to them to liberate our Lord as an innocent person; then, as one released at the Passover, as the accustomary boon to the people, even if not innocent; and, thirdly, as one scourged, and already sufficiently punished. And certainly, as Pilate supposed, in any ordinary case of envy and malice, so piteous a spectacle would have been sufficient to move them. But man's natural hatred of holiness is connected with an indefinable fear, and fear leads to cruelty; and doubtless evil spirits, as well as evil men, were most earnest for His death.

St. Chrysostom, Origen, Augustin, Cyril, and others,

confirm this view, that " the scourging" was a distinct act from the crucifixion. "This act of Pilate," says Augustin [4], " we must suppose, was for no other reason, but that the Jews might thus be satiated with His sufferings, and so desist from raging for His death." And again, " that His enemies might be satisfied with their mockeries, and not thirst for His blood." And Origen, in like manner, " that when they saw what the soldiers had done, they might pause a little from their passion, therefore he led Him forth thus crowned." Thus, while the unjust judge has not courage to acquit Him whom he pronounces innocent, even his compassions only serve to add to the afflictions and sorrows of Jesus Christ.

" *Then therefore,*" says the beloved disciple, that is, after he had delivered up Barabbas to their choice, " *Pilate took Jesus and scourged Him* (John). *The soldiers of the Governor took Jesus* (Matt.) *and led Him away within the hall* (Mark), *which is the Prætorium* (Matt. Mark), *and call* (Mark) *and bring together to Him* (Matt.) *the whole band* " (Matt. Mark): as is usual to an execution of such a kind.

And now they first of all strip naked His adorable Person; and this was of itself no slight suffering to His most Holy Soul, to have His most chaste and virginal Body stripped bare, as afterwards on the Cross. An infliction which is partly implied in the expression of " the shame" as well as the pain of that ignominious death; and which is of itself made a distinct subject of contemplation in Bishop Andrews's meditations on the Passion and Death of our Lord.

After this, as it is supposed, they proceed to bind

[4] In Joan. Tract. cxvi.

Him to a column; this St. Jerome and Prudentius [5]
mention, and the Ven. Bede likewise, probably from
them, as a pillar of marble. And this they did in order
that He might be more in the power of those that
scourged Him, which is said to have been with peculiar
severity, for the same reasons, whatever they might have
been, which led them to that singular refinement of
torture, the crown of thorns, and in order to satiate His
bloodthirsty enemies on whose account it was done.
"Behold," says St. Augustin [6], "the Lord is fitted for
the scourging; behold now He is scourged; the violence
of the stripes with repeated strokes hath broken His
sacred skin; the cruel lashes of the thongs cut His back.
Oh, sad sight, God lieth extended before men! and He
suffereth the punishment of a criminal, in whom no
trace of sin could be found." This terrible infliction we
may well suppose was that being baptized in blood of
which our Lord spake. And after that the putting on
and taking off the cloak from His bleeding body, as it
stuck to His wounds, is supposed to have added to
His pains.

Now the soldiers, after the example of their own Governor and of the Jews, began to mock and insult Him
for the alleged charge brought against Him, of His
being a King, and to make mock insignia of royalty.
"*After they had stripped Him*" (Matt.) for the purpose
of scourging Him, "*they clothed Him*," St. Mark says,

[5] Prudentius thus speaks of it, Enchiridion, xli.

> Here Christ stood bound, and to a pillar tied.
> Gave, like a slave, His body to the scourge;
> That venerable pillar still remains,
> And bears a holy Temple, teaching us
> That we may live in Him from scourges free.

"Ad columnam ligari." Bp. Andrews.

[6] In Serm. de Pass.

"*with purple;*" St. John says, "*they threw over Him a purple garment;*" but St. Matthew says that "*they put on Him a scarlet cloak.*" Some persons, and among them St. Ambrose, have imagined this to mean two different robes [7]. But perhaps the discrepancy may be easily reconciled by supposing that it was intended to represent the purple robe, but that the purple being an expensive colour, and not easily procurable, it would be substituted by some other colour resembling it, but perhaps less costly and sumptuous in its quality, such as scarlet, and perhaps it was some military cloak [8]. To confirm this it may be observed, that St. Matthew twice speaks of it under the word (χλαμυς) which signifies a military cloak. But on such an occasion they would never be content to inflict mockeries without pain, and if the rest of His body was covered with stripes, His head was the only part which was free from these marks of blood : so "*the soldiers* (John) when *they had platted a crown of thorns*" (Matt. Mark, John), of the large thorns of that country, "*they placed it about His head*" (Matt. John). Thus in addition to what He had already undergone, inflicting excruciating agony, as well as mockery, on His most sacred Person. Thus was He not in colour and appearance only, but in reality

[7] St. Ambr. transl. St. Matthew's chlamydem coccineam, and paraphr. St. Mark's πορφυραν, purpuream *tunicam*, as though this were the χιτων, or inner and close vest, the χλαμυς, being the outer and loose one.

[8] Yet κοκκινος and πορφυρα are often found together in Scripture about the coverings of the Tabernacle, and in 2 Sam. i. 24, and especially Lament. iv. 5, κοκκινος is used as a fine costly colour. It is the word in the LXX. Isaiah i. 18, where our translators render it "crimson." The French Test. renders both St. Matt. κοκκινον and St. Mark and St. John πορφυραν by the same word, *manteau d'écarlate.*

"in a vesture dipped in blood[9]," coming "with dyed garments from Bozrah[1];" and stained was "all His raiment[2]."   And now for a mock sceptre "*they put a reed in His right hand*" (Matt.), and then "*bowing the knee before Him* (Matt.) *they began to salute Him* (Mark), *and mocked Him, saying* (Matt.), *Hail, King of the Jews!*" (Matt. Mark, John.)   Such revilers would not continue in these insults without adding wanton injury also to indignities.   Then "*they took the reed*" (Matt). from His hand, "*and beat Him on the head*" (Matt. Mark); which being probably not a mere hollow and light reed, but as we shall have occasion to show, of a hard substance, must have inflicted exquisite pain by driving the thorns into His brow.   "*And they spit upon Him*" (Matt. Mark); and others "*beat Him with the palms of their hands*" (John); and others "*kneeled down and worshipped Him*" (Mark),—either an act of adoration which they showed to eastern Kings; or, as some think, from some intimation they had heard of His declaring Himself the Christ, and the Son of God.

Thus was our Lord crowned, and this was His Coronation-day.   The hall of judgment was His Kingly court, and these kneelers were His courtiers.   There was no part of His most adorable Person, but was marked with suffering and indignity.   His head was bleeding with the crown of thorns, and beaten with the reed; His Divine countenance, from the brightness of which Angels hide their eyes in adoration, before which the Heavens are not clean, was defiled with spitting, and bruised with blows; His back was mangled with the scourging of rude soldiers; His knees were already weak through fasting, and worn with kneeling.   His whole

---

[9] Rev. xix. 13.   [1] Isa. lxiii. 1.   [2] Isa. lxiii. 3.

Sacred Body was exposed to nakedness, and covered with the mockery of the purple robe, as before it had been with the bloody sweat. His tender neck was bruised and bowed with the weight of the Cross. His holy hands were at this time given to the mockery of the reed, and afterwards pierced and bleeding with nails. His eyes were hurt with the sight of horrid and malicious passions; His ears with dreadful words and revilings. His mouth was afterwards " dried up like a potsherd;" and His tongue cleaving unto His gums. And worse than the iron that held Him in chains, or that pierced His hands, those words that " like the piercings of a sword" enter the soul. For bodily inflictions we can estimate, but not so the pain of heart, and the wounds of a righteous soul, on beholding and hearing the deeds of the wicked. " The stroke of the whip maketh marks in the flesh; but the stroke of the tongue breaketh the bones.—The yoke thereof is a yoke of iron, and the bands thereof are bands of brass. The death thereof is an evil death, the grave were better than it [a]."

Let us dwell on this amazing scene. The Giver of life is called guilty of death: the only innocent a malefactor; the Saviour of soul and body is set aside for a murderer; the Author of liberty is fast in bonds. But surely He that suffers in this manner must have crimes upon Him which Pilate knows not of; the Jews know not of them; and the devil knows not of them; but eternal Justice in His own secret counsels hath laid on Him the iniquity of us all. His Sacred Body was all one wound for our sakes, because there is no part of our body, but which ministers to sin. Of us, His Israel, it is said, " from the sole of the foot even unto

[a] Ecclus. xxviii. 17. 20, 21.

the head there is no soundness in it; but wounds and bruises and putrifying sores [4]."   And therefore, when taking upon Himself our penalty, He says in our person, " My loins are filled with a sore disease, and there is no whole part in My body."   " My wickednesses are gone over My head, and are like a sore burden, too heavy for Me to bear [5]."   He wore that mock crown on account of our ambition ; and the thorns, of which it was made, were on account of those worldly cares in us which choke the good seed.   His ears were full of reproaches on account of our love of flattery ; His face was defiled with spitting on account of our personal vanity, which leads to so much sorrow and sin.   For the abuse of our liberty, He is bound to the pillar ; for the pollution of our hands, His are pierced with nails ; and for our feet that have gone astray, His are bleeding.   His shame and nakedness is to atone for our vain adornings.   His silent patience is to expiate our impatient murmurings and false excuses.   The lying accusations that are poured on Him are for our calumnious reproaches of each other.   And His tongue is dried up for our evil lan- guage.   For our desires to be glorified, and admired in the assemblies of men, He is brought forth by Pilate in derision and scorn, saying to the assembled multitude, " Behold the Man !"

When once, before this time, the multitude would have made Him a King, He avoided and declined it ; but now that His kingdom is to be one of this kind, He accepts it, and puts on His robe and crown, when it is to be a robe and crown of shame and pain ; and takes His sceptre when it is given Him in derision, the reed with which His holy Head was beaten.

---

[4] Isa. i. 6.   [5] Ps. xxxviii. 4.

And now if the disobedience of our members was thus heavy on Him, shall not we mortify the same? Woe to those subjects of a Crucified King, who do not remember these things; and practise their own members in self-denial, that they may thus yield them up to Him, who gave up His innocent Body for us. The early Christians, as we are told by Tertullian[6], refused to wear festive chaplets of flowers, from the memory of their Lord's crown of thorns. Shall we not, in like manner, endeavour to bear the remembrance of Him in all our members, if not in the suffering of pains, yet in the abandonment of vain pleasures? "Every day," says our good Bishop Wilson, "deny yourself some satisfaction: your *eyes* objects of mere curiosity; your *tongue* every thing that may feed vanity or vent enmity; the *palate* dainties; the *ears* flattery, and whatever corrupts the heart; the *body* ease and luxury[7]." We may add, that, in practising all these things, our yoke is made easy, because Christ's yoke was so heavy, for He bore our burden.

Our little self-denials are called bearing our cross, after the similitude of His Passion; and are said to be drinking of His Cup and being baptized with His Baptism. To suffer for Him, or with Him, is like touching the hem of His robe of blood, from which healing goeth forth: or might we not almost say, being hidden and protected under His garment? Our "sins are as scarlet," they are "red like crimson;" and scarlet and crimson is therobe which He wears, namely, our sins. He wears our sins, in order that we may wear His righteousness. He wears them red and crimson, but shall make them by His wearing white as snow; for He shall cast this aside, and

6 De Coronâ, ix.   7 Sacra Privata, Wed.

His Sacred Body shall be clothed with His own garment[1].
For this garment is that with which we clothe Him; but
His garment is that with which He will clothe us, who
are His Body; and His garment is "glistering and
white as snow, as no fuller on earth can whiten it!" For
it is said of His redeemed, that they have "made their
robes white in the blood of the Lamb." And so His
promise is,—"Though your sins be as scarlet, they
shall be as white as snow; and though they be red like
crimson, they shall be as wool."

He has put on our sins, we must put on His righteousness; we must put on Him, as He has put on us;
we must be in some measure like Him. He has put on
our sins in order to take their penalty; we must put on
His righteousness, in order to partake of His sanctification. Man himself can make no sacrifice acceptable to
God, for the only proper Sacrifice is that of Christ: but
what is required of us is obedience to God, and mercy
to man. For it is written, "Obedience is better than
sacrifice;" and "I will have mercy and not sacrifice."
In Christ sacrifice was combined with perfect obedience
to God, and perfect mercy to man. But as the thing
required in the typical and representative sacrifices was,
that they also should be entire and perfect: so of obedience and mercy in man, which are to set forth in us
that Sacrifice, it is required that they should be "perfect as God is perfect."

Not only our poor humiliations and self-denials,
but those evils that come to us by an unavoidable and
chastening Providence, are sanctified and blessed after a
likeness to His sufferings. As St. Cyril says[2], "Through
the first Adam we labour under the disease of disobe-

---

[1] Zech. iii. 4.   [2] In Joan. lib. xii.

dience and the curse attached to it; but by the Second we are enriched with the gift of obedience and the blessing attached to it." Or, as Origen still more beautifully expresses it, "The power of the Only Begotten was made a curse for us, being by nature a blessing: but since He is a blessing, He hath consumed, and dissolved, and scattered every curse." And St. Athanasius, not less so, says, "Darkness is irradiated by light, and 'the less is blessed of the greater;' so is our humanity blessed by His Godhead." Thus evil has become good to us. On account of His correction, it is good for us to be troubled, and His loving correction doth make us great. And because of His scourging, God doth scourge (μαστιγοῖ) every son whom He doth receive, and corrects him whom He loves. Mourning is a state of blessing, because of the Man of Sorrows. Blessed are the poor on account of His poverty: blessed are the meek on account of His silent patience. To love our enemies is to be the children of God, because it is according to the example of His Son. They that are persecuted may rejoice and be exceeding glad, on account of the agonies of mind He endured when persecuted. His stripes are healing to us. The nails which transfix Him on the accursed Tree, let us loose from the same. This is the King of that kingdom which the meek shall inherit. His robe, and crown, and sceptre, are not weakness, as they appear, but strong in that strength that overcometh the world. Never in Kingly robe, and Imperial crown, and Sovereign sceptre, were such glory, and such majesty, and such strength, as were in these.

But every instrument of our Lord's suffering was replete with Divine mysteries, to do Him honour in the sight of adoring Angels, and to speak the nature of His kingdom. As He had been before clothed with the

white robe of innocence, so He is now with the red
robe of blood.   For His kingdom is not only one of
innocence, but also one of suffering.   The purple robe
is not only the emblem of Royalty, but also of Martyrdom.   He is a King, and He is also a Martyr; and He
is the King of Martyrs.   His garment is also that
of victory; for when the Prophet speaks of Him as
coming, "glorious in His apparel," and "in dyed garments," it is as one victorious over His enemies, and
with garments dyed in their blood.   And what crown
could be more suitable to this our King (oh, awful mystery!) than a crown of thorns? whether it be as expressing that all earthly royalty must be a crown of thorns,
or rather as bearing Himself the curse of His people:
for it was meet that the second Adam should reap the
fruits of that which the first Adam planted; or whether
it be that He wore this Crown of Agony, as being that
crown which is most emblematic and suitable to the
King of Martyrs.   And the reed, which is His sceptre,
may denote the frailty of every earthly Kingdom: or
may speak the gentleness and meekness of His own
kingly sway, in distinction from that rod of iron; that
rod of eternal Judgment with which He shall break His
enemies in pieces on the Last Day.   All that are in His
presence do Him unwilling homage and obeisance in all
their purposes of dishonour, and already commence the
fulfilment of that prophecy.   For God had sworn it long
before[3], that to Him "every knee should bow,"—" of
things," adds St. Paul, "in Heaven, and things in earth,
and things under the earth[4]."   Yea, things under the
earth also; for it seems already in type and emblem to
set forth this latter; for when even wickedness is made

_____

[3] Isa. xlv. 23.   [4] Phil. ii. 10.

to bow before Him, and to personate mysterious prophecy, it is like spiritual Wickednesses under the earth, doing Him homage when they think not, and carrying on His Kingly and Victorious purposes. And observe that as the Jew did Him mock homage before, so does the Gentile now; for both shall acknowledge Him as their King; both already do so in mystery, for it is written, "All nations shall do Him service [5];" "All the kindreds of the nations shall worship before Him [6]." For in the Romans, as masters of the world, all nations do Him service. Herein is shown that strength of His kingdom, which the poor in spirit shall inherit,— unfailing charity, undisturbed meekness, and spotless innocence. And He is armed all over as Conqueror of the world with Divine armour, the helmet of Salvation, the sword of the Spirit, and the shield of Faith;—Salvation, in giving Himself up as a spotless Lamb for others; by the spiritual sword of invincible meekness; and by Faith, committing Himself unto Him that judgeth righteously. Thus He teaches His people together with Him to tread on serpents and scorpions, and all the power of the enemy; and so to be more than conquerors, through Him that loved them.

"These things," says Origen, "the soldiers did in mockery, but mysteries with regard to us were being performed thereby." "But we," says Jerome, "understand all these things mystically. For as Caiaphas said that one man must die for the people, knowing not what he said; so these also, whatever they did, although they did it with another mind, yet to us who believe they afforded mysteries." And St. Ambrose, with great beauty,—"With a motive therefore execrable, the Jews

[5] Ps. lxxii. 11.   [6] Ps. xxii. 27.

nevertheless, unconsciously, betray an issue fraught with
honour. Thus they pierce Him with thorns, yet it is to
crown Him ; though it is in mockery, yet they worship :
though in the heart they believe not, yet Him whom
they are killing they confess. They were without the
motives of a good deed, yet was not God without His
honour. He is saluted as a King, is crowned as ˏa
Conqueror, as God and Lord is adored⁷."

But in their explanation of different parts there is
some little variety among ancient writers. Origen considers the purple robe to signify the flesh subject to
suffering; for in purple Martyrs are celebrated. St.
Ambrose supposes two robes, and takes the purple for
the emblem of Royalty, and the scarlet of Martyrdom.
Isidorus of the purple robe says, " The robe of mockery
triumphed over all human Sovereignty, which was set
at nought thereby; but when it was worn by Christ it
procured strength and stability, advancing onward to
power that shall have no succession." St. Hilary⁸ considers all these things as emblems of our infirmities,
which Christ took on Himself in His own Body. The
scarlet robe the sufferings of His martyrs ; the thorns
the sins of the Gentiles ; the reed the weakness of the
Gentiles, which is made firm when held by Christ's
hand. And these two latter Origen had taken not very
differently ; " The crown of thorns," he says, "signified
the taking upon Him our sins, which the earth brings
forth as thorns. And the reed implied that vain and
frail sceptre, on which we all leaned before we believed,
the sceptre of the Evil one. For we trusted on the
rod of Egypt, or Babylon, or of any other Kingdom
opposed to the Kingdom of God; and He took that
reed and rod of a frail Kingdom from our hands, that

⁷ Expos. in Lucam, lib. x. 105.   ⁸ Can. xxxiii.

He might triumph over him with the wood of His Cross. And for that reed on which we leaned before, He hath given us the sceptre of a Heavenly kingdom, of which it is said, 'The sceptre of Thy kingdom is a right sceptre [9].'"

But St. Ambrose carries on the mystery of the crown of thorns to a sense still more sublime. "What else," says he, "does the crown of thorns, enwreathed on His Head, set forth, but that gift of Divine operation, whereby a triumphal Crown shall be sought for God out of sinners, which are, as it were, the thorns of the world?"

St. Athanasius enlarges with great eloquence on the same, in describing our Lord's contest with, and victory over, the devil [1]: "Since," he says, "the earth was polluted with blood; and thorns were springing up on all sides on account of the curse; and the devil having the hand-writing against us, had us in his power, and tyrannized over us: on this account, the Lord, in spoiling him of all things, when He went forth to death, clothed Himself with these, to show that His victory over death was for our salvation. He bore the blood in the scarlet robe; the thorns in the crown: the hand-writing against us in the reed, wherewith the devil had written down that charge against us. In order that, together with death, He might abolish these things, and cleanse the creation from them: and, instead of the thorns, might bestow on us the Tree of life; instead of the crime of blood, might, by His own blood, wash the earth and us all: and, instead of the curse, might hereafter bless those that are on the earth, saying, 'Blessed are the meek, for they shall inherit the earth.'"

Not in prose only, but in poetry also, do ancient

[9] Ps. xlv. 7. In Matt. Comm. 125.
[1] De Pass. et Cruce Domini.

writers love to dwell on these mystical allusions, whereby all that happened to Christ is made ours by spiritual emblem and figure. Thus Gregory Nazianzen, in the quaint language of proverbial sayings which he is recording, says,—

> "The thorny crown and purple robe He wore
> Are spoils of empire, which the Conqueror bore;
> The Cross His trophy: with the Tree of gore
> He triumphs o'er that Tree of sad delight:
> His nails there fix my sins, O bleeding sight!
> In those His outstretch'd arms He holds us all;
> For our luxurious tastes He tastes the gall.
> That thief is Adam, who in death believed;
> The wicked suffers, but is not relieved;
> The o'erchanging gloom of outer darkness speaks;
> Rent rocks are stony hearts His dying breaks;
> The risen Dead, which through the city range,
> Speak movement in the Dead and Heavenly change:
> From His pierced side two streams together flow,
> Baptism twofold, of water and of woe.
> When all-pursuing Time brings danger near,
> His Dying kills my death, and soothes my fear.
> His Rising bursts in twain my prison bars,
> And His Ascending bears me to the stars."

And not only are these things considered to have future references, but also to have been themselves prefigured. Thus Prudentius, in a remarkable passage, where he is speaking of the manifestations of God in the Old Testament, as shadowing forth and prefiguring the Incarnation of our Lord and the circumstances attending it, mentions an instance which he considers emblematic of His crown of thorns [2]:

> "As erst the Word, the true Irradiance
> Of the all-gracious Father, did assume
> A frame of frailty from the Virgin's womb,

---

[2] Apotheosis, C. xlix.

So ere His flesh-born days, in living trance,
Face to face seen in human countenance,
He talk'd with Moses; glassing things to come—
That He frail manhood's form should make His home.
E'en so when Godhead burst on Moses' glance,—
Making the unharm'd bush His burning lair,
Sharp-wounding thorns among and leafy hair,—
It mirror'd Godhead coming from the skies,
To put on limbs whereon the thorns should rise,
A thick-wrought crown our crimes had planted there,—
Our God in thorns of piercing agonies."

It does not appear that these inflictions, on the adorable Son of God, took place in the sight of His enemies, the Jews; for one would suppose that they did not enter into the hall of execution; and it is afterwards said that Pilate brought Him out to them. At all events, the chief design of this infliction was to satisfy them. But it appears unaccountable why Roman soldiers should proceed to such extremities of unprovoked cruelty, beyond what any wish to gratify the Jews or their own depraved wantonness could explain. "It is not said," St. Austin remarks, "that Pilate commanded the crown of thorns to be made;" although of course he must have permitted, and by his leading out our Lord with the crown upon Him, he seems to sanction it. But as Chrysostom says, "Pilate having set this charge on Him in derision, the soldiers thus in mockery deal with Him;" and he also thinks that this gratuitous and additional cruelty of the soldiers, without Pilate's command, was from their being bribed by the Jews. But the fact is, that almost all wickedness does, on consideration, appear unaccountable, and can, too often, be explained in no other way, but as the mystery of iniquity. Therefore the Fathers, instead of dwelling on ostensible causes, do attribute it to the conspiracy and instigation of the devil. "I think," says Origen, "the soldiers did this from the operation of those invisible 'rulers of the world, who stood up and took counsel against the Lord and His Anointed[3]:' that it would seem rather their delusion than that of men, of them who knew not in that dispensation the Wisdom of God; for if they had known it, they would not have crucified the Lord of glory[4]." St. Chrysostom speaks to the same effect. And St. Athanasius, in his very sublime Treatise "on the Passion and Cross of the Lord," describes the whole of it, throughout all its details, as the actions of the great enemy, and mankind as his subordinate agents, stirred up by him to answer his designs. Pursuing this subject he breaks out into this sublime language: "From hence we might see the devil fleeing, with all his host and Principalities and Powers; and the Lord pursuing with human arms the diabolical phalanx. For the interval was not long when He spoiled the enemy of all things. Being confounded he stirred all things against the Lord: the Jews to conspire; Pilate to condemn; the soldiers to mock Him: knowing not that He was doing this against himself. For malice is blind, and wickedness cannot see before it, and does not know that it is sharpening its hands against itself; for it is as if one took hold of a serpent by the hand, and wishing to cast it on another, is of course bitten himself; or seizing fire by the hand, and wishing to injure an enemy, does not know that he is setting fire to himself." It is very evident that, throughout, all the arts of the great enemy recoil upon his own head, and the very instruments of his malice become to the Author of our salvation the means of His fuller triumph and victory. The malice he kindled in

[3] Ps. ii. 2.   [4] 1 Cor. xi. 8. Comm. in Matt. 125.

the Jews exemplified our Lord's perfect charity; their inveterate cruelty, the perfection of His patience; their accumulated threats, His fortitude. His own arms were used against the Evil one, and by his own weapons he was conquered. For the stronger man entereth his place, and taketh from him the armour in which he trusted. Here the true David destroys the giant Goliath with his own sword. Pharaoh, by pursuing Israel, involves himself in his own destruction. The true Samson in His death overwhelms His enemies in the ruins of their own temple, while they are thinking to make Him the object of their triumphant mockery. The robe of derision and scorn becomes His garment of victory, and of empire: the reed put into His hands becomes the rod of iron, whereby He shall subdue the nations.

But yet—although the combination of evil powers was doubtless never greater nor more violent than on this day, nor the power of Christ more triumphant;—yet we cannot suppose them so far supernatural in their effects, that there was evinced any thing beyond those principles of good and evil, which are always in operation. The spirit of evil always attacks with the same arts, and always is overcome by the same means. Wickedness, in like manner, is always active; Christ, in like manner, is always overcoming in His members. For the account of these circumstances in the Book of Wisdom [s] must either be considered as strongly prophetic of Christ's sufferings, beyond what the known effects of good and evil can account for; or else it must be descriptive of the full development of the principles of good and evil, as they are known by the observations of the wise. For no one can read the account without perceiving that, whether intended or

[s] Ch. ii. 10 –22.

not, it is Christ and His enemies who are spoken of:
"He is grievous unto us even to behold; for His life
is not like other men's, His ways are of another
fashion. We are esteemed of Him as counterfeits——.
Let us see if His words be true: and let us prove
what shall happen in the end of Him. For if the just
man be the Son of God, He will help Him, and deliver
Him from the hand of His enemies. Let us examine
Him with despitefulness and torture, that we may
know His meekness, and prove His patience. Let us
condemn Him with a shameful death, for by His own
saying He shall be respected. Such things did they
imagine, and were deceived. For their own wickedness hath blinded them. As for the mysteries of God,
they knew them not."

"BEHOLD THE MAN."

After the soldiers had inflicted their severe treatment
on Christ,—" *Pilate therefore again went out*" (John)
—from the Judgment Hall to the Jews, taking Jesus
with him, in the hopes of moving His enemies by so
miserable a spectacle of suffering, so that they would
relinquish their murderous purpose,—"*and says to
them, Behold, I bring Him out to you, that ye may
know that I find no fault in Him*" (John). That is to
say, by this punishment which I have inflicted on
Him, you may perceive that I am satisfied there is no
charge against Him, which can warrant His death.
As he spake these words the soldiers were bringing
forth the object of their cruelties, bleeding with all the
signs of the maltreatment He had received at their
hands. "*Jesus, therefore*," says St. John, "*came forth,
bearing the crown of thorns and the purple robe. And
he saith unto them, Behold the Man!*" Very desirous

to mitigate them, and induce them to relent, on this occasion Pilate drops the offensive expression, "the King of the Jews," which he had been using in derision, and adopts a term that might conciliate their pity, towards one so unworthy of their envy. "If it is the King ye envy," says St. Augustin, "spare Him now, when thus debased. He saith unto them, 'Behold the Man!'" Very remarkable again and wonderful are Pilate's words, for our Lord had declared Himself God, and for that confession He was condemned to death; but Pilate brings Him forth to all the world as perfect "Man." As it were by a strange providence, he had before been even dwelling on this word. He spoke of Him as "the Man[6]," and kept repeating the term, saying, "ye have brought this Man[7]." And "but in this Man I find no fault[8]." It was the very term by which our meek Lord delighted to express His humiliations, "the Son of Man." And surely if any term could move all that was human, all that has left in it the milk of human kindness in man, it was this term, "Behold the Man!" Evil spirits might still go on to vent their hate, but on mankind such an appeal should not be in vain. What part is there of Him which has not already by ill-treatment evinced His perfect Humanity? To all the world Pilate has set Him forth in these words, "Behold the Man!"

But "*when the Chief Priests and* their *officers saw Him, they cried out, saying, Crucify* Him, *crucify* Him (John). *Pilate,*" as it were horror-struck by such inveterate inhumanity, answers with anger and impatience, "*Take ye Him, and crucify Him, for I find no fault in Him*" (John). Here the Gentiles crown Him, and bring Him forth to the Jews as their King: which

6 ὁ ἄνθρωπος. Luke xxiii. 6.   7 Luke xxiii. 14.
8 Luke xxiii. 4. 14.

seems mysteriously to set forth, in figure, what has ever since been the case in Christ's spiritual kingdom. The Gentiles bring Him forth as the King of the Jews, saying, "Behold the Man!" But the Jews indignantly reject Him. Thus on this occasion do they cast Him from them, and send Him back to the Gentiles: and God receives Him at His right hand, bidding Him there to rest, till He makes His enemies His footstool. "Thou shalt deliver Me from the strivings of the people; and Thou shalt make Me the Head of the heathen. A people whom I have not known shall serve Me. As soon as they hear of Me they shall obey Me [9]."

The Jews, now ashamed of their old charge, and of Pilate's contempt of them for it, as it had been shown to be so futile, and yet not willing to appear as if they had no charge at all, fall back on their own previous condemnation, which was not one suitable to be brought before a heathen Governor, for thereby they made him the judge in their own sacred matters, instead of the Word of God. "*They answered, We have a Law, and by our Law He ought to die, because He hath made Himself the Son of God*" (John). Here again we cannot but observe a Divine signification in the words of the Jews, far beyond any thing of which they were themselves conscious. "We have a Law, and by our Law He ought to die;" or He needs must die, "because He made Himself the Son of God." The words were certainly true that He had made Himself the Son of God. And if He was not the Son of God, then, indeed, He ought to die, for being guilty of blasphemy. But if He be indeed the Son of God, as He has shown Himself to be by all His miracles of mercy; then, indeed, according to their Law, He needs must die: for the whole of

[9] Ps. xviii. 43, 45.

their Law is nothing else but a testimony to the Son of God, and that He must needs die. It was the wickedness of the High Priest that led him to say that Christ must die for that nation; and it is now their own wickedness that leads the Keepers and Expounders of the Law to testify, that, according to that Law, He must die. But nevertheless it was in both cases a great truth of God. Nor is it contrary to the analogy of Scripture, to consider evil men and evil things to be thus replete with prophecy, and witnesses of God. We have dwelt upon this throughout this history, wherein we have seen that Caiaphas speaks prophecy, and the false witnesses, and Herod in his mockery, and Pilate and his soldiers by word and action, bear testimony and give utterance to the truths of God. It is in the same way observable throughout the Holy Scriptures, that not good things only (for what is good among mankind when compared with Him?) but evil things also and evil persons are made resplendent with the light of His glories. So the unjust judge is made to represent God's graciousness: the unfriendly man in bed, His long-suffering: the dishonest steward, the wisdom of His elect: Samson and saints of God, in their sins (as even David in his sin, it has been supposed [1]), typify the history of Christ, and His righteousness. All things speak of Him; hardness of heart and blindness of eyes are ever said to indicate the signs of His presence. Evil spirits are made to bear testimony to Him; they bear witness to His Almighty Power; they bear witness to Him as the Holy One of God, and as the Judge, Whose day is coming. Thus it is that the

---

[1] Apologia David Altera, ascribed to St. Ambrose.

R

prince of this world cometh, and by all his agents shall bear witness, that he finds nothing in Him.

Thus shall it be at the last, that Antichrist himself shall bear witness to His truth, and be prophetic of His coming: evil as well as good, darkness as well as light shall do Him honour; not only "day to day," but "night" also "to night certifieth knowledge."   And as it shall be so at the last, so also was it in the beginning; for thus the lie of the devil, by which he deceived our first parents, was made by the Almighty's marvellous mercy a true prophecy, by which the purpose of the devil was frustrated. For it has been well observed, man was indeed made thereby to "know good and evil," his own evil in the overflowings of ungodliness, and the goodness of God in Christ crucified. Why, therefore, may not the Jews be witnesses of God, and say more than they thought, when they said, "By our Law He ought to die, because He made Himself the Son of God?"

THE FEARS OF PILATE.

" *When, therefore, Pilate heard this saying, he was the more afraid*" (John). The expression, that "he was the more afraid," seems to imply that Pilate had been afraid before, and his whole conduct seems to indicate an unaccountable reluctance and apprehension. And as this fear is now increasing, from hearing that He had declared Himself the Son of God, this indicates that there was something about our Lord's person and conduct which filled him with some sense of awe, notwithstanding his treatment of Him. Although the name of "the Son of God" could not be to a heathen what it was to a Jew; yet an indefinable consciousness of Deity, connected with a human person, always prevailed among men, and especially at this time. Heathenism derived, in all ages, a prevailing complexion from some rays of scattered light, which fell on it from the true Religion. When the Israelites were enjoined victims of a typical or sacrificial character, the Egyptians were making such animals the objects of their worship. And now that the Jews were expecting their Messiah, the true Immanuel, the Romans were deifying their emperors, and speaking of them as gods, come down to sojourn among mankind. It is evident that Pilate had not lost the natural fear of God. And the many instances of heathens, who came first into the Kingdom of Heaven, are proofs that this fear was capable of being improved into the acknowledgment of Jesus Christ, the Son of God manifest in the flesh. Whatever the character of Pilate may have been subsequently, he does not appear at this time so hardened and lost as these Jews. To discern the Godhead of Jesus Christ did not depend on any definite instruction or previous expectation, but entirely on the state of the heart; on the eye and ear of the heart. For this reason He was more acknowledged by heathens than by Jews, as being more conscious of sin. The Gentiles, moreover, were not in this case blinded by prejudice against conviction. In every case this blindness arose from sinful passion, covetousness, envy, pride, or fear, which clouded or destroyed the power of discerning God. Add to which, that the sensation among the Jewish nation, and especially the chief rulers in it, against one so apparently helpless, and with no charge capable of being adduced against Him, was an indication of some great and hidden strength, which must have impressed the Governor with awe. Indeed, hatred of goodness is an unconscious confession of its secret power; for the fear of it exceeds all external indications of that power.

On hearing this, Pilate "*again went into the Judgment Hall*," taking Jesus with him apart from the Jews, "*and saith unto Him, Whence art Thou?*" (John) or where do you really come from; not What hast Thou done? as before, but "Whence art Thou?" For he seems convinced that He had done nothing amiss, but from whence was He? He had said before to Pilate that His kingdom was "not from hence;" and as he connected this former declaration of our Lord's with what the Jews now said, and considered His dreadful and Divine silence and deportment, Pilate's heart was opened to religious awe, and he was alarmed. It was a question of awe, and he had taken Him aside to ask Him. But how did our Lord answer him this question? we read, "*but Jesus gave him no answer*" (John).

This is now the fifth time when He observed that mysterious and remarkable silence;—before the Chief Priest, before the Sanhedrim, before Herod, and twice before Pilate. Whenever there was an opportunity to instruct others or do them any good, our Lord seems to have spoken according to the thoughts of their heart; but whenever it was merely for Himself and His own release, "as the lamb before his shearers is dumb, so He opened not His mouth[2]." "When He answered not," says Augustin, "He was silent as the sheep: when He answered, He taught as the Shepherd[3]." Without attempting to explain any thing so inscrutable as our Lord's conduct, which it is for us to adore in self-abasement, not to scrutinize; yet one cannot but notice here

---

[2] Isa. liii. 7.　　　　[3] In Joan. Evan. cxvi. 5.

that this silence is a part of that remarkable reserve, which He always maintained respecting Himself, and which we are told was the fulfilment of the expression concerning Him, that He should "not cry nor lift up His voice in the streets;"—and this in order that He might "not quench the smoking flax, nor break the bruised reed." On this occasion it is evident, that His full reply, to the question of Pilate, could be nothing less than an open confession of His infinite power and Godhead.

But still it might have been expected, that to a request of Pilate, in itself so good, our Lord would have vouchsafed a reply. But perhaps this unjust judge was not worthy of or meet for it: doubtless our Lord's silence, as well as His words, was weighed out in infinite wisdom. This silence may have been owing to Pilate's previous neglect of Christ's teaching, and of the truth. For our Lord's last words to him had been "He that is of the truth heareth My words;" but Pilate went away and gave no heed to it; he had no love for the truth, and therefore he hears not Christ's words. For, as St. Chrysostom well says, "He that had heard,—'for this cause I was born, and for this came I into the world, that I might bear witness,' and 'My kingdom is not from hence,' when he ought to have resisted and delivered Him, did not do this, but followed the violence of the Jews. For this reason he received no answer, for all his questions were but vain and idle." It may be, that Pilate had had his time of trial, and that it was now past, and the things belonging unto his peace were hid from his eyes. If Christ speaks, He can speak nothing but what is supremely good, but before the wicked He is silent. "The silence of the truth," says Quesnel, "is one of the most terrible punishments of the Divine justice in this world." This His silence may also express, by a mystery and figure, God's providence in the world; for nothing is so awful as this silence of God, whereby He at present leaves things to go on without notice. The expression, "I was even as a deaf man, and heard not," and "in whose mouth are no reproofs," may serve to describe the quiet tenor of His moral government, so awful in its silence; and in distinction from which, it is said of His final coming, "God shall come, and shall not keep silence." But even our Lord's justice towards Him is tempered with mercy, and He who bore with Judas, even to the last, will not shut the door against Pilate; for doubtless the door would be shut against him, and he would die in his sins, if he believes not as our Lord said,—"that I am He." Moreover, we may perceive, that our Lord's silence had affected him more than His words; and therefore His silence may not only have expressed His own submission to death, but may have been the greatest mercy towards Pilate. We have here two distinct trials of Pilate; one when He perceived Him to be innocent, and yet, partly from fear of the Jews, and partly from motives of private interest, sends Him to Herod, and has not courage to acquit Him. And another, at this time, when apprehending Him to be not only innocent, but also Divine; yet, for fear of Cæsar, he condemns Him, at the same time washing his hands! Of this great power of our Lord's silence, St. Athanasius says [4], "Great things and truly wonderful did the Saviour do; by silence He worked; and by not defending Himself He caused the judge to confess the conspiracy; and that he himself was influenced more by the

---

[4] De Passione et Cruce Domini.

multitude than by justice. For if He had defended Himself, He might have been suspected of fear of death; but in His silence His firmness and fortitude are cause of wonder. And for Pilate to defend Him under these circumstances, was nothing else than to confess that He who was being judged was God. Being judged by Pilate He regardeth it not; to his wife He prophesied distinctly: that by His silence He might impress him with awe at His fortitude; by His prophesying he might know that he was judging not a man, but God. For the judge feared Him that was judged. And by this fear he himself was rather judged; and in the act of judging was awe-struck at the Lord, and therefore washed his hands." To all this it may be added, that probably the guilt of Pilate would have been greatly increased, if not irreparable, if our Lord had confessed to him from whence He came.

But as the Jews had been angry at the sign being withheld from them, and said, in their impatience, "How long dost Thou make us to doubt? If Thou be the Christ, tell us plainly;" so Pilate, seeing our Lord a criminal in his hands, becomes indignant, and a little surprised, that He should observe the same silence towards him that He had done towards the Jews: *"Then saith Pilate unto Him, Speakest Thou not unto me? Knowest Thou not that I have power to crucify Thee, and have power to release Thee?"* (John.) "And in these words," as St. Chrysostom observes, "Pilate confesses his own guilt, and that he was without excuse; for he has the power to crucify or to absolve." To him, therefore, it might be said, "Out of thine own mouth will I judge thee."

"Jesus answered, Thou couldest have no power at all against Me, except it were given thee from above: there-

fore he that delivered Me unto thee hath the greater sin"
(John).   Here our Lord speaks before His judge with
Divine authority and majesty: both as a Heavenly
Teacher, informing him from whence all power flows;
and as the Judge of all men, marking the degrees of
guilt in all concerned.   And the reason why our blessed
Lord now speaks may be this, that when He was Himself slandered, He bears it in silent submission to death:
but when Pilate's arrogant words seem to claim to himself that power which belongs to God only, then piety
requires that He should speak.   There are different
modes in which this difficult passage may be understood.

First, it might signify,—'All these things are done
by the Divine permission;—this licence you have is by
God's permission.   But do not think on that account
you are guiltless: on the contrary, this it is that increases the sin of Judas in betraying Me, and afterwards
that of the Jewish nation in delivering Me to thee.   For
this licence given to the wicked over an innocent person
is their own judicial punishment.'   "This is your hour,"
our Lord had said to the Jews, "and the power of darkness."   "That thou doest, do quickly," said He to
Judas: by that permission conveying His most fearful
warning.   In like manner He said, "It must needs be
that offences come," but on that account, "Woe to him
by whom the offence cometh:" and "The Son of Man
goeth, as it is written of Him, but woe to that man
by whom the Son of Man is betrayed."   So on this
occasion they might have been restrained by the Almighty; but His withholding Hand is removed, He
gives them up to a full licence: this it is that aggravates
their guilt: this is the Divine permission and control
which our Lord so often pointed out to His disciples,
adducing the prophecies as a proof.   For this licence

of God is the comfort of the good; the sorest vengeance on the wicked.

Or, secondly, it may be explained thus: 'Thou couldest have no power at all against Me, unless it were a Divinely delegated power, which makes the sin of those who deliver Me to thee greater than it otherwise would have been, as abusing so sacred a trust; for it is written, "By Me kings reign, and princes decree justice [5]."' They who convert to their own evil purposes that authority which God hath ordained, and commit their crimes under the shadow and sanction of law, are the worse on that account. For this authority of God is intended for the protection of the innocent.

Thirdly, St. Augustin,—who considers that our Lord did in these words declare also, that which He has taught by His Apostle, that "the powers that be are ordained of God [6]:"—yet explains it rather differently from the last method. He seems to take it to mean that he who commits an innocent person to death from envy, has greater sin than he to whom God has given power under the authority of another, so as to put him to death from fear. For God had given Pilate power under Cæsar, and he was so situated as not to be free; so that the guilt more particularly lay upon the Jews, inasmuch as they were acting more spontaneously. For to act from malice and wantonness is worse than to act from fear, and under a sort of compulsion and constraint.

Another and fourth mode of interpreting it is, to suppose that it contained a mysterious allusion to our Lord's Divinity, as if He had said, 'I am not a mere man, that you as judge should have any natural authority over Me; the power now given you is by a peculiar permis-

---

[5] Prov. viii. 15.   [6] Rom. xiii. 1.

sion from on high. This it is that aggravates and makes so fearful the sin of Judas, before whom I was manifested as God, and whose guilt is therefore irremediable: and which also makes much greater the guilt of the Jews, who have come very near to the verge of that sin.' Here our blessed Lord darkly alludes to Pilate's eager and dread question, "Whence art Thou?" and hence the alarm which Pilate afterwards expressed. This last explanation the more strongly recommends itself to our adoption; as we expect some intimation at this time, however mysterious, of our Lord's secret dignity concerning which Pilate had asked. Pilate asks the Lord whence He is: and He answers not: but replies to him with the majesty and authority of God, and as Judge of all, explaining to him, that it was by a peculiar dispensation of God that Pilate stood before Him as His judge.

The various modes of understanding the passage depend on the meaning of the terms, "from above," and "the greater sin:" whether the comparison refers to Pilate or to the Jews themselves; whether it means that the circumstance rendered their sin worse than that of the Gentile, or worse than it would otherwise have been. Each clause of the sentence would be of itself perfectly intelligible, but the difficulty is in understanding the connexion of the two clauses with each other. For otherwise it would be easy to perceive that Pilate had no power, but what was given him from God; and that they who betrayed Him, or gave Him into his hands, were the more guilty. St. Cyril of Alexandria explains the clauses separately without the connexion. The latter he explains thus,—"He ascribes greater sin to him by whom He was delivered up to Pilate; and of course deservedly, for he was the origin of, and door to, the impiety against Him. But the judge is shown to be the minister of the crimes of others, and partakes of the wickedness of the Jews by his unreasonable cowardice. But who is this who delivers Him up, and to whom the chief criminality attaches ? I suppose that most venal disciple : and next to him the chiefs of the Jews and the people. But in laying down the greater measure of guilt, He had not left the head of Pilate altogether free."

One thing we may, I think, conclude, that there must be some great significancy in these words of our Lord ; and that the difficulty which we find in the interpretation of them was intended by Him, to arrest more particularly our consideration, and to lead us to search for the truth contained in them. In whatever way we understand them, they draw our attention to, and strongly mark, one circumstance, viz. the aggravated nature of the sin of the Jews. This passage appears to be the express testimony of our Lord, and His declaration respecting this circumstance, which all things tend so strongly to point out, as we shall see hereafter.

THE APPEAL TO CÆSAR THREATENED.

After our Lord had this conversation with Pilate, "*From thenceforth*," says the beloved disciple,—from that time, or from that circumstance, or on that account, as St. Augustin and some persons take it,—"*Pilate sought to release Him*." It does not plainly appear what the whole of our Lord's conversation with Pilate had been, nor what the circumstance was that now weighed so strongly on the Roman governor, unless it was that declaration of our Lord's which we have been considering, and that Pilate had been thereby conscience-stricken, and was desirous to avoid the greater guilt, as St. Austin says, of slaying an innocent man delivered to him. The attention he seemed inclined to bestow, when our Lord spoke of His heavenly Kingdom and of Truth,—and the increase of his fear when he found the Jewish charge of Christ making Himself " the Son of God,"—and his subsequent inquiry,—all indicate a mind in some degree moved ; and a little more would awaken his conscience. This is another instance of our Lord's unceasing watchfulness to do good to every one with whom He had any intercourse. But it is observable that although, before this expression of the Evangelist, we read so much of Pilate's seeking to release the Lord, yet nothing is mentioned of such attempts after this time, when it appears, from this account of St. John, that the Governor was more thoroughly and decidedly bent to release Him. Nor is there any thing stated of what space of time elapsed, while Pilate was thus determined, and perhaps more openly and avowedly endeavouring to accomplish it. But when the conscience is moved, and purposes of good are formed, it is the usual mode of God's moral Providence to allow temptations of self-interest or fear to occur, in order to try the sincerity of such resolutions. So it was now. For the Jews, seeing that he was thus more openly determined to befriend his prisoner, forgot their national prejudices, and began to alarm him with threats of an appeal to the Roman emperor,—" *But the Jews cried out, saying, If thou let this man go,*"—from which it would appear that he was now on the very point of letting Him go,—if thou let this man go, " *thou art not Cæsar's friend ; whosoever maketh himself a King speaketh against Cæsar*" (John). The terrors of the emperor, and especially of one so suspicious and cruel as Tiberius, overcame the better scruples of Pilate, having no faith in Christ's power which could have supported him in this temptation. So that he is constrained to act on a charge, which appeared to him so unreasonable, as to be a subject throughout of his contempt and derision. For instead of the evidence which should support such a charge, he had the very opposite before him. " What are the demonstrations of it?" says St. Chrysostom; "where is the purple, the diadem, the chariot, the soldiers? Has He not gone about accompanied with twelve disciples, consorting with all things the most mean, livelihood, and dress, and habitation?" But those who fear men, rather than God, are governed by a straw, by a reed for a sceptre. The subsequent fate of Pilate, who was deposed by the Roman emperor on a complaint of the Jews, has been already noticed as one of the instances where the wicked are punished by the very objects which they endeavour to avoid, and by those very instruments which they make use of to do so. This occurs so generally, that it seems to indicate a rule or principle in God's moral Government. The wicked are punished by their own wickedness: all ways of seeking for strength, and peace, and protection, excepting in God, are the ways that bear us furthest from them. This we see in our very moral nature, and in the very history of the soul of man, when it makes any thing else its choice but God alone: it is not only punished thereby, but the very object which it wishes to avoid becomes its punishment.

" *When Pilate therefore heard that saying,*" which threatened an appeal to Cæsar, " *he brought Jesus forth, and sat down on the judgment seat, in a place that is called the Pavement, but in the Hebrew,*" that is to say, in the Syriac or Chaldee, then spoken, " *Gabbatha*" (John). "A lofty place," says Bede, "formed of paving-stones, a raised and dignified station, on which the judge sat." It was now, when he was on the judgment seat, that another unforeseen check, from another quarter, was by Divine Providence sent as a warning in the way of Pilate: for St. Matthew says, " *When he was set down on the judgment seat, his wife sent unto him, saying, Have thou nothing to do with that just Man, for I have suffered many things this day in a dream because of Him.*" It has been supposed that the things which Pilate's wife saw in a dream were some intimations of the awful visitations which afterwards overtook her husband; but there is no traditional authority for this opinion: it was probably something of a higher and more mysterious nature than Pilate's own personal afflictions. It is in vain to inquire what the miraculous circumstance may have been, but it is wonderful to observe what various ways Christ makes use of, to teach all men according to their condition: the Roman Governor He instructs by His own fearlessness of death, and by His silence: and now by His wife, perhaps the only quarter from which his better feelings were accessible. In like manner, in former times, He taught the Philistines through their own prophets [7]; Chaldean astrologers He leads by a star; the idolatrous Athenians He instructs from the " unknown God [8] " of their own superstition: the sick He teaches by healing, the multitude by miracles and parables, His disciples by Heavenly doctrine, the Scribes and Pharisees by the Scriptures of the Old Testament, and now a Roman lady, who had no access to these modes of instruction, by a dream. For the Heathens had always supposed, what Holy Writ also leads us to believe, that there is in sleep some nearer connexion and communication with the unseen world; so that it became a proverb in the

[7] 1 Sam. vi. 2.   [8] Acts xvii. 23.

time of Homer, that "a dream is from Jove." The onsciousness of this is so stamped on our nature, that the most touching Tragedies, in all times, have made their appeal to our deeper feelings by the introduction of dreams. Perhaps this, and other incidents, may indicate the intervention of good spirits to save Christ, when the powers of darkness were allowed to prevail: for it cannot be supposed, as some have thought, the intervention of Satan to avert the redemption of mankind.

St. Chrysostom says of the occurrence, "Observe also another circumstance, which was enough to have recalled them all, for after these matters themselves were investigated, the dream also was of no little weight. And what is the reason why he did not himself see it? Either because she was more worthy, or that if he had seen it, it would not have been so much believed, or that he would not have declared it. On this account it is ordered that his wife should see the vision, so that it should become notorious to all. And she not only sees the vision, but suffers many things, that on account of his wife's commiseration, he might be the more restrained from the murder."

It is not very clear whether it was at this period in the narrative, or earlier in the morning, that the intelligence came to the Governor from his wife. One might have been otherwise disposed to think it was earlier in the morning; but St. John states that this was the time when he "sat down on the judgment seat;" and St. Matthew, that he was "set down on the judgment seat," when his wife sent to him. It is indeed at an earlier period in the narrative that St. Matthew mentions the circumstance, yet that is no clue to the definite time, as it is usual with St. Matthew to speak of things out of the order of time, on account of the mention of something leading to it: and accordingly, when he speaks of the "envy" of the Jews, as the circumstance which Pilate then noticed as a reason for his appeal to the people, he adds another cause of Pilate's wishing to release Him, a message of this extraordinary nature from his wife, though not occurring precisely at that time. To which it may be added that his wife says, "this day," as if the day were already in advance when she sends: and perhaps her attention would be more drawn to what was going on, as the commotion thickened through Jerusalem. Add to which Pilate was probably for a considerable time on the judgment seat.

COMPUTATION OF TIME.

" *And it was the preparation,*" says St. John, "*of the Passover* " (John). The day that now had commenced was the day preparatory to the great Sabbath of the Passover; and it was in fact, in the counsels of God, that great day which preceded the great Sabbath of the great and true Passover; during which our Lord rested in the grave. This day of preparation may be well supposed to set forth in type the whole of our Christian state, which is as it were the season and day of Christ crucified, the time of our being crucified together with Him, and preparatory to the great Heavenly and eternal Sabbath. The day of our Lord's crucifixion is the time for our crucifixion, for we must be crucified together with Him; and this life is our day of preparation, our day of preparing for the great passover, our passing over into the kingdom of Heaven, and unto "the supper of the Lamb."

"This therefore was the awful and momentous day,

which now commenced, and it was, the Evangelist adds
"*about the sixth hour*" (John), that is to say, about six
o'clock in the morning. For the most satisfactory mode
of arranging the points of time mentioned by the Evangelists, appears to be that of Dr. Townson, according to
which St. John's mode of reckoning the hours of the
day appears to be the same as our own; and is reasonably concluded to be the Asiatic, as he himself was a
Bishop in Asia when he wrote; and his Gospel has been
supposed to have been written at the request of the
Ephesians, and therefore more particularly addressed to
the Churches in Asia, so that he would naturally adopt
that computation of time which they would best understand. But the other three Evangelists appear to use
the Jewish and Roman computation of the hours. Thus,
they all three speak of the time when the sun was darkened, that is to say, twelve o'clock at mid-day, as the
sixth hour. And thus St. Mark mentions that at the
third hour, that is to say, at nine o'clock, according to
this computation, our Lord was Crucified.

The various periods of time, therefore, that mark
this eventful day are the following. At the watch
of the night, called the cock-crowing, our Lord was
denied by St. Peter. In the morning ($\pi\rho\omega\ddot{\iota}$), that is
between three and six, the Council met and delivered
Him to Pilate, and at the time of their delivering Him
up to Pilate, St. John himself states, *it was the morning*
($\pi\rho\omega\dot{\iota}a$, v. 28). And at six o'clock Pilate sat on the
judgment seat. Between this time and nine o'clock,
the condemnation of our Lord took place; and perhaps
the case of the two thieves and that of others may
have been transacted, while Pilate was on the judgment
seat, and other things preparatory to such executions.

Then ensued also the washing of Pilate's hands, the long and slow procession to Mount Calvary, and probably other circumstances which are not recorded. And at nine o'clock, the time of the morning Sacrifice, our Lord was put on the Cross. At twelve o'clock He raised the bitter cry, and the sun was darkened till three o'clock in the afternoon. And a little after three o'clock our Lord expired, at the time of the daily evening Sacrifice, and of the Paschal Lamb being slain, which was between the two evenings [9] of this day; that is to say, between three o'clock and the rising of the stars, or the setting of the sun. As if nature itself, answering to the Scriptural types, represented our Lord, the Sun of righteousness, disappearing from our sight, and the Church and His saints, or the moon and the stars, continuing to give light, the light which they derived from Him, while He is removed from human sight.

Nothing in the Gospels is without a lively interest and importance; and if this mode of computing the time be correct, the change in St. John from that of the older Jewish and Roman mode of computation, and which is that of the other three Evangelists, is curious. The Jews therefore and the Romans,—the older dispensations, and the nations at large, commenced their day in the evening, and had done so from the Creation, when "the evening and the morning" formed the day [10]. And thus night precedes day; travail precedes birth; sorrow precedes joy; darkness precedes light; earth precedes Heaven. But the Evangelist who saw the Apocalypse, who is the prophet of Christ's next Coming, and who terminates the Bible with the words that He shall come quickly; he, contrary to the older custom of his own

[9] See Exod. xii. 6, marg. reading.   [10] Gen. i.

country, adopted another reckoning, beginning at midnight; and in like manner we also ourselves begin
at midnight. For at midnight Christ arose from the
dead; at midnight we expect, and the early Christians
expected, His next coming, the coming in of " the new
heavens and the new earth." We begin at midnight,
for " the darkness is past, the true light now shineth."
The time of the Jews, *i. e.* their mode of computation,
was changed as they came out of Egypt, and that
period was made to them the beginning of months, the
commencement of the Year [11]; so our Day is changed,
when we are brought out of Egyptian bondage by
Christ's Resurrection, the beginning of our Day is
when Christ rises from the grave, the Sun of righteousness. For the darkness is already passing away, the
Kingdom of light is already begun, and the twilight of
the eternal Morning is already shining.

It appears therefore to have been six o'clock of our
time, when the Governor sat on the judgment seat; nor
was so early an hour unusual for such proceedings in
those times. Josephus states that it was at daybreak
that Herod sat arrayed in royal apparel on the judgment
seat, as is described in the Acts of the Apostles, when
he was struck by the Angel [12]. This arrangement indeed leaves a considerable space of time before the
Crucifixion, that of three hours, but such as may be
easily accounted for. It seems not unlikely, that a
good deal might have taken place at this period, while
Pilate was on the judgment seat, which would account
for the space of time allotted to it. For St. John
mentions just before, that " from that time he sought
to release Him," as if his efforts to do so were now

[11] Exod. xii. 2.   [12] Ch. xii. 2.

more decisive. St. Matthew also mentions the tumult being increased before he gave way, though he does not give the particular account of it. " Oftentimes," says St. Augustin, "Pilate treated with the Jews, wishing to release Jesus, which Matthew records in very few words, by saying, ' Pilate therefore when he saw that he prevailed nothing, but that rather a tumult was made;' which he would not have said, unless he had endeavoured much, although he leaves in silence how often he attempted to deliver Him from their fury [1]."

NO KING BUT CÆSAR.

Pilate therefore was now on the judgment seat, but had not passed the sentence; and Jesus was standing before him and all the people, as the prisoner, with His crown of thorns and His purple robe. Pilate " *saith unto the Jews, Behold your King! But they cried out, Away with Him, away with Him, crucify Him! Pilate saith unto them, Shall I crucify your King?*" (John.) with a mixture of scorn and indignation which he could not repress at the demand, and being now the more irritated as he had not courage to resist it. But the " *Chief Priests*" having found out the mode of alarming him, and losing all consideration of their own prejudices in their present exasperation, cried out, and *answered, We have no King but Cæsar*" (John). And the Almighty has taken them at their demand, as He usually does the wicked, giving them ordinarily in His providence riches, or honour, or whatever else their hearts are set upon in preference to Himself, in order that they might find their punishment therein. As before in the days of Samuel, when rejecting the

[1] De Consens. Evang.

government of God they demanded a King, God gave them a King in His anger, even so now. Their conduct now was indeed but the consummation of that their ancient sin, and the judgments that have followed upon it have been the fulfilment of Samuel's solemn forewarnings[2]. For from that time they have had Cæsar for their King, until he utterly destroyed their city; and ever since, to this day, they have lost the government of God, and the Cæsars of the world rule over them with a rod of iron. They "have no King but Cæsar." They would not receive the Prince of Peace, riding on an ass in His gentle Coming; when the "babes" sung of His Advent in the Temple; and the Prophet bade them rejoice, saying, "Rejoice greatly, thou daughter of Sion, behold, thy King cometh!" Therefore in great mourning, they shall receive their own chosen Cæsar, coming with his army and unparalleled destruction. As Moses had forewarned them, that if they would not serve God with "joyfulness and with gladness of heart," they should "serve their enemies which the Lord should send against them, in hunger and in thirst and in nakedness, and in want of all things: that He should put a yoke of iron upon their neck until He had destroyed them[3]." And that prophecy of Jeremiah, which doubtless had its fulfilment on many previous occasions, when they preferred inferior things to God, had its higher fulfilment in their fuller development of the same temper. "Be astonished, O ye heavens, at this, and be horribly afraid: be ye very desolate, saith the Lord. For my people have committed two evils; they have forsaken Me, the fountain of living waters, and hewed them

---

[2] 1 Sam. viii. 9.   [3] Deut. xxviii. 47, 48.

out cisterns, broken cisterns that can hold no water [4]." The invisible and blessed Theocracy of God they have rejected, and chosen for themselves Saul and Cæsar. Every thing that could have been done to prevent them, by warning and command, had been done in great mercy; and looking forward, as we may well suppose, to this very occasion, the Lord [5] had enjoined them, that, if they took for themselves a King, that King must not be "a stranger, but one of their brethren," and such a one as would "not multiply to himself horses," like the Roman.

PILATE WASHING HIS HANDS.

It was probably of this time that St. Luke speaks, when he says, "*And they were instant with loud voices requiring that He should be crucified. And the voices of them and of the Chief Priests prevailed. And Pilate,*" seeing the uproar that was made, and secretly alarmed at the notion of an appeal to Cæsar, "*gave sentence that it should be as they required*" (Luke). But it was now, after he had ascended the tribunal; or just before he had done so and passed sentence, that Pilate, on thus yielding, adopted that significant and striking action which St. Matthew records; and which he used perhaps in imitation of the practice of the Jews before they entered the Temple. "*Pilate therefore, when he saw that he prevailed nothing, but that rather a tumult was made, having taken water, washed his hands before the multitude, saying, I am guiltless of the blood of this just person. See ye to it*" (Matt.). A very extraordinary declaration for a judge to have made, and showing strongly the alarm of his conscience. "*Then answered all the people and said, His blood be*

[4] Jer. ii. 12, 13.　　　　　[5] Deut. xvii. 15.

on us, and on our children" (Matt.). So wonderfully was the Divine hand of awful judgment already showing itself in their most wilful expressions of wickedness; and so very mysteriously and awfully does this, and all such circumstances, bear on those numerous expressions of Holy Scripture, wherein God speaks of Himself as judicially present in the infatuation of the wicked, if in godly fear and reverence we may venture so to speak. Thus, when they sin most wilfully, their words are mysteriously indicative of their own condemnation; and they are judged out of their own mouth. Thus do they fulfil the sentence of the Psalmist [6]; " Let the mischief of their own lips fall upon the head of them that compass me about."

The action itself of Pilate was of a Jewish character, as speaking by action and sign, according to the Law: " It was not," says Origen, " according to any Roman practice, but of a Jewish character, whereby He might testify to Christ's innocence not by word only, but by deed also, and to appease them, if they would relent, if not, to condemn them. But they, not caring to be cleansed from that blood, took it upon them [7]." But what is most extraordinary is, that, like every other transaction on this occasion, he is, as it were, fulfilling, though unconsciously, the Divine word; for we can scarcely conceive but that this mysterious scene was contemplated in that Book of Moses [8]. " All the elders of that city shall wash their hands over the heifer;—and they shall answer and say, Our hands have not shed this blood, neither have our eyes seen it. Be merciful, O Lord, unto Thy people Israel, whom Thou hast redeemed, and lay not innocent blood

---

[6] Ps. cxl. 9.   [7] In Matt. Comment. 124.   [8] Deut. xxi. 6. 9.

unto Thy people of Israel's charge. And the blood shall be forgiven them. So shalt thou put away the guilt of innocent blood from among you." The Jews not only did not do this, but Pilate does it in their presence, and they do the opposite. The very command gives Divine force to both actions. The human motive in Pilate for the adoption of this strange action may have been that his conduct might be perfectly understood by all the persons of mixed languages, with whom he had to deal. And probably the "pavement" where he now stood was an open public place, in distinction from the prætorium, where he had examined our Lord; for Pilate, and our Lord Himself, seem in this place to be before all the people; as Herod was, when he sat on the judgment seat [1] in his royal robes, and made an oration to the assembled multitude in an open place;—"and the people gave a shout."

By this action the judge pronounced his own guilt, with a strange expression of remorse in the very act of crime. The numerous indications of warning from without, and these indications of warning from within, are not unlike those which Judas received; warnings, which, we may conclude, will come forth as witnesses on the last Day. In vain will he wash his hands in water, while he takes no heed to wash them in innocency; a circumstance which our own poet [2] has very forcibly pourtrayed, by representing Pilate as ever repeating that vain action of washing his hands in that place where there is no further room for repentance. However, the whole action would be well understood, merely as interpreted by that custom of sprinkling him-

---

[1] ἐπὶ τοῦ βήματος. Acts xii. 21.
[2] Spenser's Fairy Queen, b. ii. c. viii. st. 62.

self, or washing himself with water, which the Priest
did before the sacrifices. It might be mystically implied
thereby, that the Gentiles, who were represented by
Pilate, should be washed and cleansed by that Sacrifice; while the Jews took on themselves the guilt.
This St. Jerome confirms: "by the washing of Pilate's
hands all the works of the Gentiles are cleansed, and
we are separated from the impiety of the Jews." St.
Cyril of Jerusalem also [3] mentions that the water and
blood which issued from our Lord's side, was as it were
but a confirmation of this twofold declaration of Pilate
and of the Jews: "the water was," he says, "for him
who judged Him; but for them that shouted against
Him, the blood." He carries it further also, by saying
that "the blood was for the Jews, the water for the
Christians." "For nothing," he adds, "happened without a meaning." This action, moreover, seems to have
fulfilled the expression of the prophet, who, after saying
that "His visage was so marred," adds, "so shall He
sprinkle many nations [4]." And indeed it seems not improbable, that the whole circumstance might have been
prefigured by those ceremonies which are described in
the Epistle to the Hebrews [5]. "When Moses had
spoken every precept to all the people according to the
Law, he took the blood, with water and scarlet wool, and
hyssop, and sprinkled the book, and all the people."
For these requisites were all here fulfilled. Our Lord
was now standing before them in the scarlet robe, which
was signified by the scarlet wool: there was the water,
with which Pilate washed his hands; and the reed which
they put in His hand may have been a cane of hyssop,
as we find the reed seems synonymous with hyssop, on

<hr>

[3] Lect. xiii. 22.   [4] Isa. lii. 15.   [5] Ch. ix. 19.

which they put the sponge of vinegar, at the Crucifixion; at the same time the blood was that which the Jews took on themselves; and our Lord was Himself a bleeding spectacle before them, from the scourging and the Crown of thorns. So that the four mystical emblems are found together in this dread Sacrifice and condemnation.

The action is also remarkable in another point of view, as being one out of a great many circumstances that appear to have been Divinely ordered to bear testimony to the immaculate Lamb of God, proving that He was perfectly "without blemish," spotless and blameless, which was here set forth in a distinct marked action. The same was shown by the High Priest and the Council in vain endeavouring to obtain false testimony; it was shown by the declaration of Judas, that he had "betrayed the innocent blood;" by the repeated testimony of Pilate, that he could "find no fault in Him;" by the testimony of Herod, to whom He was sent; and by the expression of Pilate's wife, who called Him "that just man;" by the testimony of the thief on the cross, "this man hath done nothing amiss;" (for he had been present, says St. Cyril of Jerusalem, at the judgment;) and finally by the declaration of the Centurion, "Truly this was a righteous man." Therefore the Prophet asks, "Who will contend with Me? who is mine adversary? let him come near to Me: who is he that shall condemn Me[6]?" "Let them bring forth their witnesses, that they may be justified; or let them hear, and say it is truth[7]."

If this action of Pilate's was so wonderfully expressive and significative, no less so was the reply with which it was met by the Jews, when "all the people

[6] Isa. l. 8.   [7] Isa. xliii. 9.

answered and said, His blood be on us and on our children." It is said expressly, "all the people;" not the multitude or crowd, but high and low, rulers and subjects—"all the people." Here again, by one great and distinct declaration, they bore testimony against themselves to the following remarkable circumstance.

For we can scarcely fail to notice, that while the Jews were thus acting throughout recklessly and spontaneously, yet events were so overruled by Divine Providence, that every part of that nation should have had a voice, and share, in His death; and that owing to a variety of contingencies, apparently fortuitous. All the incidents of the trial and condemnation are striking, in this point of view, as tending to throw the guilt off the Gentile upon the Jew. On the one hand, of this nature is all that long importunity of Pilate to obtain His release by every method, by sending to Herod, by scourging Him to prevent His death, by going forth and expostulating with the Priests, by appealing to the people. The deprecation of Pilate's wife seems also, from another quarter, the voice of the Gentiles acquitting Him. And Pilate's washing his hands in the presence of them all, is, in the strongest manner, expressive of the same. On the other hand, one of our Lord's own disciples betrays; then Annas, who is designated as a High Priest[s], binds Him, and no one can tell why; then Caiaphas, the High Priest, openly and solemnly condemns Him; so do also "Chief Priests, Elders, and Scribes;" "and," as St. Mark says, "the whole Council" met together on the morning, so that the whole Sanhedrim also are guilty; then, as if by a strange and singular accident, He is sent to the king of Galilee, that the authority of

[s] Luke iii. 2. Acts iv. 6.

that part of the Holy Land might also have a share in His death. But how could it be an act of the whole Jewish people, as distinct from their rulers? It was so ordered, as if by a kind of fortuitous occurrence, that on this occasion, the only one in the whole year, even the people had the power of life and death by a custom of the Passover, when the Roman governor allowed them one prisoner. So that they also, with one voice, pronounced His death. Thus, as on one side, we have the remarkable expression of the Gentile, "I am innocent of the blood of this just person;" on the other, as if under a mysterious and Divine superintendence, these accumulated circumstances of Jewish guilt are expressed in the words of the whole people,—"His blood be upon us and upon our children." And this it is which we supposed our blessed Saviour's words to Pilate, the very few that He spake, were intended to point out, namely, the strong preponderance of guilt on the Jew rather than on the Gentile, when He said, that they, who had delivered Him up to Pilate, had the greater sin.

Thus what is very remarkable, as ever, by the Providence of God, the wicked are taken in their own craftiness; while they were thus bringing about the Lord's death, and endeavouring to thrust the act from off themselves upon the Roman, the guilt becomes thereby the more indelibly impressed upon themselves. Thus no part of the nation was guiltless; and the whole nation partook of the judgment. And the circumstance of the Jews, thus solemnly taking upon them the blood of Christ, was perhaps the more immediate cause of that impenitency which preceded their ruin,—that God heard not their prayers, according to His declaration, "When ye spread forth your hands I will hide Mine eyes from you; yea, while ye make many prayers I will not hear: your hands are full of blood[9]:" while they stretch forth their hands, imbrued in the blood of His Son. And this St. Basil observes of this passage, that "the cause is therein assigned why God will not hear their prayers, 'for your hands are full of blood.' For the very action or signs of supplication are occasions of provocation. In like manner, as if any one should slay a beloved son, and, while his hands are still stained, should lift them up to an angry father, and pray for pardon; such are now the prayers of the Jews, that whenever they stretch forth their hands, they show them to be full of the blood of Christ. For they who continue in their hardness of heart are inheritors of their fathers' murder. For they say, 'His blood be on us and on our children.' Therefore Pilate granted their request, and they obtained a victory which was the mother of their destruction." To these observations of St. Basil it may be added, that their repentance is spoken of as in some measure proportionate, "as mourning for Him," whom they have pierced, "as one mourns for his only son," and "as one that is in bitterness for his first born[1]."

But although this circumstance, which marked the accumulated guilt of that nation, may have had a reference to that visitation, when all their nation was destroyed utterly, yet it probably had also other and higher meanings, for "the blood of the Paschal Lamb was to be on every door;" "every man shall make your account for the Lamb;" expressly, "a lamb for an house." And as we observed, that all the Jews took part in our Lord's death,—excepting women, of whom not one is mentioned,—this may have signified that

---

[9] Isa. i. 15. [1] Zech. xii. 10.

every household was represented by the men. It is remarkable, too, how the very words correspond : it is enjoined, " the whole assembly of the children of Israel shall kill it[2]." And the Evangelist says expressly, "the whole assembly[3]" were met, to put Him to death.

But still, notwithstanding this marked accumulation of guilt, yet it must be remembered, that there are ever " a remnant," elect according to grace, over whom God rejoices in Holy Scripture. For it is also to be noticed, that though they thus sinned, collectively and nationally, yet, out of every class of men, there was found some one or more who bore testimony to the truth : Joseph of Arimathea, from among the rich and the noble ; Nicodemus, from among the Scribes ; the centurion at the cross, from among the soldiers ; the wife of Pilate among noble women ; the wife of Herod's steward from a king's household ; the thief on the cross, of malefactors ; Simon, the Cyrenian, of Gentile foreigners. All these single individuals from among classes who took part in His death. Thus also shall it be in the days of Antichrist, in various conditions of life, shall they that compose the remnant be found : one woman at a mill, another in the field, another in bed, shall be taken. In like manner of this act of the Jews, St. Chrysostom says, with great charity, " Although they attached that curse to themselves, and to their children also, yet the merciful God hath not confirmed their sentence, but out of them, and out of their children, He hath chosen those who should repent. For out of them was Paul, and many thousands who believed at Jerusalem."

<hr>

[2] Exod. xii.   [3] Mark xv. 1.

THE WAY OF SORROWS.

"*Then therefore*" (John) it was that Pilate "*delivered up* (Matt. Mark, Luke, John) *Jesus* (Matt. Mark, Luke) *to their will* (Luke), *that He might be crucified* (Matt. Mark, John). *They*" (the soldiers) "*then stripped Him of the purple* (Mark), *the military cloak* (Matt.), *and put His own garments on Him* (Matt. Mark), *and led Him out* (Mark), *and led Him away to crucify Him*" (Matt.). Here is our blessed Lord again in His own raiment, which, like Joseph's, was a long garment, covered with blood. But though they now took off from Him the mock robe of purple, yet they took not off the crown of torture; "for this," says Origen [4], the Evangelists do not say was taken off as well as the purple robe; "for He took our thorns on His adorable head, and lays them not aside." St. Chrysostom also observes the same; so that we may suppose, in this respect, the Man of Sorrows is rightly represented by the painters as,—when bearing His Cross, and hanging on His Cross,—with the Crown of thorns on His head.

"*And He bearing His Cross went forth*" (John). This was a refinement of torture usually practised with malefactors, to bear this instrument of their torments, the transverse beam of the cross: and in itself, therefore, a sight so ignominious, that the term expressive of the worst wickedness and degradation among the Romans was derived from it, the word "furcifer," or gallows-bearer. But in our gracious Lord, as seen by the eyes of faith, it was the true Isaac bearing the wood on which He was to be offered, placed by His Father on His

[4] In Matt. Comm. 125.

shoulders, as a King bearing the sceptre of His kingdom, the sign of mortification. "As the victim of God," says Quesnel, "He carries the wood for His sacrifice; as a Conqueror, the arms with which He is to conquer the world; as a King, the sceptre with which He is to rule His people." And this was the fulfilment of the prophecy of Isaiah, that "the government shall be on His shoulder[5]." For "His government," says St. Austin, "is the Cross; on account of which, according to the Apostle, God hath highly exalted Him. It was the very ensign of His kingdom; for you will find, on inquiry, that Christ does not reign in us, excepting through hardships; on which account it is that men of self-indulgence are the enemies of the Cross of Christ." "Here," says another writer[6], "Abel is led forth into the field to be slain by his brother; here Isaac is present with the wood, and Abraham with the ram adhering in the thorns; here is Joseph also with the sheaf seen in his dream, and the coat down to the feet smeared with blood; here is Moses with the rod, and the serpent suspended on the wood; here is the vine branch borne on the wood; here is Elisha with the wood, seeking for the axe which had sunk to the bottom and swum to the wood, that is, the race of mankind which, from the forbidden tree, fell down to hell, and through the wood of the Cross of Christ, and the Baptism of water, hath swum to Paradise: here is Jonas, from the wood cast into the sea and the belly of the whale, for three days." Here, we may add, is the captive Samson bearing on his shoulders the posts and the bars of the city of Gaza; for our Lord bore away thereby the gates of hell: here is the Levite bearing "the ark on his shoulders," for this

---

[5] Isa. ix. 6.   [6] Pseudo-Jerome on St. Mark.

Cross is the Ark of our Salvation: here is He of whom it is said, "the key of the House of David will I lay on His shoulder[7]," for His Cross is as the key that opens and closes Heaven, it is that whereby all men shall stand or fall in their eternal portion.

It is supposed that our blessed Lord Himself thus bore His own Cross, as St. John described Him, through the city, and that, when they had now come to the gate of the city, He was unable to support it: when the circumstances take place which the other Evangelists record. Probably He was at this time not only unable to support His Cross, but even unable to support Himself also. For it may be observed that St. Mark afterwards changes the expression, and speaks of their "bearing" Him to the place of execution; which, considering the circumstantial accuracy of St. Mark's words, and that he himself, as well as the other two Evangelists, had before used the other term, and said that they led Him out, would induce one to suppose that our Lord was too weak to proceed without support. But even at this moment of His extreme weakness we cannot but adore, with awe and wonder, His Divine charity, which makes even His weakness to school us in heavenly wisdom. For now, when He fainted under the weight of His Cross, and, from the sufferings of body and mind which He had undergone, was unequal to sustain this burden; yet even here He ceased not, by a mysterious lesson, to teach His true followers, and to remind them of that admonition which He had so often inculcated upon them,—"That he who would be His disciple must bear the Cross, and come after Him, and follow Him:" that as He is "King, those who would reign with Him must

[7] Isa. xxii. 22.

T

also suffer with Him ;" setting before us, in lively action, that to which He has exhorted us by St. Paul, "Let us go forth to Him without the camp, bearing His reproach." O wonderful and exceeding charity, unspeakable watchfulness of Divine teaching! O blessed privilege, to "fill up that which is behind of the sufferings of Christ!" For who can approach so near Him as to bear His Cross, and not partake of that ineffable goodness that surrounded Him? And who was that man of Cyrene? What good deed of faith had he done to Christ, or to Christ's little ones, that he, of all the sons of Adam, should have been deemed worthy to be admitted to this, the first and greatest of all earthly honours? Who he was, excepting the name, we know not, nor what he had done, for God withdraws from the sight of men, and hides, in His own Presence, those whom He most delights to honour. All that we know is that, "*as they are going out* (Matt.), *and led Him away* (Luke), *they found a man of Cyrene, by name Simon* (Matt.), *as he was coming out of the country, the father of Alexander and Rufus* (Mark), *on him they lay hands* (Luke) *as he was passing by* (Mark), *and compel him to their service that he might bear His Cross*" (Matt. Mark). And they "*placed it upon Him to bear after Jesus*" (Luke).

The reason for their laying hold of this Simon was probably, as St. Augustin suggests, that none of themselves would touch that wood, so odious and accursed ; but what they intended as shameful and painful to this poor stranger, is the highest earthly crown of greatness ; so wonderful even here is the efficacy of that Cross! He is thereby by their cruelty made meet to approach the Saviour, and to be the mysterious representative of His Church. St. Ambrose thinks that this very discrepancy in the Evangelists, who speak both of our

Lord bearing His Cross, and also of Simon bearing it after Him, tends the more strongly to set forth this mystery, that He Himself first of all lifts the Cross on Himself, and then delivers it to His members to lift. It is not a Jew who bears the Cross, but a stranger and a foreigner. Nor does he go before, but follows; as it is written, "Let him take up his Cross and come after Me." And it was probably the case, as St. Ambrose seems here to take it, that Simon did not bear the Cross together with Christ, as it is represented in pictures, but by himself after Christ. But Origen supposes that the Cross was afterwards put on our Lord Himself also. It is observed, by St. Jerome and others, that the terms Simon of Cyrene signify by interpretation "the obedient heir," which, if it could be proved, would arrest our attention, according to that extraordinary significancy which Holy Scripture indicates to exist in names; and would represent to us in a lively manner those Gentiles which were strangers, but are made heirs of the providence by obedience. But St. Athanasius takes the word Cyrenian to mean "ready," as if "ready to obedience." At all events, it represents the Gentiles, whom Christ meets coming from the countries of heathenism and idolatry at the entrance of Jerusalem, the holy city, "going," says Theophylact, "to that holy City which is above;" and delays their entrance for a while, that they may go back and bear the Cross after Him. That an instructive mystery was contained in this bearing the Cross after Christ is indeed obvious to a thoughtful mind; and most ancient writers seem to allude to it. "Not by chance," says Origen, speaking of this meeting of Simon the Cyrenian, "but hither led, according to the foreknowledge of God, and the disposing of God, that he might be found worthy of the

T 2

Evangelical Scripture, and this ministry to the Cross of Christ, by which the world is crucified unto the Saints, and the Saints unto the world[8]." And "it was not only suitable that the Saviour should receive the Cross, but that we also should bear it; fulfilling this our salutary compulsion and service." And St. Jerome,—"The Gentiles mystically receive Christ, and the obedient stranger bears the ignominy of the Saviour." And St. Hilary,—"The Jews were unworthy to bear the Cross of Christ, for hereafter the Gentiles were in faith to receive the Cross, and to suffer together with Him[9]." To these observations it may be added, in like mode of interpretation, that the mention of the sons of this Cyrenian may further imply, that if the Gentiles have not to boast of their fathers, as the Jews had, being Prophets and Apostles, yet they had sons who were disciples; according as it is written, "Instead of thy fathers thou shalt have children."

Of beautiful and touching interest is this mournful scene of meeting the Cyrenian. He with whom the Father was "well pleased," comes to the gate to meet us; fulfilling perfect obedience, yet bearing the curse of disobedience. And we meet Him at the gate, and go with Him to Calvary, that we may lay hold of the Cross, and be with Him; for we must not approach Him there without bearing some slight share of His Cross. "Here will I dwell, for I have a delight therein;" "For I know that Thou of very faithfulness hast caused me to be troubled." And "Thy loving correction shall make me great:"—"For if we be dead with Him we shall also live with Him: if we suffer we shall also reign with Him."

[8] In Matt. Comm. 126.   [9] In Matt. cap. xxxiii.

THE WOMEN LAMENTING.

And now, as Christ was thus proceeding up the way of sorrows to the place of His execution, we naturally feel desirous to know what had become of those many persons who had in some measure believed in Him, and received great benefits from Him. And we read,—*" There followed Him a great company of people, and of women, which also bewailed and lamented Him. But Jesus turning unto them said, Daughters of Jerusalem, weep not for Me, but weep for yourselves, and for your children. For behold, the days are coming, in the which they shall say, Blessed are the barren, and the wombs that never bare, and the paps which never gave suck. Then shall they begin to say to the mountains, Fall on us, and to the hills, Cover us. For if they do these things in a green tree, what shall be done in the dry ?"* (Luke). It is St. Luke alone who mentions this circumstance; and it is to be observed that, like most of the incidents and expressions which St. Luke alone records, it is of a compassionate character; such as that prayer of our Lord for His enemies soon after, which is mentioned only by this Evangelist; and also the Saviour's weeping over Jerusalem. And the expression of our Lord on that occasion, as well as the present, may serve in some faint degree to indicate one subject and cause of our Lord's inscrutable weight of agony of mind. For when He shed tears on coming near to Jerusalem, it was not on account of His own approaching sufferings, but because " the days shall come upon thee that thine enemies shall cast a trench about thee, and compass thee round, and keep thee in on every side, and shall lay thee even with the ground [10]." And now also it was for the same cause, because the days of affliction were coming on them that afflicted Him. This therefore was one subject of our Saviour's grief, His tender yearning over His own people; that wicked city was the object of all His cares. But we cannot but suppose that He who knew all things, had far greater agonies of mankind in His mind than those sufferings, very great as they were, of the Jewish siege: may we not humbly venture to suppose that He was rather thinking of those sorrows and that time, of which that siege was but the type and emblem? and that now in His grief He was connecting together those two events, which two days before He had so vividly connected together in prophecy, the destruction of Jerusalem and the end of the world? This supposition is the more probable, because our blessed Saviour uses those words of prophecy respecting it, which we know do refer to, and which will have their more entire fulfilment on the Day of Judgment; when St. John tells us, in the Apocalypse, they will say "to the mountains and rocks, Fall on us, and hide us from the face of Him that sitteth on the throne, and from the wrath of the Lamb [11]." For although what is here said of the last Day in the Revelation was literally the case, as Josephus records, in those that escaped the destruction of Jerusalem, when "they hid themselves in the dens and in the rocks of the mountains;" and although the same prophecies in the Prophets Isaiah and Hosea had their fulfilment in some nearer national calamity, yet they do also refer to the great Day of Judgment: certainly that in Isaiah very distinctly,—"They shall

[10] Luke xix. 14.   [11] Rev. vi. 16.

go into the holes of the rocks and into the caves of
the earth, for fear of the Lord, and for the glory of
His majesty, when He ariseth to shake terribly the
earth[12]." Therefore it seems probable, that as our
Lord in His prophets spoke often of some nearer
event, while in the same words He looked forward to
one which was beyond, so He was now also doing the
same: in using the same words of an event which, as it
approached more nearly, developed in stronger characters the type of the great Judgment. Quesnel alludes to
our Lord's words, as mystically containing this meaning.
"These words," he says, "are directed likewise to us,
because these calamities prefigure those of the damned
who shall seek death without being able to find it, and
shall suffer an eternal confusion." So likewise does the
other expression seem to refer not only to their temporal sufferings, but also to the final condemnation of
the wicked, viz. "If they do these things in a green tree,
what will be done in the dry?" For the "dry wood"
is a figure of the wicked, as the "dead" branches in
the parable of the vine; and as the withered fig tree.
The meaning seems to be, if an innocent person can
suffer thus in this present world, what will be the sufferings of the wicked when the anger of God comes forth
upon them? Nor is it any objection to our conceiving
this to be our Lord's meaning, that it could only be then
taken in the primary and lower sense, by those to whom
it was at first addressed, for this is the nature of our
Lord's expressions generally: for they are such as open
higher meanings to faith; and their true and worthier
sense is hidden from those who heard them. Fire
cannot burn green wood, neither can the judgment of
God those who have no sin: afflictions cannot hurt us,

<hr>

[12] Isa. ii. 19. Hosea x. 3.

excepting so far as we are sinners; these evils therefore could not hurt Christ, because He was infinitely good, but must redound to infinite good; and they are no subject for tears, excepting for the sins which occasion them, which are ours and not His. Therefore His Cross was to Him a trophy and a sceptre. He was the Tree of Life, and no fire of God's wrath can hurt Him, nor those that are found in Him. But what shall be the case when the fire of God's wrath breaks forth on the dry wood?

But with regard to this occasion, and the circumstances when the words were spoken, we cannot but reverently adore the exceeding carefulness of our Lord even now, in watching for every occasion of doing good: and the admonition we cannot but consider as intended for us all: that when we feel our human sympathies and compassions moved towards Him, at the recital of His sufferings, we are to think that He turns to us, and tells us to think of ourselves, and of our own sins, that occasioned those sufferings; that when we venture to approach, and gaze on Him, by these contemplations, we forget not ourselves also. And we may observe, in general, that whenever any strong feeling is evinced towards our Lord by His followers, that His manner was to turn and check them, by reminding them of their own frailty. Thus, when St. Peter said he would die with Him, He warned him that he would deny Him; to the man who said he would follow Him wheresoever He went, He answered that the Son of Man had not where to lay His head: to the people in the temple, who "hung on" His words, He told the parable of the man at the marriage supper without the wedding garment, and his fearful end: to the multitudes that follow Him,

He turns to say, that no one can be His disciple without taking up His cross daily.

In all the persons concerned we may see some state of human nature which requires being brought to the Cross of Christ, in order to be healed. Ardent zeal in St. Peter is here taught the danger of self-confidence; patient courage here derives the highest of all blessings and rewards in St. John: covetousness is shown in its true colours in Judas: ambition has its lesson in the crown of thorns and the robe of blood; justice without courage is shown in Pilate; injustice with cruelty in the Chief Priests; wanton cruelty in the soldiers; lastly, in all of them is shown what men may come to when they persecute and condemn the innocent blood. So likewise now affectionate feeling is shown in the women, and receives its correction in that school of all wisdom; the female sex being, as St. Cyril says, more susceptible of piety, but needing self-discipline. And Theophylact says, "Infirmity of mind, which is signified by the women, if it adopts contrition of heart, and weeps through penitence, it follows Jesus who is afflicted for our salvation." We may observe also something instructive to ourselves in this, that before the Chief Priests, and Herod, and Pilate our Lord was silent; but to these He speaks. O gracious boon! blessed indeed are they that weep, and blessed are they that mourn, for they hear Christ speaking to them! The rich and the great are regardless of His sorrows, or only know them to add to them: but God gathers around Him the women and the poor to receive His instructions, and to witness His perfect example of meek suffering. And His words are our life: He wept Himself, and He calls us to weep with Him over guilty Jerusalem, and to partake of His sorrows: but it is for ourselves we are to weep both in His and our own sorrows. The contemplation of Christ crucified is our best protection against our own calamities.

It is observable that the children sang Hosannahs to His praise [1]; the women wept; the men cried out, Crucify Him.

SECTION II.—THE CRUCIFIXION.

" They pierced My hands and My feet. I may tell all My bones. They stand staring and looking upon Me."

GOLGOTHA.

THUS was our blessed Lord dragged along, up the hill of shame and sorrows, and with Him thus conducted to execution "*were led,*" says the Evangelist, "*two other malefactors, to be put to death with Him*" (Luke), marking, as it were, by the very mode of expression, the fulfilment of that prophecy, that He should be "numbered with the transgressors [2]." For as if to add to His shame, He is put in company with them, and mentioned almost as if He were one of them. And now at length "*they had come to the place*" (Matt. Luke), or as St. Mark says, after mentioning the person who was supporting His cross, "*and they bear Him to the place*" (Mark), it was a "*place which is in Hebrew* (John) *called Golgotha* (Matt. Mark, John), *which is, being interpreted* (Mark), *the place of a skull*" (Matt. Mark, Luke, John). The spot was probably so called from the skulls, and dead bones, which remained there after former executions, as if it had been a charnel-house. It was the place of the condemned, the place where death itself appeared in the

---

[1] See Holy Week, p. 60.   [2] Isa. liii. 12.

most disgusting shape, and revolting to humanity, among the bones of the dead, and those dead under the execution of the law, the most abject of mankind; that "where sin abounded, grace might much more abound." "Jesus was, on this account, crucified there," says St. Jerome, "that where there had formerly been the place of the condemned, the standard of martyrdom might be erected." "Our bones lie scattered before the pit, like as when one breaketh and heweth wood upon the earth: but Mine eyes look unto Thee, O Lord God: in Thee is My trust[3]." But some allude to a very extraordinary tradition for the name of this place. Origen says, "of the place of a skull, it has come to us that the Hebrews have a tradition that the body of Adam was buried there; that as in Adam all die, so in Christ shall all be made alive[4]." St. Athanasius and St. Jerome both allude to the same report, but St. Jerome adds that there is no truth in it: St. Athanasius comments on the report as very remarkable, though he does not assert its authenticity. St. Basil also dwells on the same.

But as many emblems have a good interpretation combined with them, as well as an evil, it is curious to observe that St. Cyril[5] considers that the naming of this place was fulfilled in our blessed Lord Himself, as if it were the place of our Head. For Christ is "the Head of the Body, the Church." And "the Head of every man is Christ." And He is "the Head of all principality and power." Whether therefore it was the place of Adam's burial or not, it is the place of the condemned; and it has become the place of our Head, "which is Christ:" who suffered there in the place of us, who are condemned by human and Divine law.

---

[3] Ps. cxli. 8, 9.   [4] 1 Cor. xv. 22.   In Matt. Comm. 126.
[5] Lect. xiii. 22.

There are other points worthy of notice in the place of our Lord's death. " He suffered without the gate," says Quesnel, " in order to show us that we are not to expect sanctification from the sacrifices offered within that city, and that He died not for them only, but for all mankind[6]."   And there was a fitness in this, that our Lord's death should be under the open expanse of Heaven, as a spectacle to all the Angels of Heaven, and to all men.   St. Chrysostom beautifully observes, that " the Lord did not wish to suffer under a roof, nor in a Jewish temple, that you may not think He was offered for that people alone; but without the city and without the walls, that you may know it was a Sacrifice for all, and an oblation for the whole earth, and purification for all."   He also observes, that by our Lord being suspended in the air, and not under a roof, the very nature of the air was cleansed; in like manner as by the blood dropping from His side the earth derived a similar blessing[7].   In another place St. Chrysostom says, " By dying in the air He expiates the air from evil spirits, and prepares for us an ascent to Heaven."   And St. Athanasius in like manner[8] mentions that our Lord's suffering aloft in the air, was there also His " pursuing the old serpent, that from thence also He might drive him who had the power of the air, and cast down spiritual wickedness in high places.   Nor did He omit to heal the earth also.   For, by hanging on the Cross, He cleansed the air by the expansion of His hands; and redeemed the earth by the water and blood of His side, by which it was washed."   The Cross itself, as it was prefigured by numberless types, beforehand; and has

[6] On St. Matt.   [7] In Serm. de Pass.
[8] De Pass. et Cruce Domini.

become full of wisdom and instruction to after-ages: so is it in itself replete with spiritual mysteries. Well, indeed, may the very shape of the cross, extending four ways, above, and below, and on either side, set before us the depth, and length, and breadth, and height of the love of Christ. Deep fixed in earth, extending up to Heaven, in its arms embracing all mankind: fulfilling that typical prophecy referred to by ancient writers, as expressive of the earnest appeal of our Lord's tedious death, "All the day long have I stretched forth My hands to a disobedient and gainsaying people." Encompassing the world in His outstretched arms, and not that only, but also lifting up His hands to Heaven. As St. Paul says [9], "making peace through the blood of His Cross, for things in Heaven, and things in earth." And what was the nailing but that, as St. Cyril says, "His Manhood, which bore the sins of men, being nailed to the Tree, and dying, sin might die with it." Thus the Cross, which was a dead and accursed wood, being touched by the bleeding, but quickening Body of Christ, hath become the tree of Life, that tree of which David spake in the first Psalm, that groweth by the waters, the streams of Baptism. The tree which hath filled the whole earth, so that the fowls of the air lodge in the branches, and the beasts of the field are sheltered beneath its shade. Though it appeared dead wood, yet, like the rod of Aaron, it hath sprouted forth and budded, when it became the property of the true Priest after the order of Melchizedec. The dead wood hath sprouted forth with bud, and branch, and leaf. And its "leaves are for the healing of the nations." This is "the Tree of Life" by the waters that flow from beneath "the throne of God [10]:" and "the Tree of the knowledge of good and

---

[9] Col. i. 20.   [10] Rev. xxii. 2.

evil " is not far from it in the garden of the Lord: for we have thence come to know the evil of man, and the goodness of God, and yet may approach unto the Tree of Life.

THE WINE AND MYRRH.

The blessed Jesus was, we may well suppose, at this time so overcome from the agonies of His mind on the former night, and the inflictions He had already undergone, as not to be able to sustain Himself. It may have been therefore in order to support Him for His execution on account of the exhaustion which He evinced; or it may have been from mildness on the part of the soldiers; or it may be from their being mitigated at hearing our Lord's prayer for them; (but probably it was before that prayer;) or it may have been, as the expression of the Psalmist would suggest, done in scorn. " *They* (the soldiers) *gave Him to drink* (Matt. Mark) *vinegar mingled with gall* " (Matt.). This vinegar was probably the common drink or wine of the soldiers, mingled with some bitter ingredient as a restorative; and St. Mark calls it " *wine mingled with myrrh* " (Mark). Myrrh, says St. Cyril, is of the taste of gall, and exceeding bitter [1]. St. Augustin makes the same remark, and says that St. Matthew may call it " gall" from its bitterness; or that perhaps both gall and myrrh were used for that purpose. But our blessed Lord, " *when He had tasted it,*" as if not sullenly declining, and yet not wishing to receive any thing to mitigate His voluntary sufferings, when He perceived what it was, " *was not willing to drink* " (Matt.). And " *He received it not* " (Mark). Perhaps St. Mark

---

[1] Lect. xiii.

may have altered the expression "vinegar," into that of "wine," under the Divine control, to indicate that this was not the fulfilment of the prophecy, "they gave me vinegar to drink [2]." For that we find from St. John was unfulfilled, till our Lord said, "I thirst," at last, with the intention of fulfilling it; and we may suppose this to have been some bitter substance composed of gall and myrrh, either of a stimulant and restorative, or, as Dr. Hammond thinks, of a poisonous and deadening nature, and was the fulfilment of the former part of the verse, "they gave Me gall to eat." We cannot venture further into that mystery, why our Lord "tasted" and "received it not," but may humbly suppose He wished to teach us, not to lessen the sense of pain by such means when God chastens us. And the Psalmist's expression would infer, that the gall which was given to eat was, from its nauseous nature, or some other reason, intended to add to His pain. Perhaps the gall was added as something more loathsome; for no refinement of torture was omitted.

THEY CRUCIFY HIM.

And now at this place "*they crucify Him*" (Luke, John). The picture of His death is simply set forth by a Latin writer, "hanging upon the wood, attached to it with nails, driven through their hands and their feet, they were killed by a protracted death, and lived a long time on the cross; not because a longer life was an object of choice, but because death itself was lengthened that their pain might not be too soon at an end. But the Jews, in choosing this death for Him, did so only as

---

[2] Ps. lxix. 22.

being the worst of all deaths, but it was chosen by the
Lord while they understood it not; for when He had
thus overcome the devil, it was this Cross that He was
going to place as His trophy on the foreheads of the
faithful [3]."   "It was by the wisdom of God," says St.
Austin, "undertaken for our example, that we might not
only not fear death, but even no kind of death; for
among all kinds of death, none was more execrable and
more dreadful than this [4]."   And in another place [5] he
says, "Observe of what great virtue is the Cross; Adam
despised the command, taking the apple from the tree;
but what Adam hath lost, Christ hath found on the Cross.
An ark of wood delivered mankind from the deluge of
waters.   When the people of God were departing from
Egypt, Moses with a rod divided the sea, overthrew
Pharaoh, and ransomed the people of God.   The same
Moses sent the wood into the water, and turned the
bitter water into sweetness.   By the rod of wood, the
saving wave is brought forth from the Spiritual Rock.
And it was not without the rod that Amalek was overcome, when Moses was stretched forth with his extended
hands: and the Law of God is committed to the ark of
the Covenant made of wood; that by all of these, as it
were through certain steps, they might arrive at length
at the wood of the Cross."   And Theophylact observes
to this effect, that from the tree, and from the pleasure
resulting therefrom, came death; and from the Tree, and
from the pains thereon sustained, came life.   Thus did
the Lord, like Moses, seize the old Serpent, from which
human nature fled, and it hath become a rod in His
hand, the rod of God, with which He will work wonders

[3] Rabanus Maurus.   Aur. Cat.   [4] Lib. 83. Quæst.
[5] In Serm. de Passione.

in the land of Egypt; delivering His chosen out of the house of bondage, and dividing the sea as a way for His ransomed to pass over.

And "*with Him they crucify*" (Mark), or "*are cruci-fied*" (Matt.), "*two others*" (John), "*the malefactors*" (Luke), "*two thieves*" (Matt. Mark); and three of the Evangelists add, as if with a mysterious significancy, though they knew not its import, "*one on the right hand, and one on the left*" (Matt. Mark, Luke), and St. John, "*on this side and on the other, and Jesus in the midst*" (John). "*And the Scripture was fulfilled which saith, And He was numbered with the transgressors*" (Mark). Himself in the midst by way of derision, as affording Him the distinction of the most honourable position among thieves; but thus were His two asso-ciates in suffering set, the one on the right, and the other on the left of their Saviour and their Judge. So it is with those who are afflicted in this life, some thereby are brought to a sense of their own sins, and have their hearts opened to behold Christ Crucified, and are set on His right hand in glory as they were in suffering. Others are but hardened by the same suf-ferings, and not led thereby to hallow His Name. Ven. Bede applies it still more closely, to those who suffer in religion's name, but some from love of Christ, others of human glory. And St. Augustin beautifully observes, that "the very Cross was the tribunal of Christ, for the Judge was placed in the middle, one thief, who believed, was set free; the other, who re-viled, was condemned; which signified what He was already about to do with the quick and dead; being about to set some on His right hand, but others at His left." St. Hilary, also, in like manner, says, "that this showed that the whole of mankind were brought to the sacrament of His Passion; the unbelievers being set on His left hand; and those who are justified by faith being on His right hand[6]." And St. Leo observes, that by this was set forth the separation that was to take place among all mankind by His Judgment. So that the Passion of Christ contains within it the sacrament of our salvation; and of that instrument which the wickedness of the Jews had provided for His punishment, the power of the Redeemer made a step to glory. But Theophylact considers these two on the cross, to represent "the Jews and the Gentiles, both of which were transgressors, one of the law of nature, the other of the written law, which the Lord had delivered them. But the Gentile was penitent, the Jew reviled Him unto the end. In the middle of both the Lord is Crucified, for He is the Corner stone by which both are joined in one."

CHRIST PRAYING FOR HIS MURDERERS.

It was now, when they had come to the very crisis of their torture, and were crucifying Him, and, as it is supposed, while they were in the act of driving the nails into the most sensitive part of His hands, or His feet, "*Jesus said, Father, forgive them, for they know not what they do*" (Luke). By the expression "Father," was He not only preferring the highest of all claims, as the Only-begotten of the Father; but also setting forth the perfection of that Sonship, in the very image of the Father's goodness, of which He had Himself spoken; "pray for them which despitefully use you,—that ye may be the children of your Father which is in Heaven[7]."

---

[6] In Matt. cap. xxxiii. 5.　　　[7] Matt. v. 45.

' "This prayer He uttered," says St. Chrysostom, "as He ascended the Cross, not but that He might have Himself forgiven them without it; but that He might teach us, not by word only but in deed, to pray for our persecutors. And when He says 'forgive them,' it implies, if they should repent; to assist those that would repent, that after a wickedness so great, they might wash out their guilt through faith." As of old, the people were murmuring against God, when Moses struck the Rock, and the waters of salvation gushed out for them; and they were murmuring against Him, when God sent down the Manna from Heaven. Thus overcoming their obduracy by His goodness, He embraced them now in the arms of His mercy, when they were inflicting His death.

It is possible, indeed, that the prayer may have been offered in behalf of the Roman soldiers, who were engaged in inflicting on our Lord this bodily torture, and perhaps doing so, as they had before mocked Him, with merciless rigour. For they truly knew not what they did, but were only executing the sentence of the Jews, who knew better what they were about. If this be the case, it would be another circumstance, in addition to those mentioned, which tended to throw the guilt on the Jew, and to exculpate the Gentile. And this would account for the destruction which came on the Jews and on Jerusalem, as not being included in this prayer. But it seems better to understand it, that this prayer included all parties who had a share in His death, as being the first fruits of His Passion, the most availing of all prayers, the Prayer offered on the Cross. And it is for these Jews that St. Stephen also prays, in imitation of Christ; and as the prayer of St. Stephen obtained St. Paul, much more may this prayer have gained those many thousands that soon after believed. And one thing is certainly very remarkable, that as St. Paul, the chief person concerned in the death of St. Stephen, has been supposed to have been granted to the dying prayer of that Martyr; so likewise the Centurion, who, in the fulfilment of his office, must have presided over the execution of this act of cruelty, even if he did not himself perform it, is the person on this very day who makes confession of "the Son of God." This may have been the first visible answering of our Lord's prayer, and fruits of His death; and this man also, like St. Paul, more especially had "done it ignorantly in unbelief."

Nor indeed are the Jews themselves excluded from this plea of our Lord's, for we have the testimony of Scripture that they also in some sense " knew not what they did." Thus St. Peter testifies of them, "I wot that through ignorance ye did it, as did also your rulers [8]." And St. Paul, "had they known it, they would not have crucified the Lord of glory [9]." And our Lord Himself had said to them, "ye neither know Me, nor My Father [10]." And of those who should persecute His Apostles He had said, "whosoever killeth you, will think that he doeth God service; and these things will they do, because they have not known the Father nor Me [1]." They had indeed said, "this is the heir, come let us kill Him." They knew that they were murdering an innocent man; yet they knew Him only as the Son of man; and " whosoever speaketh against the Son of man it shall be forgiven him;" and therefore they were in a condition capable of pardon. They knew Him not as the Son of God, nor as such had He been fully manifested before them; and therefore they were

[8] Acts iii. 17.   [9] 1 Cor. ii. 8.
[10] John viii. 19.   [1] John xvi. 3.

not guilty of the sin against the Holy Ghost. But Judas indeed who was admitted so near to Him, might have known Him as the Son of God. For this sin therefore of our Lord's death, the Jews were admissible to repentance and pardon; and therefore the Apostles were sent to preach to them. And it was not till afterwards, when they rejected the Holy Ghost, that they were destroyed as a nation. So that not only was our Lord Himself to them the sign of the Prophet Jonah, but He Himself also, according to that sign, like Jonah, went and preached to them; with an analogous but with far greater indulgence, for He said not, "yet forty days," and the city "shall be overthrown[2]," but—yet forty years. Yet they repented not, and therefore "the men of Nineveh shall rise in judgment with this generation, and shall condemn it."   And in Ven. Bede[3] we find this our interpretation confirmed to this effect,—"we cannot suppose," he says, "that He here prayed in vain, but that He obtained that which He prayed for, in those who believed in Him after His passion. We must notice in truth, that he prayed not for those who understood that they were crucifying the Son of God, and were not willing to confess Him, but for those who knew not what they did, having a zeal for God, but not according to knowledge." "But after the Crucifixion," says a Greek writer[4], "the plea of ignorance could not profit them, when working miracles proclaimed Him aloud to be God." At all events we cannot doubt, but that this prayer prevailed mightily with God, infinitely beyond every prayer. For if others, which were but the types of this prayer, were heard on account of their faint similitude to it, as the prayer of Jonah from the

---

[2] Jonah iii. 4,   [3] Aurea Catena.   [4] Ibid.

belly of the whale; and that of Daniel from the den of lions; and that of the Three Children from the midst of the furnace; and that of Hezekiah from his bed of sickness; and that of the Psalmist which prefigured it when he said, " Thou hast heard me also from among the horns of the unicorns[5]," much more is Christ Himself heard from the wood of torment. Nay, indeed, so deep is one's sense of the mysterious efficacy of this the most availing of all prayers, that it is of itself a reason which would induce one to expect, that the restoration of that guilty nation is literally to be fulfilled, in whatever secret manner it may take place. But very awful and alarming are the grounds on which the plea of the prayer is offered; for Christ prays for them, because they did it "ignorantly in unbelief," knowing not what they did; and though we know not the full meaning of this appeal, yet we know that, " if we sin wilfully after we have received the knowledge of the truth, there remaineth no more sacrifice for sin[6]."

THE TITLE ON THE CROSS.

At the place of execution it was usual to write up the charge on which the malefactor was put to death; and we read, " *Pilate wrote a title and placed it on the Cross* (John); *they set over His head His accusation written* (Matt.), *This is* (Matt. Luke) *Jesus* (Matt. John) *of Nazareth* (John), *the King of the Jews* (Matt. Mark, Luke, John). *Now this title read many of the Jews, because the place where Jesus was crucified was near the city"* (John). It seems to have been something of a public thoroughfare, or near a road passing by, as we read afterwards of persons "passing along" that way.

<hr>

[5] Ps. xxii. 21.   [6] Heb. x. 26.

It may be observed, that all the four Evangelists agree
in giving the important title, "the King of the Jews."
Their discrepancy in other respects is nothing more
than that of some giving more words than others, and
may be accounted for by this circumstance.   Pilate, for
the more effectual expression of his anger and contempt of the Jews, who had forced him to an action to
which he was so averse, and now the more angry with
them because angry with himself, was determined that
the charge which the Jews urged might be known to all
nations, who were now met together at Jerusalem for the
Feast.   According to his direction, therefore, "*it was
written up in Hebrew, Greek,* and *Latin*" (John). "*Now
the inscription was written over Him,*" says St. Luke,
"*in Greek, and Latin, and Hebrew.*"   But though it
appeared to happen thus fortuitously, yet here again was
there a superhuman control that swayed the wild passions that dictated, and the hand that wrote the words :
the Finger of God was in it, and it was the same Hand
that wrote up the indelible characters at the Feast at
Babylon.   For, first of all, in this inscription does our
Lord claim for Himself all of us, as our King. He claims
us as purchased to Him in a higher way than any King
ever purchased a kingdom; purchased not by the death
of others, but by His own death ; a Kingdom of the
Cross obtained by meekness, and to be inherited by the
meek : a Kingdom of suffering. Death is the origin of His
Kingly power, and they who would reign with Him must
die to the world.   All this His Title teaches and claims.
But to the Jews this inscription marks in threefold characters, as indelible, their guilt, while they were endeavouring to cause, but not to inflict His death, it became
the more signally written up in the eyes of all the world
in Hebrew, and Greek, and Latin. Moreover, by being

written up in three languages, it declares to every nation under Heaven that " This is the King of the Jews." It is the execution of the Divine command,—"Tell it out among the heathen that the Lord is King." It is written in every language, for " every tongue shall confess that Jesus is the Lord." It is written in Hebrew, and in Greek, and in Latin. The law is of the Hebrews, and the Greek boasts of his wisdom, and the Roman of his power.   But they are all told hereby that the true Law, true Wisdom, and true Power, is found in Christ alone. He alone is the true King, making all to obey Him in perfect obedience, perfect wisdom, and perfect power. O wonderful mysteriousness, O mysterious Providence, swaying the caprice of men to its own great purpose! But it may be asked, why is it " the King of the Jews," and not of the Gentiles also ? for it is written, " I will make Thee the Head of the heathen." Yet this is as it were by conquest, for it is said especially, " Judah is my Law-giver ;" " Out of Judah shall go forth a Ruler ;" " On My Holy Hill of Sion have I set My King ;" " Out of Sion hath God appeared in perfect beauty."   The Jews are His by birth, the Gentiles by possession : for when it is said, " I have set My King on My Holy Hill of Sion," it is added, " Desire of Me, and I will give Thee the heathen for Thine inheritance, and the utmost parts of the earth for Thy possession." In the King of the Jews is prophecy fulfilled; the Gentiles acknowledge Him, but as King of the Jews. The Gentiles acknowledge Him, but as King of them who are of the circumcision, the true circumcision of the heart. In Judah is the true olive stock, but we are grafted in, being wild by nature. And the despised Nazarene shall be His title also : for this too the beloved disciple added, in affectionate remembrance of His early abode; for it was said,

"Shall any good thing come out of Nazareth?" and the answer was here given, "Come and see [7]." And here was it fulfilled that He should be called a Nazarene—the true Nazarite. And this despised name of contempt was perhaps written in the language alone of those who knew that country, and therefore given by St. John alone, himself a Galilean.

Here therefore our Lord preaches to all the world in silence from His Cross, when He could no longer go about and teach with language such as man never spake: and herein was it signally fulfilled,—"to whom He was not spoken of, they shall see; and they that have not heard shall understand [8]."

But the wicked, while they endeavour to extricate themselves from the net of all-involving Providence, do but tighten the knots, and render them the more inextricable. For now the Jews, being ashamed of the scorn of Pilate, endeavour to have the Title altered, as if it were only our Lord's declaration, and not their charge, and His admission, who is Truth Himself: but this their attempt marks it out to all ages as written not to be obliterated, and doubly sure. For "*the Chief Priests of the Jews said therefore unto Pilate, Write not the King of the Jews, but that that* man *said, I am the King of the Jews. Pilate answered, What I have written, I have written*" (John). There is a sort of Divine and energetic emphasis in the double declaration. For may we not reverently suppose that He who made Caiaphas to prophesy because he was the High Priest, though he knew not of what he spake, caused Pilate also to write, and emphatically to confirm what he had written, because he was a Governor, and a "power ordained of God?" That not his writing only, but his

<hr>

[7] John i. 46.   [8] Isa. lii. 15.

assertion also, as of one, though he knew not, admitting its truth, might be for ever known. And this very assertion was another instance, as throughout, of the Jews rejecting their King, and the Gentile acknowledging Him as the King of the Jews. " O the ineffable power," says St. Chrysostom, " of the Divine operation which worketh even in the hearts of those that know not of it! Was there not a secret voice in the very heart of Pilate, which sounded aloud to him, as it were, by a sort of clamorous silence ?" " Pilate," says Quesnel, "from being the Judge of Christ, seems to become His first Apostle to the Greeks, Romans, and Hebrews, publishing to them His reign upon and by the Cross." In another place the same writer says, " The Holy Ghost, Master both of the tongue and hands of the wicked, makes them to speak truth when they desire to ridicule."

With regard to this superscription it is further to be observed, that our Lord is not only " King of Salem," but as the true Melchizedec, He is Priest also. Not only as a King was He drawing the hearts of all men unto Him, by being lifted up on the Cross; but also as a Priest He was offering up the sacrifice of His own Body on the Cross. So the title on the Cross set forth His kingly dignity; and, as the Chief Priest carried on his head " holiness unto the Lord," according to the letter of the law, so " Jesus," as Origen observes, "the true Chief Priest and King, bore His title written on the Cross; and ascending unto the Father, instead of the letters and the name, He has Him Himself who is named: He bears His Father for His crown, and is rendered worthy of Him [9]." Where Origen seems to allude to that expression of St. Paul's, that "the head of Christ is God [10]." It was indeed from this His Cross that God

[9] In Matt. Com. 130.   [10] 1 Cor. xi. 3.

received Him as King of the Jews, and said unto Him, "Sit Thou on My right hand, till I make Thine enemies Thy footstool."

Of this inscription, thus done in mere derision and mockery, St. Jerome observes, that it served to prove how utterly futile was every other ground and charge that they could bring against Him, for sedition and the like. And Bede says, that "it was thus divinely provided, that not even by slaying Him could they effect it, that they should not have Him for their King: for by the death of the Cross He did not lose, but rather confirmed and strengthened His kingdom." "It showed," says Theophylact, "the craftiness of the devil's wiles against Christ, that the accusation should be written up in a threefold character; that it should escape the notice of no one that passed by, that He had made Himself a King: but what did it signify, but that the powerful, the wise, and the worshippers of God, the Roman, the Greek, and the Jew, were to be subject to His kingdom? To human eyes indeed it seemed as if His kingdom was set at nought, and destroyed, but it was rather amplified thereby." And all this, it is to be observed, is brought about by the unbelief of the Jews. When the birth of his son was foretold to Zacharias, he believed it not; but by his unbelief it was occasioned and procured that the name of the Baptist was written by himself on a tablet, as well as declared by the Angel. And now, by the unbelief of the Jews and Gentiles, it is brought about, not only that Christ should be declared King by God Himself, but that it should be written up before all people through means of their unbelief. For in writing there is conveyed a stronger and more emphatic confirmation, than in words spoken. Thus is the great purpose of God established, but by means of Jewish infidelity.

THE GARMENTS.

We come now to stand among the spectators, on Mount Calvary, not idly to gaze, but to adore therein the awful presence of God. And here a variety of circumstances occur, such as would naturally happen among the actors and spectators of such a scene; such as human motive, or fortuitous incident, might give rise to; whether it be from the exultations of gratified malice, or from wanton cruelty, or the customary proceedings of such an execution, or from the reverence and sympathy of friends. But when we discern therein God's presence, all things are changed, every word and action is weighed in the balances of God's sanctuary. For the case is, in fact, nothing else but that the Word of God had gone forth in prophecy, and that all events, though the actors in them thought not and knew not of it, were arranging and marshalling themselves in order, and coming forth at the fiat of God's Almighty Word. For, as not a sparrow falleth to the ground, nor a hair from the head, without His knowledge, much more was every incident regulated by Almighty Wisdom, and recorded with Divine purpose, respecting the death of His own Son. As He had expressly prescribed circumstances apparently most trivial in all those forms of ceremonial Worship which attended on the legal sacrifices, which were but the shadows of this Great Sacrifice; much more hath He ordained with infinite care, and in infinite wisdom, every word that should be spoken, every act that should be done in the immediate presence and offering up of Jesus Christ. And, as we reverently suppose, that all things going before, and prophetic words spoken, had an eye to this Great Sacrifice; so also may we venture to conclude that these things, which now occurred, were full of Divine import, with regard to things that were to come. Every thing is mysterious in this season of mysteries; every thing becomes Divine that approaches the Cross, and partakes of its Heavenly radiance. It was that radiance that lighted all things before, and which shall light up all things hereafter. And what there occurs, with regard to Christ's natural Body, may prefigure what shall occur with regard to His spiritual Body, the Church.

First of all, the soldiers,—as soon as they had stripped our blessed Lord of His garments, and had suspended Him naked on the Cross,—began to divide among themselves, what was their customary perquisite upon such an execution, the garment which the Holy Jesus had worn. He, like Joseph, was about to flee from this evil and adulterous world, and leave His garment in its hands. St. Chrysostom supposes that this circumstance of their sharing His garments between them was, of itself [11], " a mark of peculiar humiliation and abjectness, as done to the very vilest of men, for we do not read of any thing of the kind being done in the case of the thieves; but only to those who were so abject as to have nothing else to be divided." And, indeed, He has no earthly riches, but these poor garments, they are all He has; and even these He gives to others, and parts with them before His death, that He may die in utter nakedness and shame. He gave clothing to Adam, to cover his shame; and now takes on Himself the shame and nakedness of Adam. But those garments which He gave Adam, and these which He now bequeaths to the soldiers, are but the

[11] Hom. lxxxviii.

types of those Spiritual gifts, and that Spiritual clothing, which He has left to us, who are transgressors like Adam; who are His enemies, like the soldiers. "Such as the first man was," says St. Ambrose, "when He dwelt in Paradise; such was the Second, when He entered thither." And St. Athanasius with great beauty[1], "He laid aside His garments: for it was meet, that in leading men into Paradise, He should unclothe Himself of those garments which Adam received when he was cast out of Paradise. For when Adam sinned, and was thereafter to die, he received coats of skins, which were made of dead animals, and were the symbols of the dying which had come upon him on account of sin. But the Lord, in taking upon Himself all things for our sakes, clothed Himself with these, in order that He might also strip Himself of the same, and instead of these might clothe us with life and immortality."

These Divine garments, from the very hem of which "virtue went forth and healed them all," we may well suppose were, of all things that hand of man had ever framed, the most worthy of being expressly spoken of by all of the four Evangelists, and by the prophet beforehand. And so it is. For we read "*when they had crucified Him* (Matt. Mark) *they divided among themselves His garments* (Matt., Mark, Luke), *casting lots* (Matt., Mark, Luke) *upon them, what each one should take* (Mark). *So that that which was spoken by the prophet* (Matt.) *and the Scripture* (John) *might be fulfilled* (Matt. John), *which saith*" (John) in the twenty-second Psalm, "*They parted My garments among them, and cast lots upon My vesture*" (Matt. John). Now from the account in St. Matthew alone

---

[1] Serm. de Pass. et Cruce Dom.

we might have had some difficulty in ascertaining how both parts of this prophecy were fulfilled; for the prophecy speaks of two things, the dividing His garments, and also at the same time the casting lots for His vesture. Or some might have imagined that the prophecy only spoke in a general manner, and that a close accuracy of expression was not to be looked for; or that the casting the lots merely referred to the division of the garments, according as St. Mark's account mentions that it took place, for each, it seems, took his own part by lot. We have therefore great reason to be thankful that the last Evangelist has supplied us with these particulars. Every thing the beloved disciple speaks is so full of Divinity, that it may well arrest our devoutest contemplations. "*The soldiers therefore,*" he says, "*when they crucified Jesus, took His garments, and made four divisions, to each soldier a part.*" The soldiers being evidently from this circumstance four in number. "*And*" they took "*also His coat,*" or linen garment: "*now His coat was without seam, being woven from the top throughout the whole. They said therefore one to another, Let us not divide it, but let us cast lots for it, whose it shall be. These things therefore the soldiers did*" (John). The very nature of the garment implies, as St. Chrysostom observes, its meanness, for he says that in Palestine they were usually made of two parts. And, indeed, if they are right in their interpretation, who consider the coat of Joseph to have been of many parts or colours, then it would be the contrast to that of our Lord; if Joseph's, for its costliness, was of many colours, our Lord's, from its meanness, of one piece, "without seam." For the types of our Lord were, in many respects, "all glorious" without: but He Himself and His

Church was more especially "all glorious" within. At all events, this His garment was doubtless of a mean quality, and their casting lots for it was probably in a kind of mockery and derision, as for a thing so vile, and yet the garment of a King.

Now when our Lord was on earth, many, no doubt, thronged Him, and touched His clothes, but received no benefit therefrom, because they did it without faith and reverence: but those who did so in faith and fear, as it is said, "in fear and trembling," received inconceivable blessing. With the same spirit of meekness may we approach this subject. That this "coat without seam" or division, "woven from the top throughout," signifies the one Holy Catholic Church, is generally allowed by all, and has been ever held of old to be the case. And this is according to the analogy of Scripture, which we before alluded to, when we observed that the rending of the Chief Priest's robe signified the rending of the Jewish Church: but here it may be observed, that it is not the external robe, as in the Jewish High Priest, but the inner garment of Christ, His Church being one in spiritual and internal union.

Thus St. Cyprian explains it in that well known passage, in his treatise on the unity of the Church, wherein he says—that "in the sacrament and sign of His garment, Christ has declared the unity of His Church." It is woven from the top throughout. "That vesture," he says, "betokened unity, descending from above, coming, that is, from Heaven and from the Father, which might not be rent in any wise by the receiver or possessor, but which preserved a coherence at once entire, substantial, and inseparable. He cannot possess Christ's vesture, who rends and divides Christ's Church." And after speaking of the garment rent by

the Prophet Ahijah, signifying that the kingdom
should be rent, he adds, "But in truth, because
Christ's people cannot be divided, His coat woven
throughout and of one piece was not divided by those
whom it fell to; entire, united, knit together, it shows
the compact union of us, the people who have put on
Christ[2]." And St. Augustin differs not from this in
taking it for the unity and charity of the Church,
being without seam, and coming entire to one person.
Therefore indeed is the Church called Catholic, as
being one throughout the whole from the top, though
divided into various parts of the world; as the Apostles,
though twelve, were but one, for what they did is said
to be done by Christ Himself, and He is One; One in
Twelve. "And therefore it is," says St. Austin, "that
Christ, when speaking to all, yet speaks unto Peter in
the singular number; 'I give unto thee the keys of
the kingdom of Heaven[3].'"

But St. Chrysostom observes, that some consider it to
imply "the Divinity of our Lord, which cometh down
from above, and therefore is that robe which could not
be divided or rent. He could not, as mere man, be
destroyed by death." And St. Athanasius[4] explains
the robe, woven from the top throughout, as signifying
that "He who was clothed therewith was not of earth,
but the Word which had come from above, and therefore not divisible, but the undivisible Word of the
Father." And again he says, "The Gospel remains
undivided while the shadows are divided, the veils of
the Jewish Temple. But this," he says, "was preserved
entire by the power of Him who was on the Cross."

[2] Lib. de Unit. Eccles. Tr. v. 6.
[3] Matt. xvi. 19. In Joan. Evang. Tract. cxviii.
[4] De Pass. et Cruce Domini.

But St. Cyril of Alexandria says it may be considered as signifying "the sacred Body of the Lord, which was not formed in the natural way, but by the Holy Spirit coming down from above." And Theophylact also takes the same view, that it may be thus "considered as the most holy Body of the Lord, formed by the Power of the Holy Spirit from above, and the Power of the Most High."

But, what is very remarkable, in this great variety of interpretation, there exists, notwithstanding, much of harmony and consistency. For they who say that it signifies our Lord's Divine Nature, agree with those who consider it as His human Body, inasmuch as both are inseparably united together; and they who express these two opinions, yet both thus interpret it as of His coming from above. And they, again, who consider this robe to represent the Church, harmonize with these, because the Church is the Spiritual Body of the Lord. Nor would they differ from this who consider it may be interpreted as meaning the unity of the Church, or that love on which its well-being and life depend. Nor would this be at variance with the first and highest signification of our Lord's Divinity, for God is Love, and Christ is God: and Love and Unity is the very condition of Christ's Presence in His Church. The Church is His own Body: He is Love: and His Church is Love.

And thus considering the garment without seam as the Unity of the Church, we shall, without difficulty, admit St. Augustin's interpretation [5], that the four divisions of

[5] St. Augustin's words are, " Quadripartita vestis Domini Jesu Christi, quadripartitam figuravit Ejus Ecclesiam, toto scilicet, qui quatuor partibus constat, terrarum orbe diffusam, et omnibus

the other garments signify the four quarters of the globe, the north, south, east, and west, over which the Church will be extended; for, as he says, at the end of the world the Angels " shall gather His elect from the four winds[6]." Or, perhaps, we might venture to suppose that the four quarters of the world would be the four soldiers which divided these gifts among themselves. Of the divided garments St. Athanasius says, that " these were divisible and separated into four parts, because He carried them for the sins of the whole world, which is divisible into four parts, the east, west, north, and south ; and looking upon Him as being clothed with these St. John says, ' Behold the Lamb of God that taketh away the sins of the world.' " And this also is compatible with what we quoted before from the same writer, who explains the garments, as representing those skins with which Adam was clothed, in sign of our mortification, or of our dying on account of sin.

But St. Ambrose[7], in speaking of the four soldiers, says, " They may, perhaps, be a type of the four Evangelists, who wrote up the title which all may read." And when we consider that the number of four Evangelists has been thought to be some adaptation to the four parts of the world, there may be some secret harmony in all these, as relative, in some way, to the four divisions. And with regard to the Gospels themselves, it is remarkable how the type applies. For though the Gospels are four, yet the Gospel itself is but one ; perfect, entire, indivisible : this is the inner garment, the outer garments are the four. This oneness arises from

eisdem partibus æqualiter, id est concorditer, distributam."—In Joan. Tract. cxviii. 4.

[6] Matt. xxiv. 31.   [7] Expos. in Luc. lib. x. 115.

the very nature of what is Divine, as division arises from the imperfection of man. For as the Church is one, so there is "one Body and one Spirit;—one Lord, one Faith, one Baptism;—one God and Father of all[8];"— and so also one Gospel;—one in four: one of God, four men bearing the same: the Divine indivisible; the human divisible. And indeed the Gospel may well be considered as the clothing of Christ; as Origen considers it in his Commentary on the Transfiguration. For on that occasion it was, as one might well suppose, this very same raiment of Christ, of which He is stripped in death, which became "white and glistering, so as no fuller on earth could whiten it[9]." So are these Gospels, when illuminated by the Holy Spirit, though written by human hands, and clothing the Body of Christ, describing His human actions, yet radiant with Divinity.

Or again, from considering the one undivided robe as love and charity, that very bond of peace, which preserves the One Holy Catholic Church in unity, we are led on to consider the other garments as those diversities of gifts[1] of which St. Paul speaks when he is proceeding to speak of charity. For if the undivided robe is the Body of Christ, so St. Paul describes these diversities of gifts as representing the various limbs of the one Body, which is Christ. There is but one Spirit, one inner garment of the soul, which is love; "above all things," or "over all things," "put on charity, which is the bond of perfectness." This alone will not fail, being alone imperishable, but will cover us on that day from a multitude of sins, being Christ's own Divine robe. And therefore to "put on charity," and to "put on Christ," is one and the same thing. Nor is the interpretation of

---

[8] Eph. iv. 4. 6.   [9] Mark ix. 3.   [1] διαιρέσεις χαρισμάτων.

St. Jerome at variance with this, for he says, that the garments are the Commandments, by which Christ's Body, the Church, is covered; and the vesture is peace or unity.

But these great and Divine gifts, represented by the raiment of Christ, were shared and divided, not by good and friendly men, but by the cruel soldiers who slew Him; and so likewise, as we said before, we sinners of the Gentiles were the cause of His death; and woe be to us if we do not wrap around us His garment. This is what He has left below, Spiritual gifts for us to share, and His raiment of Evangelical righteousness; not by works which we have done, nor from any choice of our own, but, as it were, by "lot," the inheritance given us by the election of God. "It is granted," says Augustin, "not to the merits or person of individuals, but by the secret judgment of God." And St. Athanasius, "they cast lots for His vesture, and He suffereth and alloweth this, that Christ may become our inheritance;" as the Psalmist saith, "the Lord Himself is the portion of my inheritance and of my cup. Thou shalt maintain my lot [2]." Thus was Christ unclothed, that we might be clothed by Him. He has gone away, but left His clothing: left His Church, wherewith we by Him may be clothed, and put on that wedding garment, which is Divine love. For many are the diversities of gifts, but beneath all, and above all, and more excellent than all, is charity.

THE SPECTATORS.

The soldiers having now performed their work, and divided the (apparently mean) spoils, seated themselves

---

[2] De Pass. et Cruc. Dom. Ps. xvi. 6.

below the Cross to gaze on the agonies of the Sufferer. "*And sitting down, they watched Him there*" (Matt). "*And,*" in another place, "*stood the people, gazing upon Him.*" (Luke) ; perhaps at a short distance off. And beside this group of people, collected together as to a spectacle, there were others passing by, whether intentionally or by accident, who stopped to revile Him as they passed. For as St. Luke speaks of the people that stood gazing, St. Matthew and St. Mark speak of "those that were going by." For indeed St. John had mentioned that it was "near the city ;" on which account he said, that "many of the Jews read the inscription ;" it was therefore, perhaps, on a place so public, that many went by near to the Cross, so near as to read what was written on it: here therefore perhaps it was, that "*they that were going by blasphemed Him*" (Matt. Mark) ; and being, probably, near enough to address Him, were "*shaking their heads, and saying* (Matt. Mark), *Ah !* (Mark) *Thou that destroyest the Temple, and buildest it in three days, save Thyself*" (Matt. Mark). Thus wonderfully and awfully were they applying to Him, unconsciously, those very words, of His destroying the Temple, which He was in the act of fulfilling according to His promise ; and using those words not in accordance with His own expression, "ye shall destroy," but with that of the false witnesses on that morning, "I will destroy." And therein mysteriously were they acknowledging the Omnipotence of Him that was crucified, and their own impotence even in that act ; they were acknowledging, unconsciously, that although it was they who were destroying the Temple of God, as far as their own purpose and evil will went,—yet that it was He Himself who voluntarily, and of His own free accord, laid down His life, or they could not have done it. Thus, too, all things conspire to acknowledge God's Hand and Presence. "*If Thou be the Son of God*" (Matt.), they said, and thus bore testimony, while they thought it not, to the declaration for which He died, "If thou be the Son of God, *come down from the Cross*" (Matt. Mark).

Thus were they fulfilling great and Divine purposes, in that every wild and idle word they spoke was bearing witness to Christ; and sometimes were they using the very expressions which holy prophecy had put in their mouths. Little did they think that their very posture, and their wayward and passionate movements, while they spoke, were but those significant marks of scorn which were accurately pourtrayed long before by the Psalmist. Thus two Evangelists mention " their shaking their heads " as they spoke; and twice does the Psalmist mention the same circumstance, "they shoot out their lips, and shake their heads, saying³;" and "they that looked upon Me, shaked their heads⁴."

It may be here observed, that as we had each part of the nation combining in our Saviour's condemnation, so have we them all now exulting in His sufferings; if this is said of the people, the Chief Priests and the Scribes and the Pharisees also are described. For while the people were thus reviling the most holy Redeemer, "*the Rulers also, together with them, were deriding Him*" (Luke); not with those who were passing by beneath the Cross, but with the people who stood aloof: it is not said that, with the revilers last described, they addressed our Lord Himself; but whether it was from being at a little further distance from Him, or whether it was from feelings of contempt and scorn, they are not described as the common people were, as speaking to Him, but of Him,

³ Ps. xxii. 7. ⁴ Ps. cix. 24.

among themselves or with the people. For, in speaking of those who reviled Him as they passed, the Evangelists add, "*in like manner, also, the Chief Priests* (Matt. Mark), *one with another* (Mark), *mocking Him, together with the Scribes* (Matt. Mark) *and the Elders* (Matt.), *said, He saved others* (Matt. Mark, Luke), *Himself He cannot save*" (Matt. Mark). So desperately wicked is the human heart that it came to this, —that while they exulted, in triumphant malice, over Him whom they now had so thoroughly in their power, as they thought, they reproached Him with the very works of mercy He had done, even with the dead man whom He had called from the grave, which they seem to allude to.   But, as they fulfilled every other designation, so did they also mark Him out now as "the Saviour," and bear witness to Him as the true Jesus; the three Evangelists have recorded their words, "He saved others."   And as if professing themselves ready to receive that sign of the Prophet Jonas, which our Lord said was the only one that should be given them [5], though they knew not of what He spoke, "He saved others, *let Him save Himself, if He be the Christ, the chosen of God* (Luke). *Let Christ, the King of Israel, come down now from the Cross, that we may see and believe*" (Mark). Awful and portentous words! for the hour cometh, and now is, when He shall indeed come down, and "every eye shall see Him, and they also which pierced Him [6]." Yes, would another say in reply, taking up the words, "*If He be the King of Israel, let Him come down now from the Cross, and we will believe Him*" (Matt.). But still were they acknowledging Him; still using the very words of the Psalms; still bearing testimony to His assertions, in

<hr>

[5] Vol. Min. pp. 160—162.   [6] Rev. i. 7.

every word, act, movement: so does He who commands the raging of the sea control also " the madness of the people [7]," making them to speak His appointed words. " *He trusted in God,*" said they, " *let Him deliver Him now if He will have Him; for He said, I am the Son of God* " (Matt.). " Such things did they imagine, and were deceived: as for the mysteries of God, they knew them not, for their own wickedness hath blinded them [8]."

In this very mockery they confess Him the Saviour; for they say, " He saved others." They confess His trust in God, for they say, " He trusted in God." They confess His declaration that He was " the Son of God." They confess by every word and action that He was " the Prophet;" for they speak and do nothing but what He foretells of them in His word. They confess that He said, He should rebuild His Temple in three days. They bear witness by the inscription that He was " the King of the Jews." But still their words in themselves were idle, and not true. This very promise that they would believe, as St. Jerome observes, was not true; for He did more than they asked for; " to rise from the grave when dead was far more than to descend from the Cross when alive;" He rose again, but they did not believe. For as our Lord had Himself said, that if they would " not hear Moses and the Prophets," who so abundantly testified of all that was now going on; if they were deaf and blind to all they had foretold; " neither will they be persuaded though one rose from the dead." And, as to the other expressions, St. Chrysostom says, " Being the children of the devil, how do they imitate the very words of their father, for the devil said, ' If

<hr>

[7] Ps. lxv. 7.   [8] Wisd. ii. 22.

Thou be the Son of God, cast Thyself down;' and the Jews say, 'If Thou be the Son of God, come down from the Cross.' "

But St. Jerome curiously observes of this expression, that he thinks it must have been the instigation of devils which induced them to say this; for as soon as the Lord was crucified, they perceived the power of the Cross, and understood that their strength was broken, and therefore they do this that He might descend from the Cross. St. Athanasius also attributes this to the machinations of the devil; he considers that " Satan had by this time perceived from our Lord's invincible fortitude and patience that His victory was in death, and that he was himself being foiled and vanquished by his own wickedness; and suspecting that this was He of whom it is written, ' He hath ascended up on high, He hath led captivity captive,' he now turns all his arts to prevent His becoming a salvation to others by His death; for he knew full well that if He descended from the Cross, the Jews would not believe for all their saying so: he knew that the Lord dieth not, but that the death of this man would become life and salvation to all. Therefore he urged Him to come down from the Cross; and made the Pharisees promise that they would believe [9]." Certain it is that nothing ever showed more strongly the acts and instigation of the devil; while every act of Satan's was turned by a mysterious providence to the glory of God. Thus another writer suggests " that the offering Him vinegar was a device of Satan's, which he knew not that he was doing against himself. For he was giving to the Saviour the bitterness of that wrath by which he kept us for our disobedience to the law; but He received it and

[9] De Pass. et Cruc. Dom.

finished: that, in return for that vinegar which we gave to Him, He might give us to drink of that wine which Wisdom hath mingled."

The image serves beautifully to express how our evil has served to set forth His goodness: and our disobedience has been the manifestation of His sinless obedience and perfect righteousness; by the fall we have lost the crown of our own innocence, but obtained the Crown of His righteousness, by faith being made one with Him: whereby the Paradise of our disobedience has become to Him the garden of Gethsemane; bearing bitter fruits, where the "grapes are grapes of gall;" where "their wine is the poison of dragons, and the cruel venom of asps [10];" but which has become to us a better and celestial Paradise.

Nor did the soldiers continue silent spectators, where we left them sitting to watch Him at the foot of the Cross. For they also came up to join in these revilings. "*Even the soldiers also,*" says St. Luke, "*derided Him, coming to Him and offering Him vinegar;*" either in mock compassion, or, as Theophylact says, "offering Him vinegar, as if ministering to a king:" and alluding, as would appear from St. Luke, to the inscription written over His head, and the charge made to the heathen that morning, "*saying, If Thou art the King of the Jews, save Thyself*" (Luke). So was He even now, as before His trial, acknowledged as Son of God by the Jew, and as "King of the Jews" by the Gentile. "For being ignorant of the Scriptures," says Bede, "the soldiers revile Him, not as Christ, but as King of the Jews."

In the mean while our adorable Lord was hanging, in silent suffering, on His excruciating bed of death and

---

[10] Deut. xxxii. 33.

pain; and in order that the thoughts of His heart, and the weight of His sorrows, might be known to His suffering children to the end of the world, and that they might in their own evils find sympathy in His sorrows; in the same passages where His enemies are thus closely described, He Himself pours forth also His passionate complaints in His sufferings as man; and expresses the secret communings of His own heart with God, and the acknowledgment of His righteousness. "And Thou continuest holy, O Thou worship of Israel;"—"O go not far from Me, for trouble is at hand, and there is none to help Me;"—"Be not Thou far from Me, O Lord; Thou art My succour, haste Thee to help Me[1]." And again, "Hear Me, O God, in the multitude of Thy mercies: even in the truth of Thy salvation. Take me out of the mire that I sink not; O let Me be delivered from them that hate Me, and out of the deep waters."—"Thy rebuke hath broken My heart; I am full of heaviness: I looked for some to have pity on Me, but there was no man, neither found I any to comfort Me[2]." "In the volume of the Book it is written of Me, that I should fulfil Thy will, O My God; I am content to do it. Yea, Thy law is within My heart[3]." And again, as if alluding to these many manifestations of God's foreknowledge and control which were now being fulfilled before His eyes, "O save Me according to Thy mercy. And they shall know how that this is Thy hand; and that Thou, Lord, hast done it. Let them curse, but bless Thou[4]!" For in the book of Psalms we have, if I may reverently say it, the very Prayer Book of our Divine Lord Himself: which He inspired; which He Himself made use of, and has bequeathed as His own Book to His Church.

---

[1] Ps. xxii.　　　[2] Ps. lxix.　　　[3] Ps. xl.　　　[4] Ps. cix.

THE PENITENT THIEF.

Our Lord's companions in suffering had been joining also in these revilings against Him: and "*the same*" reproach which the Chief Priests dwelt upon, of His saving others and His trusting in God, "*the thieves also* (Matt.), *they who were crucified with Him, reviled Him with*" (Matt. Mark). This is the account which two Evangelists afford us; and it might be supposed by some, that although they speak in the plural number, yet they only refer to one of them; the one whom St. Luke mentions as reviling, and not to both. For as St. Ambrose and Augustin show on this passage, the plural number is sometimes used when one only is spoken of. And yet it seems better to suppose that both accounts are strictly accurate, and that by the plural number they here mean both. This seems the more reverential, and therefore the truer mode of interpretation; and so St. Ambrose and many of the Fathers consider it. For it is easy thus to understand it, that both of the thieves did at first reproach our Lord on the Cross; but that one of them, during the long period of their common sufferings, and perhaps of their common trial before their judge during the morning, had heard and seen so much in our Lord's words and demeanour, and at the same time had his heart so softened by his own afflictions, that he saw and recognized the Christ. For even Pilate, under circumstances so very different, was greatly won over in a space of time perhaps not longer. And we cannot doubt but that our Lord who, in His Divine care and knowledge, was so watchful of the heart of each, was not unmindful of this man throughout. St. Cyril speaks of the two thieves as representing the Jew and the Gentile, of which one at last repented: he and St.

Chrysostom also think that they both at first reviled. Nor is St. Augustin decidedly opposed to this supposition. Origen says, "We may suitably understand that at first both thieves blasphemed the Lord, but afterwards one of them was converted and believed: considering by himself the miracles he had heard of being done by Him, and perhaps seeing the changes in the sky and the unusual darkness[5]." And St. Ambrose, in like manner, says, "Perhaps this man also first reviled, but was suddenly converted; nor is it to be wondered at that He who forgave even those who were insulting Him, should grant pardon unto one that confessed his fault[6]." It is, in fact, but a similar discrepancy to that respecting the position of some of the women, who are mentioned by one Evangelist as near the Cross, and by another at a distance off; a discrepancy easily accounted for by conceiving that the two narratives speak of a different time.

The incident itself, one of so compassionate a character, and which could scarcely be the subject of human observation, is precisely such as St. Luke is used to select for mention. "*And one,*" he says, "*of the malefactors, which were hanged with Him, reviled Him, saying, If Thou art the Christ, save Thyself and us.*" And this he did evidently in words so loud, that the other, who was on the other side of our Lord, could hear. But he now had been probably deeply conscience-stricken, and meditating on his past life, had come to himself in the ineffable holiness of our Saviour's presence, and in the influence of His powerful grace. "*The other answering, rebuked him, saying, Dost not thou fear God, seeing thou art in the same condemnation? and we indeed justly: for we receive the just recompense for the things we have done.*"

[5] Comm. in Matt.   [6] Expos. ad Lucam.

But this man hath done nothing amiss." From which words it is evident that he had known something before of our blessed Lord, of the circumstances of His condemnation, or something else, that assured him of our Lord's innocence. And at the same time that he addressed the other thief, or perhaps at a later period, when wrapt in reflection upon himself, and upon the scene that was going on, he turns to Christ;—"When in speaking to others," says St. Chrysostom, "he finds that their hearing is stopped, he returns to Him who knoweth the hearts;"—"*And he said unto Jesus, Remember me, O Lord, when Thou shalt come into Thy kingdom. And Jesus said unto him, Verily I say unto thee, This day shalt thou be with Me in paradise*" (Luke).

By this wonderful conversion the malice of the devil was turned beyond all things to the glory of Christ. "For the devil had wished," says St. Chrysostom, "to darken and overshadow what was taking place. But what they did to throw reproach on Christ contributed to the truth. His arts were frustrated, and not only did not impair but added greatly to Christ's glory[7]." For to convert a thief on the Cross, and to take him to Paradise, was no less a miracle than to rend the rocks in twain. This instance mentioned by St. Chrysostom is but one, out of very many, wherein the evil designed by the enemy was turned into the glory of God by Christ. In order to ridicule and degrade Christ, he suggests to them to place Him between two thieves: it redounded to the highest glory of His kingdom of mercy. He instigated them to crucify Christ, rather than to put Him to any other death. No other death would have so much reached to the fulness, to the length, and

---

[7] Advers. Jud. Or. v. 3.

breadth, and depth, and height of our misery: by no other death would He have rendered it impossible for His servants to exceed Him, in degradation, and misery, and pain. The devil urged Pilate to the scorn and ridicule of that title on the Cross: it is a name written in Heaven; it bears witness to His eternal kingdom. He urged them to mock Him, but all they said fulfilled prophecy. He instigated them to add to his torments, but it only made His patience more perfect, His atonement more deeply atoning. And it has passed into an invariable law for His subjects and followers, that the evil designed against them is by Christ made their great good, if they adhere to Him. Thus was it ever of old; the sea that seemed to stop the flight of Israel, and to deliver them up to their enemies, opened the way of their salvation, and destroyed those enemies. The wilderness, where there was no food, brought Heavenly bread; where all was dry desolation there was water from the Rock, which is Christ.

The circumstance itself is in the highest degree remarkable in two points of view. For in the first place, there is no higher instance of our Lord's mercy on account of the greatness of the gift conferred; and secondly, there does not appear any greater instance of faith on record. In the depth of our Lord's extreme humiliation, when even the disciples had fled, and doubted and denied, and the beloved disciple alone of all the world was found faithful, the penitent thief showed in this instance a combination of humility, charity, faith, and fear of God, such as indicated a thorough conversion of the heart; a state of mind, which was marked by these qualities in the highest degree. At a time when, to worldly eyes, the King and the Kingdom appeared so utterly beyond acceptance and belief: as to be a matter of scorn and ridicule, this penitent acknowledged Him as his Lord and his King, as one having power to save from death. Our Lord was set before him, not in His miracles, not in His authoritative teaching, not as pointed out by prophecies, not as proclaimed by the great forerunner. But as He had said to Pilate, that he who was of the truth would hear His voice, so is He known to this penitent thief, and acknowledged; acknowledged too by a confession, almost beyond every other acknowledgment during our Lord's life. The spiritual nature of His Kingdom is acknowledged, His heavenly Kingship; He is not only acknowledged but defended, when all the world is against Him, and no other is found to maintain His cause. ·Here is humble confession of unworthiness, "we receive the due reward of our deeds;" and "he that confesseth his sins shall find mercy." Here is reverential fear of God expressed, and acknowledgment of His judgments, "Dost not thou fear God, seeing that thou art in the same condemnation? and we indeed justly:" and "he that humbleth himself should be exalted." Here is love to man shown in concern for the other thief; love to God in submission to His judgments, and in defending Christ; and "charity shall cover the multitude of sins." Here is faith of the highest kind attributing power to perform; and hope of the highest kind that looks to nothing less than a heavenly Kingdom. As the first to enter into Paradise with Christ, he is perhaps set forth as an example of that temper which is required of all who would enter there. For that man has most attained unto Evangelical righteousness who is the most thoroughly penitent, the most truly humbled; and all Christian good works lead to this humiliation. This righteousness has its foundation in penitence, and has for its crown the penitential graces. For he that hungers most, shall be most filled: he that is most abased, shall be most exalted. Here again is the fulfilment of those Evangelical requisites, to which the promises are annexed;—"Him that confesseth Me before men, will I confess before the Angels of God." Here was "the poor in spirit," the first to enter into the Kingdom; here was one that knocked, to whom the door was opened. Here was set forth before the world the highest instance of that mercy which characterizes the Gospel dispensation; here was a man at the point of death, an outcast from mankind, to whom, humanly speaking, all hope would have appeared lost, both for this world and for the next; yet more highly accepted than any child of Adam, and the first to enter Heaven. The veil was on the point of being rent in twain, our Lord was entering into His Kingdom, and this penitent thief being received with Him. He is the only one of all Christians, of whom we are sure from God's Word that he found an entrance there. This was the strongest point of view in which it could be set before all Christians, that they have a High Priest who can be touched with the feeling of our infirmities, having been Himself in like condition of suffering. Therefore to all distressed persons of all times it affords an encouragement to approach Him; it was an evidence of what would be the strength of Christians to the end of the world: that suffering would be good for them, that their own cross would open their hearts to acknowledge Christ crucified; that they who suffer together with Him, shall reign with Him. Here did our Lord afford from the depth of His own anguish, consolation to all dying persons, who shall die in Him and in His faith.

Here did He afford them most blessed assurance, respecting that intermediate state of the good, that whatever it is, it is to be with Him in Paradise. In this occasion beyond all others "deep calleth unto deep," the deep of our misery unto the deep of God's mercy.

Thus ancient writers delight to dwell on the greatness of this man's faith, and on the richness of Christ's mercy. Gregory[8], speaking of this penitent, says, "On the cross the nails had fastened his hands and feet, and nothing in him was free from punishment, but his heart and tongue, which alone remained. By the inspiration of God he offered up to Him whatever he had left free; according as it is written, 'with the heart men believe unto righteousness, and with the mouth confession is made unto salvation.' For of a sudden filled with grace, the thief both received and preserved on the cross, the three virtues which the Apostle mentions. He had faith, for he believed that He, whom he beheld dying in like manner with himself, would reign as God. He had hope, for he asked for the coming of His kingdom; and he had even in death a living charity, for he reproved for his impiety his brother and associate who was dying for a similar crime." And St. Cyril of Jerusalem says with great beauty[9], "What power, O robber, enlightened thee? who taught thee to worship that despised Man, thy companion on the cross? O Eternal Light, which givest light to them that are in darkness." .... "Be of good cheer; not that thy deeds are such as should make thee be of good cheer: but that the King is here dispensing favours." .. "O mighty and ineffable grace! The faithful Abraham had not yet entered, but the robber enters! Moses and the Prophets had not yet entered, and the lawless robber enters."

[8] Moral. xviii.[9] Lect. xiii. 31.

"I am come, who feed My sheep among the lilies[1]: I have found a sheep, a lost one; but I lay it on my shoulders, for he believeth and hath said, I have gone astray like a sheep that is lost." But none more than St. Ambrose would be moved by this touching subject; "Very beautiful," says he, "is this example of earnest endeavour after conversion, that pardon is so quickly granted to the thief; and the gracious boon is more abundant than the entreaty; for the Lord ever gives more than is asked. For he prayed that the Lord would be mindful of him when He came into His kingdom, but the Lord says to him, 'Verily, I say unto thee, To-day shalt thou be with Me in Paradise.' For to be with Christ is life; where Christ is there is life, there a Kingdom[2]." And St. Chrysostom of the same, "The devil expelled Adam from Paradise, Christ took the thief there before all the world, even before Apostles. By his mere saying, and by faith alone, he entered into Paradise, that no one after his errors should despair of an entrance there. Observe the rapidity with which he passes from the Cross to heaven, from condemnation into Paradise, that thou mightest know that it was not according to his desert, but the Lord's own clemency." "But how could he obtain access into Paradise," asks St. Gregory Nyssen, "since there was there a flaming sword that turned every way?" "It thus turned every way," he supposes, "that it might repel the unworthy, and afford access to the worthy." But Gregory (the Great) observes, that "it was a turning sword which was afterwards to be removed thence, when He should come who, by the mystery of His Incarnation, should open unto us the access to Paradise." St. Cyril of

<hr>

[1] Cant. vi. 3.   [2] Expos. in Luc. lib. x. 121.

Jerusalem also in the same manner says, "Fear not, O robber, the fiery sword, it shrinks from its Lord."

Our reflections on this wonderful instance of man's conversion and God's mercy, may perhaps be well closed with the remark of Quesnel: "One sinner is converted at the hour of death, that we may hope; and but one, that we may fear!"

THE REVEALING OF MEN'S HEARTS.

The scene we are now contemplating on Mount Calvary sets before us a great multitude, with such variety of station and character, as might almost serve to represent the diversities to be found among mankind. It is an awful reflection, when we consider that all these persons,—who were thus acting their different parts, as God had foreknown and declared, each according to the temper and the thoughts of his own heart,—were thus acting and showing their true characters in the very eye of their Omnipotent and Omniscient Judge, who hung as a malefactor before them. Thus ever in His Providence does God hide Himself, leaving men to the imagination of their own hearts; while here and there some one, like the penitent thief, is brought near to Him by affliction, and made conscious of His presence. "Here one might see the Saviour," says St. Chrysostom, "in the midst of the thieves; holding the scale of justice, and weighing faith and infidelity." And if in the case of the thieves, doubtless equally so in the case of all. For He who was on the Cross was the Judge of all men : and where He is, there is in some sense His Judgment-seat.

Here was fully manifested that great principle, which will try men through all generations, that of Christ crucified. The Cross was to be "for a sign that should be spoken against—in order that the thoughts of many hearts might be revealed." It may be perceived how thoroughly it thus served as a means of proving what was in the heart of man : and that not only in the case of the inconsiderate multitude, but even in that of the disciples themselves. For the difference between St. Peter, St. John, St. Thomas, and others was manifested and brought out, in word and action, by means of this our Lord's extreme humiliation. The difference of character, and the degrees of faith they had severally attained to, would have been, humanly speaking, unseen and unknown, had it not been for this test. For Christ having now no external evidence of a power to support them or Himself; and having in Himself "no form nor comeliness," and to worldly eyes "no beauty" for which men "should desire Him;" they were left to stand alone, excepting so far as they were supported by faith in His Godhead. Nor can we conceive any other method by which this object of their probation would have been attainable. The Cross served as a touchstone to their whole disposition, their past life, their present thoughts. And if with the disciples, still more evidently might this be seen in the case of others, that it was "set for the rise and fall of many," either as a stumbling-block for their fall in that trial, or as the power of God for their restoration. It served for a mirror wherein the inner man of the soul became pourtrayed ; set forth in the sight of God and His Angels, as in the Sea of glass before the throne of God. With dreadful truth were the Scribes and Pharisees shown therein. The vice they were addicted to was hypocrisy, the whole of their religion being directed to the eyes of men; but the case of the poor and despised Man, who apparently hung helpless before them, brought out most thoroughly the state of their secret hearts. This was shown in the undisguised exultation which they evinced at the foot of the Cross, and in the searching trial of their principles and affections which they had undergone before Pilate. And although very many circumstances, throughout the trial and condemnation, appear to have been merciful warnings on the part of our Lord, intended to recall them, yet warnings when neglected, become judgments. The multitude, moreover, who had proclaimed Him with such triumphant welcome, might have appeared to themselves and others to have been high favourers and supporters of the Messiah; and, had He now appeared in circumstances of great external pomp and power, might have claimed for themselves a reward: but of them, too, our Lord's humiliation was the test. Much indeed, otherwise, might have been alleged by some as an excuse for their unbelief; they might have pleaded deference and submission to the opinions of those set over them, as the Chief Priests and Scribes were. This might have availed in excuse for some things, but could not hold when it came to their preferring a murderer to an innocent man. That they should have believed in Christ in His extreme humiliation, might appear more than we could demand of them; but we might reasonably expect from even natural religion compassion for a sufferer and so much regard to justice as not to have made an accusation, which they knew, or might have known, to be false. And had they had but these principles of natural piety, they might have been led on thereby to something higher and better. Thus it might be shown that the Crucifixion had the effect of revealing the thoughts of men's hearts, in every way, degree, and kind. Thus were they, while they knew it not, wantonly showing themselves in the Eye of their Judge. It was the searching trial of the hearts of men which God, in His inscrutable wisdom, was making : but as it was the probation, the revelation, and manifestation of man's wickedness, so was there also in the same event combined the revelation of God's goodness ; His mercy contending with man's impenitence and cruelty. If it is in some sense like the throne of Christ's judgment, yet that throne is encircled by the rainbow, by His everlasting Covenant of mercy.

But it may be supposed that the Cross does not now answer the same purpose, which it then did, inasmuch, as we all acknowledge and worship Him, whose Divine Majesty was then hidden from men's eyes. Yet the hearts and dispositions of men are still the same; and the doctrine of Christ crucified is still the same, in the various ways in which it is presented to the mind, and manifested under different circumstances. True penitence is still put to the proof by the Cross of Christ ; true love is evinced by a conformity to Christ crucified ; nay, He Himself is presented to the eye of faith under the same condition of humiliation ; for every shape of affliction "bears about in the body the marks of the Lord Jesus :" and is identified with Him, doubtless in some very high and concerning sense, as intimated by those words, " Inasmuch as ye have done it unto the least of these My brethren, ye have done it unto Me." That mysterious indwelling of Christ in His Church so strongly promised, calls forth in a similar manner our acknowledgment of a Divine Presence, of which doubtless it may be said, " Blessed are they who have not seen, and yet have believed." In order to try their faith the Godhead was then concealed under the garb of suffering Manhood; so is it now under the poor and mean elements of Bread and Wine. The Cross is at this day, as it then was, the test of man, as well as the power of God.

Thus it is that ever since our blessed Lord was

born into the world, the remarkable prediction of the prophet Malachi [3] has been fulfilled, wherein our Lord spoke of His coming to His Church. And although that prophecy seems ultimately to refer to the Day of His final appearing; yet in earnest of that awful manifestation, it may have many previous fulfilments in all the revelations of Christ crucified. "The Lord whom ye seek," hath, as He foretold, "suddenly come to His Temple, even the Messenger of the Covenant, whom ye delight in." But so very few at His coming were able to endure that searching test of true faith, that it is asked, as if in mournful surprise at the smallness of that number, "But who may abide the day of His coming? and who shall stand when He appeareth?" This manifestation of Christ was on that day, and is on this day, so much "the discerner of the thoughts and intents of the heart [4]," that no human words can equal the Divine description, "for He is like a refiner's fire, and like fullers' soap." And, as if alluding to the long continuance of this trial it is added, "and He shall sit as a refiner and purifier of silver." This intimate approach also of Christ, whereby He, the Judge of mankind, was standing as the very witness in the midst of them, enters into this awful description; "And I will come near to you to judgment; and I will be a swift witness."

OUR LORD'S MOTHER.

That nothing might be wanting to set before us the entire description of this momentous and awful scene, the last Evangelist introduces into the picture a touching mention of those, who were nearest to our Lord in devout affection, or bound to Him by the nearest of

[3] Ch. iii. 1. 5.   [4] Heb. iv. 12.

earthly ties ; in order to record another memorable instance of our Lord's last conduct and instruction :—
" *There stood by the Cross of Jesus His mother, and the sister of His mother, Mary, the wife of Cleopas,*" the mother of James and Joses [5], "*and Mary Magdalene.*" All men had failed in this trial excepting one disciple, and yet three women are there at the foot of the Cross : women surpass men in courage ; and this is the lesson which the Cross teaches us, that God's strength is perfected in human weakness.. It may be, that they come here in attendance on, and from connexion with, our Lord's mother ; and this may be partly the cause of their patient fortitude on this occasion ; because they are together with the mother of the adorable Son of God ; because both in suffering and in sex they are connected with her. For Christ had but one earthly Parent, and that was a woman. As she was " blessed among women," because she was admitted to such near approach to the Son of the Most High; so also blessed are women, because she was among them of whom the Son of God [6] was born. Mankind in general are blessed, because Christ, as born of a woman, was the Son of Man. And women may have some special blessing, inasmuch as He was born of a woman. Human life is blessed, because He lived in the flesh : and death is blessed, because He died : so every condition of life, which approached Him, receives thereby and communicates virtue from Him. The mystery of His Incarnation and Passion pervades all things, and all things partake of radiance and of strength on earth in proportion to their nearness, by any chain of circumstances, to that mystery. Children are blessed, because He was a child ; men

[5] See page 374.   [6] See page 108.

derive strength, because of His manhood; and He draws women to Him in being born of a woman. What wonder, therefore, if they are stronger than man; and if of that little group, around His Cross, the greater part are women? And although now in the depth of His agony, our Lord does not vouchsafe to them any marks of His favour or privilege,—and indeed says nothing to the other women, but only speaks to His mother;—yet to Mary Magdalene He first manifests Himself when risen from the grave; and the same day to Cleopas, who was probably the husband of this other Mary; and, as it would seem, to this Mary herself, among the other women mentioned in St. Matthew [7]. Who then are these, and what are those qualities, which are nearest to the Cross, which is Christ's earthly throne, and the sceptre by which He reigns in the hearts of those He loves? In St. John we have calm courage, virgin purity, Divine love; in Mary Magdalene, devout watchfulness and earnest penitence; in the other Mary, faithful patience and quiet constancy. But as to the blessed Virgin herself, she is hid, as if designedly, by a cloud from our view, and of her character we can divine but little.

With this company, therefore, may we now approach the Cross, and hear our Lord's last injunctions. Two of our Lord's sayings on the Cross were addressed to mankind; one of these was the acceptance of a penitent; the other was an injunction of filial piety. The two lessons, therefore, which our Lord may be supposed to bequeath to us, as His last instructions, are penitence and filial duty. On these two all Evangelical graces may be considered to be founded. There is also something appropriate in the two Evangelists who convey

---

[7] Ch. xxviii. 9. See Vol. Res. p. 111.

to us these our Lord's last messages. If St. Luke, with a peculiar propriety, gives us the account of the penitent thief, with no less suitableness does St. John afford us that of our Lord's mother. His words are, "*Jesus therefore, when He saw His mother, and the disciple standing by whom He loved, saith unto His mother, Woman, behold thy son!*" implying thereby, that John would be a son to her. "*Then saith He to the disciple, Behold thy mother. And from that time that disciple took her to his own;*"—to his own home, we should be disposed to add; but St. Austin beautifully observes, " not to his own property, to share that with him, for of this he had none to bestow, but to his own kind offices of filial affection[s]."

Here have we in our blessed Lord the great example of filial love: and here have we also combined with it the highest sanction of human friendship ; for we read in this His last dying hour ;—" When He saw the disciple whom He loved !" " With how great an honour," exclaims St. Chrysostom, " did He honour this disciple ! But he concealed himself in lowliness of wisdom ; for if he had wished to do so, he might have added the cause for which he was loved. For it is reasonable to suppose, that there was some cause, great and wonderful. But the reason why He says nothing else to John, nor consoles him in his sorrow, is, because it was not a time for the consolation of words. However, no slight matter was it to be honoured with so great an honour." Very few, indeed, were our blessed Lord's words, but they were replete with the highest consolation and mysterious greatness. What higher earthly crown could affection bestow on the beloved disciple? And doubtless the Virgin mother,

---

[s] In Joann. ad locum.

in being received by St. John, had vouchsafed to her the figure and sacrament of some vast and consoling mystery. Infinitely great and divine was that new union of most hallowed adoption; so great and divine, that Scripture and Tradition pass over all mention of it in sacred silence. What a home was that where he was who was so fully impressed with the Godhead of his Lord; where she was who had been chosen before all the daughters of Adam, to be His earthly Mother! Imagination and thought are overwhelmed when we look into that home, where Christ's beloved disciple and Christ's mother were. Surely that place must have been the resort of holy Angels, if any habitation on earth has been meet to be so.

There seems something in the suggestion of St. Cyril [9], that—"our Lord, seeing the great trial that it was to His mother, and the great offence which the Cross of His Passion might be to her, and, as God, knowing the deep thoughts with which she was troubled, committed her to the beloved disciple, as being so furnished with Divine wisdom, that he could best explain to her the depth of that mystery." And indeed the more one contemplates the circumstances, the more do we become impressed with something of a Divine suitableness in all the parts of it, until we are lost in the mysterious harmony and wisdom of God's Providences. For where shall we find a home more suitable for the Mother of the adorable Son of God, than that of Divine love and wisdom? Where a home more worthy of the greatness, more suitable to the weakness of the blessed Virgin, when the sword pierced her soul? And for the fidelity of the beloved disciple himself, what reward could have more answered, and harmonized more

[9] In Joann. ad locum.

with his affections! Or what earthly gift have been more valued by his piety? In this disciple himself there was especially fulfilled, in this instance, the promise of our Lord; that they who sacrificed domestic comforts and possessions for His sake, should not only receive an infinite reward hereafter, but should receive also in this present time from Him, the very same things which they relinquished, in ample recompense [10]. For St. John, in following Christ, seems especially to have relinquished the comforts of a home. It is not only said that he relinquished all that he had, as it is said of St. Matthew and others, but it is expressly mentioned, that he " left his father with the hired servants." In another sense, also, he was, for Christ's sake, without the closer bonds of a domestic life, in that he was never married. In him, therefore doubtless, was especially fulfilled that promise, that such shall receive " in this present time houses, and brethren, and sisters, and mothers, and children." For though no doubt this promise has a high and spiritual fulfilment upon earth, in that " whosoever shall do the will of God," the same does become to Christ Himself, in some mysterious and transcendental manner, His "brother," and His "sister," and "His mother [11];" yet such promises do receive also, in things that are more of earth, an inferior indeed, and less plenary, but still a true and great fulfilment. And so, on that occasion, when the beloved disciple received into his home our Lord's mother, it seems to have been an earthly pledge of their higher heavenly fulfilment also; for already in this did he surely receive " a hundredfold in this present time." For he had given up a home and relatives in order to adhere to Christ, and to stand by His Cross; but, for a home and for relatives,

[10] Mark x. 30.   [11] Mark iii. 35.

like those of other men, which he resigned, he received for a home that most hallowed of all earthly homes; and for a parent one no less than his Lord's mother.

But with regard to the blessed Virgin herself, it is remarkable how Holy Scripture seems to have thrown around her a sort of holy silence; and that too, on occasions such as the present, at the Crucifixion, and also at the Resurrection, when we look with an intense interest for any thing that we can learn respecting her. There appears, also, to be a sort of mysterious reserve in what is recorded of our Lord's expressions towards her or respecting her. It was, we may venture to suppose, out of tender consideration for our weakness, and from His foreseeing that great heresy, which should arise in the Church, under the plea of doing her honour. And this will account for the circumstance, that on the few occasions, in which our Lord is mentioned as addressing His Mother, there is something different from what we should have been, perhaps, inclined to expect. For, although we know that He "was subject" to His human "parents," and that, doubtless, after some transcendent and most perfect manner of filial duty and love; yet the things recorded appear rather as merciful warnings, addressed to ourselves, than as disclosing through the veil His own human and filial affections. Thus, in the first miracle at Cana of Galilee, in speaking of His miracles, He seems to separate her interference from any control in the exercise of His Divine power: and in no less marked a manner had He done the same at twelve years of age, when engaged in His "Father's business;" and again in that emphatic declaration, made to the person who spoke of the exceeding blessedness of His human Mother, "Yea, rather blessed are they that hear the word of God, and keep it." It may be that in this way our Lord was fulfilling the perfection of that Evangelical righteousness, wherein he that loves God must love with so entire a heart as to hate father and mother (*i. e.* comparatively). However, on this occasion, when our Lord is manifested to us as speaking to His earthly Parent, His words are extremely few and short. Nor does He speak for her consolation in those high and Divine terms in which He had spoken to His disciples, when He was consoling them for His loss;—that He would send the Almighty Comforter to be with them; that He Himself would be with them; that He, and His Father, and the Holy Spirit, would make their abode with them :—but He commits her to the charge of another, as one needing human support and human comfort. It was, indeed, the very highest office of filial duty and affection, when He committed her to His beloved disciple, and at such an hour of extreme agony was mindful of her ;—but still it was human. He committed her as one human and infirm; the hallowed scene suggests the thoughts, if one may reverently venture to say so, not so much of transcendental and Heavenly, as of domestic love; of piety indeed infinitely perfect and adorable, but in actions rather filial and parental than Divine. Indeed, in the beloved disciple himself, the view which we obtain of his character in conjunction with the Virgin-mother, is rather the domestic side, than that which is represented by his emblem the Eagle, by his deep and Divine Gospel, or the mysterious Apocalypse, in which He is usually presented to us; or as reclining on the bosom of the Incarnate Word, the Ever-blessed God in the flesh. Our Lord acknowledges her not in His miracles, which were Divine; but in His agony, when she needed sympathy. Now was the time when "the sword was to pierce through her own soul;" when all that was human in our

Lord, of which she was the parent, was racked with anguish; and she who was so " highly favoured " above women, had the sign of God's favour vouchsafed to her in the greatness of her afflictions, when " the iron entered into her soul."

Of the state of the blessed St. Mary's own feelings, in these seasons of trial, nothing is told us; it is concealed from our view, in that cloud or veil which envelopes all the character of her who was " blessed among women," and is known to Christ alone. But the little which is said of her in her previous history seems calculated to teach us, that she also, like ourselves, had to learn the lesson of faith in Christ, in the breadth, and length, and depth, and height of God manifest in the Body. We are more than once told that she kept His sayings, and pondered them in her heart, and that too from His very childhood. And we may well suppose, that He who knew what was in the heart of man, and who " meets them that are worthy in every thought," being well aware of this, had trained and prepared her by His teaching and by His providence for this her trying hour, which He foreknew. There is an incident mentioned in His early years, and the only one which is mentioned, which appears to be singled out from all the events of His youth and childhood, as containing within it something especially mysterious; and the more so, when we observe that the transactions themselves are not, humanly speaking, important, on account of any results they lead to, or great principles which they convey. But the particulars of that circumstance, when considered as bearing towards the blessed Virgin, will be found to contain something extremely analogous to her present trial and position; and although the matters are in themselves very different, yet as exercising the faith of our Lord's

z

Mother, the one appears to be a sort of type of the other.· We may, I trust, venture with humility to suppose, that our Lord did thereby intend to afford her a kind of representation of this her present trial; and thereby to strengthen her towards the attainment of that faith in Him, which would diminish the severity of it. The incident referred to is the following, that when our Lord was twelve years of age, and went up with His parents to Jerusalem at the Passover, He had disappeared in the Holy City from the presence of the blessed Virgin, and had left her, for the space of three days, sorrowing for His absence and loss. And afterwards, when at length He was discovered by her, engaged in teaching in the Temple, He expressed, as it were, His surprise, that in this short and seeming bereavement wherewith she had been so much afflicted, she had not considered that it was necessary for Him to be about His Father's business, or, as it might signify, in His Father's house. Now, on reading this narrative, our first feeling is naturally something of surprise, that our Lord should have occasioned His mother that pain and anxiety, when we read her gentle expostulation,— "Son, why hast Thou dealt thus with us? Behold, Thy father and I have sought Thee sorrowing." The circumstance itself creates an apprehension that there is more in the matter than appears; especially as it is the only circumstance which the Evangelists have recorded of our Lord from His infancy to His manhood. Now the whole transaction seems calculated to train her to a trust and reliance in Him, when He should be out of her sight: and when for "three days" she should be in vain seeking for Him "sorrowing." And the state of circumstances, in her present destitution at His death, is in a striking manner analogous: for at the expiration of that time she will find Him indeed, though not in the condition of the Human Son, yet doing His Father's will, about His Father's business, sitting in His Spiritual Temple, and teaching His Church, with all power given Him in His Kingdom. If this incident, and the instruction conveyed by means of it, had not the effect of schooling her beforehand for her great trial, yet His Divine teaching on that occasion must have appeared to her such in the retrospect after His resurrection. For such are often the ways of God, seen after the events have passed, but not discovered at the time: as God said to Moses,—that He should see Him from behind when He had passed by, but should not see His Face.

Perhaps indeed it may be thus, in His moral providences and dispensations towards us, that Christ deals with us all; I mean, that often by means of matters, which are painful, and which we cannot account for at the time, He may be training us for some greater trial to ensue. It may be, too, that when our probation shall have terminated hereafter, and we are able to look back upon, and to unravel the mysterious Providences which have enveloped us in the past, we may find throughout this gracious Hand of Christ's paternal instruction and care, teaching wisdom and faith through sorrow, while we knew not of it. There is a circumstance mentioned of St. Peter in his previous history that seems, precisely in a similar manner, analogous to the events of his great temptation, and whereby he appears to have been beforehand mercifully trained and prepared for it. For on the occasion when he walked upon the sea, there appears at first the same forwardness of zeal, and the same loving confidence in venturing before the other disciples upon the wave, as afterwards led him into the hall of judgment. The same earnestness of faith and love led him on both occasions to go forth to be with his Lord, to be doing as his Lord, and to be in common danger with Him. But after he had ventured so far, there then ensued the same want of strength to support himself; and on both occasions he began to sink: on both occasions he might say, with equal propriety, " I am come into deep waters, so that the floods run over me ... O let me be delivered from them that hate me, and out of the deep waters, let not the water-flood drown me, neither let the deep swallow me up ... Turn Thee unto me and hide not Thy face from Thy servant [1]." In both temptations, if left to himself, he would have perished; in both it was his faith failed; in both he was recovered and sustained by our Lord Himself; at one time by His hand, and at the other by His look: and on the last occasion our Lord seemed to say to him, as He had said on the former, " O thou of little faith, wherefore didst thou doubt [2]?" The former seems a preparation and discipline for the latter. Now these two instances which have been mentioned, as occurring to two persons in our Lord's dealings with them in the Gospels, may be parts of a great system of God's moral Providence, in His dealings with us all; training us, and schooling us, and disciplining us in affairs of daily life, we know not why nor wherefore, but saying to us, " What I do thou knowest not now, but thou shalt know hereafter."

But there is another circumstance, wherein our Lord's conduct to His Holy Mother is recorded, which St. Austin intimately connects with this occasion, that of the Marriage feast in Cana of Galilee. He supposes that, when our Lord said, " What have I to do with thee? Mine hour is not yet come," that He spake of

---

[1] Ps. lxix. 2. 15. 18.   [2] Matt. xiv. 31.

this hour; that our Lord then meant, that when He had to make the manifestation of His Divinity, and to be as it were about His Father's business, He was not to be subject to maternal commands or wishes: but when, hereafter, in His dying agonies, He should have to suffer as man, He would then recognize His human mother in His human sorrows; and that then, when His hour should have come, she should receive the highest pledge of dutiful affection which a human Son could render: that in the midst of His deepest agonies He would remember her, and take care of her; though in things Divine He might seem to set her aside. It is thus, with some meaning of this kind, as having a reference to the present occasion of His death, that St. Augustin would explain our Lord's words to His mother, in that conversation in the Marriage feast in Cana of Galilee. This appears in some degree to sanction, and fall in with, our application of His words on the still earlier occasion mentioned by St. Luke. And both would seem to indicate, that each of our Lord's previous discourses with His mother had a reference to this the consummation of all,—this last and dying instance of filial duty. In both of those instances did He afford us an example of that most perfect goodness which He had set before us, viz. that we are to hate every earthly connexion, and hold light the most sacred of all earthly duties, in comparison with the love of God. While on this last occasion on the Cross He has afforded us His own example, that although we are to hate father and mother in comparison with God, yet that, notwithstanding, in doing so, we may give our earthly parents the strongest proofs of affection and duty. St. Chrysostom seems to adopt the same allusion and reference: "Though other women," he says, "were standing by, yet He mentions none but His mother, teaching us of the greater debt which is due to mothers. As when our parents stand in our way concerning spiritual matters, we ought not to know them; so when nothing of this kind prevents us, we are to afford all things to them, and to prefer them to every other." St. Augustin also observes, that here from His Cross, as from the chair of the teacher, the Lord would instruct us in the great lesson of filial piety. And St. Ambrose speaks with touching beauty of this affecting incident of our Lord's care, and of the circumstance, that it should be His own beloved disciple who records it [3]. "Mary, the mother of the Lord, stood at the Cross of her Son. No one hath taught me this but St. John the Evangelist. Others have written of the world being shaken in the passion of the Lord, and the Heavens enveloped in darkness; that the sun withdrew; that the thief after his confession was received into Paradise. John hath taught us that which the others have taught us not: how, when laid upon the Cross, He addressed His mother. He thought it of more moment that, triumphing over His agonies, He exhibited these duties to His mother, than that He bestowed a heavenly kingdom of eternal life. For if it was an act of piety that life was given to the thief, of much more abounding piety was it, that a mother was honoured by a Son with so great an affection." And St. Cyril of Alexandria dwells on the same most sacred instance of filial piety. He observes, that " honour to parents is of a truth the most precious kind of virtue. But not to neglect our duty towards them, although surrounded by intolerable woes, from whence could we learn this, but in and by Christ, the first of all? For that man is indeed the best who is mindful of the holy commandments,

[3] In Epistola ad Eccles. Vercell. vol. ii. p. 1140, Ed. Bened.

and is not forced from a becoming adherence to them, not in peace and tranquillity, but in the storm and flood of overwhelming calamity."

THE DARKNESS.

' *" It was "* now *" about the sixth hour "* (Luke), and *"from the sixth hour there was darkness over all the land until the ninth hour"* (Matt. Mark, Luke). That is according to the Roman and Jewish time, but as we should call it from twelve o'clock till three. The effect is thus mentioned, and St. Luke adds the sensible cause of the darkness by saying, *" And the sun was darkened"* (Luke). It is supposed by Origen [4] that this afternoon was the very period of the creation of man, the animals being created on the forenoon of the Sixth day; but there is another more palpable cause, which might be assigned for its occurring at this particular hour, which is so strongly designated. Our Lord Himself was, it is said, turned toward the west, with His back toward Jerusalem; which has been supposed by some the reason for the primitive custom of praying toward the east, on account of our Lord's Cross being turned from thence. At twelve o'clock, therefore, the sun came more in view of its Lord and Maker, and, as it were, hid his face in shame and grief at the dreadful spectacle. It was probably this which the prophet Amos spoke of when he said, "In that day, saith the Lord God, I will cause the sun to go down at noon, and I will darken the earth in the clear day [5]." The prophet Zechariah, as Gregory Nyssen has observed, may allude to the same, when he said, "It shall be one day, which shall be known to the Lord, not day nor night; but it shall come to pass that

----

[4] In Matt. ad loc.   [5] Ch. viii. 9.

at evening time it shall be light. And it shall be in that day that living waters shall go out from Jerusalem [6]." Other passages in the prophets have been supposed to allude to it, as in Jeremiah, "her sun is gone down while it was yet day: she hath been ashamed and confounded [7]." And in Ezekiel, "I will cover the sun with a cloud:—all the bright lights of Heaven will I make dark over thee, and set darkness upon thy land, saith the Lord God [8]." Perhaps these prophecies, and this event itself, both shadow forth and prefigure something else, to be accomplished hereafter.

It is matter of question how far this darkness extended. St. Chrysostom and Theophylact consider it to have been over the world; and so far distinguished from the Egyptian darkness. Origen supposes it to have been only over the land of Judea, and caused by the gathering of dark clouds. The former opinion is not, indeed, supported by any genuine and authentic evidence of the fact having been observed in other countries; neither, indeed, is there any account of it in the land of Judea, or of its having taken place at Jerusalem, beyond these statements of the inspired Evangelists. Nor surely is any needed.

Origen, who considers that it extended only over the land of Judea, adds, that, as, when Moses stretched forth his hands to heaven, darkness came over the Egyptians, who were holding in slavery the servants of God, which was an image of the future darkness which was to overwhelm the Egyptians: so, in like manner, when Christ, from the sixth hour, stretched forth His hands to Heaven, on the Cross, over the people who had cried, "Away with Him, crucify Him, crucify Him," darkness

[6] Ch. xiv. 7, 8.   [7] Ch. xv. 9.   [8] Ch. xxxii. 8.

came over them, and they were deprived of all light; an image of that future darkness which was to overwhelm the Jewish nation, who had dared to lay hands on Him "Who was the true Light." "And as the children of Israel had then light in all their dwellings when Egypt was in darkness, so," Origen adds, "shall there be light in the Church of God, while the Jews are in darkness. And as it is said, that there was darkness over the land of Judea till the ninth hour, it is evident that the light then returned, for when the fulness of the Gentiles shall have come in, all Israel shall be saved; the darkness over the land of Judea for three hours, signifying that, on account of their sins, they are deprived of the light of God the Father, and the brightness of Christ, and the illumination of the Holy Spirit[9]." This interpretation the more recommends itself, as night and day are evidently symbolical of spiritual light and darkness coexisting in the world: and the blindness of the Jews since that day, in the midst of surrounding light, is as marvellous as a supernatural darkness would be in mid-day. This opinion of Origen's agrees with what St. Chrysostom also says, "that it was a manifest judgment, in token of that darkness which should overwhelm the minds of those that were crucifying Him." The agreement of these two writers is remarkable, as there exists so great a diversity in their minds, and in the characters of their writings.

The space and duration of time is also to be noticed; it may have been the period of our Lord's extreme agony. St. Jerome expresses himself to this effect, "that the most bright luminary of the world withdrew his rays that he might not behold Him who was hanging on the Cross, and the wicked blasphemers should

[9] Comm. in Matt. 134.

not enjoy his light[10]." But it is evident, that the "three hours" have some analogous reference to the "three days," when our Lord was hid in the earth, according to the sign of the prophet Jonah. And if the space of time was for three hours, because our Lord was for three days in the darkness of the grave; then the number Three on these occasions seems to be but one among numberless instances of the same kind: and all this runs up into a still higher subject. For if this space of darkness was for three hours, because our Lord was for three days in the grave, then the question occurs, why three days was the appointed time for His sojourn in the heart of the earth? Why does the mysterious number three run into all cases, of every kind, with some significant and hidden power, in Scripture and in Nature, in all languages, and among all people, both sacred and profane[11]? The reason for all this is, no doubt, the same very deep and awful reason to which St. Augustin attributes the appointed time of the Lord's continuance in the grave. "On that account," he says, "He arose after three days; that in the Passion of the Son might be shown the assent of the whole of the Trinity. For the three days is read of in figure, because the Trinity which made man in the beginning, doth itself in the end repair man, through the Passion of Christ."

The period of the day also is probably full of great and mysterious analogies. It may bear some correspondence not only with the creation of man, as was before mentioned, but also with his fall: for as it is said

---

[10] In Matt. ad. loc.

[11] As "ter" and "tres" used to denote confirmation in poets constantly: and the mysterious proverbial expression, "numero Deus impare gaudet."—Virgil.

that Adam heard "the voice of God walking in the garden in the cool of the day," it has been thought that the crime he committed was in the heat of the day. So it may be, as Bede suggests, that the time of his crime corresponds with the period of our Lord's suffering. The same writer also notices, that when the sun was declining from its centre, our Lord died: when it was rising, He rose from the grave. A sentiment expressed by Bede is so far of weight, as he is a channel that conveys to us rather the stream of other people's opinions in earlier times, than thoughts of his own.

There is also another circumstance in the Old Testament, which we cannot help thinking of in connexion with this darkness; although it would be difficult to explain all the mysterious allusions contained in it, yet the mere mention of some will at once indicate a striking resemblance and analogy. It is when the exceeding great promise, of his seed being as the stars of Heaven, is made to Abraham; and he desires a sign whereby he may know that he shall inherit the land: when the prophecy is made that his seed shall be in a strange land and in captivity:—when the sun was going down: and also in the midst of a sacrifice. "And when the sun was going down, a deep sleep fell upon Abram; and lo, an horror of great darkness fell upon him." Again, "And it came to pass, that, when the sun went down, and it was dark, behold a smoking furnace, and a burning lamp that passed between those pieces [1]."

St. Chrysostom, according to his custom, dwells rather on the practical effects of the miracle, than on its secret causes or mysterious significations. "It was much more wonderful," he says, "that this should occur when He was crucified, than it would have been

[1] Gen. xv. 12. 17.

while He walked on earth. For it was sufficient to convert them, not only from the greatness of the miracle, but because it took place after they had spoken all they wished, and were satiated with their revilings. But how was it they were not all struck with astonishment, and believed in Him as God? Because mankind were then held by such wickedness and sloth, and the miracle soon passed away, and they noticed not the causes for which it took place[2]." Indeed, in this respect it is but the counterpart of the effect of many other miracles, taking place then in the presence of the Jews, of the Egyptians before, and of Christians now; in each case men are encompassed by a cloud of witnesses, yet believe not.

But with regard to the nature of the sign itself, no explanation of it is to be rejected merely on the ground of its littleness, or its vastness, when we speak of the Almighty; for as no instrument can be too small for Him to use in speaking to mankind, neither can any be too great; for small and great are all one to Him who is Infinite. On the one hand, the movement of a cloud over a small country were sufficient to speak to mankind; but on the other hand, it were not to be wondered at, if not our world only, but other suns and systems throughout the infinite universe, were shaken to the centre and darkened, in sympathy with their Maker's sufferings.

THE LOUD VOICE.

It might be presumptuous in us to attempt to draw near, and to venture to look into, as if we had power or thought to fathom the inscrutable depth of our Saviour's woes: which, considering that they were caused by us and were for our sakes, we ought rather with the lowest

[2] Hom. xxxix,

adoration and prostration of soul and body to hear of hiding our eyes and faces in shame. Yet the words that He uttered disclose to us at this time something of the nature and cause of His mysterious agonies. " And *about the ninth hour* " (Matt.), or " *at the ninth hour* " (Mark), *i. e.* about three o'clock of our time, " *Jesus cried out with a loud voice, saying* (Matt. Mark), *Eli, Eli* (Matt.), *or Eloi, Eloi* (Mark), *lama sabachthani? which is* (Matt. Mark) *being interpreted* (Mark), *My God, My God, why hast Thou forsaken Me ?* " (Matt. Mark.) It is evident that our Lord here speaks in the person of mankind, addressing God not even, as at other times, as His Father, but as His God. The whole circumstance is matter for silent contemplation, rather than that we should venture to say much : but it is a subject of inexpressible support and consolation, under the weight of the heaviest calamities we can endure ; inasmuch as they are not only in themselves exceeding light in comparison ; but we have this strong living evidence, that depression of mind and spiritual desertion are no proofs of the rejection of God ; but rather, like bodily sufferings, form part of that resemblance to His Son, which renders us on that account the more acceptable to our Heavenly Father.

We know not indeed what these agonies of Christ's were, nor whether this was the bitter " cup " of which He had spoken on the preceding night ; but we know that the sufferings of lost mankind consist in their being forsaken of God, nor need we entertain any fear in this life, but that of being forsaken of Him. But it has been before noticed that the expressions of grief which our Lord used, had more than once a reference to the Jewish nation ; and it is curious to observe, that Origen on this subject has an opinion, that this exclamation of our Lord in agony had some such reference. "After He perceived," says Origen, "the darkness over all the land of Judea till the ninth hour, He said with a loud voice, 'why hast Thou forsaken Me?' meaning thereby given Me up, thus emptied and desolated by such woes; so that the people which had been honoured by Thee, should receive the penalty for what it has done against Me; filling up the measure of their fathers;—that they should be deprived of the light of Thy countenance, and should be left in darkness, as having Thee their God no longer present with them." And yet the same writer afterwards adds, "perhaps on beholding the sins of mankind for which He suffered, He said, 'why hast Thou forsaken Me?' that 'I am as when they have gathered the summer fruits, as the grape-gleanings of the vintage; there is no cluster to eat.' And this because 'the good man is perished out of the earth, and there is none upright among men[3].' But you must not suppose that our Saviour thus spake in a human manner on account of the woe that had come upon Him on the Cross. For if you so take it, you will not hear the 'loud voice' by which He spake, nor seek what is worthy of a Divine voice. And from the sixth to the ninth hour, the darkness was over the whole land, but before the expiration of the ninth, the Lord cried with a loud voice, saying what is written, as if requiring that the sun should again arise on the land, and scatter from it the darkness of the three hours, as we have explained it above[4]." Thus Origen by these two passages appears to refer our Lord's mysterious woe, first of all to the rejection of the Jewish nation; and afterwards to that of the impenitent world, out of which so few would be saved by His death; and of which the destruction of

[3] Mic. vii. 1, 2. [4] Com. in Matt.

Jerusalem was the type. This is a confirmation of what has been noticed of our Lord's words to the women that followed Him. Theophylact also refers it to the Jewish nation; he observes, that "the Lord must speak this in the person of us men, for He cannot be Himself forsaken of the Father, as He said, 'yet I am not alone, for the Father is with Me.' And He may have said this for the Jews, as being Himself according to the flesh a Jew, as if He had said, why hast Thou forsaken the people of the Hebrews, that they should crucify Thy Son? So that by the expression, forsake Me, we may understand either human nature, or the Jewish people." What in truth may have been our blessed Lord's unutterable woes we know not, but this we know, that they were for our sakes. Those His dying agonies were the birth-pangs of His Church. But one feels that already one may have been speaking too curiously on this dreadful subject, although it be only to cite the opinions of great and good men.

But tenfold darker than the darkness of nature, was the darkness that clouded the heart of the unbelieving Jew. Those who stood by, as they were not awe-struck into silence and dismay by the darkness, neither did they now understand His words; for it is only His own sheep who know His voice; nor is it to be wondered at, for they had no eyes to see, and could not perceive the darkness: their ears were closed, and their heart could not understand. For when He thus cried out with the first words of that Psalm,—the whole of which we may well believe had been now passing in His mind, and the form and subject of His prayer,—either designedly or not, they misinterpret Him, thinking lightly of those words that might well darken Heaven and the Heaven of Heavens, and make the earth to shake.

"*Some of those that stood by, when they heard* that, *said* (Matt. Mark), *Behold* (Mark), *this* man (Matt.) *calleth for Elias* (Matt. Mark). *And immediately* (Matt.) *one of them ran* (Matt. Mark), *and having taken* (Matt.) *and filled a sponge with vinegar, and set it on a reed, gave Him to drink* (Matt. Mark), *saying, Let be, let us see if Elias cometh to take Him down*" (Mark); and indeed the others joined in repeating his expression, for "*the rest said, Let be, let us see if Elias cometh to save Him*" (Matt.). From the two accounts, says Augustin, we may suppose that both the man himself thus spake, and the others joined in the expression. This will account for the discrepancy, and render it more descriptive of the circumstance.

St. Chrysostom and St. Jerome both suggest, that it might have been the soldiers who thus spake, not understanding the Hebrew language; and certainly the offering Him vinegar does look a little like an act of the soldiers. And it is the same thing which St. Luke records their doing, during our Lord's agonies, "coming to Him and offering Him vinegar." But on the other hand, it hardly seems probable, that the soldiers should have known any thing of Elias. Whereas the supposition of the persons who heard it not understanding the language, might apply to the Jews themselves; for the ancient Hebrew, in which it was spoken, does not appear to have been their language at this time: and the expressions are like those of Jewish mockery, whether they understood our Lord's words or not.

"Let us see if Elias cometh!" these were probably the last words that these persons uttered on this awful occasion: for it would appear from St. John, that it was just before our Lord gave up the ghost. As being the last words therefore that His enemies spoke to our dying

Lord, they are highly worthy of our notice. The expression moreover in itself is in the very highest degree remarkable. It is recorded by two Evangelists, and the more particularly arrests our attention, when we consider the mysterious import which was connected at that time, and is still connected to the present day, with the coming of Elias; and moreover from our observing, that every thing else in the way of fortuitous incident or expression is either the subject of prophecy, or itself prophetic. "Let us see if Elias cometh!" this they had now been doing for the last three years; and this was the reason they alleged for not believing in Christ, because "Elias was not yet come." This seems to have been the objection with which they had most sorely beset our Lord's disciples, saying, that Elias was not yet come; and the understanding of which Christ explained to them, as depending on the state of the heart. And even now it is believed, that Elias will come before our Lord's Advent, and that the Jews will, in some sense, be restored by the coming of Elias. It would appear, therefore, as if the last words that they said in mockery of our Lord on the Cross, they had been repeating unto this day, "saying, Let be, let us see if Elias cometh." And this they say, unconscious of the marvellous darkness that involves them, and is spread over their hearts unto this day. But it may be asked, what do the other words signify in connexion with this allusion; "Let us see whether Elias will come to save Him," or "to take Him down?" Can it indicate that our Lord is spoken of as suffering to the end of the world in His members, until Elias shall come, and restore all things, and reconcile the Jews to the Gentiles, and the Gentiles to the Jews; the fathers to the children, and the children to the fathers? Or can it signify merely our Lord's coming down from heaven ?   Certainly the words are full of Divine import, they are still being repeated by them in every corner of the world, "Let us see if Elias cometh[5]."

THE VINEGAR.

There are as many as three occasions mentioned by the different Evangelists, when they offered our Lord vinegar on the Cross, independently of the first mention of the vinegar and gall. One of these occasions is that which we have just been speaking of, when He uttered the loud cry, and which St. Matthew and St. Mark record.   Another is that which St. John mentions at the termination of our Lord's agonies, when He said, "I thirst:" and the other is that which St. Luke speaks of, when he mentions the soldiers coming to Him and offering Him vinegar. It may be that all these accounts allude to the same transaction, that it took place when, to fulfil the Scriptures, our Lord said, "I thirst." Thus, indeed, St. Augustin considers it[6]: but I am disposed to think otherwise. The words of St. Luke rather imply that the soldiers did it frequently, and in mockery; and the excruciating thirst, which persons are said to experience in the midst of such torments, may have been the reason; for they are thus acting in a manner similar to all their conduct, if we consider them as doing this in order to add to His sufferings, by repeating the mock offer of relief. And on the particular occasion which St. Matthew and St. Mark speak of, it is indicated that they then forbore to give Him drink, saying, " Let alone," waiting to see if Elias would come. It is therefore natural to suppose that it was a little later than this,

[5] See Vol. Min. 3rd Year, 105.   [6] Cons. Ev. Lib. iii. 54.

that St. John speaks of a similar circumstance, as the solemn accomplishment of prophecy.

"*After this*," says St. John, speaking of our Lord's last duty to His mother, "*Jesus knowing that all things were now accomplished*" which had been written of Him, and which He had now completed, "*that the Scripture might be fulfilled;*"—that is to say, in obedience to the Scripture and in the Holy Spirit of God, not as seeking relief to His own suffering nature,— "*saith, I thirst. Now there was a vessel set there full of vinegar; and they filled a sponge with vinegar, and put it on hyssop, and applied it to His mouth.*"

With regard to the hyssop which is here mentioned, there is a question whether it was the same thing as the other Evangelists speak of under the name of the reed: or whether it was something attached to the end of the reed, together with the sponge. Some persons, and indeed St. Austin himself among the number, entertain the latter opinion; and think that it had some natural quality of restoring persons from fainting, or that it was of an unsavoury and bitter taste. With some reason, too, in confirmation of this opinion, it might be supposed that the hyssop was not sufficient in length for the stalk of it to be a substitute for the reed. Augustin speaks of it as a humble shrub, and as representing Christ's humility. In the First Book of Kings[1] it is described in contrast to the cedar tree, "from the cedar-tree that is in Lebanon even unto the hyssop that springeth out of the wall;" so that even in that country it may be supposed to be a small shrub. But in answer to this it may be said, that for the purpose here described, it was not necessary that it should be

---

[1] Ch. iv. 33.

any great length; and still less so for the mock sceptre, if we suppose it to be there also meant by the word "reed:" for the stalk of this shrub is about a foot and a half in length usually, and may be longer in Palestine. And the other two Evangelists use the very same word, when they speak of attaching the sponge to the reed, as St. John does when he speaks of attaching it to the hyssop. St. Matthew and St. Mark speak of having "put it about" a reed; St. John of having "put it about" hyssop[8]. "Some say," observes Theophylact, "that the reed is called hyssop, because it has leaves like the reed:" implying that they considered it one and the same thing. I am inclined to think that the reed may indeed have been the stalk of the hyssop in both cases. And that on this occasion, whereas the other Evangelists had described it under the general term of the reed or cane, St. John mentions the exact name and substance. And he may have done so on account of some mystical import contained in it, which the beloved disciple might have observed; or that he had known enough of the Divine dealings, and language of signs, to know that nothing was unimportant; or of course it might be, that he might have been overruled thus to speak without any human intention in doing so. At all events, we know thus far, that the herb was prescribed to be used in the Law; it was commanded to be made use of in sacrifices with scarlet wool, and considered as purifying. A bunch of hyssop was dipped in the blood of the Paschal Lamb, and it was with this very instrument that the lintel and posts were marked with that sacrificial blood[9]. It was also dipped in the blood of the bird in cleansing the leper[1]. To which its cleansing import, as

---

[8] περιθεὶς καλάμῳ, Matt. Mark; ὑσσώπῳ περιθέντες, John.
[9] Exod. xii. 22.   [1] Levit. xiv. 4.

used on such occasions, David alludes, when he says,
"Thou shalt purge me with hyssop, and I shall be
clean [2]." Here therefore it is used in the consummation
of the great atonement; when the sacrifice is finished,
the purification is made. So much was it the case in
this our Lord's oblation of Himself, that He regulated
and performed all things with a reverential and religious
strictness, as in an act of Divine worship; and as St.
Austin well says, "The Man that appeared was suffering
all these things, but the God who was concealed from
view was disposing them:" arranging, disposing, and
accomplishing all things according to His word, and
the types and ordinances that had gone before.

But it may be asked, as the vinegar is here given to
our Lord in answer to His cry, and as a relief from
suffering, why is it mentioned by the Psalmist with an
expression of apparent surprise or complaint, when he
says, "When I was thirsty they gave Me vinegar to
drink?" However it may be accounted for, as doubtless
it may be, in the literal acceptation, the words are very
significative in that spiritual meaning which is usually
applied to it. For is not this His complaint of His own
Israel, when He says, "I looked that it should bring
forth grapes, and it brought forth wild grapes [3];" and
"their grapes are grapes of gall, their clusters are bitter; their wine is the poison of dragons [4]?" Thus St.
Cyril says, "He asks fruit of the vine which He hath
planted; but 'their vine is of the vine of Sodom;' the
vine by nature of the holy Fathers: but of Sodom, by
purpose of heart." And, as St. Jerome says, "The
bitter vine maketh wine that is bitter, as God speaketh
to Jerusalem, 'I planted thee a noble vine: how then

___

[2] Ps. li. 7. [3] Isa. v. 4. [4] Deut. xxxii. 32.

art thou turned into the bitterness of a strange vine to Me ?' " To this, quoted by St. Jerome, we may add that expression of the Prophet Hosea [5],—"Ephraim is joined to idols ; let him alone ; their drink is sour." And here the prophet speaks of our Lord's rejecting, as well as loathing, this sour and corrupted potion, the bad affection of His people ; and this may more particularly refer to that which the other Evangelists record ; when they offered Him gall and vinegar, "He tasted thereof, and would not drink." In like manner of spiritual interpretation, Origen also says, "They who have knowledge according to Christ's doctrine, but live badly, offer unto Christ wine, mingled with gall : they who apply to Christ precepts contrary to the truth, put vinegar on the sponge, and apply it to His mouth [6]." And St. Augustin also : "The Jews themselves were the vinegar, degenerating from the wine of the Patriarchs and Prophets ; and the sponge the caverns and lurking-places of their hollow and tortuous heart." He indeed bestows on us the New Wine of His own Blood ; we give Him in return a vessel full of vinegar, sourness of heart, and bad affection.

THE CONSUMMATION.

And now, as St. Augustin says [7],—"When nothing remained to Christ of the punishments He was to endure, Death is delaying, for he beholds there nothing that is his. The novelty of the case leads to suspicion. This man, the first of all, and alone of all, hath he beheld, who hath not known sin, who is free from fault, and owes nothing to his laws." Nor indeed could death have any legitimate power over the Immaculate Son of

[5] Ch. iv. 17.   [6] In Matt.   [7] In Serm. de Pass.

God, but this alone remains of all the evils which our Lord hath taken upon Himself, voluntarily to endure for our sakes.

"*When therefore Jesus had received the vinegar, He said, It is finished*" (John). He had drunk to the dregs the bitter cup of His Father's wrath; the prophecies were finished: the work which God had given Him to do was finished: His Heavenly example and doctrine were finished: His sufferings were finished: the propitiation for the sins of mankind was finished. "*And Jesus cried again with a loud voice,*" says St. Matthew, alluding to His former "loud cry," of the desertion of God; "*and Jesus sending forth a loud voice,*" says St. Mark, or, "*and having cried with a loud voice Jesus said, Father, into Thy hands I will commend My spirit. And when He had said this*" (Luke), and "*having bowed His head*" says St. John, who, standing at the foot of the Cross, would have noticed, and ever remembered that circumstance, "*He breathed His last* (Mark, Luke), *He delivered up*" (John), or, "*sent forth* (Matt.) *the spirit*" (Matt. John). "It is commended," says St. Ambrose, "because what is commended is reserved and not lost. He commended His soul into His hands Who had promised, 'I will not leave Thy soul in hell.' And it is said, 'He delivered up,'" adds the same writer, "because He voluntarily sent it forth; and St. Matthew's expression that 'He sent it forth,' implies that it was of His own free will[8]." And this voluntary surrender of Himself, which is implied in the word He "delivered up[9]," is what St. Paul speaks of under the same term, "He delivered Himself up" as a sacrifice for us. "This cir-

---

[8] Expos. in Luc Lib. x. 127.   [9] παρέδωκε.

cumstance explains," says Origen, "that expression in the eighty-seventh Psalm, that He was 'free among the dead.' And thus the Jews might see the fulfilment of what He said when they asked, 'Will He kill Himself?' because He said, 'I will go where ye cannot come [10].' For it was evident from this, that He had power to go where they had no power to follow Him [1]."

Our Lord's cry, "I thirst," perhaps signified that human nature was exhausted, and could sustain no more, and therefore it was "finished." He received the vinegar for the last support of suffering humanity; "He shall drink of the brook in the way, therefore shall He lift up His head [2]." But when nature failed, with a loud and miraculous voice He proved that He had a power over and above nature; that He gave up His life freely; that, as He had said, "no man taketh it from Me: I lay it down of Myself. I have power to lay it down, and I have power to take it again [3]." Origen, indeed, seems to think that the circumstance which astonished the Centurion was our Lord's giving up His life to God before nature was exhausted. But would it not rather appear to be a miraculously loud voice from exhausted nature? For a person who had often witnessed death, as the Centurion probably had done, would have known that at such a time the voice and strength are gone; and our Lord had suffered the previous night, and this morning, enough to have caused death. It was before observed, as St. Mark says, that "they bear Him to the place of execution;" as if even at that time it was as much as human nature could sustain, and He was, from very exhaustion, drawing near to the gates of death.

[10] John viii. 22.   [1] Orig. in Joan. tom. ii. 174.
[2] Ps. cx. 7.   [3] John x. 18.

Thus St. Chrysostom considers it; "On this account," he says, "He cried with a loud voice, that it might be shown that it was according to His own power. For by this circumstance, of His sending forth a loud voice in dying, He most openly showed Himself to be the true God; for men when they die, are scarcely able to send forth even a slight voice." "Or," says Hilary, "He sent forth His spirit with the cry of a loud voice, as grieving that He carried not all our sins [4]." "When the flesh was failing," says St. Jerome, "the Divine voice was strong. While we who are of the earth die with the lowest voice, or with no voice at all; He who was from Heaven expired with an exalted cry." And on the expression in St. John, of our Lord inclining His head, and giving up the ghost, St. Augustin says, "Who thus sleeps at his own free choice as Jesus died? who thus at his own free will lays aside His garment as Jesus put off His flesh? How great is His power to be hoped for or feared when He judges, which appeared so great when He dies [5]." "It was not," says Chrysostom, "that He bowed His head, because He expired, but because He bowed His head He then expired; by mention of all which things the Evangelists showed that He was the Lord of all." On these words of the beloved Evangelist, of His bowing His head, Origen very beautifully says, that He was "reclining His head as on His Father's bosom."

Nor indeed do ancient writers fail to observe, that we also, from the same example, may have something of a similar resignation in death. "The Lord," says St. Cyril of Alexandria, "delivered up His spirit unto God the Father, showing us that the souls of His saints by

---

[4] Com. in Matt. xxxiii. 6.   [5] In Joan. Tract. cxix.

no means dwell among tombs, but rather depart into the hands of the Father of all, while sinners are carried into a place of punishment, that is, into Hell. He delivered His soul into the hands of His Father, that we also from this beginning in and through Him, might have bright hopes, from a settled disposition and trust that, in suffering the death of the body, we shall be in the hands of God, and in a state far better than we are in the flesh." And St. Athanasius, "In commending Himself to God, He commendeth all mortals who are quickened in Him; for we are all His members, as the Apostle says, 'we are all one in Christ[6].'" But Gregory Nyssen here asks, how it is that at the same time our Lord is spoken of as being in three different places, in the heart of the earth, as He said unto the Pharisees; in the Paradise of God, as He said to the penitent thief; and now, as He commends Himself into the Hands of His Father? But as another writer observes, "To speak distinctly, it was as to His body, that He was in the grave; as to His soul, in the place of the dead; as God, He was in Paradise with the thief, and on the throne of God with the Father and the Holy Spirit." And yet "not," as the same writer observes, "that we can consider either of these as separate from His Divinity, for in the Word they are ever united in one substance, nor can His immaculate body, or His immaculate soul, be ever disunited from the Word, being inseparably connected with His Divinity[7]."

[6] Gal. iii. De Incarnatione.
[7] Damascenus, Aur. Cat.

THE SEVEN SPEECHES OF CHRIST ON THE CROSS.

It is usual and natural for us to consider great weight to be due to dying words; but incalculably great must be the attention which is due to our Lord's last words: those injunctions which He has bequeathed to us: for He loved us as never man loved; He knew as never man knew; He spake as never man spake; He loved as a Parent, as a Bridegroom, as a Brother, as a Friend, for He spake of Himself under all these; but infinitely more as being Himself essential Love: He spake as One who knew what was in man, and saw to the end of eternity.

His words, too, on the Cross, falling into the mystical number seven, come before us as replete beyond all things with Divine doctrine and instruction in righteousness. For the number seven seems to indicate something infinite, as in that Heavenly Sabbath, of which the seventh day is the type; in the sevenfold gifts of the Good Spirit, and seven Angels, and seven Churches of God, and the seven evil spirits, and the seven deadly sins; for wickedness runs into that which is infinite in its consequences. And possibly it may signify that which is infinite—infinite in power and duration—but as connected with that which is finite; for if the number Three is infinite power, yet the number Four seems to imply universality and perfection in that which is finite, as the four quarters of the globe, the four rivers of Paradise, the four Evangelists; for these fill up and perfect the world and the Church. And the number seven is formed of three and four combined. This account, therefore, of this sacred mystical number may afford us a reason for considering these our Lord's last speeches in a sevenfold character or point of view: and at the sam time, by this explanation of that number, may serve to show that we rather suggest meanings, than limit or confine them to those only which are expressed.

Our Lord's words are as follow:

1. Father, forgive them, for .they know not what they do.
2. This day shalt thou be with me in Paradise.
3. Woman, behold thy son!
4. Eli, Eli, lama sabachthani?
5. I thirst.
6. It is finished.
7. Father, into Thy hands I commit My spirit.

First of all, we may well suppose that the duties they are calculated to teach us, for our example, are such as lie at the very foundation of true Christian obedience and Evangelical charity, as they pass from seven into sevenfold manifestation and development. These duties such as are the very groundwork of those Christian graces and tempers which we are to cultivate, seem to be the following:

1. Forgiveness of injuries.
2. Penitence.
3. Filial duty.
4. Fear of God.
5. Fulfilment of His Word.
6. Perfect obedience.
7. Resignation.

Secondly, they may be considered as containing within them the great mysteries of our faith, and doctrines emanating from the Cross, truths laid up in the Ark of the Covenant, such as these:

1. The remission of sins.
2. The intermediate state to be with Christ.
3. The Church the home of bereavement.

4. Terribleness of God's Judgments.
5. Truth of the Scriptures.
6. Justification in Christ.
7. The Resurrection of the Body.

In the third place, they may be considered as setting forth the mysterious attributes of our Blessed Lord Himself:

1. His Meditation and Intercession.
2. His Kingly Power.
3. The Son of Man.
4. His human Soul.
5. His human Body.
6. His sinless perfection.
7. His voluntary Sacrifice.

Or again, the 1st shows His fellowship with man; the 2nd, His Divine Omnipotence; the 3rd, His human relationship, the 4th, His taking on Him our sins; the 5th, His taking on Him our suffering nature; the 6th, His fulness, of which we receive; the 7th, our reconciliation to God in Him.

As these expressions become thus significative in divers senses; so likewise the Cross itself on which He dies, may be considered in various ways according to His manifold attributes. For thus His Cross becomes,

The throne of our King.
The altar of our High Priest.
The tribunal of our Judge.
The mercy-seat of our God.
The trophy of the Conqueror of death.
The ensign of the Captain of our Salvation.
The rod of His Justice against sinners.

All our reflections on the Cross of Christ, and on Christ crucified, will differ as we consider it, and all the circumstances connected with it, in either of these points of view. From either point we may safely contemplate the truth in its manifold aspects; but that point from which we look to it with most advantage to ourselves, must depend on our own individual character; on our past life, on our present circumstances of good or evil, on our existing needs of correction or assistance; on our natural or acquired dispositions; on our spiritual or temporal dangers. The various forms which the Cross assumes, may be comprehended in the seven heads above enumerated; in each of these does it appear reflected, as in a different medium.

Again; all these manifold significations in which the Cross presents itself to our devout attention, may be considered as set forth in the divers types and analogies, under which it is represented in Holy Scripture. For these various designations and offices may be considered to be represented in various figures; in each of the attributes above mentioned we shall see some corresponding symbol or Scriptural expressions.

In the first, it is "the sceptre of His kingdom," which is "a right sceptre."

In the second, it is Aaron's rod that budded, and so indicated the true Priesthood.

In the third, it is the rod of Moses, which destroyed Pharaoh and rescued Israel.

In the fourth, it is the Ark of Noah, which saved from the Deluge.

In the fifth, it is the staff of Elisha, which was laid on the dead child.

In the sixth, it is the spear of Joshua, which he stretched forth over the city Ai.

In the seventh, it is the axe laid at the root of the tree, which the Baptist spoke of[8].

---

[8] Mentioned by Irenæus as an emblem of the Cross. See Tracts for the Times, No. 89, page 34.

And if in figure and symbol, so also in the parables of His gracious teaching, shall we find the Son of Man who is now hanging on the Cross, and teaching us from thence, in a sevenfold aspect. For He is often Himself represented in His own parable: He is Himself "the man who was a king;" "the man who was a householder;" He is Himself to be found in the persons of the poor; and He has taken to Himself the place of the sinner, and expresses Himself for our sakes in the accents of penitential humiliation. The expression

"Father, forgive them," may serve to represent to us that bountiful creditor, who frankly forgives His debtor ten thousand talents.

"This day shalt thou be with Me in Paradise," are the words of that good Shepherd, who had found the sheep that was lost, and was bearing it home rejoicing to His Father's fold.

The commendation of the blessed Virgin to the disciple, when the sword had pierced her soul, is the act of that good Samaritan, who committed the wounded man at His departure to the Master of the Inn, to the Steward of His own household the Church, saying, "Take care of him, when I come again I will repay."

That cry of the desertion of God, from our Lord bearing sin, may express the humiliation and desertions of that accepted Publican, who ventured not to lift up his eyes to Heaven, but smote on his breast.

That expression of "I thirst," may be signified in the dying Lazarus, who, while angels were waiting to receive his soul into Paradise, was dying without the gate in want and nakedness.

The term "It is finished," may remind us all of the Bridegroom in the parable, standing by and saying

to the wise and foolish virgins, "It is finished,"
and passing in to the Marriage Feast.
And when our Lord commended His righteous soul into
the hands of His Father, it was as the First-born
among many brethren,—as the first of those who
are like that "good and faithful servant," who shall
enter into the "joy of his Lord," whom "He shall
appoint Ruler over all that He hath."

THE RENDING OF THE VEIL.

The sun had now been darkened for three hours
during our Lord's extreme agony, while the powers of
darkness were let loose. "*And*" when He uttered His
last cry and gave up the ghost, "*behold*," says St. Matthew, as if to imply the immediate connexion of the two
events;—and indeed St. Luke mentions the circumstance before he records our Lord's cry, as if from both
these we might conclude it to be coincident with it;—
"*behold, the veil of the temple was rent* (Matt. Mark,
Luke) *in twain* (Matt. Mark) *through the midst* (Luke),
from the top to the bottom (Matt. Mark). *And the earth
quaked, and the rocks were rent ; and the graves*" (contained in those rocks) "*were opened ; and many bodies of
the saints which slept arose*" (Matt.). But this latter
circumstance probably occurred on the following Sunday,
(as we know it is customary with St. Matthew thus to
introduce things out of the order of time,) for he adds,
"*And they went forth from their graves after His Resurrection, and went into the Holy City, and appeared unto
many ;*" which most wonderful and mysterious event we
should not have known, but for this incidental mention
of it by St. Matthew. "*And the centurion* (Matt. Mark,
Luke), *and they that were with him, watching Jesus, when*

*they perceived the earthquake, and the things that came
to pass, feared greatly and said, Truly this was the Son of
God"* (Matt.). But it was more particularly the Roman
centurion himself, as St. Mark and St. Luke mention;
"the centurion who was standing opposite to Him"
(Mark); and therefore from that position more particularly observed Him. And the thing that most of all
struck him with this feeling of awe, was that miraculous
loud cry. *"The centurion when he perceived* (Mark,
Luke) *what took place* (Luke); *that so crying He gave
up the ghost* (Mark), *he glorified God"* (Luke) by confessing Him, and *"said, Truly this man was the Son of
God"* (Mark); or, as St. Luke says, *"Certainly this was
a righteous man."* It might have been that he repeated
both of these expressions in his awe and wonder; this
would have been very natural: or it might have been
that he used the words St. Mark records, of His being
"the Son of God," alluding to our Lord's having used
that expression, but without any knowledge of its very
high and mysterious meaning; and signifying by it
nothing more, than that which St. Luke has thought
fit to express by the words "a righteous man."

Those also who before had been unconcerned spectators, or wantonly taking part in this dreadful deed,
now began to be affected at what had been done: and
partook in the feeling of the soldiers, which communicated a general awe and consternation. For St. Luke
says, *"And all the multitudes who had come together to
that sight, when they beheld what had taken place, smit-
ing their breasts,"* as in grief and amazement at what
had been done, *"returned,"* or quietly withdrew.

It is evident that this rending of the veil implies,
that not only had our Saviour entered into the Holy of
Holies, "into Heaven itself, to appear in the presence of

God for us," but that He had also broken through the partition wall or veil by which we were excluded, so that we likewise might follow Him thither. For this veil signified, St. Paul tells us, His flesh, through which, being broken in death, He of course Himself would enter into Heaven; but which being broken for us, gives us also, together with Him, free access. For we have thence, says the Apostle, "boldness to enter into the holiest, by a new and living way, which He hath consecrated for us through the veil, that is to say, His flesh [9]." Thus, in short, it signified what is expressed in the Ambrosian Hymn, "When Thou hadst overcome the sharpness of death, Thou didst open the kingdom of Heaven to all believers."

Nor does it merely signify our admission into Heaven after death, but also our having access now into the Holiest of Holies, through the blood of Christ with which we are sprinkled, for it is in this sense that St. Paul applies it in this passage. This, too, is according to the analogy of all Scripture, that expressions and emblems which are applied to Heaven hereafter, are also applied to the Christian state, as "the kingdom of Heaven" upon earth. According to this subordinate meaning, it would signify that the mysteries of God contained in the letter of the Jewish laws and ordinances are now entirely thrown open and made manifest: that we may enter into them, and partake of that inestimable grace and truth which was contained in them: that there is nothing now, which is of the nature of a Jewish rite, or lifeless ceremony; but instead of this, whatever there is in the Christian Church, contains Heaven within it, ministers grace, and is of a sacramental nature. For the way which Christ hath

[9] Heb. x. 20.

consecrated for us is "a living way." "No wonder," says Origen, "that the veil of the temple is rent in twain, which veiled the inner mysteries, so that the disciples of Christ, receiving spiritual eyes, may behold those things which, before Jesus, were shown to none." There were two veils of the Temple, he says, of which this one that was now rent was the outer veil; and by its being rent from the top to the bottom it signified, that the mystery of Christ from the foundation of the world unto the end of all things, was now manifested. " But when that which is perfect shall have come, then shall the second veil also be taken away, so that we shall behold the True Ark of the Testament, as it is in itself, the Cherubim, and true Mercy-seat, and the Manna laid up in the golden pot, and greater things than these: which were shown in the law of Moses, of which God said, ' Thou shalt make all things according to the pattern shown thee in the mount.' "

But Theophylact explains the rending of the veil from the top to the bottom, as the rending of our flesh from Adam to the last of mankind; for our flesh is the veil of our mind, and this is rent in Christ; for the veil is His flesh. And this will also fall in with the interpretation of Origen, that, on the breaking of our flesh, we shall behold that which is behind the second veil. Another explanation indeed, or rather an additional one, is also given of the rending of the veil, by Hilary, Ambrose, Theophylact, and Jerome; that it meant "the dividing of the people and departure of the guardian Angel," as Hilary says; "the retiring of the Holy Spirit from the temple," says Theophylact, "and its being polluted by the Romans;" and St. Ambrose, " the profanation of the synagogue." But still they also understand it to signify, that the veil which separated us from Heaven is done away, "namely, the enmity of God," says Theophylact, "and sin:" and that we have spiritual sight afforded us to discern the mysteries of God.

Nor is it to be wondered at, that, in addition to these signs, the earth also should quake at the death of her Lord. Perhaps it was hereby signified, that, at their hearing "the loud voice" of Christ, the dead were all moved in their graves: and that the earth herself thereby implied that she was ready to give up her dead at the call of the Lord, as she will do when she next hears His loud voice. The rending of the rock of course indicated the rending of that which is most hard in nature; besides which it may be observed, that the Rock is of itself the very type of Christ, and of Christ smitten. And the rocks here spoken of were, perhaps, the depositories of the dead; as the tombs were made in rocks. The dead are henceforth said to "sleep in Christ," who is the true Rock. Nor is it strange that on such an occurrence the good men, who had trusted in Christ, should be so re-animated as to break their bonds of death, and to rise with Him; by anticipation, as it were, of the time of which our Lord spake, when He said, "The hour cometh and now is, when they that are in their graves shall hear the voice of the Son of God, and they that hear shall live."

But yet, notwithstanding all these signs of nature bearing witness to, and suffering with the Lord, yet the heart of the Jews still continues obdurate and unrelenting; proving that of all things in the world there is nothing so difficult, no miracle so wonderful, as the conversion of a sinner. They stood now in the place of Pharaoh of old; the only effect of the miracles wrought before them was, that God hardened their hearts more and more. "O the breasts of Jews," says St. Ambrose, "more hard than the stones. The rocks are rent, but their hearts are hardened. The judge entreats; his officer believes; the traitor, by his death, condemns his crime: the elements flee; the earth is shaken; the tombs are opened: yet the obduracy of the Jews remains unmoved while the world is shaken [10]." And St. Gregory speaks much to the following effect: "The Heavens knew Him, and forthwith sent forth a star, and a company of Angels to sing His birth: the sea knew Him, and made itself a way to be trodden by His feet: the earth knew Him, and trembled at His dying: the sun knew Him, and hid the rays of its light: the rocks and walls knew Him, for they were rent in twain at the time of His death: hell knew Him, and gave up the dead that it had received. But though the senseless elements perceived Him to be their Lord, the hearts of the unbelieving Jews knew Him not as God, and, more hard than the rocks themselves, were not rent by repentance."

THE FOLLOWERS OF CHRIST.

The fierce excitement of this terrible scene is now subsiding into stillness, and we naturally look around for the faithful followers of our Lord. Stationed on a distant spot, removed from the insolence of the soldiery and the taunts of the exulting Pharisees, they had been no unconcerned spectators of this sad tragedy. "*And there stood,*" says St. Luke, "*all His acquaintance afar off;*" and "*many* (Matt.) *women* (Matt. Mark, Luke) *were beholding from afar*" (Matt. Mark), and "*seeing these things* (Luke); *such as had followed together with Him*" (Matt. Luke), with

[10] Expos. in Luc. Lib. x. 128.

"*Jesus* (Matt.) *from Galilee* (Matt. Luke), *to minister unto Him*" (Matt.); "*which also, when He was in Galilee, followed Him and ministered unto Him*" (Mark). In this general company there were some who are usually known for a more intimate and close attendance on our Lord, and who are therefore expressly mentioned: "*Among these were Mary Magda-lene, and Mary the mother of James* (*the less,* Mark) *and of Joses*" (Matt. Mark), who is called Mary the wife of Cleopas by St. John [1]; "*and the mother of Zebedee's children*" (Matt.), or "*Salome* (Mark). *And many other women who came up with Him unto Jerusalem*" (Mark). When speaking of these women, thus watching the Passion of our Lord, Origen beautifully says, "Blessed I esteem those women, who are built up to blessedness by the spectacle of the Word, and by the death of the Body of Jesus; for every thing which is in Christ, if it be beheld in truth, maketh him that beholdeth blessed [2]."

But two of the women, who are named as being with the above-mentioned party afar off, namely the two Marys, are said by St. John to have been at one time close to the Cross, together with the blessed Virgin and himself. It may have been, that at one period of this long and protracted scene of suffering, the beloved disciple had gone and brought our Lord's Mother to the place where he himself was stationed at the foot of the Cross; and with her had brought from that company the two Marys, her sister, and Mary Magdalene, to accompany and support her at so trying a scene. Or it might be, that the blessed Virgin and St. John were themselves there throughout: and that, at one time, probably near the close of the day, they were joined by those two com-

---

[1] Ch. xix. 25.   [2] Comm. in Matt. 141.

panions in sorrow, the other two Marys. For these are marked throughout for their earnest and assiduous attendance; both of them, after the burial this evening, and also when the Sabbath was past, are found separate from the others in their most zealous ministrations on our Lord; and therefore might naturally be expected to be found apart from them during this long and agitating period of our Lord's suffering; when separated from the others, who were in the distance, it would naturally be their feeling to approach more nearly to the Cross of Christ. St. Augustin indeed suggests, that they might have been first of all near the Cross, and afterwards have retired to a distance from the crowd, after our Lord had committed His mother to the Evangelist. During the six hours that our Lord was dying, this is of course supposable, and it must be allowed, that at the close of the narrative they are spoken of as " standing afar off;" but, on the other side, it appears that the mention of them by the other three Evangelists does not refer to any definite period of time; whereas the incident, wherein St. John introduces them, appears to have been a very little before our Lord's death. Besides this, it seems more natural to suppose, that if they were not near to our Lord all the time, they would rather have drawn near at His death and the termination of His sufferings, and when the violence of the scene was in some degree abated, than at that time have withdrawn farther from Him. However that may be, the discrepancy in the Evangelists, by which our thoughts become more engaged on the subject, and the natural change and movement it exhibits in such a company, tend to afford us a more lively view of this scene of awful interest, than the repetition of precisely the same account in the different narratives could have done.

THE BLOOD AND WATER.

It was now between the two evenings, the time when the Paschal Lamb was slain, between three and six o'clock, or the rising of the stars ; and it was necessary that our Lord's body should be removed from the Cross. The Divine reason for this was in order that our Lord might fulfil the type of Jonas by being three days in the earth ; the human reason, which operated on the religious scrupulousness of the wicked Jews, was that the Body might be removed before the approaching Sabbath ; and because the Law had commanded that the body of one that is hanged, which "is accursed of God," shall not remain upon the tree "all night[3]." These reasons were more especially urgent on the present occasion, on account of the importance of that Sabbath which was approaching ; for it was the Great Sabbath, that Sabbath which occurred in the Paschal week. So mysteriously and wonderfully were the Divine counsels being in every particular fulfilled ; for as the Sabbath was ever observed, because God rested on that day from the works of Creation, so was it meet that from the work of Redemption, now finished, Christ should on that day rest in the grave. And, as all things are fulfilled in Christ in their very highest sense, so it is not only the Sabbath, but the high Sabbath! "that day was" indeed "an high day." "How powerful is truth !" says St. Chrysostom, observing this, " by their zeal the prophecies are fulfilled." Powerful indeed and mighty is it; as if instinct with an unerring and heavenly strength, it moves onward, as the creative word of Prophecy hath

[3] Deut. xxi. 23.

gone forth; and all human things, as it advances, it moulds, and bears on, and fashions into great and Divine semblances, and significations, and realities: it "turns not aside, but goes on straight forward:" the designs, the passions, the accidents, the graces, the sins of men, the things of nature and the things beyond nature, it takes on the right hand and on the left, and bears on with it to its great fulfilment; they impede and stop not its progress, but are as if only made to further it, and bear witness to its unbending and unconquerable course. All are borne on together in the mighty tide of its Providence.

"*The Jews therefore,*" says St. John, "*that their bodies might not remain on the Cross on the Sabbath-day, since it was the preparation,—for great was the day of that Sabbath,—requested Pilate that their legs might be broken,*" in order to destroy any remains of life that there might be in them, "*and that they might be taken away. The soldiers therefore came;*" they were probably not those soldiers who had witnessed His death, but those whom the Governor sent for this purpose, and who knew not the fact of His dying: "*and they brake the legs of the first, and of the other which was crucified with Him. But when they came to Jesus, and saw that He was dead already, they brake not His legs;*" being restrained and overruled by the watchful hand of God, which withheld them: for He had Himself expressly promised this, saying, "He keepeth all His bones, so that not one of them is broken." "*But one of the soldiers,*" in order to be assured of the certainty of His death, "*with a spear pierced His side, and forthwith came thereout blood and water.*" To which words St. John adds a strong and emphatic declaration of their truth from his own ocular testimony, signifying thereby the vast import-

ance of the fact he declared, and the necessity of a belief in it, almost, one would suppose, beyond other
facts which he records. "*And he that saw it hath
borne witness, and his testimony is true; and he knoweth
that he saith true, that ye might believe.*"

Now some have supposed that all that the Evangelist
intended was that this blood and water was the proof of
the reality of our Lord's death: but if this flowing of
water from the heart is so, it is a proof only known to
physicians; nor does the certainty of our Lord's death
appear to be a matter ever doubted; it is also more sufficiently proved by other circumstances than it could
have been by this one alone; and, so far from its being
of itself a proof of death, Theophylact observes that it
was of itself miraculous, that blood should flow from a
dead body. From this mode of speaking one would be
naturally disposed to think that he was recording something beyond nature, rather than a mere natural consequence of death. It may have been that the Evangelist himself had no clear understanding of what it indicated; but that, being impressed with a sense of the
vast consequences and significancies of all things re-
pecting our Lord, he had no more than a general impression of something in a high degree miraculous and
mysterious. However that may be, as St. John is considered to have had beyond others an insight into the
depth of Divine mysteries [*], we should rather look to
himself to explain it, if in any part of his writings he
would afford us any clue. Now it is observable, that
throughout his Gospel he is apt to introduce references
to the two Divine Sacraments, and yet in such a manner
as not openly to display that allusion, according to the
well-known reserve, or holy modesty and reverence of

[*] "Mysteria Divina plenius penetrat," says Ambrose of St. John.

the early Church on these subjects. And it so happens that we find, in another place, he makes mention of water and blood in the same solemn and emphatic manner that he does here, and apparently in allusion to this circumstance. In his first Epistle he says, "This is He that came by water and blood, even Jesus Christ; not by water only, but by water and blood." And again, —"There are three that bear witness on earth—the Spirit, and the Water, and the Blood; and these three agree in one. If we receive the witness of men, the witness of God is greater; for this is the witness of God which He hath testified of His Son." He here speaks of the Water and the Blood as witnesses, together with that great Witness, the Spirit Himself. These things, therefore, must contain within them some allusions infinitely great. The piercing of our Lord's side was indeed the proof of the reality of His death, for it is from Him as dead that our life proceeds; but this was not the great object to which the Evangelist bears record.

He evidently alludes to the two Sacraments. The water and the blood were in Baptism, and the water and the blood were in the holy Eucharist; and these two are the life of the Church. And thus the Church, the Bride of Christ, is taken out of His side while He is asleep in death; in like manner as Eve was taken from the side of Adam, when, as it is said, "God caused a deep sleep to fall upon Adam."

This mystical and sacramental interpretation thus attributed to the whole circumstance is according to the opinion of ancient writers. St. Chrysostom simply and naturally explains the meaning of the Evangelist: "I heard it not from others, but was myself present, and saw it." "And his testimony is true, he suitably adds in mentioning this insult on Christ, not as if he was recording any great and wonderful sign, which should render his words suspected; but this he said, to close the mouths of heretics; as intimating therein future mysteries; and as himself gazing into that treasure which lay concealed therein." And St. Austin says, "That the word '*opened*' His side" (as it is rendered in the Latin version) "is full of meaning, as if it were in some sense opening unto us the door of life, out of which flowed the Sacraments of the Church; without which there is no entrance into that life, which is true life." "And this," he says, "was foreshown by Noah making a door in the side of the ark, by which those animals were to enter, which were not to perish by the flood; and by which things the Church was prefigured. On this account the first woman was taken from the side of the man, when he slept, and was called the mother of all living." And afterwards,—"This second Adam inclined His head and slept on the Cross, that from thence His wife might be formed, which flowed from His side while He slept. O death, from which the dead obtain second life[5]!" St. Ambrose also says, "From His dead body, incorrupted though dead, flowed forth the life of us all." "The water and the blood went forth; the one to cleanse, the other to redeeem. Let us drink therefore the price paid for us, that by drinking we may be redeemed[6]." Also in like manner St. Chrysostom, drawing as usual exhortations to devout practice from it,—"Since here the sacred Mysteries receive their origin, draw near as one about to drink from the very side of Christ[7]." And Theophylact; "Let them therefore blush who mix not the wine in the sacred Mysteries; for they seem not to believe that water flowed from His side." St. Cyril

---

[5] In Joan. cxx. 2.   [6] Expos. in Lucam.   [7] Hom. lxxxiv.

of Alexandria[8], too, speaks of the blood and the water as "the image and first offerings of the mystical Eucharist and of holy Baptism."

Thus did our blessed Lord "empty out all His blood upon the earth," as St. Athanasius expresses it, for our sakes. So perfect a Sacrifice, that not only all the labours of His life, but all His life-blood in death, did He entirely exhaust for our sakes. After shedding it drop by drop in His bloody sweat; and afterwards in the scourging; and then from His bleeding brows; and from His bleeding hands and feet on the Cross; not even after death did His heart-blood cease to flow for us; but now even after death did the power of His ineffable charities burst forth in a continued stream, beyond nature, and contrary to nature; blended with water, to wash and strengthen us, and give us life. Even in death His charity dies not, forgets us not, nor ceases to minister to us; nay, in death it becomes the more living, and full of all-healing, all-blessing, all-sustaining energy.

Nor is the Evangelist content with declaring his ocular testimony to the fact: he adduces also two prophecies, in fulfilment of which the two circumstances took place. "*For these things were done,*" he adds, "*that the Scripture might be fulfilled, ' A bone of Him shall not be broken;' and again another Scripture saith, ' They shall look on Him whom they pierced'*" (John). The first passage refers to that particular injunction, which was more than once given, respecting the Paschal Lamb, that not a bone should be broken[9]. And as Holy Scripture has always "eyes that look both before and after," so this circumstance appears not only to look behind as the fulfilment of the Paschal type, but

---

[8] In Joan. Evang.   [9] As Exod. xii. 46, and Numb. ix. 12.

also to look before as typical of our Lord's Body, the Church; the unity and entireness of which, so often set before us, is signified also in this event, that not a bone of Him should be broken even in death; that is, that in circumstances the most calamitous the true Church of God shall not be broken. And as that which is fulfilled in Christ and His Church is also fulfilled in His members; in allusion to some typical meaning contained in the circumstance, the Psalmist says, first of all of himself escaping from the Philistines to the cave of Adullam, and then prophetically of Christ and all Christians,—" The Lord delivereth the righteous out of all his troubles ;" " He keepeth all his bones, so that not one of them is broken [1] :" which seems to signify, that however the righteous in Christ are exercised by afflictions, they shall not be such as to break or destroy them. I find that Quesnel takes it in this threefold sense: " The Scripture," he says, " fulfilled in the figurative lamb, was only a type of the literal accomplishment in the true Lamb. It is likewise still fulfilled both in the Church, which God will always preserve entire and in unity; and in the saints, whom He fills with His strength, and secures so effectually, as not to suffer a hair of their head to perish." The other Scripture to which the Evangelist alludes, may indeed be partly that expression in the Psalms, where we read, " They pierced My hands and My feet ;" but more distinctly that in the Prophet Zechariah [2], " I will pour upon the house of David the Spirit of grace and of supplications, and they shall look upon Me whom they have pierced, and they shall mourn for Him—the land shall mourn, every family apart." Which prophecy at length, although it refers to the Jews, yet does it also describe the whole Christian

------

[1] Ps. xxxiv. 20.   [2] Ch. xii. 10. 12.

condition, which is a state of mourning and supplication; wherein it is said, "Blessed are they that mourn." But more particularly doubtless is it to be fulfilled, as St. John himself declares to us in the Apocalypse, on the appearance of the Son of Man bearing the marks of His Crucifixion on the day of Judgment, when "every eye shall see Him, and they also which pierced Him;" in reference to which our Lord Himself seems to say, that they "shall see the sign of the Son of Man;" and that all the tribes of the earth, evidently with an allusion to this prophecy of Zechariah, "shall mourn because of Him."

SECTION III.—THE SEPULTURE.

"Free among the dead, like unto them that are wounded, and lie in the grave: who are out of remembrance, and are cut away from thy hand."

THE RICH IN HIS DEATH.

It was "*after these things*," St. John tells us, while the bodies were still hanging on the Cross, although means had been taken to hasten death; "*and now* (Mark) *when it was evening* (Matt. Mark); *since it was the preparation, which is the day before the Sabbath*" (Mark), and therefore it was necessary that they should soon be removed; according to the leave that Pilate had given, before the Sabbath commenced, which was on that evening. "*Behold* (Luke) *there came* (Matt. Mark) *a rich man* (Matt.) *from Arimathea* (Matt. Luke), *a city of the Jews* (Luke), *whose name was Joseph*" (Matt. Luke); indeed he was known as "*Joseph of Arimathea*" (Mark,

John).   He "*was a counsellor*" (Luke), St. Mark says, "*an honourable counsellor*," one probably of eminence: it has been supposed that he was the Roman officer in the provinces, so named, and in Latin " Decurio ;" so Origen and others have thought : but St. Luke's words would rather lead one to infer that he was one of the Sanhedrim, for he adds that although one of them, yet "*this man had not consented to their counsel and deed.*"   He was "a rich man," St. Matthew says; and St. Luke, " *a good man and a just ;*" and that " *he also was expecting the kingdom of God*" (Mark, Luke). This expectation was attributed to the devout Simeon, who was "waiting for the consolation of Israel [1]," and seems to indicate a devout preparation of mind, looking forward in faith. " *He himself also was* (Matt.) *a disciple of Jesus* " (Matt. John), not one of the twelve, says Chrysostom, but one of the seventy : " *but secretly for fear of the Jews*" (John). St. Ambrose, indeed, applies these words of his secrecy to the act of requesting Pilate, as if he took the passage to mean, " that he came to Pilate secretly for fear of the Jews." But the Greek rather indicates that he was "a disciple in secret" for fear of the Jews, and that now " *he took courage,*" as St. Mark says, " *and went in to Pilate.*"

" *This man came to Pilate* (Matt. Luke), *and begged the Body of Jesus* (Matt. Mark, Luke). *He asked Pilate that he might take the Body of Jesus* (John). *Pilate*" expressed doubt and surprise that life should be so soon extinct. He " *marvelled,*" says St. Mark, " *if He were already dead.*" For, as Origen says, " they lived in that torment sometimes for the whole night, and even through the succeeding day." But being no doubt glad to accede

------

[1] Luke ii. 25.

to such a request, not only on account of the station and character of the person who requested it, but also because such a request implied an agreement with his own convictions, and a sympathy with the deep interest he had evinced in favour of Christ, he sent for the soldier who had the charge of the execution.—"*And having called to him the Centurion, he inquired of him whether He had been any time dead. And when he knew from the Centurion*" (Mark) that it was the case, "*Pilate gave him leave* (John), *he gave him the Body*" (Mark), or "*commanded the Body to be given up*" (Matt.) to Joseph. "It was Divinely provided for," it is said in Bede, when speaking of Joseph, "that he should be rich in order to have access to Pilate, for no mean man could have had access to the Governor: and that he should be a just man in order to receive the Body of the Lord." Indeed, we may apply in a spiritual sense also what Bede says, for he must be a just man, and one that is waiting for the kingdom of God, who is meet to receive the Body of the Lord. St. Chrysostom remarks on his boldness, " Observe the courage of this man; for he put himself in danger of death, and underwent the enmities of all, on account of his good will to Christ. And he not only dares to ask for, but also to bury the Body of Christ[2]." And indeed St. Jerome suggests that he is the person described in the first Psalm, as he who " hath not walked in the counsels of the ungodly," and the like[3]. " It was a laudable daring," says Theophylact, "for he thought not, 'I shall fall from my riches, and I shall be driven out by the Jews, if I seek the Body of one who was condemned for blasphemy.'"

This good Joseph, it may be observed, was of

<hr>

[2] Comm. in Matt.   [3] In Matt. lib. iv. ad loc.

Arimathea, or Ramah, the city of Samuel, and the place of Rachel's tomb: so that, if he returned to his home on this night, to weep for this shocking deed, there might then have been the fulfilment of that prophecy in the mourning for our Lord Himself, which was also fulfilled in the mourning for the innocent Martyrs who were slain at His birth. And if the prophecy has any relation to this occasion of our Lord's death, then it seems to unite our blessed Lord's death with theirs, and sanctifies them, and gives the hope to their death. "A voice was heard in Ramah, lamentation, and bitter weeping: Rachel weeping for her children refused to be comforted for her children, because they were not. Thus saith the Lord, Refrain thy voice from weeping, and thine eyes from tears; for thy work shall be rewarded; and they shall come again from the land of the enemy[4]." These two occasions may, at all events, be well connected together, for they shall return from the "land of the enemy," because Christ returns from thence. He returns, and therefore they return; He in them and with them: this is the consolation of the weeping mother; this is the consolation for him of Ramah, the good Joseph, who is seen as the chief mourner at the tomb of Christ; weeping for Him of whom that other Joseph had been the type, when He was sold into Egypt by his brethren; and the spirit of Rachel was weeping for Him at the tomb.

Nor was this just man of Arimathea alone in this most holy task; there came forth likewise another, who like himself also was "a ruler of the Jews[5]," and a secret disciple, to take part with him in this last duty. "*There came also Nicodemus, who at the first came to Jesus by*

---

[4] Jer. xxxi. 15, 16.   [5] John iii. 1.

night" (John), as St. John had recorded in the beginning of his Gospel; and whom he had since designated under the same description, when he spoke of his pleading in our Lord's behalf before the Pharisees[6]. The expression here "at the first," St. Augustin takes to imply, that his first coming was by night, but that he probably afterwards came frequently. St. Cyril of Alexandria thinks that the mention of the two, as coming forward, is in order to bear testimony to the truth of Christ's death, "for the Law says, by the mouth of two or three witnesses shall every word be established."

Here we may pause to observe, how, when the world seems most triumphant, then Christ's power begins most to reveal itself. Already does the power of His death begin to work, so that in His utmost humiliation, even unto the grave, the rich gain that strength and courage which they had not in His life, to confess Christ; to confess not the living Christ, nor Christ risen, but Christ crucified. To confess the Christ, when to all worldly appearance He could profit them not; and when the act of doing so was such, that all human expediency and prudence, motives which too often operate with the rich, would have condemned their interference. These were in some sense the first of Confessors. The action, too, is in this respect, like most of the best actions of the saints of God in Scripture, in that it was opposed to worldly wisdom and prudential policy. And the beloved disciple mentions expressly their former cowardice, as if to prove the greatness of their present courage. The sun had gone down to his rest: and even now, at his setting, the stars begin to come forth, and one and two become visible. Nor is their reward less marked than the de-

---

[6] John vii. 50.

voted piety of this good deed. They asked, and they received; they received no less than Christ's Body: they received Him who is the salvation of the world, the germ of everlasting life. It was Christ Himself; and the promise of God to Abraham can alone express their happiness,—" Fear not, I am thy exceeding great reward [7]."

But every thing respecting our blessed Lord is important, as containing great and mysterious principles of truth, which will be found to prevail throughout the world. And therefore we may reasonably ask, what is signified by this circumstance, that, instead of our Lord's being buried, as we might have expected, by His disciples or poorer friends from Galilee, these rich and honourable men come forward at His death; whereas no mention is made of His receiving attention from them during His life and sufferings. Perhaps the words of the prophet may in some degree afford us a clue to the explanation; for when he speaks of His being " with the rich in His death [8]," he gives us a reason for it, "because He had done no violence, neither was any deceit in His mouth." May not this therefore indicate some great principle, which was here shown in Christ, and will also be in His members? May it not signify, that although according to the pattern of Christ crucified, good men often make " their grave with the wicked," dying the deaths of malefactors, on account of the envy and hate of mankind in all ages of the world; yet, as meekness and truth (that is to say, where there is "no violence" and "no guile,") must in the end prevail, Providence has so ordained it, that at their death the rich and great come forth to do them honour. Those

<hr>

[7] Gen. xv. 1.　　　　　　　　　　[8] Isa. liii. 9.

who before could not but secretly reverence them,—being themselves, like these two, "just and good" men, but from fear of the world not openly confessing their principles, being disciples as it were in secret, as St. John says of these two persons,—yet will come forth openly, when envy has been abated by death. For as the Heathen Poet observes, "We envy and hate virtue when safe among us, but when taken from our eyes, we regret the loss." Thus the Jews slew their Prophets, but afterwards adorned their sepulchres. The good Christian must be hated by the world, but his memory is blessed. Thus even now the Kings and great of the earth do honour to those good men of all ages who were themselves rejected and hated by the world, and died by the hands of the executioner. The memory of no King is so deeply cherished and revered, even to his very countenance, as that one who died a Martyr on the scaffold. The circumstance therefore here recorded in the narrative may embody a great principle, extending to every age and clime, as connected with the doctrine of Christ crucified.

THE BURIAL.

The Scriptures have described these two persons as taking each his own separate part in these sacred ministrations. Of " *Joseph* " it is said, " *And having received the Body* (Matt) *and having purchased linen and taken Him down* " (Mark), or " *taken it down* (Luke), *he folded* " (Matt. Luke) or " *wrapped it in* (Mark) *pure* (Matt.) *linen* " (Matt. Mark, Luke). And of *Nicodemus*, that he " *came bearing a mixture of myrrh and aloes about a hundred pound weight* " (John). And then of both together, " *Then took they the Body of Jesus, and wound it in linen clothes with the spices* " (John).

Blessed indeed were these persons, although rich in this world ; and blessed beyond all things were these offerings, the linen and the spices, that were allowed to touch that most Holy Body in death.   And as the vestments in which our Lord died were the subject of sacred prophecy, it were not unreasonable to suppose that these things, that wrapped and enveloped that most holy Sacrifice, should be hallowed to sacred association, both in Scripture and nature.   This we may reasonably suppose, though we cannot venture to interpret them ; but it may not be a presumptuous or unholy task, to mention some few instances of analogy in which they occur.   May not " the linen," hallowed by this use, be the same substance which is often spoken of for sacred purposes ; such as " the linen garments of the Priests," so often distinctly specified, " the linen ephod," " the linen breeches ;" " the linen girdle " of Jeremiah[9], which was used as a sign to represent the Church of Israel ?   We may add, that in the Revelation also[10] the Angels are " clothed in pure and white linen ;" and the Church is clothed in the same, and that too, with an emblematic and spiritual interpretation, for she is " arrayed in fine linen, clean and white ; for the fine linen is the righteousness of Saints[11]."   These expressions at once connect it with the white Baptismal robe which is the righteousness of Christ.   It is remarkable, that whenever these holy coverings of our Lord's body are mentioned, they are never called " grave clothes " as in the case of Lazarus ; but are thus spoken of as " the linen clothes."

[9] Ch. xiii. 1.   [10] Ch. xv. 6.   [11] Ch. xix. 8.

Thus we find that ancient writers not only mention the analogy of this linen clothing, as connected with the Church, which is Christ's Body, but also the spiritual interpretations of mental purity, to which the figure extends. St. Jerome says, "mystically Joseph bears the appearance of Apostles, he wraps the body in clean linen; and indeed in the same, the sheet of linen, we find all kinds of living creatures let down from Heaven to Peter; from which we understand, under the name of linen, that the whole Church is buried together with Christ." And St. Ambrose, "It was perhaps that which Peter beheld let down from Heaven, in which were all kinds of four-footed things and beasts and birds, exhibiting by a figure the representation of the Gentiles." The same writer says of Joseph and Nicodemus, "one was a just man, and the other without guile. The one brought the linen clothes; the other the ointment. Nor is the distinction without a purpose: justice clothes the Church; innocence administers grace[1]."

In like manner, "the myrrh and aloes" may contain sacred import, though we cannot venture to explain what it may be. But we know, that in the gifts of the Wise Men at our Lord's birth, the gold, the frankincense, and the myrrh, the gold is considered to imply His Kingship, and the frankincense His Divinity, and myrrh His humanity. Now on this occasion the myrrh alone of these is found: it is our Lord's humanity which is embalmed. Moreover, if the Church is clothed in white linen, so also is it said of her, that "all her garments smell of myrrh, aloes, and cassia[2]." With reference to which also myrrh is often spoken of in the Canticles; and that, too, in words which, speak-

---

[1] Expos. in Luc. x. 137.   [2] Ps. xlv. 8.

ing of the Church, might also be applied to our Lord's human Person; "A garden enclosed is My sister, My spouse, a spring shut up, a fountain sealed ... Myrrh and aloes with all the chief spices; a fountain of gardens, a well of living waters .... Awake, O north wind, and come, thou south; blow upon My garden, that the spices thereof may flow out[3]." It is remarkable that the Canticles, which use so much the figure of earthly affection, speak more particularly of Christ's grave[4]. It is by mortification, by being dead and buried with Christ, that we arrive at Divine affection.

Surely of all earthly and material things, none are so worthy of our devout remembrance, as these which wrapt the Body of the God of Heaven and earth, by whose word the Heavens were made, and all the host of them by the breath of His mouth: that Sacrifice which as a sweet savour sanctified earth and reconciled it to Heaven. As, moreover, Holy Scripture passes from the figures and types to the spiritual fulfilment, and connects the linen robe of the Church with the righteousness of the saints, so also do ancient Fathers. "According to the spiritual meaning," says St. Jerome, "we may understand this, that the Body of the Lord is not to be wrapt in jewels, nor in gold, nor in silk, but in pure linen; although it may signify this also, that he wraps Jesus in clean linen, who shall have received Him in a pure mind." And Theophylact in like manner, "Let us also imitate Joseph, receiving the Body of Christ through unity, and let us lay it in the monument cut out of the rock, that is, in a soul that remembers and forgets not God, for that is a soul cut out of the rock, which is Christ. But Him we ought to wrap in linen, that is, to

---

[3] Song of Solomon iv. 12. 14—16.   [4] See Cyril, Lect. xiv.

receive in a pure body." In like manner with these ancient writers Quesnel[5] says, " Happy that person who receives the Body of Jesus Christ into a new and clean heart, which has not been defiled by sin, and who takes care to secure *the door* thereof against the spirit of the world." And in his comment of St. Mark, he says, " Whoever is dead to sin with Jesus Christ, ought, as it were, to *wrap up* Christ in his heart, by preserving Him therein with great care. To make his heart a living *sepulchre* by the remembrance of Christ's death. And to hew his sepulchre *out of a rock*, that is, to found and root it in Christ by an unshaken faith."

But it is to be observed, that these circumstances of "the linen and the spices," were not any thing peculiar to the burial of our Lord, for St. John adds, " *As the manner of the Jews is to bury;*" as if it had been Divinely provided for, that the Jewish nation should ever have observed this mode of burial, in order to do honour to our Lord's Body; enveloping it in the emblems of immortal purity and immortal fragrance, as if to represent it as incapable of corruption; and thereby they themselves also, by this mode of burial, served tacitly to express a sense of Resurrection.

Indeed, the whole of the circumstances of our Lord's burial seem to bring forth, in a strong point of view, the many other places of Holy Scripture which sanction respect paid to the mortal remains; for when brought out into light, by connexion with our Lord's history, they appear to speak of His Resurrection, and the Resurrection of our bodies also. Thus, for instance, Holy Scripture carefully records the burying of the Patriarchs, and particular circumstances connected with it; as of Abraham's purchase of the cave of

[5] On St. Matthew, chap. xxvii. 60.

Machpelah, as the Septuagint translates it, "a double cave;" the embalming and burying of Jacob; the carrying up of Joseph's bones to Canaan; the worst of curses pronounced on bad kings being, that they should not come into the sepulchre of their fathers; and also on the disobedient prophet; the piety of Rizpah in protecting the bodies of Saul's sons; and David's care in burying the bones of Saul and Jonathan. Thus does Holy Scripture raise, sanction, and hallow the feelings of nature on that subject, those instinctive feelings which have been shown by all nations, and vindicate us also in doing honour to that which has been the Temple of the Holy Ghost,—that which has been brought into some mysterious connexion with the flesh of Christ, and is to be again restored. And this opinion derives confirmation from the circumstances of our Saviour's conduct a few days previously, when He accepted and commended the good deed done to Him, in the embalming of His head and feet, assigning it as a reason that it had a reference to His burial: as if this connexion with His burial gave an especial sanctity to the deed. It is remarkable how much Holy Scripture has recorded now, after His death, of the bringing of spices, for the embalming of His Body, by three separate parties, Nicodemus, the two Marys, and the other women from Galilee. It is also to be observed, that God has caused all the four Evangelists particularly to specify the good deed, and the full name of this person who buried Christ in his own tomb, "Joseph of Arimathea;" as if in his case, also, as in that of Mary, the sister of Martha, who embalmed Him, our Lord had commanded that, "wheresoever the Gospel shall be preached in the whole world," there shall also this which "*he*" hath done, "be told for a memorial" of him.

THE HOLY SEPULCHRE.

" Now in the place," says St. John, *"where He was crucified there was a garden, and in the garden a new sepulchre, wherein was never man yet laid. There, therefore, on account of the preparation of the Jews, since the sepulchre was nigh at hand, they lay Jesus."* But as it was more particularly the act of Joseph of Arimathea, the other three Evangelists speak of it in the singular number. *" He laid Him "* (Mark), or, *"he laid it* (Matt. Luke) *in a sepulchre* (Mark, Luke) *hewn in stone"* (Luke); it was *" his own new sepulchre* (Matt.), *which was hewn out of a rock* (Mark), *which he had hewn in the rock* (Matt.), *wherein no man had been ever yet laid "* (Luke).

He was laid in a new tomb, hewn out in a living rock, for the Rock is ever put in Holy Scripture for heavenly strength; it is the appellation of God, of His Church, and of His Christ. In a cleft of the rock did God place Moses, and hide him therein with the shadow of His hand. And to His own people, to whom Christ has promised that, "together with " His " dead Body, shall they arise," He says, as with reference to His own example, " Come, enter thou into thy chambers, and shut thy doors about thee; hide thyself, as it were, for a little moment, until the indignation be overpast [6]."

It was in a new sepulchre,—new, in that it was unlike any that had received mortal remains before; and new, in that it was one in which no man had been yet laid; for it was the place for holy Angels, not for dead men's bones; and if the bones of His great type,

[6] Isa. xxvi. 20.

Elisha, gave life to the dead, much more would Christ's Body. Thus, though He had humbled Himself to be born in a stable, and through life to have no place wherein to lay His adorable Head, yet in death did God honour Him. And the grave had been hewn out and prepared for another, for no grave was due to Christ, as He had not sinned. In this rocky cave, therefore, in the inner chamber thereof, from thenceforth to be a sacred chancel or shrine, the dead Body of Christ was laid. While His spotless soul was gone to hallow and bless, for the reception of those that depart in the true faith of Him, that other and happier garden of which this was the emblem—the Paradise of the Dead.

Yet it was, indeed, in one respect, in His death as it had been in His life, that the Son of Man had not where to "lay His head." And to this effect is the remark of Theophylact: "Observe," he says, "the abundance of that poverty which He had taken upon Himself for us: for He who in life had no home, after death, also is laid up in the sepulchre of another, and being naked is covered by Joseph." But St. Augustin says [7], "On that account is the Saviour placed in the sepulchre of another, because He died for the salvation of others. For what could He have to do with a sepulchre, to whom death could not properly belong? What has He to do with a tomb on the earth, whose seat was in Heaven? What had He to do with a sepulchre, who was only in the grave for three days, not so much like one lying in death, as like one resting in a bed?" And St. Ambrose says, "Not without a purpose has one Evangelist called it the new sepulchre, and another, the sepulchre of Joseph, for a tomb is prepared for those who are under

[7] Serm de Sabbat. Sancto.

the law of death. The Conqueror of death hath no tomb of His own. For what communication is there between God and a tomb?" St. Cyril also, of Alexandria, says, with great beauty, that the new tomb in a garden signified, as it were by a type, that "the death of Christ was to us the forerunner and beginning of our readmission into Paradise. For by the death of Christ our death becomes new, and is changed into a kind of sleep,"—"a new kind of death, which does not dissolve us into an endless destruction, but brings on us a sleep full of good hope, after the similitude of Him who hath made for us the new way, that is, of Christ[8]." And St. Ambrose makes a striking observation on this subject, which will apply also to our Lord's life in many points, "The Incarnation of the Lord had every thing after the likeness of men, but this likeness was accompanied with a difference: He was born of a Virgin, with the similitude of birth, but dissimilitude of conception. He cured the sick, but by a command. John baptized with water, He with the Spirit[9]." To which may be added, that He died like men, but with the voluntary surrender of life: in His death He was powerless as man is in death; yet even in that death He was mighty as God.

THE GREAT SABBATH.

Now all these things were done in haste: it was not like the full laying out and solemn embalming of the dead; for here Death was so soon to be overcome, that the good intention was enough; He that was sleeping in death was so soon to awake, as a giant refreshed with sleep; and to come forth as a Bridegroom out of His chamber. The reason of this was, St. John says, "on

[8] Comm. in Joan.　　　　[9] Exp. in Luc. lib. x. 140.

account of the preparation;" St. Luke mentions, "*And that day was the preparation, and the Sabbath drew on.*" They were hastening on this account, but they knew not the reason of their own haste; for it was most needful, and decreed before the foundation of the world, that our Blessed Lord should rest for that day in the grave. It was not only the Sabbath, but the great Sabbath, the Sabbath of the Passover, the Sabbath of Sabbaths; and therefore, in truth, "that Sabbath was an high day."

Now this is not only in itself a great mystery, but it assists us also in solving, in some degree, a still greater mystery; though we are so familiar with the expression of it, that we do not consider how much it is so. The greater mystery I allude to is this: that the expression which hallows the observance of the Sabbath, and which is found, in connexion with it, throughout the Scriptures, viz. that " God rested on " that day, is of itself full of difficulty; for it might be supposed, that attributing rest to God is, of itself, incompatible with our notion of the Deity; for rest signified a cessation from . labour or toilsome suffering, and therefore He who is incapable of labour or of suffering, is also incapable of rest. But the circumstances attending our Lord's Incarnation, although they cannot explain (for how can what is finite comprehend the infinite?), yet in some measure account for it. It is, in some sense, like other expressions in Holy Scripture, which attribute to Almighty God human parts, affections, senses, and actions, whereby is shadowed forth our Lord's becoming man, and binding Himself with the bonds of human infirmity; becoming as one of us, in order that we may become one with Him. Now, something of this kind may be said of God's resting on the Sabbath-day, which hallowed that seventh day to holy commemoration in old time; for, notwithstanding other mysterious significations it may have contained, it was evidently fulfilled in Christ, when He rested in the grave from His suffering, and from His work that He had completed.

Thus, as Christ began His great Sabbath of rest in the grave on this evening, when the Sabbath commenced, so were we on this "day of preparation," and a little before the Sabbath, born anew, and created from His side; that we might also begin our great Sabbath of devotion together with Him, in anticipation of that heavenly Sabbath which remaineth for the people of God. Allusion has been before made to the opinion of Origen [10], that, as two kinds of creatures were formed on the Friday, both animals and man, the animals were created on the forenoon of that day; and afterwards, perhaps at the sixth hour of that day, God said, "Let Us make man in Our Image [1];" which time therefore would correspond with the time of our Lord's dying on the Cross, and His Church being formed from His side. So that on the afternoon of Friday we were at first created: and at the same period of the same day were redeemed and created anew in Christ. On the seventh day God rested from the work of Creation; and on the same day Christ rested from the work of Redemption in the grave. On Sunday God created the light; and on Sunday, Christ, the true Light of the new Creation, came from the grave. That Sabbath also, in which our Lord rested in the grave, is like our whole condition throughout our stay in this world, wherein we die to sin, and mortify the flesh, and are buried with Christ, and wait for a new resurrection. But, as our Lord said of the Sabbath, "My Father worketh hitherto, and I work," notwithstanding the rest of that

[10] In Matt. 134.   [1] Gen. i. 36.

hallowed day; so also is it with this Sabbath, which is fulfilled in us; for our old man is laid at rest, and dead with Him in the Sabbath, of the grave; but we have also a new Sabbath, wherein the new man is renewed daily in His likeness, wherein He and the Father worketh. It is to us also the Sabbath with regard to what is past; but it is not the Sabbath with regard to that which is to come: inasmuch as "there remaineth a rest for the people of God;" and therefore that rest is not yet attained.

THE WOMEN FROM GALILEE.

We are perhaps inclined to entertain some degree of surprise, at reading nothing of our Lord's disciples as taking part in this scene. Perhaps we do not sufficiently remember the extreme danger that it must have been to them to have appeared, when their Lord underwent from the hands of His enemies a death so terrible. But the women could probably approach with less danger. However that may be, we find them here, as at the Cross, in faithful attendance. Whether they or any of the disciples had the privilege of touching His Holy Body, does not appear; though we should suppose that they must have been earnest and watchful spectators of the scene. The words of St. Luke, who alone mentions them, would lead one to think that even the holy women were no more than spectators. In his account we see them entering into the inner chamber of the tomb, and taking their leave of Him there. "*And the women also,*" he says, "*which came with Him from Galilee followed after, and beheld the sepulchre, and how His body was laid. And they returned and prepared spices and ointments, and rested the Sabbath-day according to the commandment.*" And indeed their proceeding afterwards to procure spices and to embalm Him, as soon as they were at liberty to do so, would induce one to suppose that on this occasion they had no share in that act of Nicodemus. All things seem to indicate the great haste with which the burial took place, on account of the Feast that was approaching ; and partly for this reason the tomb seems to have been selected, as convenient from its contiguity.

But as every expression in Holy Scripture is well worthy of our interest and attention, we may consider this designation of the women,—" the women from Galilee." Three Evangelists at the Crucifixion especially dwell on the connexion of these faithful followers with the beloved Galilee; as—" They who in Galilee ministered unto Him," and " They who followed with Him from Galilee." And this circumstance the more arrests our notice, as Galilee is upon other occasions so pointedly dwelt upon, for whatever reasons it may be. Although most of the manifestations of our Lord after the Resurrection, which are recorded, take place at Jerusalem, yet it is Galilee that is especially marked out as the appointed scene of our Lord's appearance. There is much that we cannot account for in this strong designation of Galilee. It is the place of our Lord's own especial selection. As He approached the garden of Gethsemane on the night of His passion, He spake of Galilee and His appearing there : the Angels spake of the same and of His appearing there, on the morning of His Resurrection, although the persons addressed were to continue for the week in Jerusalem, and to see Him there. The same mention of the humble Galilee is again made by our Lord Himself. With some mysterious suitableness, Galilee was marked as the spot from whence He should commence the establishment of His Spiritual kingdom ; as it had been the scene of His earthly abode and ministry. So that His kingdom was spoken of as " beginning from Galilee to this place²:" and " The word which was published throughout Judea, beginning from Galilee³." There may indeed have been obvious reasons for our Lord's selecting the retired Galilee, as the place where He would more especially reveal Himself to His disciples, and teach them the mysteries of His kingdom, from its retired and obscure character; for the same cause, that in Jerusalem He appeared only to His faithful few, and that in the twilight of the morning or evening, or when they were assembled with closed doors, and at night. And it may be but a part of His great system of Providence, that to the few and despised, in solitary places, in darkness and stillness, He reveals Himself in mercy ; to crowded cities in judgment. But the thing to be at present noticed is this, that Galilee thus brought near unto our Lord, was the place of humility, and a name of scorn ; it was said contemptuously, as a plea for His rejection, " Shall Christ come out of Galilee ?" And St. Peter was detected as belonging to Christ because he was a Galilean : as if to be a Galilean were in some measure to bear His Cross. Blessed indeed was that poor country where our Lord was brought up from childhood to manhood, where He lived, and taught, and prayed. And the poor countrywomen, who had come up for that Feast with Him, are more objects of interest to us, than any other in this crowded town, despised as they doubtless were by the Jews. These were the women who now—overwhelmed with grief and fears, but so overwhelmed with grief as to forget their fears—were intently beholding " how our Lord's Body was laid" in the cold and rocky sepulchre.

---

² Luke xxiii. 5.   ³ Acts x. 37.

Now among these Galilean women there were two who, for their earnest zeal and devotion to our Lord, were particularly worthy of notice, the two Marys. For St. Mark mentions nothing of the other women, but specifies these two, "*And Mary Magdalene, and Mary the mother of Joses, beheld where He was laid.*" No mention now occurs of the blessed Virgin. Holy Scripture has withdrawn her from our view in an holy silence. These two Marys were probably on this occasion in the cave, together with the other women whom St. Luke mentions; but yet distinguishable from them in the greatness of their grief, and perhaps from their habitual nearness to our Lord. At all events, we soon find them together, in a most interesting and affecting mention of them that occurs in St. Matthew. And this was in fact but very similar to what we find with regard to these two women at the Crucifixion; for then we first of all find them together with the other women from Galilee, standing afar off[4]; and afterwards in another Evangelist[5] separated from them, and at the foot of the Cross. And so was it now; for while the rest of that company had now retired, as St. Luke mentions, to prepare the spices before the setting in of the Sabbath, yet these two seemed to have remained, as if too absorbed in grief to prepare those things at that time; for we read in St. Matthew's narrative, after the closing of the sepulchre, "*And there was there Mary Magdalene and the other Mary, sitting over against the sepulchre.*"

They are sitting there in the most blessed of all employments, in meditation on Christ's death; like that other good Mary, who when others were busy in minis-

<hr>

[4] Matt. xxvii. 56. Mark xv. 40.   [5] John xix. 25.

tering on Christ, sat listening to His words. "They learn," says Quesnel, " being near the sepulchre, to hide themselves from the world, and to be buried with Jesus Christ."   The star of evening had now come forth; and the same is that star which will appear earliest in the morning. " The mother of Zebedee's children," says Origen, " is not spoken of as sitting over against the sepulchre. She had perhaps that faith that enabled her to go as far as the Cross. But they, as if they were greater in love, were not wanting even to these things that followed."   But the mother of Zebedee's children was not mentioned before with these women at the foot of the Cross; but with those that stood afar off. And her retiring now might be accounted for by the absence of the blessed Virgin herself, whom St. John had probably taken to his own home; and that home was probably the house of Salome, the wife of Zebedee. But of the two Marys that continued at the grave, St. Jerome says, " While the rest were leaving the Lord, the women continued in their offices, as expecting what Jesus had promised. And on this account they merited to be the first to see the Resurrection, for 'he that endureth unto the end, the same shall be saved.' "

On this subject of the women there are many points of inquiry which arise. How is it that none of these faithful women are allowed to embalm our Lord ? His Body did not need embalming, for it was of itself incapable of corruption : and therefore He allowed them to show their good will, and accepted the good inten. tion, but needed not the embalming. And, indeed, this anointing for His burial He had graciously accepted, six days before, of one woman, the good Mary, the sister of Lazarus. And here another question suggests itself, Where are the sisters Mary and Martha ? how is

it that there occurs no mention of them? Is it possible
that tidings of these things had not reached the village
of Bethany? or can this Mary be the same as Mary
Magdalene? Or, who is this Mary Magdalene, and
what do we know of her? This is indeed a most interesting question, as every thing must be that concerns
either of these two women. It seems necessary to say
something on this subject.

MARY MAGDALENE.

There have been some who have considered that Mary
Magdalene is the same person as the sister of Lazarus
under another name; but, on inquiry, we usually find
that there is no evidence to support this opinion, either
in Holy Scripture or among the early Fathers; we are
then, perhaps, apt to dismiss the supposition altogether, as untenable and erroneous; and yet at length,
on further thought, there are some reasons which dis-
pose one not altogether to reject it. For although we
cannot find sufficient authority to support the opinion
by direct evidence, yet, when we have formed, unconsciously, a picture of Mary Magdalene in our minds,
we find that it extremely resembles that which we have
unconsciously been forming, at the same time, of the
sister of Lazarus. If any one, judging from the circumstances recorded in the Gospels, were to give an accurate description of what he supposed to be the character of either of these, it would be, in great measure,
a character of the other also; with this difference, perhaps, that with Mary Magdalene we connect something
more of penitential sorrow; with the other, that calmness of piety which belongs to one that had always
" chosen that good part which shall not be taken away
from her." And yet perhaps it may be shown, that

there is not sufficient reason for even this supposed discrepancy, either in their histories or their characters.

The few circumstances recorded of St. Mary Magdalene are such as to excite in us an exceeding interest; we behold her standing among the nearest to our Saviour's Cross, sitting the last at His grave at night, and coming the first there in the early morning; and, more than all, the circumstances of our Lord's interview with her rivet our strongest attention and emotions. So eminent among those holy women for her devoted service; and eminent, even among those holy women, in the favour and acceptance of her Lord. Now, in the previous history, we have circumstances recorded of an equal and similar interest in Mary, the sister of Lazarus. The same attachment to our Lord; the same favour expressed towards her. And the occasions on which they are mentioned, bring out the same points of disposition in both. In both the same calm, yet intense devotedness of character; in both a disposition retiring and contemplative; and yet in both, at the same time, earnest and unshrinking. We have here Mary Magdalene sitting by the sepulchre, and withdrawing from the busier company of her friends, the Galilean women, who had gone to prepare spices to do honour to their Lord. We have, on another occasion, Mary, the sister of Martha, sitting at Christ's feet to hear His instructions, and in so doing, separated from her more active sister, who was busied in preparations to do honour to our Lord, by receiving Him worthily. We have Mary Magdalene sitting in grief at His grave. We have the sister of Martha sitting in grief in the house, mourning for her brother Lazarus. Again, we have self-sacrifice and self-devotion in both; in Mary Magdalene, when she stood at the foot of the Cross, in that most trying hour, amidst taunts and revilings, unmoved: in Mary, the sister of Martha, when she seems to have sacrificed her livelihood to embalm our Lord's Body with great cost, and that in spite of the reproaches of the bystanders. In both a depth of feeling, which would be considered contemplative; and yet, in both, it was combined with a most active energy. Under circumstances of the same kind, they both come forward to our notice by a development of a similar character; and yet the conduct of each of them, under those circumstances, is different from that of others on the same occasions. Thus, at the death of Lazarus, we read of Mary, his sister, "but Mary sat still in the house," in the position and character of a mourner; but on our Lord's coming, it is said, "as soon as she heard that, she arose quickly." The earnest activity which marks this movement, displays also, incidentally, the deep and strong devotedness of her disposition; for the Jews, who knew her, concluded she had gone to sit at the grave, as an action naturally expected of her character and affections, supposing that she was going to act as we find Mary Magdalene now doing. "The Jews therefore, which were with her in the house, and comforted her, when they saw Mary, that she rose up hastily, and went out, followed her, saying, She goeth unto the grave to weep there." Now, let this account be compared with that of Mary Magdalene on our Lord's death: the one, as we observed, sat still in the house, mourning; the other now sits still at the grave, mourning. But from that posture the former arose hastily on hearing of our Lord. And Mary Magdalene is the first, on Sunday morning, before the break of day, to hasten to embalm our Lord; and, again, there is the same active intensity shown, when, on perceiving in the twilight that the stone was removed, she hastened to inform the disciples, anticipating even her companions, who waited after her at the place, and saw the Angel. Again, when they come into the presence of our Lord Himself, there is something very similar in the character displayed by both of them ; and yet not similar to any thing mentioned of any other of our Lord's followers.   At the grave of Lazarus we read, "When Mary was come where Jesus was, and saw Him, she fell down at His feet, saying unto Him, Lord, if Thou hadst been here, my brother had not died. When Jesus, therefore, saw her weeping ... He groaned in the spirit, and was troubled [6]." At the sepulchre of our Lord, and Mary Magdalene's interview with Him, we read, "Mary stood without at the sepulchre weeping;" and the Angels "say unto her, Why weepest thou ?" Soon afterwards our Lord says unto her, "Woman, why weepest thou ?" The words that follow are few, but in the highest degree expressive, and set before us, in vivid colours, the person of Mary Magdalene, when she acknowledges our Lord by the single word "Rabboni!" and our Lord replies to her, "Touch me not [7]." Words, doubtless, mysteriously and divinely intended to support the human weakness of her nature; but, at the same time, indicative of some action of intense devotedness and adoration in her. Throughout this touching scene we cannot help imagining that we see the same person again at our Lord's feet, who was weeping at His feet at the grave of Lazarus, when He was troubled and wept at the sight. There is in both a singular forgetfulness of self; the same intense but deep and calm affection of Divine Love.

To these points of identity in character may be added

---

[6] John xi. 32, 33.   [7] John xx. 17.

the remarkable fact of there being no mention made of Mary, the sister of Martha, at our Lord's Death, and Resurrection. It might indeed be alleged, that neither of her sister Martha is any thing recorded at this time, and that we should expect to find them in conjunction with each other. This is certainly an argument against the supposition we are supporting, but not altogether a conclusive one. For on other occasions we find Mary, in her conduct and actions, separated from her sister, on account of a marked difference of character. And this difference would be more strongly drawn out under these more trying circumstances. It would be the same conduct repeated, when Martha was busied about serving, Mary sat listening to our Lord: now also Martha was preparing spices, Mary sat watching. Mary Magdalene is not indeed sitting by herself; but the earnest devotedness of Mary would have knit and combined her, during this trial, with those persons in whom she would find the strongest sympathy in her affliction, or congeniality of feeling.

There still remains the question, if these descriptions are of one and the same person, why are there distinct appellations usually applied to them? But this would not be the only case of the kind in Scripture; as there occurs no distinct intimation that Nathanael and Bartholomew are but different names for the same individual, as we reasonably conclude that they are. If Mary Magdalene was a widow, and belonged to or possessed a place called Magdala, in Galilee, by marriage, she might have been generally known under that title, excepting when in the house of, or spoken in connexion with, Lazarus and her sister at Bethany. And it may be also noticed that St. Matthew, St. Mark (*i. e.* perhaps St. Peter), and St. John, who speak mostly of her, and under the title of Mary Magdalene, would naturally have known her by that name, as men of Galilee. St. Luke speaks of her under this title, not as a familiar appellative, but as a person so " called." He also mentions her as the person " out of whom went seven devils," which is the designation of a stranger; and so likewise is that other term, when he speaks of her as one " who ministered unto our Lord in Galilee."

One would indeed be glad to think that there should have been two such persons: for it is certain that the sister of Lazarus had given herself up to the one thing which is needful with singleness of heart; and also that Mary Magdalene was a person of most fervent piety. Theophylact observes, that although the Evangelists mention different women, " yet they all speak of Mary Magdalene on account of her fervent affection." And St. Augustin says of her[s], " That Mary Magdalene came without doubt, as being much more fervent in affection than the rest of the women which ministered unto the Lord: so that not undeservedly John makes mention of her, while he says nothing of those who came with her, as the others testify."

There is also another question respecting the identity of Mary Magdalene, of. not much less interest and of equal difficulty with the former; whether she is the same person who anointed our Lord's feet, at an early period of His ministry in Galilee, and who is designated by St. Luke as " a woman who was a sinner." We find that divines in our own and other countries, about the time of the Reformation, and indeed for many centuries preceding, generally agree in considering that St. Mary Magdalene is the person here spoken of; alluding to it,

---

[s] De Consensu Evang. lib. iii. c. 24.

in devotional books and hymns, as a point they had never questioned. But, on inquiry, we find that there is no intimation of this being the case, either in Holy Scripture or among the early Fathers: and although it has been a received opinion in the Roman Catholic Church, yet it is supposed that it owed its origin to nothing more than a fabulous legend, purported to have been written by a servant of Martha, the sister of Lazarus. For these reasons the supposition has been by some entirely neglected as erroneous; and certainly it must be considered incapable of proof. In the Roman Breviaries it is implied, in the services, hymns, and the like, that they were the same person; yet any supposition of this kind appears to have been carefully excluded from the Parisian. And although "the sinner," in the 7th chapter of St. Luke, is designated Mary Magdalene, in the heading to the chapter in our English Bibles; yet the service in honour of St. Mary Magdalene, which found a place in the first book of Edward, and contained this supposition, has been subsequently excluded from our Prayer Book, on account of the difficulty in which this point is involved. In the celebrated hymn, the "Dies iræ," Mary Magdalene is spoken of under this character,—"Qui Mariam absolvisti;" evidently implying that Mary was "the sinner" who was forgiven: but, as if in consequence of the doubt, another reading is found substituted for it, where "the sinner" alone is mentioned,—"Qui peccatricem absolvisti."

Now this case of doubt, whether St. Mary Magdalene was or was not "the sinner" spoken of by St. Luke, comes to us very much under the same questionable circumstances as the former case, whether St. Mary Magdalene is the same as the sister of Martha. And here again, as in the former instance, we are perhaps

inclined too hastily to reject the opinion of their being
the same, on finding that the case is not capable of
satisfactory proof: for such is the natural tendency of
a speculating and unbelieving age, to believe too little
for fear of believing too much. It may, therefore, be
desirable to state a few points to be considered in
favour of that opinion, which has come down to us by
a vague traditionary rumour.

With regard to the opinions of early writers, if there
is none in favour of this supposition, yet there appears
no distinct evidence to the contrary. Origen, Ambrose,
Chrysostom, Augustin, and others, do not appear to have
had any clear notion of who these women were, beyond
that of their own conjectures. St. Ambrose[9] suggests
that there might have been more than one Mary Magdalene; Origen, that there were three distinct cases of
anointing by distinct women; St. Chrysostom at one
time, I think, seems to suppose them all the same; at
another time as distinctly that they were not. Tertullian considers that the same person is spoken of.
All of which proves that there was no consent or traditionary opinion on the subject. Bede speaks of Mary
Magdalene as the sister of Lazarus; Thomas à Kempis
likewise considers her the same; and also designates
her as "the sinner" who was forgiven much. Gregory[1] speaks of Mary Magdalene as "the sinner, who
by loving the truth had washed with tears the stains
of crime; whose mind the great power of love had
inflamed; who retired not from the sepulchre of the
Lord when even disciples retired." But St. Augustin
says expressly that he thinks that Mary, the sister of
Lazarus, who anointed our Lord at Bethany, was the
same person whom St. Luke records as "the sinner"

[9] Exp. in Luc. lib. x. 153.　　　　　[1] In Hom. xxiii.

who anointed Him in the house of Simon the Pharisee. The reason he gives for this does not indeed appear at first sight satisfactory: it is this, that before the anointing took place at Bethany, at the time when Lazarus was raised from the dead, St. John speaks of her as the person who had anointed our Lord, and wiped His feet with the hair of her head[2]. For, in answer to this argument of St. Austin's, it might be said that St. John thus designates her, not by an action which had at that time taken place, viz. at the raising of Lazarus, but by an action for which she was afterwards known. But still the expression of her "wiping His feet with her hair," although St. John mentions "His feet" in the anointing at Bethany, whereas the other two Evangelists only speak of her anointing "His head;" yet this circumstance itself seems more characteristic of the action in St. Luke than it is of the later one at Bethany. The action of wiping His feet with her hair is in itself so beautiful and so extraordinary, that we feel a love and desire to connect it for ever with the same person: it was an action that could not have been done by a second person from imitation, and would scarce have spontaneously occurred to two different persons. But when we consider both of these anointings to have been by one and the same individual, the change that takes place in the action, that she who once anointed Christ's feet only, should now, after many expressions of His favour and approbation, venture to combine the Head also in that deed of honour, is most touchingly significative; expressive of her improved condition, of her higher acceptance, and of her overflowing gratitude for the same. Now this new case of question appears indeed greatly to increase the difficulty of the former;

[2] Ch. xi. 2. See Vol. Min. 3rd year, p. 250.

for many would be inclined to allow the former, that
St. Mary Magdalene may be no other than Mary the
sister of Martha; and many also would be disposed to
take it for granted, that St. Mary Magdalene was "the
sinner" we are speaking of. But most persons would
be very loth to suppose that the good sister of Martha
should have been "the sinner" described by St. Luke.

Our natural repugnance from adopting this opinion
arises from this, that we cannot suppose, that a person
who had been known as "a sinner," should have been
admitted into such friendly intercourse and intimacy
with our Lord, as to have been in constant attendance on Him, without calling forth the animadversions
of His enemies; that of such a person, we could hardly
have thought that our Lord would have declared, that
she "had chosen the good part;" and that the holy and
meritorious deed at Bethany of such a person should
have been honoured beyond all things in the world,
with an immortal memorial in His Church. But these
objections are by no means insurmountable. In the
first place, with regard to the term "sinner," by which
she is opprobriously designated by the proud Pharisee;
it by no means follows, that this implies that she was a
person of bad character: the term sinner is applied in
the Gospels to all who had intercourse with the Gentiles.
Dr. Hammond, although he thinks this person was not
Mary Magdalene, yet thinks the term does not imply
one of loose character. But let it be granted, that our
Lord Himself says, that "her sins are many." Or
even let it be supposed, that the term was applied to
her in the worst sense, and that she had fallen into some
notorious sin; those are not the worst persons who may
have fallen into the greatest crime: and to repent and
recover after such, indicates a very extraordinary piety

and strength of principle, as in the case of David. But
however this may be, whatever she might have done in
her past life, she must have been even at this very time
a very good person, and by no means hardened by sin;
for faith and love it is which proves the state of the
heart: these mark our acceptance with God, we are
good and bad in His sight according to the degree of
faith and love that we have; and we have our Lord's
testimony, that she had even at this time both of these;
for He says, that she "loved much;" and her faith was
great, for she believed that Christ could forgive sins.
And our Lord's own declaration of peace to her, when
He said "go in peace," was surely abundantly able to
bestow that peace which it pronounced, and might well
have conferred that calm devotion of the sister of Martha,
when she sat at His feet.   Such a person now after the
expiration of two years, might have rendered herself
worthy of a higher expression than that of her sins
being forgiven[3], even of our Lord's sanction, that she
had chosen that which she should never lose. One who
at the commencement of our Lord's ministry had received that absolution, "thy sins are forgiven thee, go
in peace," might, after faithfully attending on Him for
three years, when she repeated a similar action at its
close, have been received by the higher terms of approbation, as one who had done a good deed which should
be spoken of in all the world[4].

But still after all that can be said, we must be content to leave both points in doubt;—whether St. Mary
Magdalene is the same person as that good Mary, the
sister of Lazarus, who anointed the Lord's head at the
house of Simon the leper, on the Saturday previous to
the Crucifixion, as St. Matthew and St. Mark record;

[3] Luke vii. 48.   [4] Matt. xxvi. 13.   Mark xiv. 9.

and His feet also at the same time, as St. John mentions.   And again, whether this Mary, the sister of
Martha and also called Mary Magdalene, is the same
as that sinner, mentioned by St. Luke, who early in
our Lord's ministry anointed His feet at the house of
Simon the Pharisee in Galilee.   But we are on the
whole inclined to think they possibly may be the same
person, under different designations, from similarity
and almost sameness of character, shown in the events
recorded, between Mary Magdalene and the sister of
Martha: and in the latter case, because it seems safer
and more the part of piety to adopt than to reject, a
traditionary belief of good men, although incapable of
proof.   If indeed the whole be but the history of one
and the same individual, it affords a beautiful instance
of conversion, commencing in penitential grief which
"loved much," matured in that devotion, which had
made a full choice of " the good part," and confirmed
in perfect love; which from being conformed to the
death of Christ, came to know " the power of His Resurrection," and is led on by Him, in purified affection,
to ascend with Him to Heaven[5].

[5] The point however is so difficult to decide conclusively, that
even the same person will probably think differently at different
times.   At one time, in contemplating them, they appear all to
blend in one person and character, as they have been here described ; at another time we seem to have a distinct apprehension
of each, as not only different individuals, but as differing in disposition and circumstances.   Mary, the sister of Martha, appears
marked by a calm and holy tranquillity ; St. Mary Magdalene by
something of a self-abandoning intense devotedness ; these traits
indicate difference of character.   And again, in St. Mary Magdalene we see a person evidently thought highly of by the Jews, and
perhaps in some degree wealthy ; " the sinner " in St. Luke does
not appear to have been so esteemed by them.—*Second Edition.*

CHRIST IN THE GRAVE.

The scene therefore which we have before us, is the following. Our Lord was now laid in the sepulchre, and the entrance into the cave was again closed up. Joseph of Arimathea " *had rolled a (great* Matt.) *stone to the door of the sepulchre*" (Matt. Mark), thus shutting up the grave, "*and departed*" (Matt.). The sun had now resumed more or less of his wonted light, and was setting over the guilty Jerusalem; the uproar of the morning was changed into the stillness of the grave, and the sacred silence of the Sabbath had begun. In this now hallowed garden, the stir of the hurried funeral had given place to solitude; the Apostles had retired, and the beloved disciple had probably taken the blessed Virgin to his own home. And the women from Galilee, including Joanna, the wife of Herod's steward, perhaps Salome, and others, having in haste made preparations for the subsequent embalming, had retired for the rest of the Sabbath. But "bound to Him," says Bede, " by a closer affection," on a spot opposite to the rocky sepulchre, Mary Magdalene and the other Mary were sitting. Sitting is in that country the posture of mourners. Here, in the silence of this scene, they could recollect themselves a little, and mourn; for how many events had occurred since that time on the preceding evening! In the stillness of the scene might they look on the bloody city;—"How doth the city sit solitary, that was full of people! how is she become a widow!" "from the daughter of Zion all her beauty is departed [6]." "Righteousness lodged in it, but now murderers [7]."

But these holy women had no thought and no eyes

<hr>

[6] Lam. i. 1. 6.   [7] Isa. i. 21.

for that city, which was lying under the wrath of God; for that grave, by which they sat, absorbed all their thoughts; their hearts were with Him, who was now hid there from their eyes. The greatness of their sorrow had for awhile been mitigated, by thoughts of the stillness and ease of death, which had succeeded to His agonies; but the full sense of their bereavement was now becoming felt, in that unspeakable stillness and dread calm which accompanies death.

> At length the worst is o'er, and Thou art laid
>   Deep in Thy darksome bed;
> All still and cold beneath yon dreary stone,
>   Thy sacred Form is gone.
>
> Around those lips where power and mercy hung,
>   The dews of death have clung;
> The dull earth o'er Thee, and Thy foes around,
> Thou sleep'st a silent corse in funeral fetters wound.

Although we can ascertain so little who this Mary Magdalene was, yet we know she had been deeply afflicted; she is known as the one, out of whom went seven devils: she had been taught in affliction, the school of Christ; and by Him been delivered from her afflictions: well therefore may we conclude, that her heart was within that cold stone, wherein that sacred Body was laid. He whom she had adored as her Lord and God; had reverenced as her Deliverer: had loved as her Instructor and Guide; He, in Whose Divine Power and the ineffable sense of Whose Godhead she had found refuge, was now stiff and lifeless in the grave. "Thou art in the clefts of the rock, in the secret places of the stairs, let me see Thy countenance, let me hear Thy voice[s]." That which was a few hours since the lamentation of our Lord, His faithful follower may

---

[s] Song of Solomon ii. 14.

now take up and say, "Is it nothing to you, all ye that pass by? Behold, and see if there be any sorrow like unto my sorrow[9]?" What spot in all the world is suited for affliction and for penitence more than this? What place is there, to which their eyes can turn, but is hallowed by the recollections of Him, of His Holy teaching and His miracles, by associations of His Divine actions and words? What place is not marked with the violence and hatred of His enemies, and His undeserved suffering? But every thought of the malice of others is lost in the thoughts of Himself and of themselves. For He would never allow them to think of others and of their misdeeds; but by His unspeakable holiness ever induced men to think of their own sins; and therefore all thought of Him was connected with repentance.

But in contemplating the persons and characters of these our Lord's faithful followers, we have passed from the reflection of Himself; so weak and feeble is our nature, that we cannot dwell on the sacred vesture that enshrouds Him, nor the beloved companions of His earthly pilgrimage, nor the Angels that do His will and encircle His throne; but that we forget Him, for whose sake alone these were objects of interest to us; we weigh His words, and are wrapt around by their incomprehensible, but all-comprehending power and meaning, and forget Him that speaks. We look on the tomb that encloses Him, and while we look, we forget Him that is enclosed there. Where else shall we go but to Thee in Thy life? and where else in Thy death shall we go but to Thee?

That great stone hath hidden Thee from the world, and hath hidden Thee from our eyes. But where our

[9] Lam. i. 12.

treasure is, there will our heart be also.   If our heart be in Thy tomb, then shall faith remove that great stone, and admit us to be with Thee; and shall shut out with that rocky door the guilty world which hath brought Thee to this.   Faith shall enter into that holy darkness and silence, where Thy lifeless body is laid on the cold ground.   That stone shall not shut out the sinner from Thee; but that stone shall shut him in with Thee from that world, which hath shed Thy innocent blood.   For to be with Thee is ever blessed; to be with Thee in Thy life, and to watch Thy footsteps; and it is blessed to be with Thee in Thy dying; and to be with Thee in the grave is blessed, and maketh blessed.   Surely it is to be with Thee in this Thy grave that Thou hast invited us in, saying, " Come, My people, enter thou into thy chambers, and shut thy doors about thee: hide thyself as it were for a little moment, until the indignation be overpast[10]."

For what place is there more meet for a sinner than this ? and where else shall he meet his God but in this place ?   Lifeless Thou art now and cold, as the rock that incloses Thee, and on which Thy reclining head is laid ; and pale indeed is Thy body, which at every pore hath opened an outlet for Thy life blood, for our sakes ; from Thy hands and from Thy feet, and from Thy mangled back, and from Thy pierced head, and from Thy wounded side, it hath opened its many doors, from all of which Thy overflowing Love hath poured itself forth in blood, and hath left Thee pale and bloodless indeed.   And wrapped around in Thy sacred swaddling clothes of death, all Thy holy Form hath gone, and no vestige nor lineament remains; and even the Son of

[10] Isa. xxvi. 20.

Man, which Thou hast become for our sakes, appeareth no more.

Thou who art the Maker and Preserver of Heaven and earth, Thou who hast Thy habitation in eternity, in bliss inconceivable, and unutterable glory, hast laid all aside to become this for me. And yet am I colder and harder than that rock, on which Thy body is laid; for these rocks were rent at Thy dying; but I have watched Thy dying, and step by step followed Thee from Gethsemane unto this Thy cold tomb, but my heart is not rent; and yet all this hath been, all this is for me: but I am not moved; and on me fall the drops of Thy blood, and the cold sweat of Thy death, even as on that rock: but I am not moved.

And yet in what other place could I—who bear about me my deep and heavy sins—in what place could I meet Thee more suitably than in this? Nicodemus came to Thee from fear, under the covering of the night, and I dare only under that same covering to approach Thee: but he, in his guiltless simplicity, could endure Thine all-knowing and all-healing look, but I dare not: and though I must come to Thee, or else I die; I would fain cover myself with the night, and so approach Thee.

Where else could a sinner meet Thee so suitably as in this place? It is said that a cold rock was the place of Thy birth; and in a rock also is Thy tomb. But this Thy last abode is in some sense more suitable to a sinner, than that stable and manger wherein Thou receivedst Thy first friends on earth: for that was indeed a season of gladness, and they that came from the distant East, and the shepherds with whom Angels had associated, and the innocent animals that were in that lowly shed, were company more meet for that glad occasion of Thy birth, than that sinner who hath been baptized in

Thy blood, and yet hath crucified Thee afresh. For there in Thy holy childhood Thou seemest to invite children around Thee; and children were more meet for Thy temple than such as grow old in forgetfulness of Thee: for in Thy Temple was the holy Samuel as a child: and in Thine own Temple did the children meet Thee to welcome Thee; and little children didst Thou draw to Thee, and take up in Thine arms, and invite them lovingly to Thine unrestrained embrace; but to the double-minded sinner didst Thou turn to admonish him of the never-dying worm; and of forsaking all that he hath, and of taking up the Cross daily; setting him afar from Thee even in the greatness of Thy love; and then encompassing him most with the arms of Thy mercy, when Thou puttest him afar off, lest, unworthily, he should draw too near to Thee and die. Thy birth-place, therefore, is the meet resort for innocence; but Thy tomb is the hiding-place for the sinner: here may he find refuge who is all over putrefying sores, and hath no whole part in his body: here may he kneel by the cold stone on which Thou art laid.

This Thy dark and cold and silent bed would invite to Thee a sinner whose heart, like Thy grave, is dark and cold, and who must be silent before Thee; for how could He venture to look on Thy living countenance? Where else could he so suitably approach Thee? Not at the full daylight of that feast, where that "sinner" approached Thy feet of old; where it was perhaps this Thy afflicted Magdalene who brought to Thee the first-fruits of her repentance. For she had doubtless heard Thee in Thy gracious teaching, and she lingered not in her old paths, but bewailed in secret, and Thy Word received into the good heart brought forth fruit, and she hath brought this basket, " the first-fruits of the land

Thou hast given" her [1], and memorials of deliverance from death [2]; for she "loved much," and believed much, and these fruits of love which she brought were most acceptable unto Thee; though indeed they were none else than her silence and her tears. That ointment itself implied the fragrance of her love, which defied all cost; and the abundance of her tears showed the depth and earnestness of her penitence: and when she wiped Thy sacred feet with the hairs of her head, the greatness of that humiliation was the robe that became her in Thy presence. But the sinner who would now approach Thee in the tomb is like that cold and proud Pharisee there, who, owing much, thought he owed but little; for his heart is dry and desolate, and he hath no tears for Thy feet; and if aught could again move him to tears, it were this feeling of his want of tears. He hath no sweet ointment of love to bring Thee, and were he to attempt such an offering, his own pride is like the dead fly [3] within it —that maketh the sweetest ointment unsavory to Thee. And he hath no first-fruits to bear Thee, for " the good land Thou gavest" him hath become a desolate wilderness, and a place of unclean things; but in this desert and wilderness of his injured affections he would approach unto Thee, who art the Rock which was smitten in the desert, that he might drink of that water that goeth from Thee, and replenish the dried fountain of his tears.

Where else so well as in this grave shall he venture to approach Thee? Shall he go to Thee in that holy home of Bethany, and sit at Thy feet with that holy Mary who had chosen the good part? That sacred family were no place for him; and how could he bear to stand before that living look of Thine which readeth all things? In that house Lazarus, whom Thou hadst raised from the

<hr>

[1] Deut. xxvi. 4. 10.   [2] Ibid. v. 5.   [3] Eccles. x. 1.

dead, there sat at the table with Thee; but what if
raised by Thee, he had again turned away from Thee,
and forgotten Thee his Deliverer?, How could one be
among that company of Thy disciples and Thy friends,
who hath so long set Thee at nought? For they that
were with Thee, and shared Thy toils, and witnessed
Thy miracles, were in some sense worthy of Thee and of
that approach: and if their holiness is not as Thine,
neither are their charities as Thine, that I should be
admitted to be there, in that holy company. But here
in this rock would one draw near to Thee, whose heart
is indeed as the stone on which Thou art laid: but be
Thou laid also in his stony heart; and Thou who hast
such power even in Thy death and in Thy grave, mayest
break and rend even this his stony heart; and be even
Thyself revealed therein, Who art that hidden man of
the heart that knoweth not corruption [4].

The stillness of this Thy tomb is, in some respects,
a fitter abode for us even than that scene which is
passed; fitter even than that hour of Thine agony; for
in the calmness of this change we recognize more distinctly, and apprehend the end of all things, and that
latter end of Thee, and of ourselves, which teacheth
wisdom. It is better for us to be here, in some measure, even than in that scene in which I have attempted
to follow Thee: for there, when I was noticing at every
step the greatness of the mystery, and of the power
which ordered all things, even in gazing on Thee, I
seemed, for a while, to have forgotten that Thou wert
suffering, and I a sinner; and when I " compared things
spiritual," and perceived therein more and more Thy
Divine power which could have broken Thy bonds, and
which, in Thy weakness, was ever the most discernible,

<hr>

[4] 1 Pet. iii. 4.

—in the wonder of those contemplations my deceitful heart hath again beguiled me, and brought on me, even in gazing on Thee, and even, I might almost say, while lamenting my sins,—brought on me a fresh occasion of sin; and the very greatness of Thy love, which came down from Heaven, and restrained Thy almighty strength, bringing it down unto the weakness of a babe, hath but cooled my love towards Thee. For when I numbered the type and prophecy and figure wherein Thy Divine power was manifest; and weighed Thy deep words, and numbered Thy stripes, and paused on Thy steps, the very pursuit itself hath beguiled me: and when I called the good of all ages to be the witnesses of Thy sorrows, and to unfold the number of Thy mysteries, I myself gazed on Thee with a barren wonder; and, forgetting myself to be a sinner, and to be the cause of all these Thy sufferings, my study of Thy passion hath become to me itself a fresh occasion of sin.

" Are these things true, O my God, which I hear of Thine enduring with such long-suffering, and behold Thee sustaining with such love? If they are true, why do I not tremble all over, and burn with love and with grief? I grieve over Thee, O gracious Jesus, I grieve also on that account the more, that I—who am but dust and ashes, and, what is worse than these, a sinner, (what a sinner and how great a sinner Thou knowest)—that I should behold Thee enduring such great sufferings, and that with this my stony heart I feel not these things as I ought to feel them [5]."

Here it is no more—that " visage which was so marred" with contumelies, nor that Form which was without " beauty or comeliness" in human eyes: but Thou art become, for our sakes, even no form at all, even,

[5] Via Vitæ Æternæ.

as it were, " without form, and void," indistinguishable
even as human shape, and as the dead clod of the valley, wrapped up and laid aside as one unfit to abide
with men, and to see the light. Is it to this Thou
hast come for my sake, O my God? Is it to this Thou
hast descended from the throne of Thy glory?

But it is Thine own—Thine own most sacred Body
still, and by its apparent helplessness and repose it
invites a wretched sinner to approach Thee, and to put
his trust in Thee. It was thus when Thou wert laid
asleep "on a pillow" in the boat, and thereby leading
Thy weak disciples to have confidence in Thee: and
even then, in Thy sleep, Thy power was present to
help them; and Thou didst rebuke the weakness of
their faith, that doubted the efficacy of Thy presence
even in sleep. And if the bones of Thy prophet Elisha [6]
had such power as to restore even an enemy to life,
Thou givest hope even to me, Thine enemy, whose
second life in Thee hath become, as it were, but " dry
bones, very dry [7]." For by assuming this form of
weakness Thou dost invite the unclean sinner to approach Thee, and layest aside not Thy Godhead only,
but thy Manhood also, if I may so venture to say,
and Thy human power, that Thou mightest thus allure
him to Thee. And wert Thou alive, and I before Thee,
I might have doubted of that forgiveness which could
equal the height and depth and length and breadth of
my sins; even did Thine own gracious lips pronounce
my pardon; but these Thy many wounds, and Thy
reclining head and motionless body, are the tokens to
me of my pardon, and the seal of my hopes: for
I see therein the height and depth, the length and
breadth of Thy love.

[6] 2 Kings xiii. 21.   [7] Ezek. xxxvii. 2.

Here would I approach Thee, and kneel down at the stony bed which sustains Thee, as at a holy altar, and there will weep; and press my lips on that which wraps Thy sacred feet, and water it with these my tears. And if too hardened to mourn for any thing else, yet will I weep to think of the fickleness of these my tears, and the little stability of this my sorrow. Yea, it is Thine own gracious Self which hath humbled Thee to this, that one so unholy should approach Thee even in death : and if Thy saints are not around Thee to repel one of unclean lips from drawing so near to Thee, yet I know that the holy Angels are there, and that they are mourning at this sad sight; for it is said [8], " The Angels of peace shall weep for Thee." " And one shall say, What are these wounds in Thine hands?" and another shall answer for Thee, " Those with which I was wounded in the house of My friends [9]." Well then might they in their grief repel an unclean man, one of these whom Thou hast called Thy friends : one who hath caused Thee all these Thy sorrows, and who inflicted this death and these wounds on the Lord of life. But Thou hast given them, Thine Angels, to feel as Thou dost; Thou hast given them for Thy sake to partake of that love which led Thee to endure such things for us; and they for the love of Thee love us also because Thou lovest us, and for Thy sake will rejoice over any one that will come unto this Thy grave, to confess his sins unto Thee.

THE SINNER BURIED WITH CHRIST.

Here may one who hath crucified Thee afresh, and is indeed the chief beyond all — the very chiefest of sinners —here may he venture to draw nigh to Thee : for how can he dare to meet Thy pitying and reproving eye

[8] Isa. xxxiii. 7; LXX. version.   [9] Zech. xiii. 6.

which is conscious of his inmost thoughts and most secret sins ? In this sepulchre, as at an holy altar, may he find refuge from those accusing thoughts that pursue him : that follow after him like clamorous dogs, and come about him like bees with their stings. In this chamber would I commune with myself, and be still. If I would hide me from the eye of day, and cover me with the mantle of night that is abroad, yet even there are Thy many witnesses ; and if I go forth, the very stars in the firmament overwhelm me with dismay, when in their silent watches they speak of Thy power, which I have provoked, and of that infinite duration of years which is with Thee. But then my heart is closed, and is not softened thereby unto repentance; but here it is opened to tears at the greatness of Thy love, which is more surpassing than the greatness of Thy power.

Here may I be planted in the likeness of Thy death, so that I may ever bear about with me Thy dying. Where else should the heart of a sinner dwell but here with Thee ? For if I go forth from Thee where shall I go, where all things do not testify against me ? and while the testimony of their warnings is still in my ears, they will but tempt me again to crucify Thee afresh ; for as many things as I behold without, so many temptations are there to forget Thee and Thy wounds. Whether it be the sound of joy or of sorrow, whether of love or of hate, they find in my bosom too many that are ready to join them against Thee ; and my passions, and the evil thoughts of my heart, are but like that crowd that cried aloud to crucify Thee.

But if that is my death when I go hence, so this also is my life while I continue here : for this is the life unto which I am bound by a twofold cord, by a double dedication, for it was into this grave that I was let down at Baptism ; and that font, into which I was merged, was no other than this rock, wherein I was devoted to be in this world ever buried with Thee. And that which is our Life in the holy Eucharist is but Thy death, and this Thy Body which was given in death for me. This world, therefore, into which I am born at Baptism, is no other than this cave, wherein lieth Thy dead Body; and the stone that is set at the mouth of this cave, is in order that it might shut out the world from my heart, that I may be content to be here with Thee. And had I remembered this truth, then should I have avoided those things that pierced Thy tender heart more deeply than the spear; and planted thorns on Thy bleeding brow worse than those which made Thy face to drop with gore; and transfixed Thy hands to the Cross more keenly than these nails. Were not my heart more cold and dead than this of Thine is now in death, these pangs of remorse would wound me also with piercing agonies; but I grieve because I have lost the power to grieve; if I feel aught it is this, that I do not feel. It is my un- concernedness that fills me with concern: it is my want of fear that causes me to tremble before Thee; for so great is the abundance of Thy mercy, that nothing shall set me afar from Thee but this feeling, that I need Thee not. For that Centurion was received by Thee, and set high in Thy kingdom, because he deemed himself un- worthy to approach Thee, or that Thou shouldest come under his roof; and that woman of Canaan had from Thee the richness of Thy table, and a portion almost more than that of Thy children, because she knew her- self to be but meet to gather the crumbs under Thy table, as the dogs. And could I know and feel that which I speak, and would fain know and feel, then I am assured that I also should not be cast out from Thee.

Would that I had ever been closed about with these bars,—it is here alone that the sinner can learn true wisdom, and not in books. Those many disputations, and controversial stirrings that abound, are indeed jarring to my soul; but here I will have no ears to hear them, and with that rock will I close them out from me, that I may hear them no more: for other thoughts indeed become him, who would here wish to dwell with Thee in silence, and repentance, and tears. Nay, even those over-anxious plans of seeming good, and thoughts that trouble us, from the aboundings of iniquity, shall here be stilled in the stillness of Thy grave. Here is the place of my wisdom and my peace. Where else shall I go? I dread the stir of religion and the talk of religion, in which the love of Thee and the fear of Thee is not. Overwhelmed with doubt, and troubled at the uncertainty of varying opinions, I tremble, and know not how I shall direct my cause aright. But in this darkness I see light—in this calm I find rest for my spirit— this alone would I wish to study; and here would I desire to live. In those movements of those things that are without, I see not whether it is the Holy Spirit of God that would lead me, or the spirit of the world; but that small and still voice, which I hear in this tomb, is surely Thine; as to Elijah was that cave in the wilderness, so to me is this rocky cell in the desert of this world, where I recognize Thy voice speaking unto me.

It is in stillness and solitude, as of this Thy tomb, that Thou ever visitest the heart of man; while the world, with its loud noise, would hurry us from Thee. Many are the things that trouble me whenever I depart from Thee,—from the thoughts of this Thy death, and quiet burial, and the contemplations that are here with Thee; and even whatever of good thoughts are, by Thy Grace, planted in my heart, yet even in the workings of these there ever comes in an admixture of alloy with the world. For the secret seed of Thy Word in the heart, when it puts itself forth into the atmosphere of the world, soon degenerates into the strange vine; and the fruits are not known unto Thee as Thine own: if any desire of good had been in me, it hath soon been blended and alloyed with earthly affection, and with the wish to behold with mine eyes the fruit of my labours; and thereby I lose that eye of faith which looketh only unto Thee, and to Thy good Angels, who are with Thee in the secret place of this tomb.

But if a sinner, and one who groweth old in sin, can do any little good to himself or others, it is not by working for those ends himself, so much as by obtaining them of Thee,—of Thee who art the Fountain of all good. If the material Church and inner shrine are formed from a resemblance to these the outer and inner chambers of Thy tomb, that they may put on the similitude of this prevailing intercession, much more may this Thy grave become a Holy Church and shrine unto me; for how else can I approach Thy Father, but with Thy Body? or how else can I approach to Thee, who livest for evermore? It is to this that I appeal from Thy Judgment-seat; and I know well, that from that Thy seat of Judgment, Thou also wilt appeal to this Thy tomb: and therefore I would conform myself unto Thy death, and be buried with Thee, lest the stones of this Thy tomb should cry out against me unto the seat of Thy Judgment. For when my sins take hold upon me, and I tremble at the anticipation of that Day, and am wellnigh desolate, from the Rock of Thy tomb cometh forth the water of Thy Spirit; and therefore it is written, that the dry desert shall bear the flower, for it is replenished with the water that flowed from Thy side.

This Thy chamber of death is as that "lodging-place of wayfaring men in the wilderness [10]," which the Pro-

[10] Jerem. ix. 2.

phet of Thy sorrows longed for, "that He might go away from His people," and "weep day and night" unto Thee for their sins.   For here it is we may learn the nature of sin; and here we may weigh the world, and see what it comes to; in the stillness of this scene we hear that noise and feverish excitement of life, which we hear not when in the midst of it; when we stand aloof from the noise and turbulence of the stream, then we perceive its sound and motion; that hurry and stir of earthly things, wherein that day will overtake the world unawares.   Here buried with Thee, may we shut out its temptations.   Here is Thy sacred Body, stiff and cold; this may teach us to die to this world; this may cool in us that flesh which hath been too often inflamed by luxury or by passion; here we may learn shame for our uncharitable words, and thoughts, and deeds, from the love which flowed from Thy bleeding wounds; here may we learn the nature of ambition from Thy prostrate and dishonoured and lifeless Form.   Here may we learn godly fear; for if the all-merciful Father spared not Thee, His only Son, when Thou stoodest in the place of sinners, how shall we escape if we forget Thee ? and here may we learn godly love, for if God spared not His own Son for our sakes, there is nothing He will withhold from us if we love Thee.   And thus, as there was a Divine charity in Thy dead Body to send forth the Water and the Blood, still is there a Divine energy in Thy dead Body to give me life.

Here wouldest Thou gather us under Thy sheltering wings until the enemy hath gone by; here the true Israelite is commanded to abide in stillness with the sacrifice that is slain, and not to go forth from his house till the morning [1], lest he die with the Egyptians.   This

---

[1] Exod. xii. 22.

is that closet into which Thou hast bid us enter and to close the door, in order that in secret we may pray to Thee: this is that rock unto which Thou hast invited us to flee until the tyranny be overpast. Nay, Thou art Thyself that Rock; and the cleft of that Rock, into which Thou hast bid us flee, and concealed us by Thy hand, is Thine own bleeding side; for Thou art Thyself "a place to hide me in,"—a place to hide me, where I may be hid from mine own self, from mine own purposes, and wishes, and hopes, which have so grievously led me astray; where I may be hid from the light of day which witnesseth against me, and be concealed in the darkness of the grave with Thee.

O what place is dark enough for the sinner to hide himself in? what grave is deep enough for him to bury his schemes of selfishness and pride, his thoughts of self-indulgence and ease, his quarrels and disputes? when all these sins have brought Thee to this, and Thou art laid cold and lifeless in the tomb; that we may endure no penalty here for our deserts, but Thou wilt also endure the same with us and for us; surpassing our misery by Thy love, and our guilt by Thy holiness.

THE DEAD IN CHRIST.

Here, in the grave of Christ, our souls, being planted in the likeness of His death, shall be planted in the likeness of His Resurrection also; and it is the same with our bodies. His death is the life of our souls, and of our bodies also by His quickening spirit. This His Body is that seed of which He spake in the deep groanings of His suffering soul, which, if it die, shall not abide alone, but bring forth many seeds like unto Itself. For our vile body, if we be buried with Him, shall be fashioned like unto His glorious Body. Here, therefore, must we come, not only that we may learn to live, but also that we may learn to die, and to contemplate with comfort the death of our friends; for here may we be not only dead with Him, but in Him also dead, in some sense, with the faithful departed. It is here with Christ that we learn to reflect on the death of our friends and on our own with peace and consolation, and in the depth of this grave to learn Christian hope.

Here the solemn calm of the great Sabbath hath already begun. In the deep stillness which is here exchanged for the anxieties and agonies, and the feverish passions and excitement of the scene that has passed, we seem to participate in the awful calm of death: and as in life we mingle and blend our sympathies with the condition and state of our friends, and borrow their feelings, so in this calm we seem to partake of the stillness of those souls which are released from the body in that place, " where the wicked cease from troubling, and the weary are at rest."   And if this calm is so striking, contrasted with that which is past, still greater is that feeling of stillness in death when we contrast it with that which is to come, the great Morning of the Resurrection; deep is the suspense that watches in that awful expectation; here is that night, of which our Lord spake, wherein no man can work; He hath done our work for us; our righteousness is no longer of works, but we may rest in Him.

Blessed therefore is this grave, because we therein approach to the dead in Christ; and because this is the home where we ourselves shall have to dwell; for we, too, shall soon have to make our bed in the dark, and the grave shall close its doors about us; and before then, it is the home of our buried affections, the house of all living. Here might one pourtray human Nature itself as sitting at a tomb, for our life is a continual bereavement; and as soon as we begin to know affection, we begin to mourn the loss of it. No one can have lived for any time in the world, but his best treasures and his best affections must be with the dead. And there is no reflecting person who does not find that those parts of his life, in which he sinks most deeply into himself and the knowledge of his condition, is made up of those hours of stillness and solitude, where he seems to sit at the grave of those who were once like himself, full of the same thoughts, and feelings, and affections. Stillness and solitude is of itself like a holy sanctuary, wherein he seems to draw near to them; it is that in which they are ever found; and to draw near to them is to draw away from the world; for, wherever it is that the faithful departed are, we know that to be with them is to be with Christ.

The grave of Christ, therefore, is the best place for our abode, for this reason, that we there draw more near unto our friends that are gone, and to the place where we ourselves are fast hastening. However we may forget it for a time, yea, even in the very act of forgetting it, the thought will be brought to our minds that it is the home of us all. It is more our home, because it is more durable, more abiding and stable, than that of our sojourn in this world. It is more our home to be with them that are there, than with those that are here, on account of the greater permanence of our abode with them [2]. However man may forget it in the flow of spirits and health, yet God hath so constituted him that

[2] ἐπεὶ πλείων χρόνος,
ὃν δεῖ μ' ἀρέσκειν τοῖς κάτω, τῶν ἐνθάδε.
ἐκεῖ γὰρ αἰεὶ κείσομαι.—Soph. Antig. l. 74-6.

every sense is an avenue to the heart, and calculated to convey to him the feeling remembrance of death,—of the death of his friends, and of his own drawing near to the same; the sound of distant music or a plaintive note, a passing word, or the momentary scent of a flower, or the sound of a bell, or the retiring of the day, or the falling leaf of autumn, or a picture that has been set aside, or a lost letter that comes to view, or a sentiment that occurs in a book;—all these will touch a chord, and fill his mind with the fulness of these contemplations, of the stillness and quiet of death. Calls are they, doubtless, from our merciful Father, and the good Angels that He has planted around us;—calls that would take us from the business of the world, from the buying and the selling, and planting and building, and marrying and giving in marriage, wherein the children of this world will be overtaken by the great morning of the Day of Judgment;—calls to the awful silence of that state which is beyond the grave, to the sepulchre of Christ. "The shadows of evening are stretched out, and the day goeth away;" "the day is far spent," and Christ bids us to enter in and stay with Him.

This rocky tomb therefore we must make, in some sense, our earthly tabernacle. It is this that sanctifies here to us the thoughts of those whom we love that are out of our sight, and prepares us ourselves to die. It is here that we draw near to them with hope. It is the consciousness of their sinful flesh, and of the infirmities to which it is subject, that makes the death-bed of our friends so painful, and breaks with heavy thoughts on the stillness of that peace which surrounds them. But there are no such thoughts in this grave, for perfectly sinless is this Flesh which in death cannot see corruption; and this reflection sheds consolation both on the death-beds and on the graves of our friends.

The Wise Man hath said, that "to go to the house of mourning is better" than to go to that of mirth : "for that is the end of all men, and the living will lay it to heart." This house of mourning is no other than the grave of Christ; for it is His grave that renders blessed the house of mourning. So much is this contemplation for our soul's health in the school of Divine Wisdom, that in order to withdraw us from the stir and business of this world, God has appointed the continual returns of night, wherein we may be as in the midst of this grave, in darkness, in stillness, and in solitude; in order that He may so recall, and admonish us, every night, of the solitude and stillness and darkness of the grave. For in that return of night wherein we are continually thus laid, He has forced upon us, who are so unwilling to learn, the daily contemplation of our latter end;—of this, the death of Christ, which sanctifies and blesses that end, and of the necessity of our being conformed thereto. For night is nothing else but the due and necessary preparation for the morning: and that morning is the great Morning of the Resurrection and the coming of Christ. And so intimately is the consideration of this great morning connected with the sleep of Christ in the grave, that the early Christians used to keep the night of our Lord's rising from the grave, in prayer and watching, in expectation of His return, on that same night, to Judgment. Let us throughout the night of this world be buried thus with Christ, and watching for His return.

And if our nightly return of sleep thus resembles death, and is calculated to remind us of death; and to be sanctified and rendered solemn by that association; our Lord also, in His unbounded charities, has taken

great pains to teach us, that death also is to be considered but a sleep; that it is to be in our minds associated with sleep, and to be lightened and cheered by
that association. By so often emphatically calling death
a sleep, He has doubtless intended to alleviate and to
strengthen our minds by faith in Him, showing us
thereby His desire that we should look on death as
but a sleep, in ourselves and others. And this His own
lying in the grave sets before us in the strongest manner this truth exemplified in Himself, which He had so
often taught us in words. For although this His death
be indeed the real separation of soul and body, yet when
we contemplate Him thus lying in the grave, we are
disposed to look upon it as a sleep, because He is so
soon to awake from it : as in all other things so in this,
the example seen in Himself gives a peculiar energy
and efficacy to His own expressions, such as "she is
not dead, but sleepeth." And sleep itself, which He has
given us to be a constant image of death, seems to bring
us into a nearer fellowship with the things unseen, and
the state of dreams is like another spiritual world, like
an opening into a new and untried scene ; to represent
to us some faint image of our souls being separated from
the body, alive to a sense of joy and pain while the
body sleeps.

To be thinking of the dead purifies greatly and hallows our affections, and habituates us to think of that
which is out of sight, rather than what we behold ; and
whatever withdraws us from the grossness of sense and
sight is good for us, and is like living in the world
unseen ; it is extending our view beyond the grave, into
that state where souls live ; and prevents our limiting
that view to the things of earth after death. Again, the
rapidity with which time seems to pass in sleep, may

serve to indicate the shortness of that time which will exist before the reunion of our soul and body. For our Lord in speaking of that reunion, seems to hesitate whether He shall speak of it as a future thing, or as one already present and at hand: when He says, "the hour cometh," He pauses, as it were to alter the expression, and adds, " *and now is*, when the dead shall hear the voice of the Son of God." For a thousand years were to Him but one day. The daughter of Jairus but just dead, Lazarus in the grave four days, the Saints that arose at our Lord's Resurrection, all indicate, that out of that sleep we all soon awake, after being therein various intervals of time.

Our bodies are, indeed, utterly corrupted, and gone, and forgotten, yet not so in the Eye of God: and full of beautiful interest are those instinctive feelings whereby men have been always endeavouring, by sepulchral rites, by embalmings, and the like, to express this strong sense implanted in us, of incorruption even in corruption, of immortality in the very moment of mortality, of reunion even in dissolution.

But the dead Body of Christ is left here lifeless and untenanted, not only that His dead Body may sanctify death, but that His spotless Soul may sanctify the place of the dead. One Sacrificial animal, the sin offering, is dead in our hands: but the other is escaped and gone into the wilderness, bearing sin[3]. If the earth is hallowed and preserved from corruption, because the sinless Son of Man hath once made it His abode, and the flesh His tabernacle: no less must the place of the departed have derived some great blessing from the sojourn of His righteous Soul among them. He has not only made this world once the place of His abode, but has

____
[3] Levit. xvi. 22.

continued ever since to vouchsafe His presence to it in some high and peculiar manner, so that it is not as it was before. Thus also is it with the place of His saints, that depart hence in the Lord: for since that time, "from henceforth,—blessed are the dead," for the good to die is to be with Christ, "which is far better," and to "sleep in the Lord." It was of this that the prophet Isaiah [4] spake, "to bring out the prisoners from the prison, and them that sit in darkness out of the prison-house." This their darkness He has converted into His own marvellous light. Of this also spake the prophet Zechariah [5], "By the blood of Thy covenant I have sent forth Thy prisoners out of the pit wherein is no water. Turn you to the stronghold, ye prisoners of hope."

Well may we believe that place to be blessed, where the Soul of Christ hath been. The great Italian poet, when the scene of his poem is in the abode of the wicked, is cautious lest the Ever-blessed Name should ever there escape, or be uttered in those regions of despair: whereby he meant to imply that that awful Name would burst asunder the everlasting bars of that prison-house. How much more may we suppose that—not the name uttered by the lips, but—the ever adorable Son of God, the Soul of Christ Himself, must have been of mighty avail for good in the place of the faithful departed!

Nay, indeed, even nature itself instinctively would suggest to us this lesson of hope: for what reader has not been struck with wonder at Homer's description of the place of the dead; so expressive of demerit and the expectation of righteous judgment in man, yet not without a secret hope in God? that first and greatest of poets describes the souls of the dead as wrapt in mysterious gloom, and powerless and silent, until they

[4] Isa. xlii. 7.	[5] Zech. ix. 11, 12.

have partaken of the blood of the sacrifice. Such is the voice of nature, if it be not something greater than nature; or the glimmering light of primeval tradition, that spoke of the Great Sacrifice in the midst of that spiritual darkness, to them who wandered beneath the dim twilight of the shadow of death.

Blessed, therefore, but very awful, to the good, is the thought of that intermediate state between death and Resurrection: it is in some especial manner to be with Christ: there is something in the thought very full of awe, and trembling joy: it is also to be with Abraham and all the dead who are with Christ, as they are selected and gathered out of this evil world. The more we think of it, and of those who have preceded us there, the more do we seem to approach them, for the dwelling-place and movement of our minds depends not on bodily change of place, but on the thoughts; we are there, where our thoughts are. How aspiring, how exalting, how calming, how quickening, how hallowing is the contemplation, that before the rising of another sun, we may be in that country of the faithful departed,— if found worthy to be there!

Other Catholic Churches, amidst their many corruptions, have inherited, not more sober, yet perhaps in some respects deeper and livelier thoughts of the dead than ourselves. We find the following striking prayer on the departure of a soul, in the Breviaries:

"I commend thee to Almighty God, dearest brother, and to Him, whose creature thou art, I commit thee: that when thou hast paid the debt of humanity, thou mayest return unto Him who hath formed thee of the dust of the ground. As thy soul goeth forth from the body, may the bright company of Angels meet thee; may the judging senate of Apostles succour thee; may the triumphant army of white-robed Martyrs welcome thee; may the band of glowing Confessors, crowned with lilies, surround thee; may the choir of Virgins receive thee, singing jubilees; may the embrace of Patriarchs bind thee in their bosom of blessed repose; mild and joyous may the aspect of Jesus Christ appear to thee, and award thee a place for ever among them who wait upon Him. Mayest thou never know what is terrifying in darkness, or sounding dismally in the flames, or in torments excruciating. Let foulest Satan with his attendants retire from thee: may he tremble at thy coming among Angels that attend thee, and for ever flee away into the vast deep of everlasting night. Let God arise, and let His enemies be scattered: let them also that hate Him flee before Him. Like as the smoke vanisheth, so shalt Thou drive them away: and like as wax melteth at the fire, so let the ungodly perish at the presence of God: but let the righteous be merry and joyful before Him. Let all the legions of hell be confounded and put to shame: and let not the ministers of Satan dare to impede thy journey. May Christ who was crucified for thee, deliver thee from all torment. May Christ deliver thee from eternal death, who deigned to die for thee. May Christ the Son of the living God place thee for ever within the green and pleasant places of His own Paradise; and may the True Shepherd recognize thee among His sheep. May He absolve thee from all thy sins; and set thee on His right hand in the inheritance of His elect. Mayest thou behold thy Redeemer face to face: and for ever standing in His Presence, mayest thou behold with blessed eyes the very Truth. Set among the companies of the blessed, mayest thou enjoy the sweetness of Divine contemplation for ever and ever. Amen."

HYMN ON FUNERAL RITES OF THE DEAD.

As our object throughout has been rather to set forth the thoughts of others than our own, and to revive the reflections of better times, we cannot perhaps better conclude, than by attempting to translate that very beautiful Hymn of "great and grave Prudentius," the poet of Martyrs.

O God, the fiery Fount whence souls descend,
   Who dost the twofold element combine,
Living and dying dost together blend,
   And mould in one,—the human form Divine.

Thine are they both, our Father Thou and Guide,
   The wondrous chain is form'd by Thee alone;
Bound at Thy will together they abide,
   And flesh and spirit serve Thee, two in one.

But when asunder rent they part in twain,
   Then man is all dissolved, and seen no more;
Dry Earth the mouldering clay receives again;
   Air bears the soul unto the viewless shore.

Thus all that is created must decay,
   And yield to wasting change and withering eld;
Things closest knit must vanish all away,
   Break the live bonds which erst the texture held.

This is that death, which Thou our gracious God
   Hast come to vanquish, from the pitying skies,
Forming a road, which Thou Thyself hast trod,
   Whereby the perish'd limbs again may rise.

What though immortal seeds are bound with frail,
 Closed in its prison-house and chains of earth—
The mightier part within us shall prevail,
 And vindicate its own ethereal birth.

If the free Will embracing low desire
 Wallow in grovelling thought and things below,
The soul shall sink, weigh'd by the earthly mire,
 And its immortal birthright shall forego.

But if the soul, true to her fiery birth,
 Refuse the foul contagion of the clay,
The Heav'n-born guest shall wing the laggard earth,
 And to the stars the associate frame convey.

What though we see the body sink to sleep,
 Resign the passionate mind, and void remain,—
A little while shall break its slumbers deep,
 And the assembling senses meet again.

The ages soon shall come, when friendly heat
 Shall these dry wither'd bones again resume,
The life blood seek again its ancient seat,
 And animate again with glowing bloom.

The buried carcases which lifeless lay
 In mouldering sepulchres and charnels cold,
Soon on the gales of Heav'n shall wing their way,
 Companions to the souls they held of old.

Hence on the dead we tend with holy pains,
 And when we would in vain the life recall,
Cherish with honours sad the dear remains,
 And duly deck the solemn funeral.

Bound in the whiteness of the winding-sheet,
 As in its swaddling bands we lay the dead,—
Myrrh, with Sabean odours blending sweet,
 Hold the cold sleeper of the silent bed.

For what do mean our beauteous monuments,
  And carved stones, which seem their watch to keep
Over the dead,—but that in those still tents
  The inmate is not perish'd, but asleep?

Such the providing care that Love shall take,
  Which dwells in Christ, believing, at His breath,
All things shall in an instant be awake,
  Which now are held in the cold arms of death.

When bodies of the Dead unburied lie,
  He who takes pity on their poor remains,
To Christ who died he shows that charity,
  And Christ that liveth shall reward his pains.

Love, while for others, for itself it sighs;
  For 'neath one melancholy lot we groan,
We recognize our kindred obsequies,
  And in another's death grieve for our own.

That aged saint and venerable lord,
  Sire of Tobias, whom the Angel led,
Instant arose from the untasted board,
  And first would tend on the unburied dead.

When ministers attendant stood around,
  The cups untouch'd and viands did he leave;
Instant he rose, on duteous service bound,
  To dig the grave, and then return'd to grieve.

Vast his reward;—Heav'n shall the deed repay,
  And healing Raphael upon earth is seen;
His eyes, which long had lost the visual ray,
  Touch'd with the gall behold the light serene

E'en then our Father hath His children taught,
  How bitter is the cure to the dark soul;
How keen the remedy to wakening thought,
  When the light breaks, and spirits are made whole.

He taught us thus that he who, Heav'nward bound,
  Would see hereafter His celestial reign,
Must pass through night, and bear the grievous wound,
  Train'd by the sufferings of this world of pain.

Death is more blessed for these short-lived woes;
  Through dissolution's pangs and fleshly jars,
Arduous the way that opens to repose,
  And pain doth pave the pathway to the stars.

But bodies that have learn'd daily to die,
  Here shall again return in happier years;
And that reunion in the blissful sky,
  Shall never know decay nor parting tears.

The face now tinged with that pale livid hue,
  Bred of disease and hastening to the tomb,
More beauteous than each flower, shall wake anew,
  Mantling with blood of never-dying bloom.

Envious Old Age shall then no longer prey
  Upon the alter'd brow which once was fair;
Nor Leanness, with its gradual dry decay,
  Shrivel the arms, and leave the forehead bare.

And fell Disease, who with relentless pains
  Lays waste the limbs, and taints the panting breath,
Then shall be bound amid a thousand chains,
  Torturing himself in never-dying death.

The Flesh triumphant from the realms of day,
  Exulting in new life's perennial flow,
Shall see his foe for ever pine away,
  Himself the prey of self-inflicted woe.

And ye, surviving friends that throng the tomb,
  Why mingle here those sounds of idle wail?
Why, with loud tears and desolating gloom,
  Blame ye God's righteous laws that must prevail?

Be still, thou sad lament; and ye that mourn,
   Suspend your tears; ye mothers, weep no more;
Mourn not those pledges from your bosom torn,
   Death hath a new and better life in store.

E'en as the seeds beneath their parent earth,
   All dead and buried for awhile remain;
Then greenly rise unto a second birth,
   And meditate again the golden grain.

Receive him, Earth, unto thine harbouring shrine,
   In thy soft tranquil bosom let him rest;
These limbs of man I to thy care consign,
   And trust the noble fragments to thy breast.

This house was once the mansion of a soul,
   Brought into life by its Creator's breath;
Wisdom did once this living mass control,
   And Christ was there enshrined, Who conquers death.

Cover this body, to thy care consign'd;
   Its Maker shall not leave it in the grave;
But His own lineaments shall bear in mind,
   And shall recall the image which He gave.

The full-appointed times e'en now are come,
   When God Himself shall every hope fulfil;
Thou must give up from thy sepulchral womb
   The shape I yield unto thee, and am still.

For what, though Time consumes unto a span,
   Wastes e'en these bones which unto thee I trust,
Till what remains of that which once was man,
   Is but a little handful of dry dust:

And what though wandering blasts and moaning gales
   Shall bear that dust throughout the empty air;
It shall not be that God's own promise fails,—
   It shall not be that man hath perish'd there.

But while Thou dost recall, and thus remould
  The perishable body, Father blest,
In what pure region of Thy heavenly fold
  Wilt Thou the unshackled spirit bid to rest?

Shall it, like Lazarus, reposing lie
  On the blest bosom of that ancient Sire,
Where afar off, enclosed 'mid flowers on high,
  The Rich man saw him from his bed of fire?

O Saviour, we would follow Thy commands,
  Who, conquering death, hast won a passage free,
Where on Thy steps, through Eden's blissful lands,
  The associate of Thy Cross doth follow Thee.

Lo, to Thy faithful opes the ample glade
  And shining path of Thine own paradise;
And we may enter in that verdant shade
  Wherein no more the deadly serpent lies.

Lead, gracious Guardian, as Thou knowest best,
  Guide a poor soul, Thy servant, to Thy fold;
Conduct her in that natal seat to rest,
  Which she, an exiled wanderer, left of old.

We on the dear remains and cover'd bones
  Will drop the violet and vernal leaf;
And on the title cold and silent stones
  Shed liquid sweets,—and seek in Thee relief.

INDEX OF TEXTS.

PSALMS.

PSALMS.

PROVERBS.

ECCLESIASTES.

SONG OF SOLOMON.

ST. MATTHEW.

CHAP.	VERSE	PAGE
xxv.	10	367
xxv.	31	62. 70
xxv.	40	328
xxvi.	3	97. 162
xxvi.	13	394
xxvi.	31	79
xxvi.	32	401
xxvi.	34	120
xxvi.	33	72
xxvi.	55	196
xxvii.	19	107
xxvii.	25	168
xxviii.	20	26

ST. MARK.

CHAP.	VERSE	PAGE
i.	12	10
i.	20	334
i.	24	133
iii.	35	334
iv.	38	426
v.	39	438
vi.	20	202
vii.	11	134. 178
viii.	18	51
viii.	34	273. 275
ix.	3	228. 308
ix.	6	28
x.	14. 16	422
x.	30	334
x.	32	52
x.	38	222. 227
xiii.	35	120
xiv.	9	415
xiv.	2	167
xiv.	30	120. 280
xiv.	37	121
xiv.	51	69. 80
xv.	1	92
xv.	41	107
xv.	47	107
xvi.	9	107

ST. LUKE.

CHAP.	VERSE	PAGE
i.	11	23
i.	18. 63	299
i.	42	330. 337
ii.	4	192
ii.	13	36. 373
ii.	19	337
ii.	25	384
ii.	34, 35	325, 326. 336
ii.	42. 49	338
ii.	49	335
ii.	51	335
iii.	2	89
iii.	6	146
iii.	8	184
iv.	9	314
iv.	30	43
vi.	36	45
vii.	37	410
vii.	38, 39	422
vii.	47, 48. 50	415
viii.	2	410
ix.	23	280
ix.	29	206
ix.	55	59
ix.	58	280
x.	19	231
x.	34, 35	367
x.	42	405. 414
xi.	7	241
xi.	22	237
xi.	26	175
xi.	28	335
xii.	10	292
xii.	8	322
xii.	44	368
xiii.	1	202
xiii.	32	203
xiv.	11	321
xiv.	26	336
xv.	5	367
xv.	10	427
xvi.	8	241
xvi.	19, 21	177
xvi.	31	313
xvi.	21	367
xvii.	28	436
xviii.	5. 7	241
xviii.	13	367
xix.	22	247
xix.	42	175
xix.	43, 44	277
xx.	21	188
xx.	41	143. 152
xxi.	17	132
xxii.	19	429

II. TIMOTHY.

CHAP.	VERSE	PAGE
ii.	9	94
ii.	11, 12	276
ii.	12	273. 322
iii.	12	210

HEBREWS.

CHAP.	VERSE	PAGE
iv.	9	399, 400
iv.	12	329
v.	7	14. 22
v.	8	21
vi.	4, 5	51
vi.	6	175
vii.	17. 24	150
viii.	5	371
ix.	19	265
ix.	24	369
x.	19, 20	370
x.	26	124. 294
xii.	1	147. 348
xii.	2	121. 221
xii.	6	229
xii.	17	175
xiii.	13	274

ST. JAMES.

CHAP.	VERSE	PAGE
ii.	5	108

I. ST. PETER.

CHAP.	VERSE	PAGE
ii.	23	231
iii.	4	424
iv.	8	321
v.	5	30

I. ST. JOHN.

CHAP.	VERSE	PAGE
i.	5	77
ii.	8	259
iii.	2	146
v.	6. 7. 9	379
v.	16	175

REVELATION.

CHAP.	VERSE	PAGE
i.	5	198
i.	7	146. 312. 383
iv.	6	66
vi.	15	278
vi.	16	55. 278
vii.	14	228
xiv.	13	440
xv.	6	390
xix.	8	390
xix.	13	224
xxi.	1	259
xxi.	2, 3	197
xxi.	23	27
xxii.	2	285
xxii.	11	175
xxii.	20	258

THE END.

www.ingramcontent.com/pod-product-compliance
Lightning Source LLC
Chambersburg PA
CBHW051944150726
47999CB00004B/1244